good vibrations
a history of record production

Design: David Houghton
Printed by: MPG Books, Bodmin

Published by: Sanctuary Publishing Limited, 82 Bishops Bridge
Road, London W2 6BB

Copyright: Mark Cunningham. First edition 1996. This edition 1998

Photographs: sourced from the following individuals and
organisations. Their assistance is greatly appreciated: 140dB
Management, AIR Studios Ltd, Apple Corps Ltd, Roy Thomas Baker,
John Beecher, Dean Belcher/Opal, Steve Benbow, BMG, Alex
Bowling, John Bradley, Sheila Bromberg, CliveBubley/Joe Meek
Appreciation Society, Stuart Colman, Anton Corbijn, Andre Csillag,
James Cumpsty, Mark Cunningham, Gus Dudgeon, Andy Earle/HK
Management, EMI Records Ltd, EMKA Productions/Pink Floyd Music,
Rob Finnis, Juan Gatti, Ronald Grant, Erich Gruenberg, Ross Halfin,
Hansa Ton Studios, Paul Hardcastle, David Hentschel, Simon
Heyworth, Dezo Hoffman, Hotwire Records, Steve Howe, Island
Records Ltd, Jeff Jarratt, Chris Kempster, Craig Leon, Gered
Mankowitz, David Mason, Linda McCartney/Robbie Montgomery
Associates/MPL, Dennis Muirhead, Charles O'Connor, Denis
O'Regan, Phonogram, Barry Plumber, PWL, Redferns, Mick Rock,
Savage & Best, Miki Slingsby, Martin Smith, Solid State Logic,
Soundfield Studios, Ringo Starr, Sterling Audio, Tascam, Trace Elliot,
Derek Varnals, Mike Vernon, Chris Walter and ZTT

ISBN: 1-86074-242-4

good vibrations
a history of record production

mark cunningham

forewords by alan parsons & brian eno

about the author

Born in 1963, Mark Cunningham was professionally engaged throughout the late 1970s and 1980s as a professional bass guitarist, singer/songwriter and record producer at all levels of the music industry.

By the early 1990s, he had turned his attention towards journalism, particularly in the fields of professional audio and concert production, and quickly earned a favourable reputation through his work for specialist magazines including *Sound On Sound*, *Pro Sound News*, *Lighting + Sound International*, *Live!*, *Making Music*, *The Mix*, *Audio Media*, *Total Guitar*, *Bassist*, *Rhythm*, *Billboard* and *Music Week*, and mainstream titles such as *Mojo* and *Q*.

The original May 1996 release of *Good Vibrations – A History Of Record Production* resulted in an invitation to give a series of lectures on record production at the University of Westminster in London. This project was quickly followed by his work as Editor on session bassist/composer Mo Foster's Sanctuary book *Seventeen Watts?*.

Between May 1997 and January 1998, Mark rose from a freelance position to that of Editor with industry magazine *SPL*, and finally, with the formation of his own company Pulse Publications, he became Publishing Editor of the live performance trade journal *Total Production*.

Mark Cunningham is an associate member of Re-Pro (The Guild of Recording Producers, Directors & Engineers) and BASCA (The British Academy Of Songwriters, Composers And Authors). He lives in Essex with his wife Paula, twin sons William and Jordan, and daughters Rosalie and Lucinda.

For Paula and my own fab four –

Rosalie, William, Jordan and Lucinda.

And in loving memory of

Robert William Cunningham (1926-1983),

who never knew me as a writer.

acknowledgments

Two years on from completing the first edition of *Good Vibrations*, I am reminded of the arduous but immensely enjoyable exercise that lay ahead of me when I originally planned this project. You have in your hands the result of around two and a half years' research and countless interviews which I hope will prove as intriguing to you as it still is for me.

None of this could have happened without the many people who, either by direct or indirect means, assisted me with this project and its associated developments. Firstly and foremostly, I owe everything to my wife and best friend, Paula – thank you for your understanding, and for instilling in me a spirit of determination and sense of purpose which grows with every passing year. Endless gratitude to my mother, Joan, for her continued love and unflagging support. Special thanks to Mr Brian Wilson of sunny California, who granted me valuable time for vital interviews, and whose song title was borrowed with maximum respect.

A big thumbs up to David Woodley for helping to get the ball rolling back in 1994, and to Kate Stevens for her invaluable transcription skills when copy deadline fever reached panic stations. A golden plectrum to John Hill for being John Hill. A jester's cap to Mo Foster for lifting my spirits with an endless source of bad jokes (hi Kay!). Major appreciation to Andy (and Fiona) Lenthall and PH for sharing the dark hours of late 1997 and going for the big one!

Gestures of varying proportions go to the musicians, engineers and associated friends with whom I have worked over the last twenty years and learned much from. Mucho gracias to all of my journalistic co-conspirators, especially Ian Gilby, Dave Lockwood, Matt Bell, Paul White, Diana Scrimgeour, Phil Ward, Andy Wood, Chris Kempster, John Offord, and Rob Alexander. Extra thanks to Jerry Gilbert (and John Roden) for the initial break. Last but not least I raise a glass to Penny Braybrooke and Jeff Hudson at Sanctuary Publishing who gave their support.

All that remains is for me to doff my cap to the producers, engineers, artists, equipment manufacturers and others who have contributed in the form of vital interviews, information, photographs and establishing contacts. The value of their support cannot be overestimated. In alphabetical order (deep breath), they are:

140db Management, Stuart Adamson, Malcolm Atkin, Geoff Baker, Roy Thomas Baker, Lin Barkass, Martin Barre, John Beecher, Hal Blaine, Les & John Bradley, Chuck Britz, Sheila Bromberg, Gerry Bron, Dave & Julie Bronze, Joe Brown, Mark Brzezicki, Stephen Budd, Richard James Burgess, Jean Jacques Burnel, Shirley Burns, Tony Butler, Eamon Carr, Clem Cattini, Ed Chalpin, Graeme Clark, Tony Clarke, Martin Colley, Phil Collins, Stuart Colman, Alan Crowder, Jackie Da Costa, Peter Filleul and Chris Hook at Re-Pro, Malcolm Davies, Saul Davies, Barry Devlin, Bernard Doherty and all at LD Publicity, Tom Dowd, Gus Dudgeon, Jim Ebdon, Geoff Emerick, EMKA Productions, Brian Eno, John Entwistle, Stuart Epps, John Fean, Rob Finnis, Ted Fletcher, Flood, Gordon & Hilary Giltrap, Kevin Godley, Paul Gomersall, Larry Gott, Ginny Goudy, Ian Grant, Erich Gruenberg, Paul Hardcastle, Dave Harries, Heart Radio, David Hentschel, Richard Hewson, Simon Heyworth, Paul Hicks, Tony Hicks, Chas Hodges, Annie Holloway at The Producers, Trevor Horn, Steve Howe, John Hudson, Jim Irvin at *Mojo*, Andy Jackson, Al Jardine, Jeff & Elfie Jarratt, Glyn Johns, Kenney Jones, Norman Jones, Carol Kaye, Adrian Kerridge, Gary Langan, John Leckie, Alvin Lee, Owen Leech, Craig Leon, Larry Levine, Jon Lewin at Confederate Broadcasting, Judy Lipsey, Jim Lockhart, Mike Love, Phil MacDonald, Ron & Russell Mael, Manfred Mann, Sir George Martin, Tony Martin, David Mason, Kathy Mason, Joe B Mauldin, Sir Paul McCartney, Linda

McCartney, Karla Merrifield at Studio One, Peter Mew, Jonathon
Miles at Soundfield Studios, Mojo Workin' International, Mono Music,
Robbie Montgomery, Dennis Muirhead, Larry Mullen Jr, David Neal,
Jeremy Neech, Charles O'Connor, Paul O'Duffy, Eddie Offord, Hugh
Padgham, Pino Palladino, May Pang, Rick Parfitt, Alan Parsons, Les
Paul, (L'il sis) Tina & Phil Pearlman, Poole Edwards Publicity, Simon &
Christine Porter at Duroc, Cozy Powell, Guy Pratt, Bobby Pridden,
Phil Ramone, Chris Rea, John Repsch, Jay Reynolds, Robobuild, Ulle
Ronnback, Stan Ross, Francis Rossi, Allan Rouse, Fiona Sanders-
Reece, Joe Satriani, Sidney Sax, Martin Scott, Ronnie Scott, Jill
Sinclair, Chris Slack, Solid State Logic, Keith Smith, Martin Smith, Zak
Starkey, Sterling Audio, Stephen Street, Derek Taylor, Chris Thomas,
Michael B Tretow, Bjorn Ulvaeus, Midge Ure, Derek Varnals, Mike
Vernon, Tony Visconti, Martyn Ware, Bruce Watson, Paul Weller,
Snowy White, Paul & Margo Wickens, and Muff Winwood.

contents

foreword
to the 1998 edition

Although the scratchy, honky sound of old wind-up gramophones seems a far cry from the quality of sound we can achieve with Nineties audio technology, we must remember that the early days of music recording started with attempts to give the impression that our living room had become the location where the performers were playing – an illusion. The purpose – as it still is now in many genres of music – was to recreate exactly the natural acoustic balance of the instrumentalists and vocalists such that the listener would be literally transported to the studio or concert hall.

In the Fifties, this goal of recreation gave way to what I would call "creative cheating", but still the aim was an illusory result. In reality, the likes of Bill Haley and Elvis had absolutely no chance of their unamplified voices being heard over the thumping din that their backing bands were producing. A remarkable invention, already well-known to sound recordists, the microphone, had matured in real world circles from a device used for "Public Address" to a means of completely remodelling the balance between instruments.

The Beatles were one of the first to recognise the creative potential of manipulating sounds artificially in the studio. As their career developed, they layered take after take, performance with performance, onto an ever-increasing number of tape tracks, placing great demands on the available technology. This was the just the beginning. From then on, most rock and pop artists became accustomed to using the recording studio as a tool – an instrument within itself. Recording and production technique could have a dramatic effect on the finished results – so much so that in many cases the studio effects actually became an integral part of a composition. What would 'A Day In The Life' have been with no studio gimmickry?

Modern music owes a great debt to the behind-the-studio-glass "magicians" who discovered that as long as a "soundscape" could be imagined, with a few "tricks" and "sleights" it could probably be brought into your home, your car or your local fast food restaurant. But unlike the illusions of Harry Houdini and David Copperfield where the question, "How did they do that trick?" is rarely answered, in the coming pages you will get a real insight into some of the secrets that helped shape some of the greatest illusions of all – the ones we call pop records.

Alan Parsons

foreword
to the 1996 edition

Until the late Sixties, the recording studio had been a passive transmitter. A band went into the studio with the aim of getting a well-rehearsed, pre-existing song on to tape as faithfully as possible. "Fidelity" was a big word then. But after witnessing the achievements of a handful of visionaries, people began to see the studio as a labyrinth of possibilities and started experimenting with echo, reverb and tape repeats to make more of their sound, something that didn't originate from the band. But nonetheless, the feeling was still that the act of imposing the music had already happened before you got into the studio.

I was always fascinated by records that had a very distinctive sonic identity, like Phil Spector's records which had a peculiar usage of echo and reverb. That was what drew me in and intrigued me, more so than the melody, lyrics or rhythm. Of course, the psychedelic era was all about people inventing new worlds of sound, and my impulse to become a musician came when I realised it was possible to make different kinds of music.

At the time, I was a painter at art school, trying to create visual atmospheres and I became drawn into music by sonic atmospheres and textures. Suddenly, I thought this is the best way to paint: painting with music. I was never a great painter, but with tape recorders and studios, I found that I was doing all the things I wanted to do as a painter...but better.

Brian Eno

introduction

It was at senior school at the age of eleven when the concept of record production hit me between the ears. Already able to fumble convincingly on guitar, bass and drums, I was shown a copy of Mike Oldfield's recent *Tubular Bells* album with the explanation that it had been recorded by a genius who could play a zillion instruments. What, all at once? And what on earth is a double-speed guitar? Until that point I had assumed that all records were made entirely by groups of people, together in one room. I was also the same person who took it for granted that electric guitarists plugged straight into the mains, but thankfully never tried it myself. The time for enlightenment was nigh, and after investing in a second-hand Akai four-track tape recorder, I discovered for myself the mighty power of the *overdub*!

Hard to conceive is the notion that only fifteen years prior to the legendary beat boom, multitrack recording was a mere flight of fantasy in the mind of American guitar icon, Les Paul – his milestone sonic achievements being the most significant since Edison invented the tin foil phonograph in 1877 and, in effect, became the world's first record producer/engineer.

In these sophisticated days it is easy to forget that most of the greatest recordings of the Sixties – the era in which many modern-day techniques and principals were born – were made on four-track equipment in straightforward environments. Today, artists are generally expected to deliver one album and around four singles (normally from that album) each year. In the case of Kate Bush, Pink Floyd and Dire Straits, the gap between albums has tended to be as great as five or more years. In contrast, the normal requirement of an artist in the Sixties was two albums and anything up to six singles (*not* taken from the albums). The focus is now clearly on the performance of the song and the sound surrounding it, rather than just the words and music. And even though the enabling technology has improved beyond Edison's wildest imagination, the making of recorded music often takes longer to perfect because the barriers have been lifted. How does one perceive a *good* production today? It's a good question.

As we roll at a thunderous pace towards the new millennium, musicians are faced with seemingly endless possibilities when it comes to making records. Tape, the standard recording medium for more than forty years, is now virtually obsolete as, in this digital domain of hard-disk recording, computer sequencing and MIDI (Musical Instrument Digital Interface), the number of tracks we can utilise is theoretically infinite. The producers and engineers who, little more than thirty years ago, were anonymous back room boys on meagre record company salaries, are now revered like the pop stars themselves. And, whereas the general record-buying public were in complete ignorance of the way their favourite artist made those groovy, space-age sounds in the monochrome era, even today's amateur musician and casual listener has an insight into the creative and technical elements of recording – thanks to genuinely affordable home recording systems and the plethora of specialist and consumer magazines now widely available. The times surely have a-changed.

It is my relentless fascination for the recording process which moved me to write *Good Vibrations – A History Of Record Production*. Indeed, as a producer myself during the Eighties, I had often searched in vain for such a book – I never dreamed that I would personally fill this literary void! In doing so, many of my long-standing questions about record production and how it has matured over the decades have been answered by the people who were directly responsible for some of the true rock and pop classics. Collectively, they have helped me draw a line of progression from the rock 'n' roll era, Sixties pop and psychedelia, through to the conceptual, glam and punk rock of the Seventies and out to the electronic-obsessed Eighties and the current environment which, through the new communications revolution, is already witnessing a change in the way records are not only made, but also listened to.

I do urge you, however, to regard this as a *generic* history of record production. It is not *the* history – common sense would suggest that it would take at least another two volumes of this book to cope with that task. Therefore, *Good Vibrations* does not promise all things to all people, and while the making of a number of classic tracks are closely analysed as technological milestones, there will undoubtedly be an omission of many worthy records, artists, producers and engineers – a point underlined to me through reviews of the first edition. But in the cases where those artists are absent, one can be reassured that many of the techniques revealed in the case studies of others will apply generally, across a variety of musical disciplines and countries. Whilst a study of the origins of reggae, hip hop, rap and other ethnic production styles would be most valid (and I cannot over-emphasise their importance), I have felt it appropriate to focus simply on mainstream rock and pop, and acknowledge the advances, working practices and influences in that context. Another key aspect is that this book is mostly interview-based and from inception its existence was always going to be determined by the availability of individuals for discussion. The content of this book is, therefore, unique and almost wholly based on the recollections and experiences of those who were there, as intimately told to yours truly.

Mark Cunningham
Thorpe Bay, Essex
March 1998

chapter one

let there be sound on sound

"What we hoped to hear was 'Hello, hello, hello, hello, one, two, three, four, testing' played together. If it did that, then we could go on until the neighbours complained! And lo and behold, it worked!"

Les Paul on his invention of tape multitracking

Anyone who has derived enjoyment and, indeed, a living from recorded sound owes a debt of gratitude to Thomas Alva Edison who in 1877, invented the world's first record and playback machine. Built by assistant John Kruesi from Edison's specific instructions and drawings, the cumbersome device was completed in New York on 6 December, 1877 and consisted of four key components: the phonograph, with a mouthpiece connected to a diaphragm and a central stylus; a four-inch diameter grooved brass cylinder, mounted on a threaded shaft and turned by a handle; a tin foil phonogram, made by the indentation of a recording on to the foil-covered cylinder; and a phonet – a stylus and diaphragm assembly enabling the tracing of engravings on the phonogram and their transmission.

To make a recording, Edison projected a loud vocal signal into the mouthpiece of the phonograph while turning the handle simultaneously. The vibrations were then conveyed via the diaphragm and stylus to the foil which became indented with a number of small marks. In order to reproduce or play back the signal, the phonet's stylus made contact with the revolving cylinder and followed its indentations whilst vibrating its own diaphragm. Depending on the speed at which the crank handle was turned, a recording would last for around two minutes.

Edison's first successful recording was of his own *a cappella* rendition of the nursery rhyme, 'Mary Had A Little Lamb', an account of which appeared in *Edison And His Inventions*, a publication by JB McClure. In it, Edison explained: "I was singing...to the mouthpiece of a telephone when the vibrations of the wire sent the fine steel point [the stylus] into my finger. That set me thinking. If I could record the actions of the point, and then send that point over the same surface afterwards, I saw no reason why the thing would not talk. I tried the experiment and found that the point made an alphabet. I shouted the word 'halloo! halloo!' into the mouthpiece, ran the paper back over the steel point and heard a faint 'halloo!' in return! I determined to make a machine that would work accurately and gave my assistants instructions, telling them what I had discovered...the discovery came through the pricking of a finger." The inventor filed his new contraption with the Patent Office on Christmas Eve, 1877 and within twelve years, commercial recordings would be made available for public consumption.

For many years after Edison made those first tentative steps, the challenge for anyone involved in music and audio was to improve the fidelity of the recording medium. Several improvements evolved during the first half of the twentieth century, but the first major breakthrough to affect the creative use of sound and indeed launch the notion of record production as we know it today came in 1949, in Chicago, with the invention of sound-on-sound tape recording. Like the tin foil phonograph itself, this occurred as a complete accident at the hands of an electronics genius who had both Edison's scientific curiosity and the musical dexterity of Django Reinhardt: Lester Polfus, known to us all as Les Paul.

A highly gifted guitarist who turned eighty years of age in 1995 and was more recently inducted into the New Jersey Inventors' Hall of Fame, Paul will always be known for the legendary Gibson electric guitar he designed and gave his name to in 1952, and to some degree this fame has overshadowed his enormous contribution to studio technology. Born in Waukesha, Wisconsin, Paul's inquisitive nature and eagerness to learn was apparent from an early age, and as a schoolboy in the depressed Twenties he would while away the hours tinkering with the most unlikely toys – his gramophone, piano, radio, telephone, harmonica and, of course, guitar – "all the weapons I needed to go out and rattle a lot of cages". Something of a boy genius, it wasn't long before his teachers ran out of things to teach him. "I asked my teacher at grade school how, when I pressed my finger on a record and slowed it down, the pitch changed," he recalls. "I was just a kid, but they marched me to the library where I met the professors and they began to tell me what digital and analogue meant, and in no time I was building my own recording machines and broadcast stations. One of the things I made really early on at about the age of about eleven was a disc recorder, using a Victrola gramophone pick-up arm and a Cadillac fly wheel, and that was the same recorder I used on my first-ever radio broadcast in 1929."

Paul's early successes as a musician were based on his enormous popularity on American radio where he would be in regular demand as the writer and performer of kitsch product advertisements, as well as providing the guitar backing for Bing Crosby, Nat "King" Cole and other greats of the era. In 1944, as an army soldier, he also appeared on what has been credited as the original rock 'n' roll record – the live 'Blues Part 2' by Jazz At The Philharmonic – when he performed under the pseudonym, Paul Leslie, to avoid military regulation problems. After signing with Capitol Records in 1947, Paul chalked up a number of his own hits (later with his partner and future wife, Mary Ford), recorded in a studio which he installed in the garage of his Los Angeles bungalow. The state of the art equipment was built to his own design and so well regarded by the fledgling record industry that various top artists of the day, including The Andrews Sisters, were virtually queuing at Paul's studio door.

It should be noted that Les Paul's early voyage into layered sound began in 1930 when he became the first known person to record a multi-instrumental performance by building up several guitar tracks on the outside and inside bands of an acetate disc. "I took my ideas for multitrack recordings around the record companies but they could only see the novelty value," he says. "They certainly didn't look upon it as the way of the future." Nevertheless, Paul's brainwaves did filter through the industry and in 1931, the opera singer, Laurence Tibbett superimposed a baritone vocal line on top of his original tenor performance for the recording of 'The Cuban Love Song'. Mike Oldfield's multi-instrumental feats on 1973's *Tubular Bells* were also pre-dated by thirty-two years when jazz musician, Sidney Bechet took sole responsibility of two saxophones, clarinet, bass, piano and drums on his version of 'The Sheik Of Araby'. An absence of backing vocalists on one session in Chicago in December 1947 later gave Patti Page good reason to duplicate her own voice. Mercury Records, seeing this as little more than a gimmick, was to market the record ('Confess') as performed by Patti Page And Patti Page. A similar PR approach was reserved when for Page's follow-up record, 'With My Eyes Open, I'm Dreaming', she used the overdub technique to create four-part harmony. But it is vital to understand that the standard medium for recording at this time was still acetate disc, which Paul continued to use to its creative limits for his Capitol record releases throughout the Forties.

"I got into playing many different parts, using only one guitar to play basslines and drum parts by tapping or beating the strings," he says. "I even got it to sound like a xylophone or a marimba, and all these different sounds were generated by one guitar. I had two disc machines and I'd send each track back and forth. I'd lay down the first part on one machine, the next part on the other, and keep multiplying them. In other words, I would record a rhythm track on the first disc, then I would play along with the rhythm track and lay the needle down on the second disc which would simultaneously record me playing along to my rhythm track. The second disc would now contain two guitar parts. Going back to the first machine, I would put the needle down onto the disc and record, say, a bassline along with the music from the second disc. Then for other instrumentation, I would just repeat the process, *ad infinitum*. It was very interesting because it was in my garage in Los Angeles that I stumbled across and invented all those things that you hear on the recordings like disc delay, echo, phasing, multitracking and recording at different speeds, on records like 'Chicken Reel' and 'Lover'. So I was very excited because it was something new and different."

At this point, Paul had only ever *seen* a tape recorder. Namely, the AEG/Telefunken-manufactured Magnetophon which was commercially launched in 1937 and notably used during World War II by German radio stations for propaganda broadcasts. He certainly had not *used* one. But it was while working with Bing Crosby in 1949 that Paul's future, and the future concept of recording, would change forever. "Bing came over to my house and said, 'Les, I've got something for you in the car'," he recalls. "I figured it was going to be a truckload of cheese, because we were doing a radio programme for Kraft. I never dreamed that Bing would have in his car something far more precious than that. What he had was one of the very first '300 Series' tape machines made by Ampex. We carried it through the backyard to my garage and I looked at that Ampex machine for maybe three or four hours, and finally I ran into the house and said to Mary [Ford], 'Hey, have we got something here!' We weren't nailed down to recording in a garage anymore. We could go anywhere."

Paul realised that by adding a fourth head to the Ampex machine, sound-on-sound recording would be possible. "I always recorded my guitar direct to the tape machine by plugging it into the mixer," he says. "It was a mono machine and I had to put the last parts down first. The least important parts went down first and the important parts last. In the beginning, the recordings were just of me playing on my own, but I added Mary later on. Recording these songs in a backwards order, if you like, was terribly interesting because you would play the third part first, the second part next and the first part last. And I would go down as many as thirty-seven generations before I finished a recording, but the quality would start to deteriorate."

Knowing that a truly flat frequency response would be impossible to achieve, Paul concentrated on the electronics to ensure that the "head hump" was at a minimum and the linearity of the tape machine and mixer was as flat in frequency response as possible. "The acoustics in the room are not flat, the vibrations of the strings on a guitar are not linear, your ears are not linear, neither are your speakers or earphones," he reasons. "So there is almost nothing flat in frequency response, other than electronically. But that is not going to be the final result anyway, so I had to be very careful to design equalisers and amplifiers, to provide the headroom and the ability to get the correct results. I also had to change the curve of the tape machine. Today, there are frequency tone recordings that are used to align machines, but back then every studio had to invent its own. In doing all of this, I was able to go down many generations of recording and still keep the sound relatively clean." So crystal clear were the results of Paul's labours that his ten-inch album, *New Sound*, was seized upon by hi-fi manufacturers and retailers as a test disc with which to demonstrate the quality of their gramophone products.

In Search Of The Fourth Head

A conniving approach helped Les Paul acquire the elusive "fourth head" for the Ampex, which led to the birth of real multitrack taping. "When Mary and I hit the road with this 300 tape deck, I thought, 'How am I going to get a fourth head?'" he says. "I ended up calling Ampex and told them that I blew a head, and they agreed to send me a new one. I really didn't know at that point if it would work but on paper, on the back of an envelope in fact, it seemed to me that it would. I was totally convinced it would until we were driving all the way from California to New York. By the time we got to Chicago I wasn't so sure anymore, 'cause Mary was asking me all the way across the desert, 'How do you know if it's gonna work or not?' We depended on the tape machine because it was the only thing we had to do the type of thing that I was doing in my garage, which was making radio programmes for NBC and records for Capitol. I was doing them on acetate but now I packed this all away and said we were going to do them all on the tape machine with four heads on it. Mary was very concerned and, of course, she had a legitimate reason.

"I picked up the head from Ampex when we reached Chicago and immediately mounted it. The first thing I did was record me saying 'Hello, hello, hello, hello...', and then I rewound the tape and explained that I was going to use the fourth head to record me saying, 'One, two, three, four, testing.' What we hoped to hear was

'Hello, hello, hello, hello, one, two, three, four, testing' played together. If it did that, then we could go on until the neighbours complained! And lo and behold, it worked!"

By spacing the heads on the Ampex, Les was able to achieve tape delay – a technique that was still essential to the recording process until the development of purpose-designed effects units in the Seventies. "I was having a drink in a tavern with my buddy and telling him that I was still trying to figure out how to achieve tape echo. I told him to picture himself in the Alps, shouting, 'Hello,' and then hearing the echo return...'Hello, hello, hello...'. That's what I wanted, but I didn't want an echo chamber. If that was the case, I'd record in the bathroom. I didn't want reverb. It was just a clean, repeat echo I was looking for. He said, 'What do you mean, like if you put a playback head behind the record head?' My God, that was it! We both jumped out of our chairs and went to the other side of town to my house, and within twenty minutes we had 'Hello, hello, hello...' all over the neighbourhood! Suddenly, that opened up a whole new world.

"The repeating of the delay was a matter of choice, as to how much delay you wanted and how much repeat you wanted, although the timing between each delay was about one-tenth of a second to avoid a reverb effect. It was very easy for me to space the heads on a disc recorder, but on a tape machine I didn't have that privilege because you just can't take a head and move it further away or closer to the preceding head. So what I did was change the speed of the tape machine. If I wanted the echo delay of my voice saying 'Hello' to be faster, I'd just change the speed and consequently tape delay was born."

'How High The Moon'

Relocating from LA to Jackson Heights in New York in 1950, Les Paul's discovery of tape delay, coupled with the ability to layer sound on tape, was the key to his and Mary Ford's most successful record, 'How High The Moon', which was to occupy the Number One position on the American chart for nine weeks in the spring of 1951, and launch to a bewildered public the concept of sound-on-sound recording. Along with Paul's dynamic guitar solo which would become the premier reference point for all of the early rock 'n' roll guitarists, his technique for recording his partner's voice defied tradition. "The unwritten rules stated that a vocalist should be placed no closer than two feet away from the microphone," he says, "but I wanted to capture every little breath and nuance in Mary's voice. So I had her stand right on the mic, just a couple of inches away. Then, what happened? Everybody started to record vocals in that way!"

For many years, Paul employed the use of only one microphone, an RCA 44BX ribbon mic, changing over to a Neumann around 1952. "The earphones we used were US Air Force earphones, and the frequency response was something like 250Hz on the bottom. If we were lucky we got a pair that went to 5kHz on the top end."

In those early days, it was very easy for a work of recorded art to be spoiled by accidental sounds leaking on to a multitrack master in the making. Especially when Les was on his twelfth-generation overdub and a loud truck passed his garage. "Many things would happen to drive me mad and call a halt to a take," he admits. "Either someone would knock on the door, the phone would ring or the fire department or police would drive past with their sirens wailing. The fellow who lived upstairs above us in New York had a weak bladder and Mary and I would time our recordings around his regular trips to the bathroom. I knew that he always went at around two o'clock, for example. He always made a noise when he got up and walked across the floor, so we knew better than to record. We knew the schedule of the aircraft in the area so we recorded in between that. But what we couldn't do was predict when there was going to be a fire. We lived across the street from a firehouse, so we did have some opposition. But I guess we made it!

"The man and his wife upstairs must have wondered what in God's name we were all about. We rented the basement and that's where we lived and recorded, underneath their home. They would hear Mary screaming, 'Look what you're doing to me.' It was a lyric from a song, but maybe the fifth part of the recording, and they don't hear any of the music because we were wearing earphones. So they never heard any more than one part at a time and people living around us must have thought we were pretty strange! They didn't have a clue about what we were doing until we were more than thirty dubs down and they heard the song. I remember playing in Las Vegas one time and a lady knocked on the door and said, 'I'll sure be glad when you've finished "Whispering".' I was working on 'Whispering' out there and I was adding parts, but the motor would break down and I'd have to get a new one. Then something else went wrong and I had a real tough time with that particular song. I went back and re-recorded parts, but tape would spill out all over the floor. A million weird things were going on."

Surprisingly, it was years before the rest of the recording industry caught on to the power of multitracking, the first two-track, stereophonic reel-to-reel tape recorder being introduced in 1954. "The real fun of the early multitrack recording period for me lasted only about five years," Paul recalls. "I was out there all by myself with no one trying to copy my ideas or follow me. It took about five years for people in the industry to figure out that it could be used for purposes other than just Les Paul and Mary Ford.

"At one time, around 1951, I played for the BBC at the London Palladium and they asked me if I would demonstrate on television how we made a multitrack recording, step-by-step. This was where we recorded on disc, then they had me go down the hallway with the disc, down some stairs with the cameras following me, to another disc machine where I recorded another part. The two machines weren't even in the same room or on the same floor. It was a terribly interesting show that the BBC conceived and had me do. It must have taken hours and hours of planning to do this and they did an excellent job of showing the British viewers how multitracking was born. Somewhere in their library, the BBC has that programme but I have never seen it. For many years the broadcast industry would not accept tape as a medium; our shows were not allowed to be played from tape. They had to be transferred from tape to disc. Even the early Ed Sullivan shows were not done on tape."

The mid-Fifties advent of the eight-track recorder had most studios perplexed as to what to do with this new technology. "I remember walking down a hallway with an engineer and saw a plastic bag over the top of an eight-track tape machine," he recalls. "He said, 'Look what you started, Les.' And I saw this machine and said,

'What's it doing in the hallway?' He said, 'What are you gonna do with it?' He didn't think there was anyone else out there that could use it apart from me and Mary. People just did not have the foresight that multitracking, this tool, could be used in so many different ways. And it was so terribly important for other things than just to do a multitrack recording of a guitar and a voice. So it took about five years before they began making background recordings and putting a singer on later. They did that with Ray Charles, Patti Page and a lot of people, but it wasn't really done seriously for quite a few years."

The Les Paulverizer

In the early Fifties, Les Paul and Mary Ford would often record up to four songs a day, as well as making fifteen-minute radio broadcasts which showcased Paul's songwriting and scriptwriting talents. "We knew the limitations of what we had and we didn't have that many things to mess our heads up," he says. "Now you can go down to the store and buy millions of toys, boxes and footpedals, whatever. But we were very limited in what we had, so we had to make it work. On one of the radio shows I said that I invented the gas guitar just in case there was a problem with electricity and I didn't want the electric company getting a monopoly. I was into spoofs."

It was one of these spoofs that led to yet another Les Paul invention, the Les Paulverizer – the recording device attached to his guitar that enabled him to record and play back numerous guitar parts live on stage to the astonishment of his audience. "It started off as a radio sketch about this mythical device," he remembers. "All I told them was that I got my invention, the Les Paulverizer, and with it I could take Mary's voice and make it sound like The Andrews Sisters or even Bing, or turn my guitar into an orchestra. I was the guy who invented The Chipmunks. I suggested to my friend, David Seville that he do something like that and he made a hell of a lot of money out of the Chipmunks idea."

Six years after his original radio broadcast scam, the Les Paulverizer did, in fact, become a reality and Paul gave a prestigious demonstration on stage to an audience which included President Eisenhower and Vice-President Nixon among its number. "I got a

LET THERE BE SOUND ON SOUND

call from Vice-President Nixon and some other people, saying that they'd like to have me play for the President of the United States," Paul says. "I told Mary it would be a great opportunity to try out my Les Paulverizer. She said, 'Are you crazy? Surely you're not going to experiment and try this out on the President?' But the darn thing worked! It was the funniest thing that ever happened and, yes, we had a lot of problems with it but in the end it worked out very well and I've got a lot of good memories about that whole period. We could suddenly do on the stage what we achieved in our basement."

As early as 1952, Paul envisaged a time when digital recording would become a reality. "All my close friends and confidantes knew that the things that are so commonplace in studios today would eventually happen," he says. "I gave an impromptu speech at the AES [Audio Engineering Society] show in front of Sherman Fairchild, Major Armstrong and some of the smartest people in the business. I was scared to death standing up in front of all these high profile people and it was not a speech I was prepared for. But I said, 'There have been some things I've been bitching about and you're the guys I'd like to talk to. I am so fed up with gouging out acetate with a needle. It reminds me of a farmer with an ox, ploughing up his field. This is the crudest way of making a record that I can think of. Why don't we stop it now? Don't lay tape on me because tape won't be here tomorrow.' I asked the 800 people there with their bald heads to get their act together and make better speakers, better amplifiers and a different way to make a recording machine, other than analogue. I now see all of my original dreams coming true and it makes me feel mighty pleased."

In 1953, Paul's career as a recording artist began to take a downward turn after his last Number One, 'Vaya Con Dios', and the emergence of rock 'n' roll shortly afterwards put paid to any meaningful chart comeback. But the Les Paul name will live on in the hearts and minds of guitarists and recording technology historians forever. Even in his Eighties, he can often be found jamming at his New York club, Fat Tuesday's, while back at home in New Jersey, his Les Paul House of Sound is one of the most spectacular recording complexes in the United States. "I still get a lot of fun out of music," he told me in 1994. "I moved to New Jersey from California many years ago and built this big, big estate with thirty-four rooms to incorporate some beautiful film, video and music recording studios, and we can do just about anything we want. But we only use it for our own stuff. It's been an interesting life and even though I've been in this game for seventy years it doesn't make any difference, I just keep going."

Hail, Hail, Rock 'N' Roll...And Elvis

The roots of rock 'n' roll can be traced back as early as the mid-Forties when artists ranging from Joe Liggins And His Honeydrippers to John Lee Hooker and Arthur Smith And The Crackerjacks began to develop new stylings from a melting pot of blues, country, bluegrass and "big band" jazz music. But it was not until Bill Haley And His Comets' Number One hit, 'Rock Around The Clock', that the phenomenon really hit home, even though the song which shook the world was originally intended as a B-side.

On 12 April, 1954, immediately after signing to Decca, Haley and his band waltzed into the Pythian Temple studio (a former dance club) on New York City's West Eightieth Street to make history, at a time when the grey-haired engineers who had persevered for years to reduce the amount of·distortion on recordings were now scratching their foreheads in response to the requests of the new artists who yearned for a grittier sound. Milton Gabler, the producer responsible for turning Billie Holiday's career around, was put in charge of the session and insisted that the band assemble themselves on the studio stage as if they were playing live, and let the acoustics take care of the big sound.

Haley was due to cut two tracks that day – 'Thirteen Women' and the less-favoured 'Rock Around The Clock' – but because of Haley's late arrival at the studio, Gabler made it clear that the band would only have time to record the former. However, having cut the first song and with around ten minutes left, Haley suggested that they make a speedy run through of 'Rock Around The Clock', and after playing no more than a couple of verses for balance, the classic-to-be was recorded in one full take, but not before the engineers were shaken by the threat of the lively meters peaking into the red. The producer may have preferred the A-side, but it was 'Rock Around The Clock' which received the most airplay, even though it only scraped into the American Top Thirty upon its release. But its inclusion in the movie, *The Blackboard Jungle*, fuelled the imaginations of both British and native youth, forcing its triumphant reissue in the summer of 1955.

A myth was perpetuated in the media that the great artists of the period would spend only an hour or so in the studio and, as if by magic, record a whole batch of classics as though the creativity was available on tap, to be turned on whenever required. This was clearly not the case, but guarded secrecy surrounding those who actually made the records would prevail until around the late Seventies when it became known that some producers would order the engineers to form a composite master from the best sections of various takes – something only the tape medium would allow. Many of the producers and technicians of the day emerged from War service engineering duties, such as radio communications, and became familiar with the finest amplifiers, compressors and microphones in the world. At the end of World War II, much of the military's audio equipment began to be sold off at bargain basement prices and the servicemen who had developed an interest through their military work took the opportunity to invest in such quality equipment and start their own independent recording studios. The equipment boasted just the right qualities for the embryonic, rough and ready rock 'n' roll music which began to find favour during the early Fifties.

While studios such as Owen Bradley's prolific Nashville operation, Bradley's Barn, had only basic recording equipment, the reliability of the Telefunken, RCA and Columbia microphones so common after the War was key to the sounds the record-buying public adored. Previously used in the military and also for general broadcast and theatrical applications, these microphones could be purchased second-hand for little more than $25 each. That the originals now sell for anything up to $10,000 is evidence enough of their long-term appeal. The engineers realised that these mics could tolerate high volume signals and were virtually indestructible. The drummer on many early rock 'n' roll sessions, Buddy Harman, once recalled to *Nashville's American Federation Musicians' Magazine* that often only one mic would be used to record the drums and an upright bass, with one instrument on either side of the mic. Although little separation was possible, the pulse of the drums on one side would drive and accentuate the bass on other – a happy accident which was to be developed further by the engineers.

No documentary of the birth of rock 'n' roll would be complete without acknowledging the influence of Elvis Presley who did more to change the course of popular music and youth culture than any other individual entertainer in the twentieth century. But it could be argued that if not for his fateful meeting with Sam Phillips in 1953 at his Memphis Recording Service studio, pop may not have become so vital to modern life.

Formerly an engineer at the WREC radio station in Memphis, blues aficionado Phillips opened his studio at 706 Union Avenue in January 1950 with the aid of technical expertise from his broadcast buddies, not that he was a shrinking violet himself when it came to electronics. A two-year loan enabled his purchase of recording equipment. At first, sceptical of the reliability of tape, which was still regarded as a secondary medium until the mid-Fifties, Phillips submitted his recordings to sixteen-inch acetate discs. Whereas the normal cutting speed at the time was thirty-three rpm, Phillips, striving for the best quality reproduction, recorded everything at seventy-eight rpm before making an acetate master on his Presto 6-N lathe and turntable. He obviously saw something in the New Jersey manufacturer, Presto, for his studio consisted mainly of its products including a portable five-input mixer with four microphone ports and a fifth which incorporated a multiselector input/output toggle switch. At this stage in Phillips' business, portability was a prime concern as he earned a fair proportion of his income from transporting his equipment to outside locations to record weddings and other social events.

Phillips eventually turned to magnetic tape in the winter of 1951, using Crestwood and Bell tape machines before buying the Presto 900-P recorder which allowed him to record at either seven and a half or fifteen ips (inches per second). The higher speed, however, was not an option to Phillips who, because of the high price of tape was forced to remain extremely frugal with the amount he used on a session until business boomed. As a result, several hours' worth of early Presley outtake tapes were sacrificed to be reused for other recordings – much to his later regret. A significant studio upgrade occurred in 1954 with the installation of two Ampex 350 tape recorders – a console model and a rack-mounted version used predominantly for the slapback tape delay echo for which Sun became famous. Almost twelve months later, he traded in his Presto board and purchased the RCA 76-D broadcast console which embellished any passing signal with the warm tube coloration characteristic of the period.

The Sun Records label was formed by Phillips in March 1952 after Leonard Chess passed on the opportunity to release his Memphis recording of Walter Horton and Jack Kelly's 'Blues In My Condition' and 'Sellin' My Stuff'. Two months later, Chess would sign Chuck Berry to his label and begin Chicago's important contribution to rock 'n' roll history. From the beginning, Phillips was experimental in his approach to capturing abstract results from his basic tools. For Sun's first actual single release in April 1952, Johnny London's 'Drivin' Slow', Phillips conjured the distant highway sound from London's saxophone by suspending a hollow booth-like object above the player's head, to give a dark, reverberant effect. This was part and parcel of the dark, raw, ethereal and often eerie Sun sound – the perfect ingredients with which to launch a rock 'n' roll icon.

Presley's relationship with Phillips began with the singer's recording at the studio of two songs ('My Happiness' and 'That's When Your Heartaches Begin') as a birthday present for his mother. Although a little rough around the edges, Phillips sensed Presley's potential and in June 1954, he invited him to audition for Sun Records. With the now legendary guitarist Scotty Moore and upright bass player Bill Black as experienced sidemen, Presley ran through several numbers at his debut session before he and Phillips suggested trying 'That's All Right', a nine-year-old hit for its writer, Arthur "Big Boy" Crudup – then Presley's biggest inspiration. It could be said that Presley "produced" himself on this day, for his choice of B-side for his debut single was 'Blue Moon Of Kentucky', originally recorded by Bill Monroe as a bluegrass 3/4 ballad, but this time given Presley's full Crudup treatment, prompting Phillips' enthusiastic cry, "That's a pop song now!" This was the very session at which Phillips introduced the slapback delay sound, used not only on Presley's five Sun singles, but also many recordings by the label's other rock 'n' roll greats, including Jerry Lee Lewis, Roy Orbison and Carl Perkins.

But Presley's success had an unexpected negative effect on the Sun label's business. Demand for the singer's records had become so acute that Sun was having to order re-pressings at a fast rate, paying cash on delivery. The record distributors, however, would not bring forward the normal ninety-day payment to Sun and this left Phillips with a major cashflow dilemma. After considering all his options, he eventually decided to save his skin by selling Presley's contract to RCA in November 1955.

For Presley's first single on his new label (where he would remain in America until his death in 1977), RCA producer, Steve Sholes was adamant that Phillips' sonic treatments be adhered to as closely as other studios would allow. Recorded in a converted church in Nashville over two days on 10-11 January, 1956, 'Heartbreak Hotel' signified Presley's transition from a unique rockabilly singer to a dynamic and impassioned rock 'n' roll performer. In attempting to recreate the Sun echo sound, Sholes relied on the ambience of the cavernous recording venue rather than the tape delay method, giving the impression that the song had been recorded in a desolate haunted house. To augment Presley, Moore and Black on these sessions (at which several songs including the B-side 'I Was The One' and a cover of Ray Charles's 'I Got A Woman' were also recorded), Sholes hired drummer Dominic "DJ" Fontana, veteran guitarist Chet Atkins and piano player Floyd Cramer, plus a gospel vocal trio. One problem facing Sholes was Presley's tendency to get carried away with the music and wander away from the microphone, leaping in time to Fontana's hard-hitting beat. Rather than spoil the singer's fun, Sholes decided to position three microphones around Presley to capture his quivering voice, no matter where he strayed. The results were breathtaking.

Two songwriters who became heavily linked with the Presley legend were Jerry (Jerome) Leiber and Mike Stoller. Already a huge success with regular American chart entries to their credit, Leiber and Stoller were overjoyed when Presley recorded their 'Hound Dog' in July 1956 and when later contracted to RCA themselves, the duo made the major commitment to write for the star on a regular basis. One of their first commissions was to pen new songs for Presley's second movie, *Jailhouse Rock*, and the duo spent the last few days of April 1957 overseeing the recording sessions at Radio Recorders in Hollywood. Although Steve Sholes was Presley's official A&R man – effectively the producer – Leiber and Stoller's guidance became critical to the end product and they quickly became regarded as the production team.

On many sessions up until 1962, when the partnership with Presley subsided, Stoller would contribute piano while Leiber handled matters in the control room. Leiber says, "It was always the A&R man who made a choice of song for the artist, then get the artist familiarised with the material before hiring an arranger who in turn would instruct a session fixer to book the musicians for the session. Things were very organised, particularly with RCA, and not very conducive to artistry. You know, there wouldn't be much room for manoeuvre or making changes to plans two-thirds of the way down the line. As for the songwriters, well, you wouldn't normally see them at a recording session. It wasn't a team effort on the day of recording – that all happened beforehand. But we did get involved and although we didn't intend to be record producers, we did make our feelings and suggestions known to the studio people and the artist because we had firm ideas about how our songs should be performed, even though in the case of 'Jailhouse Rock', we didn't get any extra money for giving such advice! So after a while, not only would we write and arrange the songs, we also worked them up with the artist and directed the recording. Basically, we knew how to make great songs into great records."

Like many stars with rags to riches careers, Presley's original hungry attitude and persona began to change once international fame and wealth came to his door. John Lennon once acidly remarked that "Elvis died when he joined the Army [in March 1958]", intimating that his rocking qualities had dissolved in an ocean of simpering ballads. Of course, this is a highly subjective matter but it is true that apart from his acclaimed performance on the *Elvis* TV special in late 1968, Presley never truly rekindled the raw urgency that first made his name at Sun Records. Leiber and Stoller, however, went from strength to strength as songwriters and producers both during and after breaking away from the Presley camp. Their work with Atlantic Records artists such as The Coasters, The Isley Brothers, Ben E King and The Drifters – whose 1959 hit 'There Goes My Baby' is widely known to be the first rock 'n' roll/R&B track to feature an orchestral arrangement – helped to shape the musical environment of the late Fifties and early Sixties.

Some of the engineers who drifted into rock 'n' roll work came from the film studios in Hollywood, which for some time had used echo chamber effects for cartoons, and they quickly realised their value for pop music. That echo could help to "beef up" small bands of only three or four musicians was a revelation, so much so that amplifier designer, Ray Butts started to build his products with integral echo facilities for guitarists, and later inventions like the WEM Copicat (a stand-alone tape-based echo unit) offered a variety of delay times at the push of a button.

Stuart Colman, who helped to incite a rock 'n' roll revival in the Eighties as the producer of all of Shakin' Stevens' greatest hits and now lives in Nashville, says, "I was making an album with Jeff Beck a few years ago and, being a huge Gene Vincent fan, he wanted to recreate some of those vintage sounds that were made at Bradley's Barn. I discovered that the delay time used there was 130 milliseconds and that was exactly the timing of slapback that fitted the tempos that were common then. Now, of course, you can vary a delay time to very exact distances but Bradley's Barn had a separate tape machine for nothing but delay, but they also fed the delayed signal into a live room before it came back on to tape, so it was a two-handed operation and it cracked like a whip! 'She's Not There' by Santana and Steve Miller's 'Abracadabra' are great modern examples of where that type of echo has been introduced during a guitar solo and the effect is astonishing. So all these years later, those old methods are still viable for making tremendous pop sounds."

At the end of the Fifties in Norfolk, Virginia, Gary "US" Bonds and his producer, Frank Guida put in place new sound characteristics which were at the heart of Phil Spector's and, much later, Bruce Springsteen's work. At the forefront of all of Bonds' records – including show-stoppers 'New Orleans' and 'Quarter To Three' – was a strange "outdoor" sound, featuring double-tracked vocals squeezed to the hilt with compression. Contrary to ridiculous media hype, these tracks were not recorded in the middle of a field. A record shop owner, Guida made his records with local musicians in a studio to the rear of his premises (Frankie's Birdland), issued them on his own LeGrand label and sold them as part of his stock.

With little FM radio in existence, such records were recorded in mono for AM broadcast and cut as loudly as possible, often with the meters pinned in the red. Guida would instruct his engineers to not only move the record and playback heads of a tape machine apart, but move them within 360° so that the azimuth of the sound changed and affected the pulse on the vocal to give a more exciting effect.

Holly In Clovis

In the same year that Les Paul chanced upon the sound-on-sound recording technique, a skinny thirteen-year-old from Lubbock, Texas was making his first appearances as a country and bluegrass singer/guitarist. Nearly seven years later, in January 1956, Buddy Holly signed to Decca Records and recorded his first single, 'Blue Days, Black Nights' at Bradley's Barn with Jerry Allison on drums, Sonny Curtis on guitar and Don Guess on bass. Within five months of its release, however, Holly and Decca parted company due to mutual dissatisfaction and he travelled with Allison to Clovis, New Mexico to meet independent producer and engineer, Norman Petty, at his studio. Together they would form one of the most successful partnerships of the rock 'n' roll period.

Although Holly died along with fellow stars Richie Valens and The Big Bopper in an aeroplane crash on 3 February, 1959, his backing group, The Crickets continue to work both on stage and in the studio, most recently with Nanci Griffith and Stuart Colman. Bass player, Joe B Mauldin joined the band in February 1957 and, later to become a second engineer himself in the early Sixties at California's Gold Star Studios, was fortunate to take notice of the techniques used by Petty during the making of such hits as 'Peggy Sue', 'Oh Boy' and 'Maybe Baby', until the team broke up in October 1958.

"I had known Buddy for some time in Lubbock," says Mauldin. "We went to the same high school, although he was a couple of years ahead of me, and I had seen him and Jerry performing in town. I was playing with another group at the time and Buddy had Don Guess playing stand-up bass like me. A bit later, Don decided that he wanted to do something other than just be a bass player, so he went and quit. Then Buddy and Jerry came by one day and asked if I'd care to fill that slot in the group because they were gonna be big stars. I said, 'How long do you think it's gonna take?' He replied, 'How long did it take Elvis?' I thought that boy sure had a lot of confidence so I was willing to give it a try. Decca had dropped Buddy and that was the reason for forming The Crickets. Buddy recorded 'That'll Be The Day' for Decca just before I joined and there was a clause in his contract that stated that he couldn't re-record that song for another record company for five years. So he said, 'Okay, Buddy Holly won't record it, The Crickets will.' The record [released by Brunswick] was never credited as Buddy Holly and Decca didn't even realise it was him singing on it until a year or so had passed."

Up until joining The Crickets, Mauldin had only ever recorded at radio stations in the Lubbock area, whereas although Holly had already recorded in Nashville, he had become frustrated by the tense, conveyor belt attitude of the engineers towards the young talent. "It was the kind of situation where someone would say, 'Hurry up, we've got another band coming in,'" Mauldin recalls. "Buddy wanted to check out Clovis to see how relaxed he could be over there, so that's kind of what started the ball rolling for The Crickets."

According to Mauldin, Norman Petty's greatest strengths as a producer and engineer were his intense analysis of sound and attention to detail. "He was quite particular about everything coming back from the tape exactly the way it sounded in the studio, as if you were right there listening to it," he says. "With the guitars, Buddy would play his Stratocaster through a Fender tweed-covered amplifier, and Norman would have a couple of mics on the amp to record the electric sound. But then he would also take another mic and put it up near the strings of Buddy's guitar, even though they weren't making much noise, so that he could get the sound of the pick on the strings. He would put Buddy out there on his own without even running his guitar through an amplifier. I thought that was unusual and the end result that came out of the speakers in the control room really sounded like you were right in front of Buddy, listening to him play."

Having previously enjoyed moderate success with his own Norman Petty Trio and Buddy Knox And The Rhythm Orchids, Petty was among the new breed of technicians who took the rock 'n' roll sound to new heights, using Les Paul's overdubbing principles, even though he was yet to invest in a multitrack recorder. Comments Mauldin, "Norman's mainstay tape machine was a mean momma Ampex 600 portable which allowed him to remove it from the studio and take anywhere he wanted. But he also had an Ampex 327 mono machine on which he made duplicate copies. He recorded us in mono and would use the two machines, playing back on to one the music he had just recorded while recording a new part along with it. Most of the time, Buddy, Jerry Allison and I would go out into the studio and record the guitar, bass and drums all at once, with an occasional piano part played by Norman's wife, Vi. Then, if he wanted the pick sound, like on 'Everyday' where it is quite evident, he would overdub that and mix it into the overall sound. It was very effective."

'Everyday' featured another original and much copied sound, care of Jerry Allison's knees, as Mauldin explains: "He had some tight Levi's on that day and we had been rehearsing with Norman listening behind the console. Buddy was playing his guitar and I was playing the bass as normal, and Jerry was sitting there just patting his knees. Norman happened to hear that and said, 'Wow, let's put a mic down between Jerry's legs and we'll use that sound as the drums.' So it was a spur of the moment thing which worked out real well, and that's all the percussion there is on 'Everyday'. That wasn't an overdub either, it was all done live."

To avoid instrument leakage on other mics, Holly and Mauldin were often sandwiched between acoustic screens, while on some numbers, including 'Peggy Sue' and 'Not Fade Away', Allison set up his Pearl drum kit in a completely different room. "There were some pretty elaborate mics at the studio," says Mauldin. "At the time, the

Telefunken version of the Neumann U47 was Norman's favourite for vocals, sometimes on the guitar and as an overhead mic for the drum kit, and it's good to see how that mic is back in vogue today. We used a little Stevens tie microphone on my stand-up bass, a tiny thing that was just as big as the end of your thumb. That was a good mic for the bass because Norman could get it into the f-hole of the instrument. He also had an RCA 77 and a 44, the big old thing that the announcers used to use in the Forties, and he would use that a lot on the kick drum, with an Electrovoice RE15 on the snare drum."

The Clovis studio consisted of two buildings and could be regarded as the original residential studio. Upon entering the first building, one would be greeted by a reception area, behind which was the small control room. "Norman's console was positioned so that as he sat there, he had to look over his left shoulder through the window to see us playing in the studio," says Mauldin. "He had one Altec 604 speaker for mono monitoring and the mixing console was a four-buss operation which went into a mono mix."

The main studio to the right was designed by Petty himself, influenced by the acoustic properties of some of the large New York studios. Also on site was a small apartment where the band and Petty would sleep after sessions. "It was real convenient for us," Mauldin recalls. "We couldn't work during the day because the building next door was a garage where Norman's father worked on automobiles and trucks, hammering away and using electric wrenches, so there was always a lot of noise going on. We would spend the day time working in the yard, or playing around or swimming, then record at night when his parents had gone to bed or had quit working or whatever."

In the garage attic was the studio's echo chamber which, again, Petty built himself. At one end was an Altec 604 speaker with two Sennheiser microphones at the other, picking up whatever sound was being fed in. Mauldin believes that the crispness of the echo sound on Holly's recordings stems from the use of the Sennheisers which produced a sharp, brilliant sound, and have since become favoured as overhead mics. "I think Norman may have over-compensated on the top-end frequencies, anticipating that he was going to do some overdubbing," he says, "because the more generations of recording you use, the less top end you'll be left with. He also used filters to eliminate tape hiss. We didn't have noise gates or Dolby noise reduction then! We knew that whenever we were overdubbing, we had to get as much down in one take as we possibly could, to avoid too many overdub generations, otherwise it might damage the quality of the end product."

During the recording of 'I'm Gonna Love You Too' for The Crickets' second album, an invasion of the echo chamber triggered mass confusion inside the control room. "We had a cricket in the chamber and we couldn't get rid of it," says Mauldin. "We began recording but had to keep stopping the takes because Norman would say, 'Ah, there's that cricket again!' We had to go and try to find it up in the attic, but every time we looked, the cricket shut up and we never did find it. It just so happens that the recording of 'I'm Gonna Love You Too' has four cricket chirps at the end which are in tempo with the song, but that was a complete fluke because Norman let the tape run to allow the echo to die off."

It was common belief for many years that The Beatles introduced the trend for late-night/early morning sessions, although Mauldin is quick to dispel the myth. "We had unlimited time and there was nobody with their thumb on a stopwatch saying, 'Hey, you boys have got to quit at twelve o'clock!'" he recalls. "We went in there and never kept any kind of record of how much time we were spending on a song. I guess that was how we came up with some of those great sounds. We were never under any kind of pressure from anybody so we could pretty much do as we pleased. You know, if we decided that we wanted to stop and eat something after recording for a couple of hours, we would. It was real relaxed and it was great to be able to work at our own pace."

Mauldin's fondest memory of working with Holly and Petty is of the session for 'Well All Right', which turned out to be a much simpler acoustic guitar/bass/drums arrangement than Petty had in mind. "Buddy was just going to use his Gibson acoustic but Norman had some plans to overdub a few things later on and make some changes to it," he says. "But when we finished the take that was used, we said, 'Wow, that sounds just great as it is, it doesn't need anything else on it.' We all agreed so we left it alone and I thought Buddy did a phenomenal job of playing that acoustic."

While Petty's producer role is now cast in historical stone, Mauldin insists that The Crickets' sound was the result of a democracy: "He gets a lot of credit for production, but we were all producers on those records. No one person was actually the beginning or the end of the production. Not that anybody ever mentioned the actual word 'production', because we all looked on the process of recording very differently back then. Norman started out strictly as our engineer and as we began to feel comfortable with him, we asked if he would be interested in managing us, so he began to have more control over what was being done and who was doing it."

chapter two

atlantic crossing

"When the three of us worked on a project, if one of us had an idea, the other two would ask how they could help...it was like a board meeting about what we were each going to do."

Tom Dowd on Wexler, Mardin & Dowd

"I wanted everyone to listen to this masterwork and I felt like I had all the power of the world in my hands."

Brian Wilson on 'Good Vibrations'

For some considerable time, the Americans led the way in pop music production and many years would pass before the British industry as a whole caught up and latched on to their artistic and technical innovations. Over in the States, three people to enjoy the most consistent commercial success with the new technology were Jerry Wexler, Arif Mardin and Tom Dowd – the triumvirate production/arrangement/engineering team responsible for Atlantic's incredible record of R&B and soul classics in the Sixties. Even today in the Nineties, Dowd's advanced years do not prevent him from opening his mind to contemporary rock bands such as Primal Scream who benefit from a little of the fairy dust magic that made Aretha Franklin, Wilson Pickett, Otis Redding, Booker T And The MGs and Ray Charles legends. And that is just a small portion of names from one of the most glittering credit lists in the business.

Dowd joined Atlantic Records in 1947, initially as a freelance engineer, and having worked with every conceivable recording format he is one of the few engineers and producers from the period to remain active in an industry which has seen enormous changes in technology over the last half-century. Essential to the tight Atlantic sound (and that of Bill Haley's early Philadelphia recordings), Dowd became one of the original pioneers of eight-track recording when, in 1957, he received only the third-ever Ampex machine of its kind (Les Paul and songwriter Mitch Miller owned serial numbers 0001 and 0002).

"I was anticipating things," he says. "The people at Atlantic Studios were sensitive to stereo, and we were recording stereo or binaural tracks as far back as 1952. That's when I set up the initial mono and stereo simultaneous recording consoles so that anything we were doing in the mid-Fifties was recorded on both one- and two-track. There was a great deal of controversy among engineers, predominantly about the signal-to-noise ratio not being good enough on three-track on quarter-inch or half-inch. They were intelligent arguments from an engineering point of view, but at the same time I knew about the problems involved in getting a good mix to produce the best results on disc. I couldn't understand how Les Paul was getting such wonderful, wonderful quality when I could hear Mary Ford simultaneously doing three voice parts and Les playing three, four or five guitar parts. But that's when I found out about the eight-track machine and how he was using it creatively for layering. Until then, all the engineers were saying that tape was noisy, but no one said, 'Oh, that Les Paul record is no good, it's got too much hiss on it!' So suddenly all these so-called technical geniuses were having to eat their words.

"Hearing what Les was doing prompted me to think we could make superior records if we were to record on multitrack tape, because instead of reacting to the mix and trying to capture the performance in one hit, we could enhance it, relive it, improve parts, and generally make a better tape for transference to disc. But hardly anyone appreciated the power of eight-track. They didn't realise that an hour after the session or even the next day, you could sit down and push up the level of the bass or the guitar on a particular recording to create a whole new different mix that would make a much better LP or forty-five."

234 West Street, NYC

By 1958, when most of the major American studios were still pondering over whether to progress to four-track, Dowd was already making eight-track hit recordings, his first being LaVern Baker's Bessie Smith tribute album, quickly followed by The Coasters' 'Charlie Brown', 'Yakety Yak' and 'Poison Ivy', 'Splish Splash' and 'Queen Of The Hop' by Bobby Darin, and 'What'd I Say' by Ray Charles. All of which were recorded at New York City's celebrated Atlantic Studios at 234 West Fifty-Sixth Street where Tom was now part of the staff as the house engineer and resident electronics boffin. "The studio was used as an office in daylight hours, then they would push the desks and chairs into the corner, and bring out the mics and stuff to make a studio in the night time," he says. "When they moved to another office, they gave me that room and I designed a new thirty-five by forty-five foot studio with the space that was available, so that we could accommodate the bigger sessions we had been doing outside at Capitol or Coastal Studios. We would often record twelve or fourteen string players, four horns, six rhythm players, five background singers and one principal, simultaneously. That's where we recorded things like 'Stand By Me' by Ben E King and The Drifters' 'Save The Last Dance For Me', 'Up On The Roof' and 'On Broadway', all between 1960 and 1962."

Atlantic Studios boasted possibly the world's most famous echo chamber but, as Dowd explains, there was absolutely no science behind its eccentric tiled design. "I bought lots of boxes of leftover tiles from local hardware stores because I only wanted fractured pieces," he says. "We intentionally had the most non-symmetrical room in the city! We did everything the total opposite to what a carpenter or mason would do. We made that room so screwed up that the only thing level was the floor, and the ceiling and four walls had nothing in common with symmetry whatsoever! When we put the tiles on, we did it in such an erratic fashion that no two pieces looked the same. I mean, it was a nightmare of a room, aesthetically, but it was a nice echo chamber. Ultimately we changed over to the Neumann EMT chambers because in order to make another chamber similar to that would have been so expensive."

"Columbia Records on 799 Seventh Avenue used to use the stairwell for their echo chamber. They'd have to wait until everyone left the building after office hours and they would put a microphone up on the eighth floor and wheel a speaker out on the landing of the third floor and another up between the fourth and fifth floor, and so on. They would experiment to see which way sounded better for the strings or the vocal or whatever. But things got so expensive that it was a totally uneconomical use of space. The best chambers, I think, were the ones owned by EMI out in California. They were wonderful, but they weren't designed to be echo chambers because they were the part of the original air conditioning installation in the circular building. When the air conditioning needed to be replaced, they realised that they had engineered themselves into a corner and couldn't get the units out without dismantling and removing them piece by piece. So they quickly vacated the space and the EMI engineers designated it echo chamber land."

Between the late Forties and early Sixties, most studios continued to produce recordings on hand-me-down equipment, acquired from radio stations. One of the first innovators in purpose-designed recording consoles was Bob Fine who quietly revolutionised that side of the industry at the turn of the Fifties. But when Atlantic graduated to eight-track, Dowd was forced to design his own console for the studio. "As soon as Atlantic gave me the opportunity, I started building a console that was simultaneous mono and stereo," he says. "No one knew what the hell eight-track was, so I had to build a console that would work with that format. We were still using tubes [valves] and if you sat behind a twenty-position desk, you'd get sunburn on your kneecaps from the heat coming off of the tubes. It was ridiculous. There would be 400 or 500 volts floating around on the power supply and somebody could have got electrocuted trying to replace something. But, hey, it's a lot safer now."

In 1966, a fresh-faced Tony Visconti – later to become one of the most successful British-based producers of the late Sixties and Seventies – made his first visit to a recording studio at the invitation of his friend, Bruce Tergessen who had just joined Atlantic as a junior engineer under Dowd. Visconti looked around in awe as he viewed the empty control room and can remember in crystal clear detail what he saw. "My whole perception of how records in the big league were made was wholly based on what I gleaned from that visit and it was like being in a palace when the King was away," he recalls. "The eight-track machine had eight faders which were just potentiometers for the microphones. There was no EQ on the board and the microphone gain went directly to a track. If you wanted to put two or three mics together, you had to go through another section of the board called a network, which we might call a buss or group output nowadays. Back then, they were still only using two mics on the drums – a kick drum mic and an overhead which picked up the snare, cymbals and toms. They insisted that the drums were always recorded in the same spot – you were never allowed to play them anywhere in the studio other than in a reserved space which Tommy Dowd had built to create some really great sounds. So in actual fact they never networked any more than two mics, or maybe three for a horn section. The net was just three faders going to one fader.

"They never believed in EQ except in drastic situations when they used their three Pultecs and stuck some enormous, GPO-like telephone cables into the patch bay on the wall. It was so primitive. Their philosophy was, 'Use the right microphone for the right job.' So if you were getting a bad vocal sound, that meant you were using the wrong mic! They'd record everything almost raw, right on to the eight-track."

Monitoring, Visconti says, was strictly mono with one loudspeaker positioned in the centre of the control room; stereo mixes could only be checked for accuracy after the actual mixing was complete. "Next door to that studio, they had quite a sophisticated mixing suite which was the very antithesis of the studio control room," he says. "They had three speakers: a stereo pair and one mono speaker, because they still believed in mono. And they were probably American speakers, like Altecs, because British products had not yet reached American shores. There was a nice little board with a sophisticated EQ but no echo plate."

Until the late Sixties, there was a marked difference between the production and engineering methods in America and Britain, almost as if there was an impervious technological barrier set up in the Atlantic Ocean. Although it was America which embraced eight-track recording many years in advance of the Brits, Dowd believes it was the latter who displayed a superior understanding of the recording arts. "I tip my hat to the training that the British engineers had and their degree of proficiency, because in America, a lot of the people who aspired to be engineers didn't know as much, but they flew by the seat of their pants and made it work," he admits. "On the first encounter I had with British engineers, when I stepped into a session at Advision Studios in London for the first Yes album with Eddie Offord, I quickly became aware that they knew more than I did. I just thought, 'What am I doing here?'"

One of the recording industry's biggest controversies of the mid-Sixties concerned the broadcast of stereo records on AM radio. EMI, for example, would provide American AM stations with stereo albums to be played on their mono equipment, only to hear vocals drop out of the records during broadcast. This was particularly noticeable on Beatles tracks and a cause of great embarrassment to producers. Says Dowd, "The people at Capitol were listening and saying, 'But it's not cutting in and out,' but they were listening in stereo. George Martin and I joked about it once or twice. He was booby-trapped on one or two of the Beatles albums by the inconsistency of manufacturers at the time. Unfortunately, the tape machine manufacturers in those days were designing the engineer's tape machine, and didn't realise that producers would want to bounce from track to track. The sync or record heads were not always the same polarity, so when you bounced something from one track to another, as long as you listened to it in a stereo configuration you never heard a phase shift. But when you took that stereo product and played it in mono, there would be places where a voice or instrument would drop out in the middle of the recording and come back again at the point where parts had been bounced from one track to another to form a vocal or instrumental track. It was insane that all of these people spoke the same language but couldn't understand each other.

"Many of the equipment designers didn't spend five minutes in the studio and think how someone might start abusing a machine to make it do something it wasn't supposed to. But I wasn't afraid to open the seam on the equipment and get inside and say, 'This is what I want it to do. What if I change this or change that?' All of a sudden, people were asking how I got some effect and I'd say, 'Oh, I had to modify the equipment.' Suddenly it became the vogue and we were no longer going to be handcuffed. When I compare the naivety of the business back then to the amazing advances we are enjoying today, it's rather like the difference between the Wright Brothers flying the first aeroplane and a supersonic jet. They both leave the ground but they have nothing else in common!"

Wexler, Mardin And Dowd

Aside from the talented roster of artists, Atlantic's magical hit formula can be largely attributed to the awesome partnership of producer Jerry Wexler, arranger Arif Mardin and engineer Dowd. "There was a wonderful chemistry," says Dowd. "When the three of us worked on a project, if one of us had an idea, the other two would ask how they could help and it became a collaboration. Maybe not all three of us were in love with the same song or arrangement, or even the same take. But something would inspire one of us and the other two would say, 'Go ahead and do it.' I think Arif and I deferred to Jerry because he was closer to most of the artists at the outset than we were, and he would do the preliminary work with them. But then there were times when Jerry might send me to Memphis with Wilson Pickett or send Arif someplace else with Bette Midler. We would all meet up again back at base five days later. I would have my two cuts and Arif would have his and Jerry would have some cuts with Aretha Franklin, and Jerry would say, 'Hey Dowd, whaddya say, let's put some horns on this one? Mardin, how about some strings on this one and when we get them together then we've gotta come up with some background?' It was like a board meeting about what we were each going to do. We'd have our individual responsibilities and get on with the job.

"Arif is an immaculate arranger and conductor, and he'd even be writing melodic parts while the tape machine was in record. He'd be writing the paste-on arrangement before the previous take was finished, and then suggest how that earlier take should be re-recorded to fit into what he was writing at that moment. There were times when Arif and I would be in two different cities, maybe in Memphis and Muscle Shoals, and I'd call Arif to ask what he was doing with strings.

I'd say, 'I'm sending you a song that I'd like strings on,' and I'd sing him a line over the phone that he'd write down and modify. By the same token, he might ask what rhythm section I had and say, 'I need a song at this tempo, in this key, a blues progression with an instrumental in C for twenty bars. Can you send me a track?'

"If Arif was doing something and he realised that the people he had working in New York were not right for the song he wouldn't be afraid to ask me to make a track for that song in Memphis, even though I wouldn't know the damn song. He'd just say, 'I'm looking for a two-beat, funky-sounding track.' And he could then finish it the way he wanted. But he'd never embarrass people by saying he could get something done better elsewhere. We were constantly switching hats. For one Aretha Franklin session at Criteria in Miami [in October 1969], Jerry sent me the tape to put the horns on 'Rock Steady' and 'Don't Play That Song', and took another copy of 'Don't Play That Song' for Arif to put strings on. And when the record came out it was the first time I knew there were going to be strings on it. Neither Arif or I knew the other was going to put their parts on until the finished record came out, yet it sounded so planned."

Franklin's 'Respect' may remain a much-covered classic of its time but Dowd concedes that it was recorded rather hastily after sessions broke down at Rick Hall's Florence Alabama Recording Emporium or FAME Studios in Muscle Shoals, Alabama – the venue for James And Bobby Purify and The Jackson Five's earliest hits. "We came back to New York and recorded 'Respect' along with some additional songs for the album [1967's *I Never Loved A Man*] with an amalgamation of musicians from Muscle Shoals and Memphis, along with some New York people who we thought were worthy," he recalls. "On that session, it was Roger Hawkins [drums] and Jimmy Johnson [bass]. Jerry Jemmott and Tommy Cogbill, from the Memphis section, were also playing bass on some of those things."

The unique identity of Alabama's finest studio players and the stark difference in style to their Memphis and New York counterparts, provided Wexler, Mardin and Dowd with a diverse range of musical flavours to work with. "When we were recording Percy Sledge and Aretha, we would use people from Muscle Shoals or Memphis," says Dowd, "because these were musicians who were around the same age as the artists, in their early to late twenties. They had grown up in this culture where black and white music was mixed, and you didn't have to be black to play black music, just as you didn't have to be white to play white. People in other parts of the United States were listening to something coming out of the South, not realising that some of those musicians were white."

Although officially signed to Atco – an Atlantic subsidiary label – soul giant Otis Redding was to become an important part of the Stax establishment and his greatest work, the album *Otis Blue/Otis Redding Sings Soul*, was recorded by Dowd at Stax's Memphis studio in two days in a break during a national tour in 1965. Says Dowd, "The record company called me and said, 'Otis is coming in for the weekend and he has to leave by Sunday, but we'd like to make an album with him so we can put out a collection of all new songs rather than an album of his singles.' So I took a Thursday night flight into Memphis so that I was ready to start promptly at ten am on the Friday morning. We had the finest musicians money could hire, people like Steve Cropper, 'Duck' Dunn, Al Jackson, Isaac Hayes, David Porter and Booker T. On horns were Bowlegs Miller, Wayne Jackson, Paki Axton, Andrew Love and Floyd Newman. Booker T was the band and The MGs, or Memphis Group, were the horns.

"Otis was a very controlled person and even though it was myself and Jim Stewart (Stax A&R man) in the control booth, no one person actually produced him as such. We all gave an equal amount to the overall sound. He would save up all that emotion and energy, that others might use in demonstrating, stomping and screaming, for when he was going to sing. The Stax studio was actually a 4-500 capacity theatre with the seats pulled out so it was a pretty big room, with a sloping floor. It was easy to isolate sounds without having to use screens. You'd just keep the musicians far enough apart from each other and it was okay. The vocal was always recorded up at one end of the room and Otis learned very quickly after we had recorded once or twice how to fade in and out of a mic, or sneak up on a microphone. Otis was the ultimate artist. Every now and again, he would stop a take and say, 'We've got to do it again because I messed up.' He'd say, 'If you guys can play the song that well, you can do it again one time for me.'

"Down at Stax, they had two or perhaps three Neumanns of the U47 or U87 variety, an RCA 77DX, an RCA 44BX, one or two Shures and an AKG, although it was not a microphone-rich studio. When we had the five horns up, more often than not there would be two microphones for the five horns, and whoever was in the control room would say, 'Second trumpet, back off the mic a little, baritone come in a bit.' Once they heard a playback, the horn section would re-position themselves and perform dynamically around the mics. Once the musicians found a good position, they'd remember it and return there."

Fiery Cream

When Dowd worked with his first fully-fledged rock band, he couldn't have hoped for a more formidable line-up than Eric Clapton, Jack Bruce and Ginger Baker who, as Cream, were the original rock supergroup. 'Sunshine Of Your Love', 'Strange Brew' and 'Crossroads' remain icons from the early progressive rock era. But the sessions for the *Disraeli Gears* and *Wheels Of Fire* albums at Atlantic in 1967 and 1968 proved to be something of a culture shock for Dowd, who was not prepared for the huge live sound of the band. "They were a powerhouse!" he explains. "My biggest concern was how I was going to isolate Ginger from the guitar and bass. When the roadies were setting up the equipment and I saw those double speaker cabinets for the bass and the big Marshall guitar stack, I thought, 'That's all well and good, but where do I put these things so at least I can get a sound on the drums!' Then I saw the drum kit go up with two bass drums and five cymbal trees, and I thought, 'Oh God, I'm gonna have guitar and bass spilling down every damn drum mic.'

"I just made them feel comfortable and tried to keep them as far apart as I could in that studio that I'd designed for Atlantic on Sixtieth Street. They had Ginger in one portion of the room and I had the guitar and bass amplifier stacks positioned at ninety degrees to where he was playing so that Jack and Eric could stand in front of their amps and still have eye contact with each other and Ginger. There was no need for earphones although ear protectors would have been a good idea 'cause they were so loud!" Surprisingly, Dowd chose not to use limiters. "Glyn Johns and I discussed this at length but I very seldom used limiters on anything except vocals, and that was just to cut the peaks down. I would just ride the peaks with my hand on the fader after I'd heard a song once or twice to get a feel for what the band were doing. I preferred it that way."

Having been used to recording on four-track for previous releases back in England, Cream must have acknowledged Atlantic's eight-track capabilities as a luxury. Their presence at the studio, however, was the result of a complex political situation, as Dowd explains: "Ahmet Ertegun [Atlantic's president] had made a negotiation with Robert Stigwood the year before when The Bee Gees were signed and RSO was starting. In this particular era, there was little give and take between European and American musicians when it came to the nationalism factor, and if a five-man American group were going to appear in England, then we had to allow for a five-man group from England to come here for an equal amount of time. There was a very hard-nosed attitude on the part of both countries and the unions. Cream came over to the States to promote their first album, *Fresh Cream*, and they had a thirty- or thirty-two-day visa and work permit, and I think they toured for about twenty-three days, with the occasional day off. Ahmet called me up in the middle of the week and told me that the band had three days left and he had promised Stigwood that we'd record them. He said, 'They'll be here tomorrow. Make an album.' So the next day, their roadies were moving in at ten am and the band started at about two pm, and we recorded throughout the rest of that day, and the following two days. Then on the Sunday afternoon at around five pm, a limousine driver came walking into the control room and said he had to take three guys to the airport. I said, 'Here they are,' and pointed to Ginger, Jack and Eric. I said, 'Hey you guys, you gotta catch a plane.' So they got in the limousine and left me to mix the album [*Disraeli Gears*]. I didn't see them again until after it came out!"

Cream's follow-up album, *Wheels Of Fire*, was recorded under more scheduled circumstances during two weeks in 1968 at Atlantic Studios. During the period between the making of the two albums, Atlantic's control room had undergone a facelift which allowed total blackout, save for the twinkling controls on the console. "We had the console raised about five feet from the studio floor so we'd be looking down into the studio," says Dowd. "It was an enormous control room and everything in it was black, and all of the lights were pinspots. This meant that the musicians looking in would not see a bunch of gawking, yawning, sleeping people hanging on to telephones or drinking coffee. But unknown to us because of the loud music, there would be all kinds of people quietly sneaking in behind us in the dark to catch the session.

"Linda McCartney [then Eastman] was occasionally around to get some photographs and she'd say, 'Tom, do you mind if I turn the lights up a bit for the camera?' The band didn't mind so we'd turn the lights on and we'd suddenly realise there about fifteen people crashed out against the wall digging the session. There was Janis Joplin and all kinds of people, but it wasn't that we weren't going to allow them in, it's just that you were intent on recording with your head down, and you'd never know when somebody came in on their hands and knees and snuck up on the floor! It was absolutely insane!"

Whether back in the Sixties or in today's environment of electronically-delivered perfection, Dowd has always maintained that feel and emotion should be the overriding factors when laying down a track, and his hatred of clinical musicianship has occasionally led to control room wars. "I've had some wonderful marriages with artists but also some disastrous ones where that particular partnership just wasn't meant to happen," he says. "I come from a strange musical and ethnic background, so I am sensitive to classical music, but also to swing and blues. I can't stand time-corrected tracks or sterile, vertical recording. It has to have a horizontal motion, it has to be going somewhere, from the first note to the last. I will raise hell with a band over the principle of contributing to anything sterile. A lot of people don't realise before they work with me that I'm going to get in their face for being a perfect time-keeper or memorising parts.

"When I record, if I have my way and I am working with a single artist, not a band, before I give a chord chart and sheet music to the musicians, I let them see what the lyrics are so that they learn what the piece of poetry is about that they're playing to. If you just put the music in front of them, they won't even listen to what the song is about, so they'll invent melodies that may not have anything in common with the lyrical subject. So I like to think that if I'm on a session with six or seven musicians, if the vocalist didn't show up, each of them could sing the vocal. If they know the song well enough to sing the vocal, then their playing won't get in their own way. A lot of artists don't appreciate that point. For the most part I try to make the musicians more sensitive to the song they are playing on and get the music to flow, rather than like a metronome. So it expands, dilates, contracts, lives and breathes."

Ramone: A&R Man

Eight-time Grammy award winner, Phil Ramone began his career in a small New York demo studio before landing a job at A&R Recording which, along with Bell Sound and only a few others, was one of the most prolific independent studios in the Big Apple of the Sixties, competing for chart places with their major rivals Atlantic, Columbia, RCA and Decca. Ramone, who broke into production with the 1969 *Midnight Cowboy* movie soundtrack and went on to produce such major names as Billy Joel, Paul Simon, Barbra Streisand and Frank Sinatra, learned how to run a session from his mentor of the time, Bill Schwartau who made the important point that a young engineer should learn how to cut a disc before recording the music. "Cutting discs taught me all about sibilance and all the things that you really were frightened of," says Ramone. "I learned how to put bass on to a record, how to make a forty-five sound so loud that the juke box would come to life. How to make a record that works on radio, so that ours was slightly louder and attracted more attention than someone else's. In those days, we used to do three hour sessions, and half an hour overtime was considered a sin. In three hours you were supposed to cut at least four songs, so an album, on average, would take two days at the most – maybe three, and after that you edited and did anything else that was possible.

"As an engineer I was constantly looking at the clock and you had to be able to get a balance in an amazingly short time. If you couldn't balance a rhythm section and pull up a good level on the horns within five minutes, you were not considered good enough to work with the pros. So the clock often determined what a record would sound like. That kind of schooling or, at least, that level of stress has thankfully disappeared from the modern world. By the time I started to get going in the studios, a great many of the older, wiser engineers began to tire of the lifestyle associated with their work, and it gave my colleagues and I the break to experiment with the R&B or jazz dates, as they were then called, which took place between ten pm and four am. We were working with three- and four-track at A&R and the sixteen-input console we had was pretty far out for its time, with four Pultecs and a couple of limiters. The rest of it was down to miking technique and I learned such a lot from just watching Bill Puttnam, Bill Schwartau, Al Schmitt, Tommy Dowd and Don Fry who had the patience and the humour to deal with me. I was a maniac who wanted to record every day and be a musician, I wanted to understand songs and be in the studio with everybody. So I never left the studio."

Phil Spector's Wall Of Sound

In the early Sixties, Phil Spector single-handedly changed the face of American pop by providing a mesmerising new soundtrack for the lives of lovesick teenage bobbysoxers. His phrase, "Wall of Sound" became the trademark by which he will always be remembered, its unique, dense style, indelibly linked to the man who many regard as the first "personality" producer. Spector's musical career began in 1957 at the age of seventeen as a member of The Sleepwalkers, alongside future Beach Boy Bruce Johnston, Kim Fowley and star drummer Sandy Nelson, but he quickly moved into production when he formed The Teddy Bears the following year to record his first hit song, the much imitated 'To Know Him Is To Love Him', at Hollywood's Gold Star Studios – later to feature largely in the Spector legend.

Much of Spector's early success was as a songwriter and while working as an apprentice with Jerry Leiber and Mike Stoller, he co-wrote the Ben E King classic, 'Spanish Harlem'. But it was after he broke away from the Leiber/Stoller empire in February 1961 that he began to find his feet, producing the first-ever recording of 'Twist And Shout' (by The Top Notes) and 'Second Hand Love', a major hit for Connie Francis. The next 18 months were crucial to Spector's eventual success. With entrepreneur Lester Sill he formed his own record label, Philles, and formed an alliance with songwriters Barry Mann and

Cynthia Weil, with whom he would enjoy a string of international hits. The notoriety as a determined but unpredictable individual which Spector earned around this period came as a result of forming a new line-up of The Crystals for the recording of Gene Pitney's 'He's A Rebel' when touring commitments made the original singers unavailable. Without hesitation, Spector brought in three new girls for the session at Gold Star, including Darlene Love. This was the beginning of the girl group phenomenon which would explode in 1963 with further hits for The Crystals ('Da Doo Ron Ron' – co-written with Jeff Barry and Ellie Greenwich – and 'Then He Kissed Me') and The Ronettes ('Be My Baby' and 'Baby I Love You'), and become compounded by the monumental *A Christmas Gift For You* album, which has been subsequently re-issued as *Phil Spector's Christmas Album*.

Spector's grand production style, which was developed over the course of 1962 and 1963, was clearly a result of the merging of both his artistic vision and the physical properties of Gold Star Studios, which was established by engineers Stan Ross and his builder co-partner, Dave Gold. The recording engineer who worked on virtually all of Spector's 1962-6 boom period classics, Larry Levine, says of the studio, "The control room at Gold Star was the single greatest listening area that I've ever been in. Dave didn't have any formal audio qualifications *per se*, instead he designed the studio by feel. He would occasionally turn to reference books to discover some facts and figures on acoustics, but generally he used his own initiative based on where he thought things ought to be. Consequently that control room sounded like no other. There was a problem in that what you heard in there was not a true sound. The acoustics coloured the sound but what you ended up with was a big, beautiful sound, even though it sounded completely different in another room. When a session was going well, it was the most thrilling sound imaginable."

The console was a custom twelve-channel creation, built by Gold with assistance from Bill Puttnam at United Audio who was responsible for the technical qualities of a number of studios around the Los Angeles district. At the beginning of the Spector period, Gold Star employed an Ampex three-track tape recorder which allowed sound-on-sound overdubbing, and monitoring was provided by three

Altec DE loudspeakers. Used in line with the three-track machine was a further two-track and a mono machine, and by late 1963 the studio wisely invested in a new four-track Scully recorder. Even when the studio could offer full stereo capability, Spector chose not to move away from the mono format. Levine reports that the producer once told him, "I don't care how close you come, you can never balance those channels precisely. With mono I have it locked in."

Sonically, the Wall of Sound was a combination of Gold Star's echo chambers and Spector's desire to record large numbers of musicians without any form of acoustic isolation, inside a small room with a ceiling height of fourteen feet. "The lack of isolation between the musicians had a lot to do with the unique results," says Levine. "Those ideas came from Phil's mind and as engineers, Stan Ross and I helped wherever we could, but it was the room itself and the juxtaposition of the musicians themselves which were the leading factors in creating what became known as the Wall of Sound. But as well as being a great sound it was also the bane of Phil's career. His regular complaint to me was that he hated not being able to get a consistent drum sound from one session to the next. He always compared his work to what Motown was doing, where they would have the drum kit nailed down in a permanent place to achieve that consistent sound, whether it was a Four Tops or a Miracles track.

"A lot of the sound qualities of the studio area could be put down to the acrylic paint which coated the walls. It was a now-outlawed lead-based paint which made the sound bounce all around the room, giving it a really crisp feel. Because of the small dimensions of the studio, it was subject to resonance depending on which instruments were played in certain areas and also the keys in which the songs were played. It was normally the guitars which had the most effect, with open chords or strings obviously omitting a louder sound than when there were fretted chords or closed notes. So whenever an acoustic guitar played a closed string, we would have to open up the microphone a little more to get the desired level, but in turn that would let in a little spill from the drums."

Spector made heavy use of his regular session musicians, including drummer Hal Blaine and bassist Carol Kaye – otherwise known as the Wrecking Crew. "We were all basically jazz and pop musicians playing shows at nightclubs, and we were lucky to get the studio work because a lot of the producers wanted people who could play the new rock 'n' roll styles," says Blaine. "We came along as a bunch of people wearing denims and T-shirts, as opposed to blue blazers, and all of a sudden we got known as The Wrecking Crew because the older, more established musicians thought we were wrecking the business! Little did they know that we were all extremely schooled and learned players, but they soon discovered. One thing led to another and pretty soon we were doing all the TV shows and movie scores, as well as working for Phil."

Spector's sessions normally began with him listening to the guitarists, who generally worked from the beginning to the close of each session. Kaye, who worked regularly as a guitarist for Spector before switching to bass, remembers a late 1964 session for The Righteous Brothers' 'You've Lost That Lovin' Feelin''. "I played acoustic on that track using my regular Epiphone Emperor jazz guitar, the box that Phil would never do a session without," she says. "He loved its sound and he dumped a lot of echo on it, so my rhythm sounded like sixteenth notes, which was kind of the glue between what the bass and drums were playing. You can hear me doubling with Ray Pohlman on the montuno middle bass line. The Righteous Brothers were right there in the studio, singing live to our backing, although I'm convinced they overdubbed a better vocal later. That song had its own electric energy and we were bristling with the music. There was a lot of echo in the headphones but somehow we all managed to play together."

Adds Levine, "Phil would get the guitarists to play the patterns he heard in his head, then change and modify these ideas as things progressed. When he was satisfied that he had something he could work with, he would add the piano to that mixture. The drums were always the last element to consider. In order to affect the drum sound I had to try balancing the other instruments against the kit. It wasn't like today where the drums are recorded in total isolation and they can be placed anywhere you want in the mix. I had to get enough presence on the drums while still being able to hear the other instruments. So it was always a compromise."

The first major Wall of Sound breakthrough, Levine claims, came during the recording of Bob B Soxx And The Blue Flames' 1963 version of 'Zip-A-Dee-Doo-Dah'. "When Phil cut 'He's A Rebel' at Gold Star he instinctively knew that this was the studio in which he wanted to work because for the first time he was hearing the sounds that he had imagined for so long," he says. "He came back to Gold Star to make 'Zip-A-Dee-Doo-Dah' and by the time I had worked through and balanced all the instruments on the session, everything was so over-amplified that I knew I'd never get anything usable on tape. This was about three and a half hours into the session and I knew Phil was just about ready for a take, so I was too afraid to do anything about it. But I had to! I finally summoned up the courage to kill all twelve channels on the board and Phil looked at me as if I had gone mad, screaming at me, 'I was almost there. How could you do that?' I explained the overload problem and started bringing up the channels one by one and balancing them until I had a good level. I had brought up all the microphones except Billy Strange's lead guitar when Phil just shouted 'Yeah, that's the sound!' I said, 'Well, I still don't have Billy's mic up yet.' He said, 'No, don't bring it up, that's the sound I want to record. Let's record now!' Hence the weird sound of the guitar, but that's what we did and we got it down in one take."

When Spector began working at Gold Star (which sadly burned to the ground in the Eighties), he used a basic rock 'n' roll line-up of piano, guitar, bass and drums, with the occasional addition of horns. This later changed when his vision for massive productions dictated that he multiply the instrumentation several-fold. "Tons of people came to watch us when we cut 'River Deep, Mountain High' for Ike And Tina Turner," says Kaye. "There was a crazy amount of musicians on the session and I was one of four bass players. There were two acoustic basses, a Danelectro and me on Fender."

"Phil started to bring three pianos, four or five guitars, two or three basses and then it was only natural in his mind to have three drummers," says Levine. "But they weren't always playing the same part – he'd maybe have one drummer doing a standard kind of rhythm pattern and the others doing fills of some description. If an artist friend dropped by on a session, it wasn't long before Phil had him join in on some kind of percussion instrument."

"On the great Sonny And Cher sessions with the arrangers Jack

Nitzche and Harold Batiste, Sonny used to love to sit in with the tolerating percussion section," Kaye continues. "He would try so hard to play on the beat, but damn, he just couldn't do it and inevitably Phil had to call him into the booth for an imaginary phone call while counting us off for a good take."

Levine often had cause to alert Spector that a maximum of twelve microphone inputs prevented all twenty-four musicians being heard clearly. "Sometimes there might be an acoustic guitar playing and I wasn't able to have a live mic on it, so he never got heard," he explains. "I mentioned this to Phil on a number of occasions and even suggested that the guitarist in question might just as well go home. Phil would say, 'No, nobody leaves. This is the sound I want, so everybody must stay.' His philosophy was that even if we couldn't hear the guitar in the booth, the sound might just change, however subtly, if that musician walked out."

One might assume that all it took to control the levels of such a large number of musicians, all playing simultaneously, was a little compression. Fortunately for the Spector sound, as it turned out, Gold Star was not wealthy enough to afford such a luxurious item. "We didn't have a lot of the tools that some of the other studios could take advantage of," insists Levine. "If we had access to that kind of equipment, then I guess we would have used it and the Wall of Sound might have sounded a whole lot different! We also didn't have equalisers that did a great deal. They were very basic units which would give us broad frequency curves at three, five and 10kHz – nothing like the facilities that are common today."

Inside the control room, Spector could not bear to stop a session until he achieved an end product – much to the annoyance of The Wrecking Crew. "I was playing electric twelve-string while eight months pregnant and after sweating for two or three hours with no break, I had to scream at Phil to give us a break or I was going to wet my pants!" remembers Kaye. "He dutifully called a break and the guys later thanked me, the bums! The sessions were too long and sometimes boring but we were professionals and they paid well too. We played our asses off for them and they couldn't have done it without us."

Devastated by the cool commercial reception in the United States to his self-proclaimed masterpiece, 'River Deep, Mountain High', Spector unofficially retired from production duties at the end of 1966 and did little of any consequence until March 1970 when The Beatles' then business manager, Allen Klein hired his expertise to make a coherent album (*Let It Be*) from the ragged "live" tracks recorded during the band's January 1969 'Get Back' sessions. Not only did Spector painstakingly edit and remix the tracks, he also embellished songs such as 'Across The Universe' and 'The Long And Winding Road' – to Paul McCartney's endless fury – with heavenly choirs and a fifty-piece orchestra.

Spector's volatile artistic temperament, no less due to his increasing paranoia, was something to which Abbey Road Studio's technical staff and regular orchestral players were unaccustomed. His presence during the mixing sessions in Abbey Road's Room Four was normally accompanied by a burly bodyguard and his manic insistence that echo should adorn every instrument was met with quizzical stares from those who felt he was going too far with The Beatles' style. Nevertheless, Spector must have impressed George Harrison who invited him to produce his best-selling 1970 triple album, *All Things Must Pass* (which included 'My Sweet Lord').

Just a few months after joining the Abbey Road Studios team on 15 February, 1970, future hit producer John Leckie received a major injection of experience as the tape operator on the sessions for *All Things Must Pass*. "I worked on nearly all of that album which was recorded mostly in Studio Three from April right through the summer of 1970," he recalls, "during which time Phil always turned up in a white chauffeur-driven Rolls-Royce with an armed bodyguard – this was viewed by several staff as being sinister, threatening and quite unnecessary."

Leckie backs up the theory that Spector's sound had less to do with the studio itself than the large amount of musicians playing together simultaneously in the same room. On most tracks, there were three drummers (Ringo Starr, Alan White and Jim Gordon), two bassists (Klaus Voormann and Carl Radle), two pianists (Gary Brooker and Gary Wright), two organists (Billy Preston and Bobby Whitlock), four acoustic guitarists (Badfinger), two electrics (George and Dave Mason), Bobby Keys on sax and Jim Price on trumpet, with much of the recording going live to tape.

"There were also a lot of overdubs with strings, guitar solos, vocals and backing vocals, and some of this work was done at Trident which was the only studio in 1970 with sixteen-track facilities, and that was important for things like the massed 'Hare Krishna' vocals on 'My Sweet Lord'. Phil was used to the 'what you hear is what you get' idea of recording and would expect the reverb and delay effects normally only heard through the monitors during recording to be put on tape. At his request we would have two or three machines running for tape echo delays, and a lot of time was spent working delay times out via the monitor. The next day, we would come in and Phil McDonald would pull up the faders and put all the reverbs and delays back into place because they weren't on tape. Of course, it never sounded exactly the same as the previous day, and Spector would know that and so he insisted that the effects and music were as one on the multitrack. So on things like 'My Sweet Lord' and 'Wah Wah' a lot of the reverbs were recorded. It was, of course, the album which defined George's double-tracked slide guitar style and also the one which enabled him to record all the songs that he was never free to do with The Beatles."

Leckie says that, as an engineer, it was never safe to assume anything with Spector. "When he said, 'Run the tape,' you would need to know what song he was talking about. He'd say, 'Play that song again!' and you'd rewind to the beginning of the track you'd just been working on and hit the play button, only to hear him yell, 'Not that song, the other one!' It was hard to know what was going through his mind most of the time." Which is why Leckie's blood ran cold when a control room incident resulted in Harrison's track 'Awaiting On You All' appearing in a shorter form than desired on the final album.

"We were working with 3M eight-track machines on which the tape wound past the record head, around a roller and past the playback head in a kind of elongated 'S' shape," says Leckie. "Running at fifteen ips, you had a good half a second between playback and record which obviously was a consideration when dropping in. You really had to drive these machines and slow them down before you slammed them into fast-forward. I was having a few problems controlling one of these machines and kept complaining to the famous maintenance guy Eddie

Klein (now the manager of Paul McCartney's private studio in East Sussex). He said 'Oh, don't worry about it, I can't fix it now.' Five minutes later, during George's vocal overdub on top of the finished track, complete with strings and horns, I pressed fast-forward and stop, and the tape went flying across the room. My heart was in my mouth. Imagining being on the receiving end of Spector's legendary temper, I panicked and said in a quivering voice, 'It wasn't my fault, Eddie said it would be all right!' Fortunately the tape was retrieved and I think Phil McDonald got me round that one, but I suspect part of the recording may have been damaged amidst the chaos."

Immediately after the Harrison sessions, Leckie worked with Spector yet again on the *Plastic Ono Band* albums by John Lennon and Yoko Ono. "John's album was a much more stripped down affair with just piano, bass, guitar and drums, recorded live and often in one or two takes," he says. "Yoko's album took much longer than John's, and both were recorded simultaneously with the same band. Yoko would essentially scream over the top of blues jams, and we'd spend about three weeks editing them. I suppose what we did was the forerunner of sampling because we would copy a vocal line from the multitrack on to quarter-inch and splice it into place at John and Yoko's instruction. It was a way of forming a composite article from half an hour's worth of improvised music. John was very spontaneous as an artist but I remember him being incredibly disciplined in the studio, as was George, and both of them were good at taking instructions and respecting Spector's wishes."

Rock 'N' Roll Nightmare

It was a long-standing ambition of Lennon's to record a whole album's worth of rock 'n' roll standards which had inspired him as a young performer and who better to produce it than Spector? The trouble was, both men were strong, determined characters who shared a vicious, prima donna-like temper. Worse still, one significant stumbling block was the heavy trauma they were each currently experiencing in their personal lives, made no better by a vast consumption of alcohol. The ensuing sessions in October and November 1973 resulted in scenes that would make Spinal Tap appear tame by comparison.

Estranged from wife Yoko Ono, Lennon was accompanied in LA by assistant and confidante, May Pang, with whom he had an affair during his infamous "Lost Weekend". As the production coordinator on a daily basis, she was well placed to witness the odd couple's behaviour. "They got on great when it came to co-producing the previous albums, but this time John gave Phil total control," she recalls. "Phil was saying, 'Are you sure you want me to have sole control?' John said, 'Yes, all I want to be is the singer in the band. I don't necessarily want to have to play rhythm guitar.' Phil would say, 'Okay, if you're sure now.' After hearing that more than just a few times, a few alarm bells started going off in my head.

"We had quite a good set up out there in LA with our own engineer, Roy Cicala and Jimmy Iovine as assistant. The studio was set up for eight musicians and Phil was saying to John on the first day, 'Don't worry, I'll take care of everything, just be there.' But instead of the eight, there were all these people were coming into the studio saying, 'Phil Spector's session, yeah?' I was wondering just what was going on and did a head count. There were twenty-seven musicians in this studio waiting to do a Spector session on the first day. Everybody was scrambling to make the session work. Then Phil arrived, two hours later, dressed as a karate expert. It was just so surreal and it ended up being total chaos. You know, there may have been ten people all playing one note. And ten very famous people too but nobody knew what they were supposed to be doing. John was floored by all these musicians, like Jesse Ed Davis and Steve Cropper on electric guitars, three acoustic guitarists, two bass players [including Klaus Voormann], a whole horn section, Hal Blaine and Jim Keltner on drums. Larry Carlton was there, Dr John, Barry Mann and Leon Russell on piano, Jeff Barry playing tambourine, Michael Hazelwood on acoustic. There wasn't any really special playing on it though, and Phil certainly wasn't utilising Leon Russell's piano skills to their full extent. If I said Steve Cropper's on it, you'd say, 'Where?'"

Despite Pang's desperate efforts to namecheck the musicians on the album sleeve, there were simply too many people to deal with. The flowing alcohol also caused problems. "Phil would get through at least a bottle of Courvoisier a night," she says. "Then we got thrown out of A&M Studios because everybody got drunk out of their minds and someone poured some liquor down the console. They just took to the drink that was around while waiting for something to happen. We transferred to the Record Plant and Mal Evans (ex-Beatles roadie) and everybody was there, even Phil's mother was in the control room. They were doing a playback and I heard this noise go off, a real loud bang. Of course, I stupidly went running towards this sound and everyone else is ducking under the mixing console. I saw Phil looking a little surprised with a gun in his hand and John was holding his ears. I'm screaming, 'What happened?' John looked over to Phil and said, 'He shot off the gun, that's what happened!' John said, 'Listen Phil, if you're gonna shoot, shoot me, but don't fuck with me ears 'cause I need them to listen to the music, right?' Of course, we thought they were just blanks until the next night when we were having dinner with Mal and he showed us the bullet. Bullet?! We were both a little upset by that."

The episode concluded in dramatic fashion when Spector disappeared with the master tapes, and allegedly falsely claimed that he had been in a car accident and taken to hospital. "I asked Capitol how much had been paid off the session bill so far," says Pang. "They told me only $120 but that was impossible because of the amount of sessions we'd done. Phil had actually made a deal with Warners and they had paid the bill, even though neither party had a legal right to do such a thing. However, he still had the tapes and we couldn't get through to him for a long time. That's when he claimed he'd had an accident and people were saying he'd had a hair transplant and all sorts of bizarre things. It was just Phil being weird."

When Lennon finally received the masters in June 1974 he could not believe his ears. "They were very sloppy," Pang continues. "You couldn't do any overdubbing because every track was leaking on to the next and it was very painful to John, particularly as it was the most he'd ever spent on doing an album. Phil could spend money like there was no tomorrow. It was a very bad memory. That's why the rest of the album was produced by John. It was a shame because one of John's favourite songs was 'Angel Baby' but it really hurt him to listen back to some of his vocal tracks and hear how drunk everybody was."

Motown Mystery

A chapter on the development of American record production in the Sixties could not pass without substantial mention of Berry Gordy Jr's Tamla Motown empire which was responsible for some of the best-selling classics of the day, by Smokey Robinson, The Four Tops, Diana Ross And The Supremes, The Temptations, Marvin Gaye, Stevie Wonder and more. One might say that the Motown Sound as a subject deserves a book all of its own and, true enough, there have been in-depth studies of the company. But we are dealing here with the physical production of records, and the *true* story of the making of Motown's hits has been so guarded by those close to Gordy that it is difficult to know exactly what happened, when and, more importantly, where.

Motown began operating from its Hitsville office and studio base at 2648 West Grand Boulevard, Detroit in 1959, fuelled by Gordy's dream to be a successful songwriter. He achieved that ambition quickly and a whole lot more besides. The wider understanding is that all of the company's major hits up until the late Sixties were cut at Hitsville by black artists, black session musicians and black producers – none more successful than the crack trio of Eddie and Brian Holland and Lamont Dozier, whose innate ability to mould hit after hit, with production line ease, was a major influence on the British team, Stock, Aitken and Waterman in the Eighties. Hitsville's resident engineers, Laurence Horn and Mike McClain originally worked with a three-track tape machine but had progressed to a pair of Ampex eight-tracks by 1965. The relatively small recording area was a significant factor in the Motown Sound – with little room for amplifiers, the guitarists were required to DI their instruments straight into the console, from which a mix would be played back to them through a single loudspeaker for monitoring purposes. The standard line-up of Motown's rhythm section was bass player, James Jamerson, drummer Benny Benjamin, pianist Earl Van Dyke and guitarist Robert White, aka The Funk Brothers, who by the nature of their contract were required to remain on call in Detroit. Soundchecking at the start of each session was largely determined by having Jamerson and White set their own instrument volume levels and hell was to pay if ever they adjusted them during a take. A gantry of microphones was a standard fixture in the centre of the studio and unlike Atlantic Studios where it was frowned upon, Motown made excessive use of limiting in order to regulate the dynamics of vocal recording from artist to artist.

The crisp, high end bias of Motown's product can be attributed not only to the musicians and the studio characteristics, but also to two other important factors: firstly, the extensive equalisation hardware which outweighed every other known American studio, with control over various parameters of bass, middle and treble both in the recording and mixing stages, at a time when just bass and treble functions were the norm. Secondly, Gordy made his music for transistor radio, which by 1963 had almost totally replaced the tube format, and it was important to Gordy that Motown's records sounded outstanding on portable radios and in cars. To this end, Gordy invested in a vinyl disc cutting machine and ordered an average of twelve slightly varied mixes of each new title, before "auditioning" them on a small transistor radio system in Hitsville's quality control department. Perfection was invariably guaranteed.

But much confusion surrounds exactly how much of the classic Sixties Motown material was actually recorded by the Brothers in Detroit. In his 1985 book, *Where Did Our Love Go?*, Nelson George made a minor reference to demo sessions in New York and Los Angeles, while concentrating almost wholly on the supposed productivity of Hitsville. What I found hard to understand was that despite the two and a half years that George claimed to have spent writing and researching his book, he spectacularly failed to address the importance to the Motown legend of the Los Angeles scene of the early and mid-Sixties, and by not doing so, contributed further to the public's belief that Detroit was where it all happened. It is acknowledged that from 1968, much of Motown's activity moved to Los Angeles, but there is now evidence to suggest that even as early as 1963 (when Gordy allegedly bought a large estate in the Hollywood hills), mainly white session musicians from Phil Spector's Wrecking Crew – including Hal Blaine and (black) Earl Palmer on drums, bassists Carol Kaye and Ray Pohlman, guitarists Tommy Tedesco, Bill Puttnam, Mike D'Asey and Al Casey, and horn players Plas Johnson and Steve Douglas – were creating hit backing tracks in Los Angeles.

It is claimed that regular sessions were recorded by Motown engineer, Armin Steiner (who was not mentioned in George's book) in his Formosa garage prior to him running Sound Recorders studio and, later, Sound Labs. In an interview with *Modern Drummer* magazine, Los Angeles drummer, Earl Palmer once said, "My first association with Motown was through two guys, one who is still producing for them now, Hal Davis. We used to do an awful lot of Motown stuff, and at the time we didn't know it. We knew it was Motown, but we didn't know who the artist was going to be on it. We heard these records and tapes come back and knew it sounded familiar, but we knew we hadn't recorded with The Temptations or with Diana Ross. We were doing a lot of tracks out here and two girls by the name of The Lewis Sisters were singing on them...in an old ramshackled house behind Sunset Boulevard."

It appears that for many of the tracks, The Lewis Sisters' vocals were replaced by the Motown artists once the tapes reached Detroit. "We never knew any of the titles," says Hal Blaine. "We understood that after each session, Armin would book a flight back to Detroit and would have two first class seats – one for him and the other for the tapes. Detroit would then try recording the same songs with different vocal groups and then release the versions that they thought worked best. Lester Sill was heavily involved in those days and prior to his death he verified our recordings [Wrecking Crew colleague, Carol Kaye is in possession of a letter from Sill on Jobete Music stationery, dated 12 July, 1989, which reads: 'Carol Kaye has played bass on several Motown hits that were cut between the years 1963 to 1969'] and my understanding is that Berry Gordy himself admitted in recent years that the earlier Motown recordings were, in fact, done in Los Angeles by us.

"Listening to the records on the radio, like 'Baby Love' and some others from that time, we just knew it was us. But word got out that it was Benny Benjamin who was the drummer and Jamie Jamerson on bass, and a lot of books and television special have claimed the same thing. But we knew differently. I later worked with Jamerson when he moved out to California but we never got to discussing any of this stuff. Armin Steiner definitely knew because he engineered the stuff but I understand that he is a little afraid of getting involved in the debate. There were no contracts and we did them on the 'toofer' basis: two tracks for $35; it was just prior to every session being subject to contracts."

Carol Kaye insists that it is her bass playing and not Jamerson's which is heard on The Four Tops' 'Reach Out I'll Be There', 'Bernadette' and 'Standing In The Shadows Of Love', The Supremes' 'Baby Love', 'You Keep Me Hangin' On' and 'You Can't Hurry Love', Stevie Wonder's 'I Was Made To Love Her', Mary Wells's 'My Guy'...the list goes on and on, and substantiates the claims of Blaine and Palmer. It is no wonder that Kaye received the red carpet treatment on a curiosity visit to Hitsville to see how the other half lived, so to speak. Of the session for 'Reach Out I'll Be There' (ironically considered one of Jamerson's greatest bass lines), Kaye says, "'Reach Out' was a typical LA Motown rhythm section cut with horns. I did some ad-libbing with the sixteenth note bass line which was typical of the sixteenth note style I played then and much different to the linear James Jamerson styles. It fitted the pick style I used which was very fast, faster than fingers. The part was indicated in the first two bars as usual, with breaks mapped out, but I had to make something out of it. I consider what I did on 'Bernadette' to be much better although the feel on 'Reach Out' was very good, with Earl Palmer on drums. For 'Reach Out', we heard Detroit's songwriter demos first and it was one of the West Coast guys, Hal Davis, who produced the rendition you hear with us playing [George's book states it was produced by Lamont Dozier and Brian Holland]. The Detroit crew did many fine hits but I think that there is a fear of losing the Motown 'ownership', started by Berry Gordy's second wife. I'm sure that even the lead singers had no idea where their tracks came from in the Sixties and there's a secrecy for some reason that surrounds the real truth. Maybe it's to protect producer monies or protect them from being sued by someone concerned."

Ultimately, Earl Palmer's black pride got the better of him and he quit working for Motown. He said in *Modern Drummer*, "I began to feel that Motown was a company that was supposed to be a very black company and they prided themselves on the Motown sound, the black sound and all of that...but for a time there, the operation was more white-run than it was black, which smacked of hypocrisy to me. I think

I voiced that a couple of times and that was the end of my association with them." As a bassist myself, I find it alarming that many players automatically cite James Jamerson as their biggest influence through listening to the Motown catalogue, yet they either do not appreciate, or refuse to acknowledge that at least some of the time, they most probably drew their influence from a white woman, namely Carol Kaye. And so the emotionally-charged Motown debate over who did what and where continues.

Inside The Symphonic Mind Of Brian Wilson

1966 was a watershed year for record production, largely due to the acute sense of competition felt by the main innovators on either side of the Atlantic: in Britain, The Beatles; in the United States, building on many of Spector's philosophies, The Beach Boys. Behind the Californian surf sound of 'Help Me Rhonda', 'California Girls' and 'Surfin' USA' was band member, songwriter and producer, Brian Wilson who, from the band's second album, *Surfer Girl* (1963), displayed a rare talent for vocal arrangements and an understanding of recording techniques, borne of a fascination with the work of Spector.

From the outset of his professional career as a Beach Boy, it was clear that he was quite different to his relatives in the band, showing signs of being a musical visionary as early as 1962. While his relatives were keen to negotiate the rigours of touring as the ambassadors of clean-cut, all-American pop, Wilson, the member upon whose talents the group's success ultimately rested, did not weather the road so well. A troubled flight to a show in Houston in December 1964 encouraged his decision to quit live performance the following year and concentrate wholly on production, while the rest of the band conducted business as usual out in the public eye.

Once inside the recording studio, Wilson gradually forged an obsession for sculpting music which exceeded the general requirements of the listening audience. By late 1965, he was no longer satisfied with assembling a selection of audience-pleasing surf songs for the next album. In his mind, the studio was, like a guitar or a piano, another musical instrument – one which could (and would) be responsible for creating the sound landscapes of 'God Only Knows',

'Wouldn't It Be Nice', 'Let's Go Away For Awhile', 'Caroline No' and nine other tracks on the *Pet Sounds* album, released by Capitol on 16 May, 1966.

Wilson was now taking his craft to an entirely different plateau, driven by his obsession with being the best in his field, or at least delivering the highest quality he could muster. It was listening to The Beatles' *Rubber Soul* album, prior to the Christmas of 1965, which fuelled his desperate sense of competition. "Being competitive got me into trouble," he says. "I thought I was a real big shit until I ran into some even bigger shit! *Rubber Soul* was really the main motivator for me making *Pet Sounds*. The Beatles rarely, if ever, put filler stuff on their albums and it really hit home with *Rubber Soul*. Now I wanted to go the whole nine yards. I had a burning, overwhelming need to better them and make music on a real deep level. But that's such a weird trip in life to go through. It forced me to go further than even I thought I could."

This creative battle, however, was not the only ingredient behind *Pet Sounds*. Like The Beatles, Wilson's recent intake of LSD had expanded his musical sensibilities. He was now hearing, seeing and feeling rich textures and full arrangements which he would turn into reality on tape. For *Pet Sounds*, Wilson dispensed not only with the traditional "beach bum life" lyrical themes of Mike Love (hiring in Tony Asher as a temporary wordsmith and sounding board), but also with The Beach Boys' instrumental services. Instead he hired the best California session musicians available, including Carol Kaye, Hal Blaine and keyboard player Larry Knechtal.

Apart from 'Sloop John B' and the title track which were taped the previous year, the album was recorded between January and April 1966 at Western Recorders Studio Three, Sunset Sound and Gold Star, all in and around Hollywood. The album's backing tracks were recorded on three- or four-track machines (depending on the studio) and the rich, spacious vocal sound can be attributed to the fact that the backing was always bounced on to a single mono channel on an eight-track machine, allowing a luxurious seven tracks for the boys' vocal workouts.

Although a fine bass player himself, Wilson decided to leave those duties to the more experienced Kaye. "Sure, I could play bass," he says. "But I could see the bigger picture if I left that to someone else so that I could stay in the control booth and produce the session." That he had suffered hearing loss in his right ear as a child did not affect Wilson's acute detection of performance glitches from the hired hands. "I guess I have at least one good ear!" comes the ironic understatement. On many of the sessions, Wilson arrived at the studio with just a simple chord framework and an idea of what he wanted from the musicians. Although ready and willing to match the sounds in Wilson's head, reaching the destination was often difficult and tiresome, as Kaye remembers. "Brian was illiterate in music writing and would put the stems on the wrong side of the notes, with very strange rhythm notation and wrong keys," she says, "so we would have to re-write his stuff. But I'd say that aside from a very few licks, it was all his. Certainly nothing came from the other Beach Boys, it was all Brian. We would rarely see Mike Love, Dennis or Carl, although they'd stop by once in a while just to say hello. Carl [who died during the revision of this book] was very nice and twice I saw him overdub his twelve-string in the booth, plugging directly into the board, and he played adequately. I also played some overdubbed guitar parts on *Pet Sounds*, after playing Fender bass on all but one cut on the album. I thought Brian had cut a masterpiece.

"I'm really surprised that Brian didn't take arranging lessons and wind up scoring movies like Quincy Jones did because he could have done it. Why he stayed with just records is beyond me, but maybe he didn't have the self-confidence to learn the nuts and bolts of writing music. He could really have contributed to the movie and TV world. But at least he did set some fine standards. Once in a while he would overstep his time while recording with us and forget our Union-regulated five-minute breaks. But he was always very nice, very self-composed, with clear ideas about the kind of records he wanted to make."

Despite the widespread allegations of his "fragile mind" and drug-tormented behaviour, Kaye insists that in the studio "Brian was strong, sane, level-headed, and appeared just the opposite to us. He was *not* fragile at all, but sort of bull-headed, strong and very self-confident, so [the accusations are] totally wrong according to what we all remember him as being."

One key factor of Wilson's work was his gross impulsiveness, which was in evidence when he cut his own arrangement of the traditional West Indian folk song, 'Sloop John B', an earlier hit for The Kingston Trio. Beach Boy Al Jardine originally took the idea of recording a version to Wilson. "We were working on some other material at the time and I said to Brian, 'Hey, I know you're not into folk music, but I think you should hear this song, because if we put our own arrangement on it, our own style, I think it will be really successful,'" says Jardine. "I played it to him in the key of E and put in a little minor change which I thought sounded interesting, but Brian just looked blankly at me, as if to say, 'Well? So what?' So we went back to the other stuff we were doing. About twenty-four hours later, I got a phone call asking me to show up at Western. I was just expecting to do the work in progress, but Brian had already completely arranged my idea for 'Sloop John B' and framed it in the Beach Boys style. Not only that, the backing track was also recorded, which was miraculous when you consider the production. So my idea must have made an impact on him. All we had to do was just show up and sing. I mean, we are talking about a very short timespan here!

"I was flattered, but at the same time devastated because I wasn't given the opportunity to do the lead vocal. Brian auditioned all of us at the microphone; we all had a crack at singing a verse, but he wasn't satisfied and ended up doing it himself. Of course, I was accustomed to singing it in the folk style, so I wasn't prepared for the pop approach which I now understand. I'm sure that if Brian hadn't been working so fast, we might've sat down together and structured something whereby I could have sung the song. But he was on such a creative roll, like a sponge, absorbing every little influence and idea. It didn't matter where an idea came from, he still owned it. His attitude was, 'It's mine. I'll mould it into my own shape.' He was very demanding, like an impresario who had to have it his own way, but he made it."

In common with his colleagues and some of the world's greatest admirers of *Pet Sounds*, Jardine firmly believes that 'Sloop John B' (issued as a trailer single from the album) should have been kept off the track listing. "I'm proud that I contributed to *Pet Sounds*, although I am surprised that 'Sloop John B' ended up on it. To this day I cannot reconcile that. Paul McCartney and I have discussed this and he too has the same complaint. That song belonged on the previous album, *Summer Days (And Summer Nights!!)*."

'Good Vibrations'

During work on *Pet Sounds*, a new song was occupying Wilson's imagination even though it was not destined to feature on the album. 'Good Vibrations' was the culmination of Wilson's acid-drenched desire to set new standards in production and develop recording as an art form. He later described 'Good Vibrations' as his "pocket symphony", the record by which the creativity of all others – including The Beatles – would be measured throughout the psychedelic era and beyond. This was Wilson at his creative peak and suddenly anything was possible.

The first takes of 'Good Vibrations' were recorded on 18 February, 1966 at Gold Star Studios – one of several aborted attempts to perfect the recording during the *Pet Sounds* sessions. No fewer than sixteen more sessions were to follow at Gold Star, Sunset Sound, Western and Columbia between 9 April and 1 September, at a reported cost of between $50,000 and $75,000, before Wilson could breathe his sigh of relief and wallow in the inevitable anti-climax he must surely have felt. Mike Love recalls that 'Good, Good, Good Vibrations', as it was first titled, started life at Gold Star as "a very R&B flavoured track, almost like it might have been performed by James Brown's Famous Flames. The bass was really cranking." Larry Levine says, "Brian originally came to Gold Star because he idolised Phil and I was Phil's engineer. I worked on one of the 'Good Vibrations' sessions just before the song really had any shape to it. I don't think Brian had much of a concept of the song at that point – all he seemed to have to go on was a feeling for what he wanted to achieve."

Once the album was completed, Wilson focused his complete attention on this new song and set about recording a number of whole sections to be edited together later. Like *Pet Sounds* and the Spector classics before, the backing track on each take was recorded live, yet Wilson paid no heed to the "rule" that the musicians should be isolated from each other to avoid acoustic spill. This was wholly intentional, contributing to the thick texture of the often haunting backing.

"All we did was separate the musicians into two different categories: one positive and one negative," explains Wilson. "I then took the whole thing and crammed it into one. The first part of the record was done exactly like that. There was no real isolation between the musicians. A lot of people thought I was pulling some kind of magic trick, but it really wasn't like that. People were also telling me that I shouldn't be doing a record like this, you know, it was too modern, too long, not commercial. But it was like I had tunnel vision, I had to keep going until I was was fulfilled.

"I was very Spector-influenced at the outset of 'Good Vibrations'. I thought 'River Deep, Mountain High' was a good record. I just believed in Phil Spector's records. I cut 'Do You Wanna Dance' on four-track at Gold Star, with a really good Spector timpani drum sound. Putting the whole thing together for 'Good Vibrations' was an odd experience. We recorded the verses at Gold Star, and the chorus vocals at Columbia. The mixing was hard work with all the changes that needed to happen within the movements and mood changes, like dropping voices out and bringing different instruments like the Theremin or the cello or Larry Knechtal's organ up in level here and there. But this was what production really meant to me."

Among all the other innovations that Wilson inaugurated with the recording, the cellos as a rock 'n' roll rhythm instrument was probably the most revolutionary. "The Crystals' 'Da Doo Ron Ron' was a good reference point for me," says Wilson. "There were triplets all over the place on that track and I took that idea for the chorus of 'Good Vibrations', with the cello playing the triplets."

Along with millions of other cinema-goers, Brian Wilson had heard the eerie sound of Professor Theremin's pre-synthesiser electronic invention on the soundtracks of dozens of horror and thriller movies, such as *Spellbound*. But he was the first to incorporate it into a rock track on *Pet Sounds*' 'I Just Wasn't Made For These Times', using it to even greater effect on 'Good Vibrations'.

"When Brian brought this thing into the studio, I couldn't believe it," Western Recorders' engineer, Chuck Britz remembers. "All it had were two little arcs and a vibrator in the middle. I thought the idea of using it was a little old fashioned but Brian demonstrated it for me and told me he wanted to use it in a different way to the movies. Paul Tanner was the guy who played the Theremin on the track at Western Studio Three and the result was amazing."

Carol Kaye insists that despite her ability to help with arrangements, her picked bass line was Wilson's invention, note-for-note: "Brian had such definite bass ideas. He liked me to have more of a treble sound on my Fender Precision than I personally liked and used on other people's sessions, and I used a Fender Concert amp with an open back four by ten-inch Utah speaker cabinet, the same set-up I used from 'Help Me Rhonda' through to 'Heroes And Villains', and all the other stuff in between like Simon And Garfunkel's 'Homeward Bound'. The speakers were usually miked with a Shure 545 which worked best when centred on the cabinet and placed back about one and a half feet, although some engineers liked to stick the mic right on the grill, up high on one speaker. I also used a Gibson Maestro fuzz box for a fuzz bass line which never made it on to the released single. It was just another experiment that Brian wanted to try."

(Those interested in discovering the discarded experiments from these sessions should invest in a copy of Capitol's 1990 CD re-mastering of the *Smiley Smile* album which includes several fascinating outtakes as proof that Wilson was indeed in total command of his orchestra. Indeed, *Pet Sounds* fans will also do well to purchase the wonderful *Pet Sounds Sessions* EMI boxed set which was finally released in 1997 after a long delay. The set features outtakes, alternate mixes and both mono and stereo versions of the original album.)

On the original backing tracks of 'Good Vibrations', there were generally two percussionists, Larry Knechtal on organ, one guitar played by either Glen Campbell or Barney Kessel (subject to their availability), Hal Blaine on drums and Kaye on Fender bass, doubled by Lyle Ritz on upright bass. The string players, Theremin, horns and reeds, including sax player Steve Douglas, were all overdubbed later. "Sometimes you'd see horn and sax players on the sessions with us, but rarely because Brian layered them," says Kaye. "Brian would take over the mixing console once Chuck Britz had done a preliminary set-up, then he directed us from the booth via intercom or waving motions."

Once the magical backing track was approved by the ever-discerning Wilson, it was time to bring his Beach Boy colleagues off the road and into the studio for the vocal sessions which Mike Love describes as "an exhausting experience at the hands of the master. I was around for one of the sessions and actually came up with the lyrics and melody line for the 'I'm pickin' up good vibrations' part. But I just had a 'let's wait and see attitude', so I left Brian to his own devices and didn't attend any more backing sessions until it was time to record the vocals which was difficult enough on its own because he worked us into the ground. Brian was listening out not only for the resonance of the four voices working off each other but also the feel, timbre and quality of every single note. He'd say, 'Stop! Do it again!' over and over, which we all thought was a little obsessive, but we figured he knew best. Quite often it took about thirty or so overdubs of the same little piece of the chorus before he was satisfied."

After months of sessions, 'Good Vibrations' was finally completed at Columbia Studios with Wilson taking masterful charge of the editing together of three distinct sections. "We made the final mix to mono and it was just so beautiful," he says. "It took a while but when I finally got there it was the ultimate feeling of fulfilment, exaltation. I wanted everyone to listen to this masterwork and I felt like I had all the power of the world in my hands."

Al Jardine's first reaction upon hearing the completed record was one of amazement and disappointment. "I heard flaws in the tracking, EQ changes that I didn't think belonged there and without the vocals it is very noticeable," he says. "But it's really because different parts were recorded at different studios, on different boards. I've never had cause to discuss this with Brian though. We were zooming along so fast that we never had the time to review a situation or analyse why something sounded the way it did. Of course, the final single was edited and you can tell that by listening to how it changes colour in various places. It's clear in one place and then it suddenly sounds muddy. I assumed that Chuck or someone had done something on the board, but it never went away!"

The critical acclaim which followed the release of 'Good Vibrations' encouraged Capitol Records to announce the December arrival of the next Beach Boys album, *Smile*, even before it was recorded. Despite re-arranged deadlines which continued into the late spring of 1967,

Wilson constantly failed to deliver, his sense of perfection becoming a major stumbling block. What the album did promise, however, was 'Heroes And Villains', vocally and instrumentally even more complex than 'Good Vibrations', and based on Wilson's vision to create a three-minute musical comedy, set in the Wild West. The version that eventually surfaced as a single was a comparatively under-produced re-invention of the original recording which began in May 1966, but was not completed for another nine months. Wilson insisted that a re-recording take place at his new Bel Air mansion. In haste, a studio was assembled and because of the absence of an echo chamber, the tracks were played through speakers in his emptied swimming pool with the reverberation picked up by microphones.

Another song to be recorded in early 1967 was 'Mrs O'Leary's Cow', a dark, eerie instrumental track which has found a place in Beach Boys lore as the mythical 'Fire'. For fear of "scaring the public" with what he calls "bad, demonic vibrations", Wilson saw fit to destroy the tapes before they could be made available to Capitol. Carol Kaye was once again the bassist in residence. "It was a realistic, beautiful piece of music with cellos, and Brian had us all doing 're-building' tool sounds like sawing and rivetting," she says. "Lyle Ritz got to 'play' a jack-hammer. We were getting paid for this! The cellos on 'Fire' were gorgeous and sounded like real fire engines at written points. I heard he burned the master after the Malibu fire which I saw start up the hill as I rounded the bend on the freeway into town from Camarillo on my way to master the *Joe Pass Guitar Style* tape. A camper had burned some trash which quickly caught the whole hill on fire due to very strong Santa Ana-like winds. Coincidentally I heard that Brian was worried about fire of some sort. I don't really know why he burned such a gorgeous master – it was his best work yet."

By the summer of 1967, Wilson gave up his self-inflicted production race and admitted defeat upon hearing The Beatles' next work – *Sergeant Pepper's Lonely Hearts Club Band*. "The game was up when *Pepper* came out," he sighs. "I threw in the towel but my mind was already in too much of a bad state to compete," he says of his health, which by then had succumbed to an out-of-control drug habit. For several months, *Smile* remained but one of Wilson's more experimental whims, much to the anger of Love who accused him of "fucking with the successful Beach Boys formula" and making "ego music". Pressurised into assembling an album's worth of material for release in late 1967, Wilson set about assembling the arty but ultimately uncommercial *Smiley Smile* from its ashes. His search for even greater heights in studio production, it seemed, had already climaxed.

"It was like Brian had given up and become withdrawn from everyone, and then we gained a little more control," reflects Mike Love. "Carl Wilson and Bruce Johnston later produced some of The Beach Boys' albums and Brian took a supporting role." Over recent years, through collaborations with artist/producers such as Don Was, Jeff Lynne, Van Dyke Parks, there has been more than a little evidence to prove that the genius of Brian Wilson is still alive. More than thirty years may have passed since he carved his *Pet Sounds* masterpiece, but those who know him believe that he still has the potential to unleash another timeless work of wonder from his unique, symphonic, and ultimately unpredictable mind.

America's Real Hitmakers

Summing up the professional and personal qualities which each gave Spector and Wilson a special edge, and the relationship she enjoyed (and endured) with them as a session regular, Carol Kaye says, "They were free to exploit their own individual talents and experiment – Phil for his overall recording sounds and Brian for his vocals, arranging, songwriting and producing. Brian could (and should) have gone on with his creative musical career. He could have done anything he wanted with some musical education grounding, to allow him to physically write music because he had some great sounds in his head. Phil was more the producer, he did some fine writing and knew what a hit should sound like. People have labelled him as being nutty and stuff, but he was always nice to me. I always thought him to be very artistic but tons of people started leeching off him later. He might have got too pre-occupied with his identity as a hitmaker. When the Lennon things [*Rock 'N' Roll*] didn't really come off that great, he got very upset and tense. I felt sorry for him because they were his comeback sessions. I think Phil should have gone on to other things because he had such a lot of talent, but that damn Hollywood star stuff probably put a lot of pressure on him.

"Phil kidded a lot and liked to have fun with the musicians, as did Brian sometimes, but they both realised our total professionalism in spite of some weird kibitzing, plus they knew we all worked for everybody and were the finest musicians available. They weren't the only fish in the sea for us. So they really did appreciate and respect us...until they both got filthy rich."

Bands had a long wait before they could force the hands of record companies and producers to allow them to perform on their own records. For many years, until well into the Seventies, the session musician remained all-important to the hit sounds and the reputations of the artists. When Kaye entered the studio world on a Sam Cooke session in December 1957, the standard musician rate in America was $42 for a three-hour session and by 1966 it had risen to $64, although Kaye stresses that musicians were paid either double or triple scale for ninety-five per cent of sessions. Today's equivalent standard rate for a three-hour session is $225.

While Kaye remembers the camaraderie of her fellow musicians in Los Angeles and the atmosphere of the session world with fondness, she believes that the massive success which came to the artists and producers, and the infiltration of the drug culture, led to intolerable ego problems and a social breakdown in her world in the late Sixties, prompting her escape from mainstream pop sessions in 1970. "Even a lot of the studio musicians started bragging a lot," she says. "This had a lot to do with securing future 'accounts' because we never knew when this whole thing would stop. In the end, I had to stop myself and get out. It got real crazy, you know, it was like movie star time. Crime was beginning to get heavy in Hollywood and several musicians were getting mugged. So by 1970 I had quit the record scene altogether and went back to mostly TV and movie work.

"People on the outside form fantasy opinions, especially if turned on by the drug-filled lives of the music stars, thinking music in the studios was a continual rush. It was not a continuous rush but deep down hard work, putting up with idiotic, talentless A&R men who would insult you because they had the 'account'. If it wasn't for us, most of those so-called stars wouldn't have had any hit records. It really was the studio musicians who created most of the Sixties' golden oldies you hear now, not only in our performances, but our creativity, creating instant arrangements, or deviating from a corny arrangement to create a hit. It was a cut and dried business, not how one Detroit musician put it as 'Riding bareback on a camel'. Listeners fall in love with the identity of the good music, thinking we must all have had a ball! I threw three dinner parties and went to two others where we sat around and talked shop or fell asleep because we were always so tired. Six hours' sleep was like the Garden of Eden if we could get it. We used to do as many as four or five sessions a day. Now most musicians are lucky to get that many in a month, or in some cases, even a year. I was making more money than the President of the USA! Our world was a coffee world but we later saw all the drugs and the marked decline of studio music of which ninety-nine per cent is totally gone now, with Hollywood still trying to live off its lies.

"We couldn't believe how gullible the public was to believe everything they were told by the music press. People had this crazy idea that the hits of the Sixties were mostly cut on drugs. We would shake our heads at the way the fans started taking drugs to emulate the stars. But those hits were cut by people who took care of their families, usually well-experienced big band or jazz musicians who were thrilled to death to stay home and off the road to be with their families while earning a fantastic living. Our studio life was a serious, military-like business, very self-disciplined and carefully guided to the hit-making process which was the goal of everybody in those days. We liked it that way because it was very logical and orderly. Our talents and abilities were traded for excellent unheard of monies which helped us raise our families. We stayed away from all the bullshit for the most part, although some present-day, older musicians are very jealous of our success. If they only had the inclination to work hard and stay straight and sober, maybe they'd have done it too."

chapter three

england swings

"The first producer I ever worked with was Joe Meek and his studio in Holloway Road wasn't like any of the studios you'd see today. It was a real egg box studio but he was an advanced craftsman in the making of pop records. He was quite famous in the local community, people knew of his studio. Consequently I went there in 1964 to make my first record which was a version of Chuck Berry's 'Maybelline' and I have a clear memory of his old RCA mixers with big knobs on them. The place was rife with these knobs and pre-amps."

Steve Howe

Despite the presence of some home-grown talent in the shape of Cliff Richard (now Sir Cliff) and Adam Faith, the British record charts at the turn of the Sixties largely reflected the superior production efforts of the American market, and would predominantly remain so until four young Liverpudlians turned the tables in 1963. But before the rise of Beatlemania, one rare independent producer was unwittingly preparing us for a colourful new era of sound.

Joe Meek's achievements are regarded by many as the catalyst for the experimental approaches which typified the latter part of that swinging decade. Although the general public will remember him for the schizophrenic behaviour which led to his murder of his landlady and subsequent suicide in 1967, the recording fraternity views him as an enigmatic visionary who was simply years ahead of his time. His studio at 304 Holloway Road, North London consisted of a number of rooms above a leather goods store, with a control room which resembled an eccentric electrical hobbyist's den. Not the kind of place one would associate with barrier-breaking sonic achievements, perhaps, but it did produce the most enduring instrumental hit of all-time, 'Telstar' by The Tornados.

Throughout his youth, Meek experimented with electronics, building crystal and television sets and capturing sound effects on acetate discs. His entry into the professional world came in 1953 when he was hired by IBC Studios in London to assist with the recording of Radio Luxembourg's live shows on location and when based at the studio itself would operate as balance engineer on a wide range of sessions. Influenced by the new R&B sounds emanating from American shores, in contrast to the more staid British scene, Meek made the decision to leave IBC to set up his own studio in a tiny flat in Arundel Gardens where he would form ambitious plans to record the most mystifying music of early Sixties Britain. Soon, with the help of business partner, Major Banks, a new record label, Triumph Records, was born, along with a production company (RGM Sound) which would establish Meek as the nation's leading independent producer, much to the anguish of Decca, EMI and Pye: the top major labels of the day. An early sign of Meek's success was his move to new premises in Holloway Road where he was based until his tragic death on 3 February, 1967.

One of the few privileged individuals allowed access into Meek's creative cockpit was Ted Fletcher, who has since carved a niche in today's world with his JoeMeek brand of retro studio equipment, which borrows much from the old master's flavoursome technology. Fletcher was introduced to Meek through working alongside his future wife Barbara and brother Guy in the vocal trio, The Cameos, who after a brief audition became Meek's regular backing singers. "'Telstar' had just made the charts, so he was really on the rise," says Fletcher. "We thought he was quite shy and retiring, and when he spoke, which wasn't often, it was in a funny, squeaky voice. He wasn't a very big guy and neither did he seem the forceful character he turned out to be. It wasn't until later that we realised he was prone to such awful tantrums and threw bits of equipment around the place, so that you had to dodge them! That was the dark side of his character. But generally, outside of sessions, he was a very quiet bloke in his dealings with people on the periphery of the business."

A civil engineer by day, Fletcher made his interest in electronics known to Meek and gained a rare insight into the producer's techniques as he helped out around the studio. "I was into building amplifiers, mixers and various things, and we began to exchange bits of information. He was very open and forthcoming about the gear he made for his studio, and stuff he was working on. He also talked to me about the way in which he was recording which was fascinating to me. This was, I discovered, quite unique, because he never discussed this with anyone else."

With increasing venom, Meek became obsessively paranoid about the steps record companies were taking to discover his control room secrets. "He was convinced that people were bugging the studio and stealing his ideas," Fletcher recalls. "He was particularly paranoid about Decca who he did some work for. He hated Decca and believed that some of their guys had got into the studio during the night and planted microphones in the wall, then plastered over them."

New World Records

Coming at the dawn of the space age as a tribute to the newly-launched satellite, 'Telstar' was unlike any other record of its time. Its atmosphere had as its foundations an unreleased album Meek had produced in 1960 called *I Hear A New World*. A rare stereo production, it is believed by many to have been the world's first concept album – an early Sixties *Dark Side Of The Moon*. It was an album which merged strange sound effects with simple melodies, performed using unorthodox instruments, such as the new Clavioline – the battery-powered keyboard which provided 'Telstar' with its sonic hook and was later used on Del Shannon's 'Runaway' to provide the fairground-style solo flourishes. In creating this other-wordly electronic concoction of echo, reverb and severe limiting, Meek pre-dated the efforts of Tangerine Dream and Jean Michel Jarre by fifteen years.

Although he never took a hands-on role during any of Meek's sessions, Fletcher often stood inside the control room while his boss single-handedly engineered and produced hits such as John Leyton's 'Johnny Remember Me' and 'Have I The Right' by The Honeycombs. Fletcher casts his mind back to the pre-beat Boom era of the early Sixties and builds for us a picture of Meek's palace: "The main studio itself was on the third floor and the fourth floor attic was used by Joe as a reverb chamber. The control room was a very small room of about eight feet square. In one corner was a single Tannoy Lockwood speaker enclosure and in another corner was an EMI BTR-2 machine, so that was half the room taken up straight away! There was a bench, like an ordinary workbench, with a few bits of gear on it. One of the bits was a Lyrec two-track tape machine and next to it were some things which might be described as mixers or equalisers, but they were all open without any form of casing. It literally looked like a workshop because nothing had its cover on. Even the BTR-2 had its amplifier drawers hanging out. It was totally disorganised. I don't know what the floor looked like because you couldn't see it. As soon as you set foot into the room you were up to your ankles in lengths of quarter-inch tape with tape boxes lying all over the place. That was the first thing that struck you – all this tape!"

When it came to overdubs, Meek's equipment was used to full capacity in the most ingenious way. "The technique that he used for most of the time while I was there was to lay down the backing track on the full track of the BTR-2 so that the recording occupied the full quarter-inch tape in mono," Fletcher explains. "The advantage in recording on the BTR-2 was that it had a tremendous overload margin and was much better than the EMI TR50 he had previously been using. He would then remove the tape from the BTR-2 and put it on to the Lyrec machine where he would erase one half. There would still be the original backing track on the one half of the tape and he would add to that either the lead voice or backing vocals, depending on the song, on the other half of the track. He would then mix the backing track and the vocal track together live while he was recording another part, and send all three elements back to the BTR-2, live in mono on full track. He was pretty sensible because the backing track had only gone through one generation and yet he had two overlays and an original –

three separate recordings.

"If he had everything he wanted by then he would do a final mixdown with additional compression and EQ, often changing the speed of the recording by wrapping editing tape around the capstan wheel! Most people would have found it difficult to be consistent with the speed but he was very good at it. Occasionally, if he was going for a bigger production, he would repeat the exercise so that he had five separate recordings, but everything had to be mixed at the same time because you couldn't approach overdubs in the way we can today. Of course, it's hard to imagine how someone could have worked that way and achieve big hits. But he did."

It is believed that Meek built some form of echo chamber in his attic, although no one other than the highly secretive Meek would have seen it. For tape delay, he used a Vortexian unit and whenever a certain quality of vocal delay was required but could not be achieved within his limits, he would either build a unit which would match the sound in his head, or he might take the easier route and book time at Abbey Road or Decca to make use of their famous echo chambers. "He was a real innovator and I had never seen anything quite like it, but I was quite inexperienced then having just come into the business," says Fletcher. "I had never set foot inside a recording studio before I went to Joe's. To me it was all new so I didn't realise that nobody else recorded things in the same way he did. I simply assumed that this was how everyone must do it. Because we were on a busy street, recording would occasionally have to stop if a heavy lorry went thundering past."

Meek's close-miking techniques were often carried out to the extreme. "He used to suspend a Neumann U47 inside the piano either at the front or the back, depending on who he was recording," says Fletcher. "He had an old player piano with the player parts removed and put drawing pins in the hammers to make a very bright, tinny sound which was fantastic. With guitar amplifiers, he would generally hang a microphone over the amp then cover it with blankets, so that the whole thing just looked like a pile of blankets on the floor. In the middle of that was the amp and microphone! Drums were always very difficult because the studio was so small. I only saw about three or four sessions with drums and the drummer [normally Clem Cattini] was very cramped. The drums were normally recorded in the same space we did the vocals, often miked with a Reslo RBT ribbon mic. The studio was essentially a bedroom with blankets and egg boxes hanging on the walls. The vocal mic, a U47, was suspended on a really huge stand. The mic had a massive pop shield on it and the technique was to get as close to it as you possibly could, virtually touching the pop shield with your nose."

The Honeycombs' 1964 Number One, 'Have I The Right', was famous for its heavy stomp sound. "He got everyone who was in the studio on that session to climb up the stairs and stamp their feet like crazy," remembers Fletcher. "But it still wasn't as heavy as he hoped for so he got my brother Guy to hit a tambourine right against the microphone, as hard as he possibly could! That mic certainly took a beating, and when the session ended we noticed that the mic was full of dents. He once told me that someone who had been around while he was recording 'Have I The Right' went back to The Dave Clark Five camp and told them about the stomp sound which in turn gave them the idea for 'Bits And Pieces'. He was pretty upset about that."

Meek's hit-making abilities appeared to dry up by 1966, as psychedelia began to rear its head and, ironically, employ many of the strange sound qualities he had introduced six years earlier. It was at this time that Fletcher's partnership with Meek foundered. "The last time I spoke to him was about six months before he died," he says. "He phoned me to accuse me of running a studio in competition with him and using his ideas, which was ridiculous. All I had was very basic equipment that we just used for fun really and it was certainly not used commercially. He got really paranoid about the fact that I even had a tape machine, but he was like it with everyone and he got progressively worse as time went on. He was becoming increasingly detached from the real world. The last few sessions we did for him were very difficult because he was so moody. He'd be nice as pie one minute and then fly off into a temper the next. But he was being ganged up on by the establishment, there's no doubt about it. People started to refuse to release his records. We did quite a lot of stuff towards the end that never saw the light of day. Nobody with any power in the business really liked him because he was independent and successful at it too."

Session players who remember Meek's odd ways of working

include veteran guitarist, Joe Brown who played on many of the producer's sessions. "He was crazy, and it never seemed to matter to him where in his place you played," says Brown. "I used to do sessions with my Vox amp up there and on the very first occasion I put the amp down and said, 'Right, how loud to you want me to play?' He said, 'Play as loud as you like, it doesn't matter.' I thought that was great because I was so used to being told to turn down in studios. Then after the session was over, I grabbed my amp and took it to another gig, but when I got there to set up, it wouldn't work and I was in a real panic. So I looked in the back and noticed that Joe must have clipped some bulldog clips to the speakers, then direct injected the sound [DI] into his desk. When I pulled the clips off at the gig, it worked fine, but it did puzzle me."

Bass player, Chas Hodges, better known now as half of the Cockney duo, Chas And Dave, remembers Meek for the presence he was able to achieve in his productions. "He was the first person I ever worked with who close-miked a drum kit and he used to stuff blankets into the bass drum to get a nice thud," he says. "Joe produced all the recordings by my group at the time, Mike Berry & The Outlaws, which included about eight singles. One of them was 'Crazy Drums' on which the intro sound effect was done by putting a clock spring on a record player pick-up arm and twanging it. He was just into doing things differently and it caught on.

"But 'Johnny Remember Me' was probably the biggest success I was connected with as a session bassist. One of Joe's brilliant ideas was to DI the bass guitar into the desk and he was an innovator in that respect. It was a far better sound and, of course, it removed any risk of spill on to other microphones. For that record there was a little room for the drum kit, the female singer was in the kitchen, the violinists were upstairs in the loft area and I was in a booth right next to Joe's control room, so I could clearly hear and play along to the rest of the music. There were no headphones. Everyone playing on the track had their own speaker near them wherever they were in the building."

"Joe used to leave it to ourselves to get the right kind of performance going," says Clem Cattini, the session drummer credited with more chart records in the Sixties and Seventies than any other in Britain. In 1961 he quit Johnny Kidd And The Pirates to become both

Meek's house drummer and a member of The Tornados. Cattini says that Meek would brief his musicians about a new song simply by singing ideas over unrelated backing tracks. "The melody would never fit the chords on the tape he was playing, so we would all sit around and try to figure out the chord sequence," he says. "The tape was really only a guide to the style. There was normally only one mic on my snare drum, one on the bass drum and an overhead mic. Joe actually preferred me to play the bass drum case rather than the drum itself to get a better thud sound. I'd just put the pedal up against the case and play it as I would the drum. It was a bit difficult at times because the pedal would wobble about but we managed to tape it to the floor.

"I was working almost exclusively for Joe then. The other producer I worked with was EMI's Peter Sullivan who did Johnny Kidd And The Pirates and went on to join Decca and produce Tom Jones. Peter and Joe were not necessarily similar as characters but, like Joe, Peter broke rules and if an engineer told him that he couldn't have something sounding a certain way because it wasn't in the manual, Peter would tell him to throw the manual in the bin...or words to that effect! Both Peter and Joe went against all the traditions of recording and I think that is why they did so welll."

Joe Brown made his first record as an artist at Decca Studios in 1959 and by also working as a session guitarist, became so fascinated with the process of putting sound on tape that he soon invested in his own home studio facilities – one of the first artists of his generation to take such a step. With his band, The Bruvvers, Brown would play new material on the road for several weeks to gauge audience reaction before recording. "If it went down well, we would knock it on the head for a few weeks so it didn't get stale," he reveals. "Then we'd get in the studio, set the gear up and record it. When we did 'A Picture Of You', we played the song through once and the control room team said, 'Oh, that sounds good, we'll do a take now.' So they switched the tape machine on and when we finished it, we put our guitars away and went into the control room to ask for a listen. They said, 'We can't do that, we've taken the tape off the machine.' It was that quick, so we never even heard the record until it came out."

Another band whose choices of singles was largely dictated by feedback at gigs was The Spencer Davis Group. Bass guitarist Muff Winwood, brother of Steve and later a successful producer, says, "We weren't writing anything afresh in the studio – we had been playing our stuff and trying it out on audiences well in advance. We'd come in with our ten songs or whatever and there would be very little fine tuning, so the band would record everything within four or five takes. 'Gimme Some Lovin'' was written one afternoon, specifically for a single, and we had to record it the following week. So we played it twice at every gig from that night onwards. It had not only gone through its routining and arrangement in the rehearsal room, it had also been played at least fourteen times at gigs before we recorded it. We got to the studio and, bang, down it went in no time. We were only playing small clubs, but it was the audience reaction which helped you to decide which tracks to record and that was very important, and part and parcel of playing live. That was our own primitive form of market analysis! People would come and tell you which songs they liked after the gig, you know, 'I liked that solo, you sing that one very well,' and that was great. You knew before you made the record that people were going to like it that way. These days, people have a lot less concrete evidence to suggest that their new record is going to be a hit."

The simplicity of recording bands in the early to mid-Sixties owed much to these tightly honed stage performances, and Winwood draws comparisons between a mastering session of that period and modern-day BBC Radio One live sessions, where the results rely on expert engineering techniques. "The engineer on a lot of our records was Adrian Kerridge and he used to tell us what he could cope with, but I don't ever recall a time where we were not able to do something the way we wanted to do it," he says. "We would sit down and listen to a playback and if there was something about it we didn't like, the engineer would try and do something about it. But I can never remember us being particularly caring about a record. We'd worked on our songs so much live that as long as they sounded good when we transferred them to vinyl, that was all that counted. We only really needed a good engineer to record the performance and it always seemed to be done without any arguments and done well. I think the most telling thing about it all was that we cut an album in two days. What I find difficult to get my head around is why it takes three months to make an album today, when it used to take two days and record buyers were just as excited."

Although Joe Brown was rarely let inside the control room to hear his finished recordings, he insists that even at the outset of his career as an artist he maintained a certain amount of control over the choice of material and the way it sounded. "Obviously, people like Larry Parnes would come up with songs that had been written for me but if I really didn't like something, it wouldn't happen," he says. "I had terrible rows with people who tried to tell me what to do in the studio, especially later on. I had a blazing row with one of my managers once and kicked him out of the studio because he wanted me to do a crappy song that his mate had written. But everyone gets talked into doing things they don't want to do at some point, and sometimes they don't even realise it. Few people in the business really cared about creativity and if you said that you wanted to spend some time getting a decent sound, the managers wouldn't consider that was important. No one really looked at sound as being a crucial part of what was going on because the whole emphasis was on getting the song on tape. As long as they could tap their foot, or tap their wallet, the managers would be happy. Back then, it was just a record."

Decca Days

Along with EMI's Abbey Road and Pye, Decca was among the most influential record company-owned studios in London during the Sixties, with a steady stream of hits by The Rolling Stones, Tom Jones, The Moody Blues and scores of other British-based international artists. Like its rivals in the capital, Decca's history stretched back several decades before the golden age of pop began to change its previously staid working practices and a new generation of engineers and producers shocked its old-timers with comparatively strange ideas about sound. Situated in West Hampstead, Decca operated three studios in its Broadhurst Gardens building. The control room and studio area in Number Two studio, the venue for most standard rock and pop sessions, had a low ceiling, around sixteen feet from the floor, and the recording space was approximately twenty-two feet wide by forty-five feet long – large enough to comfortably accommodate a rhythm section and horns. Visual access from the control room to the studio itself was through an oblong window. The much larger Number One studio could accommodate up to ten times as many musicians and control room access was via a flight of stairs which overlooked the studio. Bigger still was Number Three studio which regularly housed full orchestras and rarely were pop records made there, except when orchestral arrangements were required.

Gus Dudgeon began his engineering career as a tape operator at Olympic Studios in Barnes but it was while working at Decca as a staff engineer – which he joined in 1962 – that his ambition to become a producer began to take shape. He narrowly missed engineering The Beatles' failed audition session for Decca, but *was* in attendance for The Rolling Stones' audition in January 1963. Dudgeon admits to harbouring an early "fear" of the mixing console and despite his eventual success as Elton John's long-time producer, never regarded engineering as being a stepping stone to greater heights. In the beginning he was grateful that Decca even allowed him the responsibility of a session. "It was more of a responsibility then because you had to turn out a specific amount of material within a given time," he says. "Sessions were exactly three hours long and if you went into overtime it would cost a bloody fortune, so you had to negotiate with the musicians at the session which was always a hit or miss situation because they were invariably committed to work at another studio immediately afterwards. Going into overtime was very uncool, so you had to be there on time, ready to deliver. It was white knuckle recording because you had to sit there with your hands and fingers on the faders, ready to catch that guitar solo. You had to move things within a track, so it was about as hands-on as you get. The whole idea of spending a day on a vocal track was completely ridiculous – it never occurred to anyone that it would become the norm."

The lack of headroom provided by the consoles and tape itself presented largely unsurmountable obstacles when attempting to form big sounds. A general policy for Decca engineers was to place no more than four mics on the drums, and as long as cymbal crashes poked their way through the drum kit balance, that constituted a workable soundcheck. Unlike today where a snare drum mic is normally placed as close as one inch away from the top skin, engineers would keep them much further away for fear of either the sound exploding in the control room or, worse still, a drummer hitting the mic with his stick. Veteran blues producer and one of Dudgeon's contemporaries at Decca in the Sixties, Mike Vernon says, "I learned a lot from Jack Clegg and other senior engineers about microphone technique and how to set up mics for drums. With Gus I learned things about using mics at angles, coming in at the side of something or further away to give it more space. There was also the ambient technique of having a second mic further away, but you had to be careful that by using more than one mic close to the second that there wasn't a phasing problem."

Vernon is particularly grateful of the insight into analogue tape editing which he gained while at Decca, a technique in which he is now regarded as an expert. "Arthur Bannister taught me everything I know and my first editing job was with Arthur for a twenty-record boxed set of Sir Winston Churchill's pre-war and post-war speeches which came out just before his death in 1965," he says. "Churchill had re-recorded these speeches on to acetate disc at his home at Chartwell and we also had some BBC recordings of his actual wartime speeches. Our job was to de-click, de-cough and de-splutter these recordings. Anything that shouldn't be on the discs was to be removed to make the speeches more coherent, because when Churchill delivered these speeches to disc in 1953 or 1954, he would read and take long pauses in between phrases and sentences. The knowledge that I picked up on that project proved to be invaluable throughout my career. Nowadays, if I'm working in analogue format, I don't have the slightest fear of taking a chinagraph pencil and razor blade to a piece of two-inch or quarter-inch tape. I have often seen people building a sweat up prior to editing who have to keep washing their hands because they are literally dripping with the fear that they might be about to chop out something important by accident. It's an art that you have to learn."

After his early period as an office boy at Decca's head office at Albert Embankment, Vernon moved into studio work in West Hampstead as an assistant to producer, Frank Lee on sessions for Mantovani, Stanley Black, Frank Chacksfield and Gracie Fields. "I accompanied Frank with my notepad and stopwatch," he recalls. "One of the major tasks I had was to follow the score for the benefit of the engineer. The recording was done directly to two-track because in Studio Three, the largest studio where we did all the orchestral recordings, they didn't have a multitrack machine when I started. The four-track machine was in Studio Two and we used that on the first John Mayall album. So I had to sit there with the score which had been given to me by the arranger and I would have to warn the engineer if there was a solo coming up or a bank of French horns coming in so that they could push up the appropriate faders at the right moment. We would have three or four trial runs at this and sometimes I would miss it or the engineer might be too slow. Sometimes we would edit together the best parts of two or three takes, however, that was often dangerous because in those days we didn't have click tracks. But it was usually Ronnie Verrell playing drums and he was a champion timekeeper."

The rivalry between engineers at Decca and EMI's Abbey Road Studios stretched back to before World War II, when the two companies battled it out for the major share of the recording business, and both parties went to great lengths to protect their technical trade secrets. "Equipment was house-made and we were not about to tell people on the outside what we were doing to create a particular sound," says former Decca engineer, Derek Varnals. "But we were still curious to know how people like Norman Smith and Geoff Emerick were getting their sounds at Abbey Road, just as I'm sure they wondered about us,"

At one point in 1964, Decca dispatched its in-house producer, Peter Attwood, and ex-Shadows drummer, Tony Meehan, to conduct a tour of studios in America to discover how the Americans made their distinctive records, but they returned with only a list of microphones. "With a few exceptions, they were the same microphones we already had, so Decca went out and bought a couple of each of the absent mics, and started making some records with them," says Varnals. "But they didn't make anything sound any different! Of course, in those days, a record largely sounded the way it did because of the musicians and the room in which it was recorded. The studio environment was all-important in the Sixties. Back then, a Decca engineer could play an EMI record and tell which engineer had recorded it, because they would each have their own style, and which studio at Abbey Road had been used, because they had their own sound. You could also do that with Decca records. But I'd defy anyone to be able to make the same kind of educated guess today."

By 1967, it was apparent that Decca's die-hard engineers of the older generation had become too old and detached from the progressive pop world to have anything in common with the new breed of engineers, like Vernon and Dudgeon, and the young birds were preparing themselves to leave the nest. "Frank Lee, for instance, was stuck in a time warp, recording people who had been with Decca for twenty-five years or more and were getting well past their sell-by dates," Vernon comments. "This was the age of The Rolling Stones, yet this had no bearing on the corporate mentality. Frank was also beginning to upset a few people. He was in Decca's Studio Three with me one day doing an album session with Stanley Black and there was a serious amount of competition between Black and Mantovani. Frank was prone to nodding off to sleep in the studio and he did it this day in the middle of a song that we had been routining. In the midst of the take he woke up and thought we were still rehearsing it, and leaned forward and pressed the talkback button which immediately aborted the take. As if that wasn't bad enough, he announced, 'That's great, Monty, let's take one!' Of course, Stanley just freaked and stormed out of the studio. Frank had totally screwed the whole session."

It was Glyn Johns who began a future trend for engineers to leave the staid security of salaried positions and branch out as freelancer, then going further by jumping a perceived barrier between engineering and production. Johns began with IBC Studios in Portland Place as a trainee in 1959 and by the mid-Sixties had worked with almost every hit producer in Britain until he realised that not only could he earn more money by becoming a free agent but he could also do a better job than most of those "so-called producers". "I was fed up working for idiots," he explains. "The producers were mostly the record company A&R men whose egos were so huge that they'd let a mistake or bad decision pass rather than admit they were wrong. It was people like myself and the arrangers who really produced the records. Of course, being a member of staff at IBC, I just had to swallow all this but when it dawned on me that I could make a living on the outside, I was off like a shot. The only trouble was, the studios I was allowed to work in were limited because many had the rule that only their staff could operate the equipment."

"Glyn had a great reputation and it was no surprise to any of us that he became the favoured engineer of The Who and Led Zeppelin," says Gus Dudgeon. "He came in to Decca for a couple of sessions and we were a bit taken aback by the fact that he was working on our holy ground, using our desks."

Clem Cattini backs up Johns' tales of unimaginative, clueless producers. "I worked with hundreds of producers who didn't really know what they were after," he says. "I once did a session for Dick Rowe at Decca where we were recording an album with the Irish tenor, Josef Locke, and we were halfway through a track when the producer's switch went on and stopped us. Dick said to Ivor Raymond, the musical director, 'What is Clem playing at the start of this number?' Ivor said, 'He's tacit,' [signifying a player's silent part in a score]. Dick replied, 'Well, could you ask him to play it a little quieter, please?' There was another incident with Dick when something wasn't sounding right and we suggested a key change. He said, 'No, but I think it could go up a *crochet*.'

"But Dick was a very clever man because he could tell a hit record, even though he passed on The Beatles which he never lived down. He may have been devoid of any real technical or musical knowledge, but he was really a punter which put him in the position of instinctively knowing what the public wanted. Wally Ridley was a producer who didn't really know about rock 'n' roll. When I made 'Shakin' All Over' with Johnny Kidd, the label credited Wally but he wasn't even on the session. It was actually produced by Peter Sullivan who was his assistant. Wally was more of a classical producer and he wasn't enamoured with the idea of working with us. Of course, 'Shakin' All Over' went to Number One and suddenly Wally Ridley appeared to produce the follow-up, 'Restless', which was just typical!"

Mike Vernon's first production credit on Decca Records was for an album recorded in a one-day session by Texan singer and keyboard player, Curtis Jones which also featured Alexis Korner and Jack Fallon. A number of other small blues projects followed, such as an Otis Spann album with Muddy Waters, but it was as the producer of John Mayall's Bluesbreakers in 1966 that Vernon made his name. "I had submitted some demo acetates to Decca of The Yardbirds when

Clapton was still in the band, but they were rejected because they had signed the Stones and didn't want another band of that ilk for a while," he says. "So working with Mayall, with Clapton on guitar and Gus engineering, was an absolute joy but pressurised because we had to do so much in a short space of time. The allocation of studio time was very tight and everybody wanted to get into Studio Two where all the pop stuff was made, like 'It's Not Unusual' [for which Tom Jones recorded his lead vocal in the tape cupboard in one take!]"

The *Blues Breakers* album with the famous *Beano* cover was recorded within four days. "When Clapton first plugged in his guitar and played it was deafening," says Vernon. "Much louder than anyone had expected him to be because it was in a confined space. Gus reacted more acutely to this than I did because he had always been used to recording session players who never played at that volume. Gus said, 'My God, can you turn it down?' but Clapton said, 'Well I can't because then it won't sound the way I want it to.' So between us we decided that it would be best to put the microphone about four or six feet away from the Marshall stack instead of up close like we would normally do it. I remember thinking at the time that Hughie Flint wasn't a very good drummer, but that was a personal observation during the sessions and I kept it to myself. I suppose if you compare him to the guys who followed him, Aynsley Dunbar and Jon Hiseman, he wasn't that good.

"We recorded it on four-track and had drums and bass together with the occasional basic rhythm guitar or keyboard on one track. The vocal had its own track, and the solo guitar, harmonica and organ were spread between two tracks. I have been horrified to listen to the stereo versions of some of the early records I was involved with, where the drums were all on one side. But most American records, like Motown and Stax, were also like that. On one occasion I had the drums left and right, but the snare was on one side and the bass drum was on the other. I think I was experimenting for the sake of it."

Meanwhile, Gus Dudgeon had decided that unless he made a concentrated effort to exceed his assistant status and prove his worth as an engineer, he would fade into obscurity. His first break came when Jack Clegg feigned sickness in order to let him take the reins of a Marianne Faithfull session. At the same time, engineering wizard Bill

Price had joined Decca from an electronics career at Plessey. "That Bill was ten times more clever than me, but was my junior, put a rocket up my arse and I realised that I had to do something with my career otherwise I would be swamped," says Dudgeon. "One of the earliest sessions I engineered was 'She's Not There' by The Zombies which went to Number One in America. The engineer who started the session got drunk in his lunch hour and was taken home in a cab, so I was left in charge. After the record became successful, a guy from *Cashbox* in America came to the studio to present the band with an award. The Zombies were thrilled shitless to have been honoured in this way and I remember looking at the plaque and thinking, 'I'd quite fancy one of those.' That sowed a seed in my mind as I began to set my mind on the future."

Around 1966, Dudgeon found himself working the console for producer Denny Cordell on Moody Blues sessions and learned a valuable lesson when his big ideas got him into hot water. "There was one track called 'Fly Me High' on which I had done a particularly good job, without Denny's input and the support of the band," he says. "I was thinking that I had got a great sound, but the band wanted everything changed. By the time Denny arrived the whole thing had been carved up and I was getting more and more depressed. But Denny couldn't hear anything wrong with it. I said, 'I think it sounds terrible.' At which point he flipped out and shouted, 'Where the fuck do you think you're getting off, it's their record!' So we really fell out, which was a shame because he used to specifically ask for me to engineer for him. Behind my back, he called head office and demanded that I be taken off the session. So I got a tongue-lashing from them for treating one of their best clients badly. I went back in with my tail between my legs but to my amazement, Denny apologised and he asked me to play me what I thought the track should sound like. He agreed that it was several times better and that I was right to stand up to the band."

Key to Dudgeon's next important phase was David Platz, the owner of several independent production companies including Denny Cordell's Straight Ahead Productions, who had been impressed by Dudgeon's covert work on The Strawbs' debut single (while still contracted to Decca) and offered to help launch his production career in 1968. "Both Denny and Andrew Oldham told me on separate occasions me that I shouldn't be bothering with engineering because I had too many ideas, and that I should look towards production. Andrew gave me the tip that if I did head that way, I should always demand a royalty. I had to find out what a royalty was! So when I did finally make it into production, I had this fixation that if Andrew got a royalty, I should have one too!"

As soon as Mike Vernon left Decca to pursue his independent production career in February 1968, he too addressed the issue of royalties, but his were backdated. "I went to Hugh Mendl at Decca to see if I could get something more out of what I'd done while I was there," he says. "I had worked on some very important product like Ten Years After, Savoy Brown and John Mayall, and I was now asking for a royalty. About three months later, he came through and a contract arrived for a very small percentage. Thanks to Hugh, every three months I receive a royalty statement and cheque from Decca for all of my production work with them and it has been quite profitable at times."

One studio which became synonymous with Dudgeon's early productions after leaving Decca was Trident in Soho which had been set up in 1968 by Barry Sheffield as one of London's first eight-track facilities. "Somebody tipped me off that Trident was the new happening place to record in town," he says. "I had been having trouble finding studios that I liked to work in and even some of the independent ones had a kind of a corporate feel to them. I wanted to escape from the starchy, Decca-type environments and find a nice, funky place where my lack of mechanical ability wouldn't be challenged so I could just get on with it. I knew that was possible because that's how Denny worked; he knew nothing about the technical side of making records, but that didn't prevent him from getting the results he wanted. But although I was in a position to be able to sign up acts through Platz to my own company, Tuesday Productions, I couldn't find anyone for about nine months."

Dudgeon then discovered folk singer/guitarist, Michael Chapman and scored a deal with EMI's new underground music label, Harvest, for his first album which was also notable for Mick Ronson's debut as a session guitarist. In June 1969, only weeks before the first moon landing, Dudgeon produced David Bowie's 'Space Oddity' at Trident which marked the start, as they say, of two rather brilliant careers.

The Musicians' Union And Overdubbing

Up until around 1972, the Musicians' Union kept a tight rein on the activities of producers and its members in every studio, to ensure that each session started and finished at fixed times, allowing musicians sufficient travelling time between other studio engagements in London. One area of recording in which the MU exercised its power was overdubbing which in nearly all cases was strictly forbidden.

"If you wanted to do overdubbing of any sort, you had to seek permission from the MU but it wasn't always granted," Gus Dudgeon says. "Sometimes, we could only get permission to do a vocal overdub if we produced a doctor's certificate to prove that the singer was too ill at the original session. There was a Lulu session at the peak of her success where she got stuck in a blizzard in Glasgow and couldn't get down in time, and halfway through the session the musicians got up and walked out because she wasn't there performing. The artist had to be seen to be performing in the booth at the same time as the musicians. The assumption was the entire performance all went down at the same time but that gave us problems because there were some artists who were either too nervous or untalented to be able to deliver under those circumstances. So we used to have to resort to covert night time sessions behind locked doors.

"There were one or two musicians around who were wise to this, like Jimmy Page and Big Jim Sullivan, and were prepared to go along with this. We were always shitting bricks that we were about to be found out at any moment and at one time, Decca Studios was actually blacklisted by the MU when they discovered that some of the rules were being broken and we couldn't get any session musicians in. Eventually, I think the MU relaxed their rules when they realised that they were so uncreative and that they were up against some severe opposition, even though they still had the power to walk in and call a halt to things to supposedly protect the interests of their session musician members."

Respected as one of the great new guitar talents in the mid-Sixties,

Steve Howe was occasionally asked to play on sessions, one of which was in 1967 for Mark Wirtz's *A Teenage Opera* which included the Keith West hit single, 'Excerpt From A Teenage Opera', otherwise known by its chorus as 'Grocer Jack'. "One night, Mark showed up for an evening overdub session at Abbey Road Studio Three at around ten-thirty and a chill went down my spine," says Howe. "I said, 'Where is everybody?' He said, 'Oh, this is just a guitar session.' I thought, 'Jesus, just guitar?' So I went in and he told me he wanted me to play this tune. After I'd got it down okay, he said, 'I want you to play this again identically.' So I had to take out all the difficult nuances in my playing and literally duplicate the part in terms of the notes, timing and feel. That was the first ever time I double-tracked anything professionally. It was so exciting and felt to me that I was breaking new ground."

The power of the session musician was at an all-time high between the early Sixties and mid-Seventies, before the use of synthesisers began to replace a number of human roles, not least orchestration. Record company A&R men and many independent producers virtually outlawed some band members from playing on their own records and in the extreme case of The Love Affair, the lead vocal was performed by a session singer. Even The Beatles were not immune to such measures at the start of their EMI recording career: their first single in 1962, 'Love Me Do', saw Ringo Starr temporarily replaced by session drummer Andy White and relegated to tambourine. And had it not been for Pete Townshend's wrath in the face of producer Shel Talmy, Keith Moon would have sat on the substitute's bench while Clem Cattini played his parts.

"I try not to think about Shel too much!" The Who's John Entwistle says. "He also wanted to bring Jimmy Page in to play guitar and The Ivy League on backing vocals, but we rebelled against that and didn't want to know. Jimmy got relegated to just playing a fast drone on 'Bald Headed Woman', the B-side of our first single, and The Ivy League sang on 'I Can't Explain'. But we wouldn't have anymore of that after those numbers and we finished off the rest of our first album in three days doing it all ourselves. Shel signed us to a deal which was crap, where we got five per cent of seventy-five per cent and he got half of our five per cent. But we realised that Glyn Johns was doing most of the work on the sessions and Shel was getting that for doing sweet FA so we got out of that as quickly as we could. Whenever I met him he would apologise profusely, but the next day we'd be hearing from his lawyer asking for more money."

Joe Brown says the widespread use of session players was not necessarily a reflection of a lack of musical talent on the part of bands, but an indication that producers wished to get the most from short sessions by employing specialist expertise. "You were booked because the producer knew what he wanted and you fitted the part," he says. "So they'd wheel you in and say, 'Joe, have a listen to this.' So you'd hear a backing track or a demo and sort out the key, then you'd have a couple of runs through before they went for a take."

After Clem Cattini quit working as Joe Meek's house drummer in 1965, he launched himself as one of Britain's busiest session musicians – the UK counterpart to America's Hal Blaine – and there is every chance that at least a handful of records in every pop collection features his work. "I would drum on lots of demos down at Southern Music's studio then get calls from the producers asking if I would play on the masters," he says. "I was working every day and there are many records that I'm on that I don't even know about. With The Kinks, I was drumming in place of Mick Avory because it was a normal financial decision rather than artistic. I am told that I played on 'You Really Got Me', 'All Day And All Of The Night' and 'Dedicated Follower Of Fashion'. Dave Davies and Pete Quaife both acknowledge that it was me, although Ray Davies says it was Bobby Graham. But I don't know for sure. I do remember going in and recording lots of Kinks numbers, and I certainly played on all of the *Kinks Kontroversy* album.

"I did so many songs at so many sessions – four songs a sessions, three sessions a day for seven days a week – that they all sounded the same to me in the end. I do remember things like 'Hurdy Gurdy Man' by Donovan and 'Tossin' And Turnin'' by The Ivy League because I was part of the band, and also 'Let's Go To San Francisco' by The Flowerpot Men, who were in fact The Ivy League under a different name. I played on Marc Bolan's records but I didn't even know until the producer told me later because the system was like a conveyor belt. A lot of the producers were unsure as to what they wanted from us, because everything was being pioneered and there was no standard to go by. So we were often asked to copy the style of a certain record, just because it had been a big hit."

In 1966, Cattini earned the notoriety of instigating the standard approach of completely removing the front head from a bass drum and putting a blanket inside it, to allow closer miking. He was also known for insisting on foldback headphones for studio musicians. "We always had such trouble hearing each other," he says. "I used to complain terribly, saying, 'How can I play with the band if I can't hear them?' I was once asked, 'What do you want in the cans?' and I replied, 'Can I have the strings a bit quicker, please?' because the strings always lagged behind the rest of the musicians, time-wise."

Despite John Entwistle's criticisms of Talmy, both he and Mickie Most are credited by Cattini as being the most intuitive independent producers he ever worked with. "They had an ear for a hit song and that was their strength," he says. "You can be the greatest musician in the world but that doesn't mean to say you can pick a hit record from twenty songs. Mickie would even let some mistakes go by on a session because although he wanted a perfect take within reason, he was more into the feel of a performance. If the atmosphere was right on a record, that's what counted."

A Time For Experimentation

Gradually, from late 1965, artists began to look for new ways in which to express themselves on record, instead of relying on straightforward guitar-bass-keyboard-drums arrangements and recording methods. This was the beginning of the psychedelic period, although many of the ground-breaking tracks and albums were not created in a haze of pot smoke and LSD, as legend will have it. Admittedly, some bands did dabble, but most of the advances were simply the result of friendly competition between bands, studios, producers and engineers who saw the creation of "way out" sounds as a means of one-upmanship. The studio hardware used to forge such inventiveness largely remained the same as it had for some years, but now the control room teams were forced to wrack their brains to see how they could push its capabilities to the limit and, in doing so, ignore virtually everything they had been taught as trainees.

"New Sounds" was the key phrase by the summer of 1966 as The Beach Boys and The Beatles (whose mammoth achievements in this area are covered separately) began to defy all logic in recorded sound, and both acts were responsible for introducing a new palette of exotic instrumentation to the rock masses, such as the sitar, tabla and Theremin, and sound effects.

Even the normally stiff-shirted music company executives were beginning to turn on to a different lifestyle, according to one member of staff at Dick James Music in the Sixties – Stuart Epps. "It was an amazing time in 1967 around Soho, Denmark Street and that area," he recalls. "Hippie times. We used to get accountants coming in one day in a smart suit, collar and tie, really straight. The next day, one of them would have freaked out overnight and he came in wearing beads and lighting joss sticks in his office."

"Everybody seemed to know everybody else in those days and there was a sort of cross fertilisation of ideas," says producer and artist manager, Gerry Bron. "I wouldn't say we were copying each other, but there would always be occasions when someone would say, 'John Mayall did this great thing at Olympic last night, let's do something like that.'"

Before he joined Yes in 1970, Steve Howe had amassed considerable studio experience as a member of The In-Crowd, Tomorrow and Bodast, and on several sessions at Abbey Road oversaw the engineering prowess of Geoff Emerick and Ken Scott which helped to shape the new approaches in recording during the heady 1966-7 period. "Something new and exciting began to happen in the studios then," he says. "I felt a familiarity with engineering people, mainly because I wanted to learn from them. Before I started performing, before I made my first record, I was very interested in recording, definitely. I was fascinated by the sounds of the records I was listening to. When I think retrospectively, it seems to me that I not only heard the guitar and wanted to play it but also the things that happened in sound when it was recorded were very interesting to me from the beginning. But I also realised how much patience engineers needed then because it had to be one of the most gruelling jobs in the world, having to sit through an entire session and all the hassles that went with it! It was a bit like flying a jumbo to Australia and they were always being asked to respond to huge challenges."

Mike Vernon always hated the sound of drums and often asked engineers to look at ways of recording them differently. "They had a very compressed flavour about them which I wasn't crazy about," he admits. "You always had to try and be aware of what the engineer was doing. One wondered whether things sounded the way they did as a result of what he was doing on the board, or because of the mic positioning or even the drummer himself. There was an element of creative experimentation with regard to mic positions and how you contained the sound without it exploding all over the place. But more often than not we came unstuck because we might not achieve what we were looking for, and sometimes achieved the opposite! We tried a lot of things with bass drums with padding here and there, sometimes with the front heads on, sometimes off, and that's still done today. But people are more inclined to say, 'To hell with all that, let's just use the kit to trigger samples.' With bass players, we'd try different things like get them to play with a pick or a matchstick. If we were overdubbing guitars we might shove them out in the corridor and put the amps in a lift shaft. I've even recorded guitar amps out in the open air, which is not much use I have to say. But most of the time we went back to basics. Most of the time, innovative sounds have been created by using certain musicians playing in a unique way in a special environment, rather than messing around with mics and mixing desks. If you wanted a big, spacious, cathedral-like sound, recorded acoustically, people would go and record in a church to overdub things. You had to decide in your own mind what you wanted."

An increase in the level of bass on records also became noticeable in the mid-Sixties, as many an owner of frail Dansettes and radiograms will recall. Influenced by the deep tones of Atlantic, Stax and Motown, bands looked towards bringing the bass guitar to the fore, much to the envy of lead guitarists, while nervous cutting engineers struggled to contain the lower frequencies at the mastering stage. Normally, a bass solo would not have constituted part of a hit single's formula, but The Who's 'My Generation', produced by Shel Talmy and released on Brunswick in the autumn of 1965, spectacularly broke the mould. Bassist John Entwistle explains the solo's evolution: "The first version we did was without a bass solo, but because of the playing style that I had developed, Kit Lambert [manager and executive producer] thought it would be a good idea to incorporate something that would showcase my playing. Another reason was to balance up the shots we got on TV. Bass players in those days got a standard two shots if they were lucky. There would probably be a close-up of the hand and then a fleeting glimpse in a long shot. Unless you were also the vocalist, you were practically unseen. So the bass player's lot was not a happy one but Kit was keen to balance it up.

"I played that solo on a Fender Jazz Bass with tapewound strings through a Marshall 50 watt amp and a four by twelve-inch cabinet. The bass solos on the earlier takes were much more complicated and I played them on a Danelectro medium scale bass which had a much more piano-like sound. The trouble was that the strings I used on it were so thin that I kept on breaking them. We recorded during the day and to finance the sessions we were playing gigs nearly every night, but inevitably I would break a string. The next day after one such gig, someone said we had to record 'My Generation' again but none of the music shops had any replacement strings, so I had to go down to Marshall's and buy a new bass for £60. I ended up with three Danelectros, all with busted strings! In the end I busted my last string and there weren't anymore in the country. So I thought, 'Fuck it,' and bought myself a Fender Jazz Bass and a set of La Bella strings, and played the solo with that. But it was a different sound and a simplified, slowed down version of the solos on previous takes."

Entwistle claims that the lack of bass on records up to that point could be attributed to "stick in the mud" engineering. "Most of the time they would insist I played with a plectrum because they couldn't get a decent sound if I played with my fingers," he explains. "They didn't know what to do with the treble end of my bass and ended up with a huge amount of bottom end which was only half of my sound, and then they pushed it into the background." Due to a disagreement with Talmy, Pete Townshend produced The Who's follow-up single, 'Substitute', which although bereft of a similar solo, featured an even more intense bass sound, largely due to a little pre-planning on Entwistle's part. "We went back to Olympic to record that one and I had with me a two pick-up, medium scale Gibson bass and managed to find a decent set of Gibson wirewound strings that vibrated properly," he says. "The session was going well, they'd previously balanced everything and it was all going through the mixer at the same time. Then when I felt that we were ready for the master take and it came to what was going to be Pete Townshend's guitar solo in the middle, I turned the bass up and there was nothing the engineer could do about it."

The Who's all-time classic rock opera double album, *Tommy*, was recorded at IBC Studios over six months between late 1968 and early 1969, this time produced by Kit Lambert. To this day, Entwistle remains disappointed with the album, citing the unfriendly equipment and environment of the studio, and Lambert's naive production. "Compared to the effect the stage performances had on people when we played, the album was a real let-down," he says. "We had great plans for overdubbing loads of little parts that we felt were important to Pete's lyrical ideas, but Kit was more interested in capturing a live performance from us than what could be done technically. I mean, we had eight tracks at our disposal and most of the time there were three blank tracks. But it took a long time to do. You got a very woolly bass sound at IBC. It sounded great there in the studio through the big Lockwood monitors, but thin and weak when you played it anywhere else. They were more concerned with getting depth on the record than a good bass sound. You could feel the bass but it wasn't really there. I think Kit had learned a bit about recording by the time we made *Tommy* but if anything compromised it, it was the studio equipment."

Muff Winwood believes that his dominant bass sound on The Spencer Davis Group hits, such as 'Keep On Running' and 'Gimme Some Lovin'', had more to do with the interplay between him and drummer Pete York than studio technique. "Pete was much more of a jazz drummer than a rock drummer, and he had a smaller kit than most rock drummers," he says. "So by accident, we developed a technique where my bass had a greater role in driving out the rhythm. This allowed Pete to be a little more flowery and inventive with cymbals, rather than being restrained with the bass player doing little lines alongside the guitarist. So it came about for those reasons and I tended to almost strum like a rhythm guitar on a lot of songs, playing eights like a rhythm part, just hitting one string, sometimes two."

Winwood also says that the leakage of instruments on to different mics and tracks often helped to add an interesting flavour. His younger brother, Steve Winwood's classic, overdriven Hammond organ sound on 'Gimme Some Lovin'', for example, was affected in this way and so could never be accurately reproduced a second time. "A lot of the sound was down to Steve's settings and we miked the organ's Leslie speaker in the traditional way, but it is important to realise that there was also a rhythm guitar and percussion on the Hammond track," he says. "There was also the general leakage of other instruments that the studio would give, even if acoustic screens were used. So there was a kind of relationship between the organ and the rest of the instruments on the same track which is bound to affect the harmonics of the organ. It's got to sound different. If you're recording the same organ and same Leslie speaker today, you'd give it its own track, more likely two tracks, and the result will be entirely different. There has to be a harmonic difference. Whether the lack of technique gave it a better sound to what today's high-tech technique can achieve is just a matter of circumstance."

'Gimme Some Lovin'' was later remixed for the American market which required a fatter sound with extra percussion and additional backing vocals from Steve Winwood's newly-formed Traffic. The result, although bigger, did not boast the previous forceful, raw sound. "The Hammond was dirtier and more dominating on the earlier version because Steve was playing chordal fills and as soon as we put backing vocals on the top, everything was smoothed over," explains the elder Winwood. "Sounds are equal to the relationship between each other. It doesn't matter how much time you spend on getting a great sound on one instrument, the moment you place it alongside another instrument in the mix, its sound in relativity changes, relative to the one it's playing next to. That's why I was always amazed at the amount of time people would spend getting the sound right of one particular instrument – you know, the drum sound, the bass sound, whatever. It was the sound they all made when played together that was most important."

Muff Winwood left The Spencer Davis Group in April 1967 to assist the band's manager, Chris Blackwell with his new label, Island Records, before branching out as the producer of many successful acts including Sparks, and is now head of Sony's Soho Square label. "Chris had been working with a lot of Ska and Bluebeat artists, and he wanted to make it into much more of a proper UK A&R-based mainstream rock label, and he asked me if I would be a part of it," he says. "We knew that when Steve formed Traffic that the band was going to be on Island, but that The Spencer Davis Group wasn't. My job then was as an absolute jack of all trades. I went round the BBC plugging, went to studios with the artists, did some A&R work. Just like the independents do now. There were only three or four of us but we did everything. Spencer was annoyed that Blackwell seemed to encourage the split with Steve and I didn't relish the thought of staying with Spencer and Pete, and effectively cutting the ties with my brother. So it was a fairly straightforward decision. I wouldn't have joined Traffic, that's for sure, because Traffic was bass-less. Steve was doing all the bass parts on his organ pedals and that's the way he wanted it. Besides, I found the challenge of developing this new record company really interesting."

One of the most profound effects of the era, phasing, made its most obvious early appearance on The Small Faces' 1967 Immediate single, 'Itchycoo Park', which was recorded by Glyn Johns at Olympic. Applied to the whole track at the end of each middle eight section of the song the phasing had a most peculiar affect on Kenney Jones's drum fills. Although attributed to Johns, he claims it was his assistant engineer, George Chiantz who worked out the method using three tape machines. "George had been attempting to create this effect all morning and by the time I arrived for the session, he had it all figured out and played me something which knocked me out," says Johns. "So when we cut 'Itchycoo Park' I played an example of phasing to the band and they loved it." Small Faces frontman, Steve Marriott, had an altogether more colourful explanation for the effect when he was interviewed shortly after by BBC radio presenter, Ray Moore. "I pissed on the tape," he grinned.

It was the Small Faces' move from the Decca label to Immediate which provided the band with a perfect opportunity to explore their musical potential and make records which were not necessarily aimed at the Top Ten. "Out of that period came 'Green Circles', 'Tin Soldier', 'Here Come The Nice' and a lot of great album tracks," recalls Kenney Jones. "That gave me an opportunity to be dynamic and think big with my drumming, playing like I really meant it. That's when I started getting heavier and almost think classically. So that's how that style came through. The songs that were being written by Ronnie Lane and Steve lent themselves to that approach. One of the great things about the band was that we never told each other what to do, our individual parts just happened and gelled beautifully. Any arrangement was a pure natural groove and I was left to do my own thing. The guys used to let me experiment, knowing that when the tape machine went into record, I'd put the cream of all those ideas on the final track, and the phasing effect we used was a brilliant way to capture the mood of the moment."

Producer and engineer David Hentschel, who began his career at Trident Studios in 1969, became a huge fan of manual tape phasing and used it frequently in his work during the Seventies. One way to achieve phasing was to have two identical tape copies of a performance playing on machines that were synchronised together as closely as possible. If the engineer retarded the tape spool of one machine, the combined sound of the two recordings would go in and out of phase, and frequencies would be cancelled. "To get that really tight phase, rather than shifting the varispeed knob all the time, we would wind editing tape round the capstan to make it acentric, so that it would wobble all the time and give that constant variation," he says. "It was a killer sound! Modern phasing using digital equipment isn't a patch on the old method. There was a beautiful warmth about the sound."

One of the greatest exponents of phasing, flanging, stereo panning and all of those queasy psychedelic effects which shaped the musical environment of the mid to late Sixties was Jimi Hendrix, whose *Are You Experienced?* album (produced by Chas Chandler and engineered by Eddie Kramer) made an enormous impact when released in 1967. Hendrix's yearning for experimentation was neither an accident nor a means by which to join the freak-out bandwagon; it was a direct result of a curiosity borne of his pre-fame years spent as a session guitarist, under the management of producer Ed Chalpin.

In late 1964, after touring with such luminaries as Sam Cooke, The Isley Brothers, Wilson Pickett and Ike And Tina Turner, Hendrix joined New York R&B band Curtis Knight And The Squires as a guitarist and multi-instrumentalist. Knight introduced Hendrix to Chalpin who at the time owned one of the most technically advanced studios in the Big Apple: PPX. Chalpin not only recorded Hendrix with Knight, but also used the guitarist's talents on a wide range of sessions. It was a relationship which helped steer the guitar icon towards his eventual success as an artist in his own right. "As a session player, Jimi took directions easily and for a musician at that time he had an unusually good personality," Chalpin says. "He had a great sound – he did what was asked of him and then innovated right there on the spot. While all this was going on he was also arranging the songs and even co-producing them. Even back then, when his hair was still straight, Jimi was playing with his teeth! It was a great showpiece that no one else had seen before. I don't recall any of that stuff where he used the mike stand as a slide, maybe that came later. But he used his teeth on 'Drivin' South', on which Curtis is talking to Jimi and saying, 'Look, he's doing it with his teeth, y'all. Eat it, Jimi, eat it!' Apart from Johnny Starr on drums, Jimi recorded all the instruments on those Curtis sessions. He often did overdubs with a different guitar each time, so that he could vary his sound. A lot of the sounds and techniques on the 1966 recording were similar to things on *Are You Experienced?*, so Jimi certainly soaked up a lot of knowledge of the way we worked at PPX."

The 1965/66 Knight/Hendrix sessions were recorded on four-track at PPX Studios. By the time Hendrix returned to PPX in July 1967 to fulfil a further session obligation to Chalpin, he had turned the pop world upside down, not only with *Are You Experienced?* but also with his new, flamboyant look...complete with his famous Afro perm. "One day that July when Dick Rowe from Decca was visiting me at the studio, there was a knock on the door and to my total surprise it was Jimi," says Chalpin. "He looked a lot different with his big Afro hair and costume, and he also had a couple of groupies following him around. When Jimi came back, we had progressed to ten-track recording. We were the only ones in the country with ten tracks because we customised the tape heads on the Ampex equipment, and used our own custom console, along with the best quality Neumann microphones.

"Jimi said, 'Man, I heard the recordings you were playing to this guy of me playing with Curtis from the past. Put it away and let me re-do it all with my wah-wah pedal.' I was not acquainted with a wah-wah at that point. He said, 'You'll hear what I can do with this thing and you'll go crazy about it.' After re-recording one song, he continued to play different stuff for hours and hours, giving it the full treatment, feedback and all. He was one of the world's true originals."

Stoned, Fuzzy Logic

Essentially a straight-ahead R&B act, Decca's most successful group, The Rolling Stones, were rarely a vehicle for complex production values. But in 1965, they recorded what was to be the first Number One single to feature a fuzz box-driven guitar, soon to become a sound source for guitarists such as Jimmy Page, Jeff Beck, Eric Clapton and Jimi Hendrix. By this time, the Stones were no longer tied to Decca's studios and in the previous year had recorded their cover of Bobby Womack's 'It's All Over Now' at Chess Studios in Chicago which began a trend for them to record in America whenever they were there on tour.

When the Stones reached Florida during their third North American tour in May 1965, Keith Richards strolled into a local music emporium and treated himself to a Gibson Maestro fuzz box. Inspired by the recent Martha Reeves And The Vandellas hit, 'Dancing In The Street', Richards conjured an infectious riff overnight and coined the phrase 'I Can't Get No Satisfaction', relying on Mick Jagger, who originally "heard" the song as a country number, to complete the lyrics. (Some sources claim that at least part of the song refers to male frustration over the "unavailability" of a woman during her monthly cycle. Others have said it relates to Brian Jones's violent clashes with women.)

Five days after Richards rolled out of bed with the riff in his head, the band convened to Chess Studios to record tracks for their next album, *Out Of Our Heads*, and a version of this new song was attempted with a horn section playing Richard's riff accompanied by Jones's harmonica wailing. Although steadfastly unconvinced that the song was worth progressing any further, recording continued in Hollywood's RCA Studios where Charlie Watts converted to playing a double-time rhythm and Richards decided to try playing the riff with his new fuzz box. Everyone in the studio, including producer Andrew

Loog Oldham and engineer Dave Hassinger, praised the energy of the newly recorded version and insisted that 'Satisfaction' be the band's next single. Everyone except Jagger, that is, who still believed it lacked commerciality, and Richards, who claimed the new fuzz sound was too gimmicky for the band's own good. Yet the single, which was released in July 1965 and became the band's first American Number One, sports one of the world's most famous rock riffs and at the very least typified the very essence of the Sixties Stones more than any other song.

After a half-hearted brush with psychedelia, by way of *Their Satanic Majesties Request,* 'Jumping Jack Flash' signified the Stones' return to rock roots, but with a harder edge than ever. Recorded at Olympic Studios in the spring of 1968, 'Jumping Jack Flash' was written mostly by Jagger against Richards' riff, and heralded the beginning of the band's lyrical obsession with things demonic, as was evident by their moody promo film. The single was recorded at the same time as their highly acclaimed album, the acoustic-flavoured *Beggars Banquet,* from which came 'Sympathy For The Devil'. This was the band's last album to feature Brian Jones, while both 'Jumping Jack Flash' and *Beggars Banquet* were to benefit for the first time from the expertise of top "feel" producer Jimmy Miller, who had impressed the band through his work with The Spencer Davis Group and Traffic. Miller's recent death prevented an inquiry into why Richards' guitar appeared to go out of tune during the break before the last twin verse of 'Jumping Jack Flash'. But studio legend has it that this *faux pas* happened as a result of a stoned Brian Jones falling against the four-track machine, affecting the tape speed during Richards' guitar overdub.

A rare short film entitled *One Plus One* was produced during these Olympic Studios sessions and remains a fascinating insight into not only the way the band recorded, but also the general state of recording technology in the late Sixties. Jimmy Miller was to continue as the band's producer through what is regarded as their peak period, working on *Let It Bleed* (1969), *Sticky Fingers* (1971), *Exile On Main Street* (1972) and *Goat's Head Soup* (1973). When asked why Miller was not present for the recording of 1974's *It's Only Rock 'N' Roll,* Richards commented, "We wore him out."

A Little Help From An English Friend

Tony Visconti was another producer to come to prominence in the Sixties, even though he did not originally intend to have such a career. A native New Yorker and self-confessed high school dropout who found success in Britain, Visconti was one of millions of would-be rock stars to be influenced by his country's first sight of The Beatles in 1964. Together with his first wife, Siegrid, he began writing "very British-sounding tunes" which caught the ear of the powerful Richmond Organisation publishing house which also owned Essex Music in London and recording sessions at RCA Studios in New York followed. "As Tony And Siegrid we made some very bad records including a minor hit called 'Long Hair'," he says. "It wasn't the big hit that everyone thought it would be and my publisher, Howard Richmond, was leaving messages for me to call him. I eventually got together the nerve to reply, telling him I'd go to see him that afternoon. He said, 'Tony, I've been listening to your demos and I think they're absolutely great and I think you know how to make records. But I don't like your songs, so I'm gonna drop you and Siegrid as an act. Instead I'd love you to be my house producer.'

"But I wasn't really sure what a record producer was. They were the ones behind the glass who sat next to the engineers and spoke to you through the playback speaker in the studio. But you never *met* them! At first, I thought Howard meant that I was to be the engineer but, no, he meant the *other* guy! So they set me up in a little demo studio in Columbus Circle, New York, right above Atlantic Studios and I developed some local New York talent with a two-track machine with a simul-sync third head, plus a mono machine, bouncing tracks from one machine to the next. My friend at Atlantic, Bruce Tergessen played my demos to all people like Ahmet Ertegen and Tommy Dowd, and so I started my career as a producer by getting second-hand advice from the biggest people in the industry."

In 1967, Visconti met his Essex Music counterpart, Denny Cordell in the offices of the Richmond Organisation and the Anglo-American connection began in earnest with a Georgie Fame session at A&R Studios for the track, 'Because I Love You'. "Denny was the first Englishman I'd ever met in my life," he recalls. "We took an instant liking to each other and I remember being transfixed by his accent. He was in New York to record a track for Georgie and he told me that his musicians included Harvey Brooks on bass and Clark Terry on trumpet. I asked him if I could see the charts, the arrangements, and he said there weren't any. I said, 'What do you mean, there are no arrangements? How is anybody going to know what's gonna happen?' He said, 'I'll just roll a joint, play them the demo and they'll figure out their parts that way.' But we didn't do things that way in New York. First of all, it was booked as a strict three-hour session and guys like Clark Terry were gonna need music charts. Denny turned white and it was about an hour before the session was due to start, so I got him to play the demo and I asked him what he liked about it. He said, 'Well, I like the brass and bass parts.' So I wrote them out and he was astounded that I was trained and could actually write music! So I took these parts off and wrote a chord sheet, bass lines and trumpet parts. I didn't have time to write out a drum part, but by then that was the least of our worries! I xeroxed all this stuff and brought it to the studio where the session went very smoothly and within the given three hours, Denny had a master recording.

"When the session was over, Denny took a long look at me and asked if I would like a job as his assistant. He said, 'I need a guy like you. I can't read music, I can't play an instrument and I often find myself at a loss for words when I'm trying to explain things to musicians. But you translated my ideas immediately on to notepaper and really helped me out of a potentially embarrassing situation.' I told him I was interested, but then he said that while he was over in the States he was planning to interview other people. He said that he wanted to go out to LA to ask Phil Spector to work as his assistant! I said, 'Denny, you have some pair of balls, man!'"

A fortnight passed before Visconti was to receive the Transatlantic telephone call which would change his life. "Denny called me when he got back home and asked how long it would take me to get over to London and work with him," he says. "He told me he'd have the Richmond Organisation pay for the ticket, so I told my boss and told him that Denny had asked me to work for him and that I'd stay for around six months and learn how the British make records. Then when I returned to the States I'd be a much better record producer. He scratched his beard for a little while and said, 'Go with my blessings.' So I was loaned to Denny Cordell for six months but stayed three years!"

Cordell had already achieved acclaim for his production on Procol Harum's 'A Whiter Shade Of Pale' earlier that year and was also now working with The Move, whose 'Flowers In The Rain' had been earmarked as a single but had been virtually shelved by Cordell because of its arrangement. But Visconti saw through it and suggested a new treatment with a traditional woodwind section which would be recorded at double-speed in the middle section to lend an unusual flavour, just right for the psychedelic period and the perfect single to kick off Radio One's first broadcast on 30 September, 1967. Visconti had the opportunity to shine again the following year when Cordell was experiencing problems with the mix of Joe Cocker's version of 'With A Little Help From My Friends'. "Denny knew it would be a big hit but he just couldn't get the mix together," he says. "I don't know if it was the varying dynamics of the track that presented a dilemma or what, but he had gone to America where he overdubbed some backing singers and tried to mix it over there, but still no joy and he was getting quite irate about it. Then he went away on holiday for a few weeks, during which time David Platz [then head of Essex Music] began to panic that this hit might not happen if we didn't get it out soon, and I was pressured into mixing it while Denny was away. I must have done a good job because it was my first involvement with a Number One single and the first thing Denny knew about it was when he got back!"

Early on in Manfred Mann's career, during his HMV and Fontana periods which included the hits 'Do Wah Diddy Diddy' and Bob Dylan's 'Just Like A Woman', his band had been produced by John Burgess and Shel Talmy. But in 1967, their manager Gerry Bron took over the production duties for 'Ha Ha Said The Clown' at Philips Studios in London's Stanhope Place, which in the Eighties was to become Paul Weller's Solid Bond Studios.

"I think it took Manfred a while to understand the flexibility that multitrack recording gave you when mixing," says Bron. "Like most people at the time, we were working on four-track then, bouncing three tracks together on one track and then overdubbing. We had been working on 'Ha Ha Said The Clown' and Manfred phoned me up at about eleven-thirty pm and said, 'This is absolutely no good at all, this is terrible, we will have to do it again.' He told me that there wasn't enough bass in the mix, but I assured him that the bass was on a separate track. He said, 'Are you sure about that?' I said, 'Of course I am sure,' and he went and had another listen. Ten minutes later the phone rang again and he said the same thing, that it wasn't going to work, and was I absolutely sure that when we mix it across there is going to be enough bass? I emphasised that we could mix it anyway we liked, but he still rang again, way past midnight, saying that he didn't believe me and I could imagine his mind ticking over, trying to work out how it might be done. The very next day we went back to Philips where I did a mix and the bass was at just the right level. Manfred has got the most incredible musical ability and as far as I am concerned he is the best musician I have ever worked with. I think that overdubbing him over lots and lots of tracks, which he never had before, just gave him that chance to develop a new approach to his music which emerged in a big way in the Seventies."

After briefly working with Denny Cordell on the failed single, 'So Long Dad', Mann himself took over the production duties in 1968 and continued to do so until the group's demise in June 1969. His philosophy was simple. "'Mighty Quinn' was the first one we did ourselves because although we had used several producers we were still having the same level of success," he says. "So we figured that maybe that was more to do with us. In the early period we produced some music, some bluesy, jazzy stuff, on albums that was really very good, but we were not able to translate that to our main activity which was the singles. It was our own choice to record the Dylan songs ('Just Like A Woman' was one of several) and I still record them to this day. They were great songs and sometimes Dylan did them in such an idiosyncratic, personal way that there was room to move them into another area. You can't do that with an Elton John song because he's already done the definitive version. Dylan never seems to have done the definitive version. He's done the Dylan version but there's always another way of doing it. I once read that of all the covers he had heard, he preferred ours to anyone else's."

'Nights In White Satin'

Working alongside Mike Vernon, Gus Dudgeon, Bill Price and future Queen producer, Roy Thomas Baker, as a fellow Decca staff member during the mid-Sixties was Tony Clarke, who in 1967 became a key element in The Moody Blues' dynamic transition from an R&B group to proto-symphonic rock stars. As A&R manager Dick Rowe's assistant, Clarke had been asked to listen to a quarter-inch tape containing five Moodies' demos with a view to producing masters. "One of them was a guitar and vocal demo of 'Nights In White Satin' which I then picked for the band to record," he recalls. "Dick said, 'They owe us £5,000, so see if you can get it back.'"

'Nights In White Satin' and especially its parent album, the conceptual *Days Of Future Passed*, marked a significant shift in style for the Birmingham band following the September 1966 departure of original members Denny Laine and Clint Warwick. With singer/guitarist Justin Hayward and bassist John Lodge in the frontline, and with Clarke producing, the band moved towards a more fulfiling musical direction. "*Sgt Pepper* and *Pet Sounds* were obvious inspirations, and so was Richie Havens," notes producer Clarke. "But there was another, more curious album which turned all of our heads, titled *Cosmic Sounds*. It was filled with the most unusual music I had ever heard in my life, full of different moods and very cleverly done, sounding not unlike today's computer music, only the 1967 equivalent."

During the previous year, Decca had formed the Deram label upon which to issue product from its more "progressive" roster – its first signing being Cat Stevens. "The head of the album department, Hugh Mendl, wanted some kind of a fanfare to accompany the label," says Clarke. "So they did albums called *Strings In The Night* and *Brass In The Night* which were light orchestral productions featuring the double stereo imaging principles that were part of the Deramic Sound System, and we were going to be doing something along those lines.

"Those orchestral albums were quite revolutionary in some respects because the actual recording level that Michael Dacre-Barclay and Terry Johnson managed to get on to the disc was substantially higher than any on other previous record," agrees Mike Vernon. "They were experimenting with levels to tape and then levels from tape to disc." From a production point of view, Clarke would cross the echo returns of instruments on one channel over to the opposite channel to give an impression of width and separation – important elements in the new Moody Blues sound.

"The original idea we had was for the Moodies and an orchestra to record Dvorak's 'New World Symphony' as an excuse to show off that effect," explains Clarke. "I was then asked to consider doing a 'Young World Symphony', but the band thought this was going a little too far. Even so, we went into the studio with that understanding and quickly laid down three tracks, one of which was 'Nights In White Satin'."

Hayward's 'Nights In White Satin' was recorded in Decca's Studio One in October 1967 and mixed for a single in one afternoon and evening session, two months before it was to receive an epic orchestral overdub for the extended album version. "We brought in arranger and conductor, Peter Knight, with whom we discussed the orchestration and additional passages. On the day of recording, the London Festival Orchestra overdubbed on to the band's track which was running in their headphones. That studio was just about big enough to accommodate the orchestra. We had three bowed double basses and one of the players was positioned in the doorway because we were that pushed for room."

The control room equipment configuration in October 1967 included a twenty-channel mixing console which was originally designed for four-track recording but modified later for eight-track. It had four groups of five faders and any group could be attributed to a choice of two tracks. 'Nights In White Satin' required three generations of four-track recording: Clarke and engineer, Derek Varnals recorded on a one-inch Studer four-track on which the backing track would fill one whole four-track tape, before balancing the mix and bouncing over to one track on a half-inch Ampex four-track. A further reduction mix was carried out and sent back to the Studer for further overdubbing before the final mixdown on to an EMI BTR-2 machine. "The Moodies all performed live as a five-piece on the backing track and as much went down as possible, including backing vocals, on the first four-track before bouncing down," says Clarke.

"Then we added guitar and Justin's lead vocal."

Despite the aural suggestion of a distant choir, Varnals maintains that only the band members played a part in the vocal tracks. "There was no choir involved," he insists. "The backing vocals which take the top of your head off are a result of a blend of their vocals and one of the two acoustic echo chambers on the roof of the studio building, and I still find that shivery effect pleasing even now. We had EQ on the echo send and return, and that affected which frequencies reverberated longer than others. It was also important to record the various effects on the voices and instruments as they went down rather than add them in the mix, because it meant the band were reacting to these enhanced sounds on the backing vocal overdubs. There wasn't even tape speed involved – John Lodge could really get up that high, above Justin and the others. The vocals were recorded with four of the band behind two Neumann mics in a straight line, facing the control room window, and then tracked about three times."

When completed, Clarke's enthusiasm for the classic-in-the-making single was greeted with a lukewarm reception from the stiff old guard at Decca. "I couldn't get anybody to listen to it at first," he says. "No one was interested because they felt it was too long, too slow, no one could dance to it and they didn't know what it was about. Of course, when it went to the top of the charts in America they soon paid attention."

The Moody Blues were the first pop artists to take advantage of Decca Studios' new Scully eight-track recorder in April 1968, when they used it to complete a number of tracks for their follow-up album, *In Search Of The Lost Chord*. "Suddenly, we had four more tracks to play with," says Derek Varnals. "So we thought we'd add a few more voices."

The Ancient Sampler

Since the Eighties, artists and producers have reaped the benefits of digital samplers which have provided authentic reproductions of real and synthesised instruments, as well as a whole world of "non-musical" sounds, at the touch of a keyboard. But the principle of sampling was already in place in the Sixties – the flute sounds, for instance, heard on The Beatles' 'Strawberry Fields Forever' were performed not by a flautist but by the use of a controversial home organ-looking instrument named the Mellotron. To be entirely accurate, however, the origin of sampling goes back even further to 1949 (what a year that was!) when Harry Chamberlain developed his namesake, the Chamberlain, in California. The Chamberlain was a revelation to American businessman, Bill Fransen who took a model to London in the early Sixties. Here was an instrument which was capable of reproducing the sound of anything that could be recorded on to tape: each note on its keyboard pushed a length of tape over a replay head to activate a sound, made possible by a motorised spindle and pinch rollers. Les Bradley, and his brothers Frank and Norman, came into contact with the instrument in May 1962 when Fransen ordered seventy matched tape heads from their Bradmatic electro-mechanical company, and they almost immediately formed a new company (Mellotronics Limited) dedicated to the design of the Mellotron and improving on Chamberlain's theme.

The tapes or "analogue samples" of instruments and sound effects were first recorded at IBC Studios, often using name session musicians, then the company rented premises a short walk away in Portland Place where it installed its own recording equipment. The stability of the Mellotron's pitching of sounds remained a problem even at the time of its 1963 launch and it was not until the introduction of the Mark II Mellotron in 1964 that Bradley – who sadly died in 1997 – and his team felt they had achieved their real aims. The Mark II gave the user access to six banks of sounds, such as violins, guitars, organ, saxophone, flute, piano, trombone and vibes, and the keyboard was split into two thirty-five-note sections, with each note capable of playing one of three selected sounds, this time recorded on to 3/8" tapes.

While it was Graham Bond of the Graham Bond Organisation who has the distinction of being the first musician to use a Mellotron on a pop record (on the 1965 Columbia track, 'Baby It's True'), it was Manfred Mann who had the first major chart success with one, using a Mark II to replicate a wind instrument sound on his band's October 1966 single, 'Semi-Detached Suburban Mr James'. "Whereas nowadays there is a new instrument coming out every week, in those days there were very few," says Mann. "So I suppose anything that came out would be interesting. There were basically only a few versions of an organ and a few electric pianos, so anything new was considered interesting. The Mellotron had a particular grainy sound that was very good and I always liked it. We weren't being terribly clever. We just put a microphone up against it and recorded it. In those days, though, we were interested in anything that made a record sound different."

"They were one of the first bands to really use the Mellotron intelligently," the Manfreds' producer, Gerry Bron says. "But it had a lot of disadvantages. It was rarely in tune, partly because the speed of the tape was not very well controlled, and when you pressed your finger on the key, it only lasted as long as the tape came out of the spooler, although I was a fan of the sound. Manfred's real classic was 'Ha Ha Said The Clown' on which he played a whole series of bits on the Mellotron. My first wife played violin and she had a good ear for pitch, so she noticed that some parts were slightly out of tune and said, 'You can't put that out!' But to me it sounded sweet and unusual. I have yet to find a sampler or a modern sound module which can faithfully recreate the Mellotron sound because it was so unique. But it was so enormously heavy that three or four people could barely move it."

One month after the release of 'Semi-Detached Suburban Mr James', The Beatles recorded 'Strawberry Fields Forever' which featured probably the most famous Mellotron figure of all-time. "It was around at Abbey Road and mainly for sound effects and jingles and things like that," George Martin recalls. "It was a bastard of an instrument really, an early attempt, I saw, at a synthesiser, although the sounds were hardly authentic. I mean, the sound we used on 'Strawberry Fields' was supposed to be a real flute, but no flautist would ever play like that. But it was a great sound and it's impossible to hear it another way now. Instead of using the Mellotron to reproduce authentic instruments, we took it for what it was and used it more interestingly."

In the hands of Mike Pinder, the Mellotron gave the music of The Moody Blues a whole new character on 'Nights In White Satin' and *Days Of Future Passed*. Pinder had worked for Mellotronics' parent company, Streetly Electronics, as its chief Mellotron demonstrator, and by the time he joined the band in 1966 he knew the instrument inside out, prompting the band's purchase of a second-hand Mark II that year. "Because Mellotrons did not travel very well, Mike was having an especially robust model built for touring work at the time we recorded *Days Of Future Passed*," Tony Clarke says. "I think it took several albums to get the Mellotron sound right. We had it positioned down on the three-tiered stage in Decca Studio Number One and basically took a jack feed out of it, and plugged it straight into the desk via a microphone line."

Although Mellotrons fell out of favour in the Eighties, not least due to the advent of hard-disk sampling, they have once again found favour with artists such as Elvis Costello, Kula Shaker, Michael Jackson, Lenny Kravitz, Julian Cope, Paul Weller, Oasis, Pulp and Paul McCartney who, in 1994, bought the original Mark II used on 'Strawberry Fields Forever' to add to his already impressive Mellotron collection. Martin Smith is an aficionado of the instrument and has played a major role in the instrument's recent re-birth, having co-formed Mellotron UK in the early Nineties as a maintenance service for existing owners. "There is something about oxide scraping across tape heads which to some people is more appealing than sterile digital sampling," he explains. "People criticise the out-of-tune characteristics of the Mellotron, but if you get a room full of sixty orchestra musicians, they will also be slightly out of tune with each other. So in that respect, the Mellotron is authentic, only it produces a sound that makes the hairs on the back of your neck stand on end!"

Black Magic Mac

As the Sixties drew to a close, the focus of progressive music shifted away from the psychedelia which had flavoured many British bands' recordings between mid-1966 and 1968, and moved back into the more basic blues arena which provided a backdrop to an explosion of virtuosity among musicians. One of the greatest exponents of blues guitar at this time was Peter Green, whose Fleetwood Mac brought the blues to the masses by way of commercial success with 'Black Magic Woman', 'Need Your Love So Bad' and the haunting instrumental 'Albatross'. That their producer was Mike Vernon came as no surprise

The father of multitracking, Les Paul, seen in his garage studio in the Forties (left) and with his eponymous guitar in the Nineties (right)

Norman Petty, the man who shaped the Buddy Holly sound

A modern view of Sun Studios as a popular Memphis tourist attraction

The control room of Norman Petty's Clovis Studio

Modern-day rock 'n' roll producer, Stuart Colman (left), working with Sonny Curtis on a new Crickets album

The enigmatic Phil Spector

The Beach Boys, Phil Spector and Motown were all graced by the musicality of LA's first call session bassist in the Sixties, Carol Kaye

Pet Sounds by The Beach Boys ranked Number One in *Mojo*'s 100 all-time best albums survey in 1995. This copy is autographed by Al Jardine

(L-r) George Harrison, Billy Preston, Eddie Klein (now manager at Sir Paul McCartney's private studio), Klaus Voorman, Phil Spector, Ringo Starr and Gary Wright at Abbey Road, 1970, recording Harrison's *All Things Must Pass*

Another New York minute for Phil Ramone, the Pope of Pop

Lamont Dozier, one third of the hit Motown production and songwriting trio, Holland-Dozier-Holland

The Beach Boys, 1996: (l-r) Bruce Johnson, Al Jardine, Mike Love, Brian Wilson and Carl Wilson

Dave Harries and Adrian Kerridge – two cornerstones of the British recording industry in the Sixties

(L-r) Mike Vickers, Paul Jones, Manfred Mann, Tom McGuinness, Hal David and Burt Bacharach (at the piano) in session

Joe Meek outside his Holloway Road studio

An advert from the 1965 issue of *The Stage*, promoting the features and benefits of the mighty Mellotron

Joe Meek in his Holloway Road studio control room, one year before his death

Derek Varnals remixing the documentary album, *A Conversation With The Blues*, in Decca's Studio One control room, mid 1964

Joe Brown achieved fame both with his Bruvvers and as a session guitarist for Joe Meek

Now head of Sony's Soho Square Records, Muff Winwood reflects on the simplicity of recording in his Spencer Davis Group days

(L-r) Martin Smith, Les and John Bradley – the trio behind two generations of interest in the Mellotron

Joe Meek backing vocalist, Ted Fletcher, now designs his own Joe Meek audio equipment

(L-r) Hank Marvin, Cliff Richard, Bruce Welch and engineer Peter Vince with Abbey Road's first dedicated eight-track mixing console upon its introduction in 1968

to those who respected his earlier blues projects, but the path which enabled Vernon to work with Green and co was as chequered as the band's history itself.

While at Decca, Vernon and partner Neil Slaven (both still regarded as Britain's foremost authorities on the blues) formed their own collectors' label, Blue Horizon, and issued recordings of artists including Hubert Sumlin (recorded in Vernon's bedroom on a Grundig portable tape machine) through the magazine, *R&B Monthly*. One of the label's greatest admirers was John Mayall who after falling foul of his deal with Immediate Records in between Decca contracts, recorded a set of "downhome" blues tracks at Wessex Studios for Vernon's operation. Another Blue Horizon fan was Mayall's one-time guitarist, Peter Green who saw appeal in the label's low-key image. During the summer of 1967, Vernon became instrumental in the formation of Fleetwood Mac when he introduced guitarist Jeremy Spencer to Green and Mick Fleetwood, and within a month the band made its debut at the Windsor Jazz And Blues Festival. Soon, Vernon took the band into the studio to record several tracks, including 'I Believe My Time Ain't Long' and 'Ramblin' Pony', then took the tapes to his bosses at Decca with the proposal that they distribute his label.

"Bill Townsend, the managing director under the chairman Sir Edward Lewis, said, 'Sorry, we don't give people their own labels, old chap,'" says Vernon. "They had fought with Andrew Loog Oldham over the same issue with The Rolling Stones who wanted their own label, but they had a good deal with Decca. I wasn't going to be brow beaten in that way because Peter desperately didn't want to be on the Decca label. I told Townsend that the artist and his management wanted this situation with Blue Horizon, although what I meant was *I* wanted it because I was Peter's representative. I felt very put out that they wouldn't consider the label idea, having worked with them for five or six years and put in an enormous amount of effort. I was on a salary which had risen, but I wasn't getting any royalties from the hits I was producing at that point."

The situation for the band was quickly rectified, although it put Vernon's job at Decca at risk. "I went to see Derek Everett at CBS and offered him distribution of my label with Fleetwood Mac as the lead act, because by then the band had played at Windsor and were creating a buzz," he says. "Everett was prepared to go with me on it as long as there was a honeymoon period during which a few records would be released with a Blue Horizon logo and if it looked like being a success, they would then give me a proper label. I thought this was the best I was going to get so I agreed. By the time the second Fleetwood Mac single, 'Black Magic Woman', was due to come out, the band had really gone from strength to strength and become a major club act. The whole Blue Horizon thing suddenly blossomed into something quite substantial. Prior to 'Black Magic Woman' coming out on the actual Blue Horizon label I was told that I couldn't work for Decca as a staff producer and have my own label with CBS. I told them that it was their own fault because they turned me down. I was forced to leave but I was offered the opportunity to sign with them as an independent producer, which I did. So I continued to produce many of Decca's acts, like Bloodstone and The Olympic Runners, well past the time of Fleetwood Mac and Chicken Shack."

After the release of 'Need Your Love So Bad', which featured a string arrangement courtesy of Mickey Baker – of Mickey And Sylvia fame – Fleetwood Mac returned to CBS Studios in New Bond Street in October 1968 to record yet another classic: 'Albatross'. "It was a one-off," says Vernon. "I guess it was a creation that Peter, John McVie, Mick and to a lesser extent Danny Kirwan had been working on. Jeremy wasn't involved in it at all. The floating slide guitar was Peter's, not Jeremy's, and like most of the Blue Horizon recordings, it was recorded with Mike Ross engineering. 'Albatross' was a departure from what the band had been doing but in a way it pre-empted what they were going to do, because 'Man Of The World' was just as much of a departure. I personally liked it but then I was a great fan of Santo And Johnny's 'Sleepwalk' and 'Albatross' was not dissimilar in some respects. Every band has to develop and Peter was an extremely creative individual who felt that if the band was going to have a future, they couldn't continue to ape Elmore James and BB King. It was within all the members to develop in that way and it was Peter who was the driving force behind getting it out of them. None of us thought that 'Albatross' was going to be the massive Number One it became, in fact we thought it was a risk to bring it out as a single. But it paid off and worked."

Unfortunately for Vernon and his brother Richard, who became a partner in the label, the pressures of running a newly successful company meant that some aspects of their business began to slip by them. Aspects such as Fleetwood Mac's recording contract. "We discovered after the event that their contract had expired, and suddenly there were a few people around who decided to exploit our naivety," he admits. "The band had a fairly heavyweight manager, Clifford Davis, and he sharply informed us that we didn't have a contract any longer, although it would be okay for the next single, 'Man Of The World', to go out on Blue Horizon. He suggested that we renegotiate, but then Reprise came into the picture and offered them a gigantic deal, and Davis never came back to us. Had he come back I'm sure that CBS would have matched the deal because they wanted to sign the band."

But to the Vernons' horror, 'Man Of The World' appeared on Immediate. "I was incensed because I had been promised on numerous occasions that it would come out on Blue Horizon," says Vernon, "and we had even paid the bills on the assumption that the band were still under contract as normal. 'Man Of The World' was the last session I did with Fleetwood Mac. I had produced about seventy-five per cent of it but the last twenty-five per cent was taken away from me when Immediate got involved. There was no way that I was going to come to the studio and finish it off when that all blew up. It left a very nasty taste in my mouth because it wasn't as if we hadn't done anything for the band. It was all so unnecessary and a classic case of what a Number One single does to the behaviour of business people. CBS were mad as hell at us for letting things slip and were getting ready to sue because they thought we were taking a backhander. But Peter was very unhappy about how it turned out and I don't think he wanted to leave Blue Horizon. He certainly wanted me to continue producing the band."

Going Underground

It was while producing Manfred Mann that Gerry Bron discovered the outrageous Bonzo Dog Doo-Dah Band after the Manfreds' temporary bassist, Jack Bruce's (then still with Cream) recommendation. The

Bonzos has already recorded one album for Parlophone, *My Brother Makes The Noises For The Talkies*, which had, in industry-speak, stiffed. But Bron quickly came to their rescue. "I went to see them at a club in Manchester and thought they were absolutely terrific but, of course, they were just a stage act," he says. "The way they played instruments really badly was very funny, but to make them into a meaningful recording act was quite a different matter entirely. So I made some demos with them in a small studio in Rickmansworth and persuaded Liberty to sign them, at a time when none of the traditional record companies wanted to know. The demo sessions were hysterical. They were trying to get rid of the ukelele and banjo player, Vernon Dudley Bowhay-Nowell, who looked a complete arsehole and didn't have the faintest clue about how to play. I stopped them in the middle of one chorus and said to him, 'Vernon, you are playing completely the wrong chords.' He looked at me very sheepishly and replied, 'But the others won't tell me what the chords are.' I couldn't believe it – they had been playing this particular song on stage for the previous six months and all the time he'd been playing it wrong! I got the other guys to show him the correct chords but he still couldn't play it right. That was the thing about the Bonzos, they could sit on stage and do completely the wrong thing musically and everyone would sit there killing themselves laughing, not realising what was going on. Neil Innes was the only true musician among them and he helped to pull the whole thing off in the studio."

Sensing that significant public interest was on the horizon, Bron eventually produced the band's *Gorilla* album and made the heavy suggestion to Liberty that at least 20,000 copies should be pressed for release in October 1967. "I was sure it would sell like the proverbial hot cakes," he says. "But they just couldn't see it being that popular and pressed only 1,000 which absolutely killed it. I took Liberty to be a forward-thinking, progressive label but in this instance I was wrong."

At the very end of the "swinging" decade, Bron proved to be a leading figure in the booming progressive rock market, both as a manager and producer, when he helped to establish Philips's Vertigo label to compete with EMI's Harvest. Now a producer manager, he says, "Olaf Wyper had taken over at Philips and they were prompted by the success that Harvest had achieved with Pink Floyd and some other interesting bands. The bands that Olaf was interested in signing, like Uriah Heep, Colosseum and Juicy Lucy, were all managed by me and so they asked if I would be interested in bringing them to this new label, Vertigo. I thought it was a great idea because I had already failed to get some of them signed to Harvest. I later formed Bronze Records for exactly the same reason and I think we were a bit more far-sighted than some people. The problem being that most record companies just didn't understand that sort of progressive music."

Free's 'All Right Now'

A terminally infectious riff, a fluid and memorable solo, and one of the most potent rock 'n' roll vocal performances of the last forty years were all the ingredients needed to propel Free's 'All Right Now' into the history books and give Paul Rodgers his greatest success as a singer/songwriter. Like Clapton's 'Layla', Deep Purple's 'Smoke On The Water' and Led Zeppelin's 'Stairway To Heaven', it belongs to an elite club of Seventies rock gems which continue to defy trends and generation gaps, and still sound as fresh as the day they were recorded.

Co-written with Free bassist Andy Fraser, 'All Right Now' was produced by the band and John Kelly during sessions for their third album *Fire And Water* at Island Studios in Basing Street, West London. It was released on Island Records in June 1970 and with enthusiastic radio coverage it quickly rose to Number Two in the singles chart, with only Mungo Jerry's 'In The Summertime' preventing it from occupying the top slot it so deserved.

Confirming that the best songs are often the quickest to write, Rodgers says that this classic was virtually written to order. "The whole song was orientated around the idea that it should be a singalong," he recalls. "Free was basically a blues band but for some reason we started to get larger audiences as we brought in our own songs. One of the numbers in particular that survived and stayed in the set despite the fact that we were writing our own songs was [Booker T And The MGs'] 'The Hunter'. It was a very big song up in Sunderland, they loved it and always asked for it. We used to love playing it but I also thought that we needed another 'Hunter' in our set, but one that they could sing in the audience and be a part of. We were in a dressing room somewhere and I remember discussing this with the others.

"Right off the top of my head I said, 'Look, lads, it needs to be a really simple chorus...something like 'All right now, baby it's-a all right now.' They said, 'Yeah, great,' and I grabbed a guitar, worked out the chords on the spot and we had the chorus immediately. Andy Fraser and I were writing a lot together at the time, and he took that away with him and came up with the verse riff. I worked on the lyric which came very easily and was based on my imagination, although that kind of liaison has probably happened to all of us at some time. It was supposed to be something that anyone could relate to and it just flowed out naturally because I knew where I wanted to end up with it. It was a little bit cheeky I suppose."

Unaware that this song would soon represent the peak of their career, Free decided to debut it at the beginning of their next gig and were taken aback by the reaction. "There weren't many people in that night but they were dancing and enjoying us," says the singer. "The first time we played 'All Right Now', it sounded a bit of mess, frankly. At the end, I asked the audience if they had any requests and they all asked us to do 'that first song' again. That was amazing that they even remembered it from ninety minutes before. I thought, 'Wow, it must be pretty good then!'" This was also the general consensus of the hordes gathered at the Isle Of Wight Festival in the August of that year when the number was one of the event's major highlights.

Still no more than a contender for the next album, 'All Right Now' was recorded on the then standard eight-track format in a brisk one-day session during the spring of 1970. "We were very excited when it came to laying it down," says Rodgers. "We did the basic track and everyone was very pleased. After recording his pretty tasty bass line, Andy put some keyboards on and then it was time for me to do the vocals. Chris Blackwell [Island Records' boss] walked in with a gorgeous girl right in the middle of my vocal take and I was feeling good about it all. We were always trying to write the best song we could but until then we didn't anticipate that this would be a single. When Chris came in that day, though, he was adamant that it should come out as soon as possible."

However, one problem had to be solved – the problem of length. In its original album track format, 'All Right Now' was far too long to be considered for airplay and both a large section of Paul Kossoff's masterful guitar solo and the final verse refrain would have to be sacrificed before making a seven-inch possible. The result was one of the slickest jobs ever undertaken with a razor blade and editing block.

"The edits certainly had not been decided on during the recording, but we were very happy with them," says Rodgers. "We were very idealistic about our music and wouldn't normally have considered editing anything, but even we could appreciate that this was way too long for a single. So we agreed to attempt an edit and if it sounded kosher, we'd go along with it. And it sounded great, totally seamless. Whenever I hear it now, I am conscious of the edits but it doesn't worry me."

The main guitar riff written by Fraser and played by the late Paul Kossoff on his 1960 Les Paul Sunburst (with a Marshall stack) may at first appear incredibly simplistic, but it is virtually impossible for one guitarist to absolutely recreate it live. One reason is that Kossoff double-tracked his Les Paul and played slightly different parts on each side of the stereo picture (use your pan knob to hear the difference). But that's not all the story, as Rodgers explains: "That was no ordinary A chord – it was a heck of a job. Paul would put his little finger across the E string on to the fifth fret and get an extra A, which was an amazing thing. Because we had a three-piece instrumental line-up, Paul used to add a lot of things that guitarists in four- or five-pieces wouldn't bother with, but we had to put things in to fatten our sound.

"Pretty much all the guitarists I've worked with since Paul have played a fair approximation of the riff, including Brian May and Steve Vai. They all have a tendency to not change anything because they view it as a classic, and they play the solo almost note for note. But the main riff has always been a little bit elusive for most people."

1970 was not the only year which saw 'All Right Now' riding high in the singles chart. It reappeared in 1973, 1978 and 1982, each time with marked success. Its last appearance came in 1991, this time in a Bob Clearmountain-remixed format (ambient drums, cleaner sound) which was never to Rodgers' taste. "There were some very strange things going on with that and it was far too clean," he says. "But I had nothing to do with it, no one called me and told me they were remixing the stuff and would I like to come down to the session. It was done and released before I even knew about it. I don't know why they can't leave these things alone. I guess it was some marketing ploy but I don't know if the punters actually want that." It was recently estimated that the record is played on radio somewhere in the world every forty-five seconds. How does that make Rodgers feel? "Absolutely incredible! I received an award recently from BMI for one million airplays. That edit came in handy, didn't it?"

chapter four

abbey road and the beatles

"George Martin is one of my great heroes. Any engineer or producer that has ever walked the earth owes him a lot of thanks for his perseverance with The Beatles and what they brought to us changed all of our lives. Just about anybody who had adventurous ideas was motivated by what George and The Beatles were doing."

Phil Ramone

"EMI Studios was maintained so well that it was like working in a hospital. There would be guys in white coats buzzing around every morning and the place was pristine clean. It wasn't the funky, creative, cool and groovy atmosphere that people assume it was. EMI was looked after better than any studio in the world has ever been looked after."

Manfred Mann

Electric And Musical Industries Limited, better known as EMI, celebrated its 100th anniversary in 1997 – its history beginning with the formation of the Gramophone Company in December 1897, which later merged in April 1931 with its rival, the Columbia Graphophone Company and labels Parlophone, Regal and Zonophone to establish "the greatest recording organisation in the world". Over its distinguished life, EMI has received unbridled acclaim for its work and achievements, but it is doubtful that even with the passing of another

100 years, few achievements will come close to matching the significance of the company's two most enduring assets: Abbey Road Studios and the most successful group of all-time, The Beatles.

Despite the steady growth of the broadcast and recording industry, nowhere in the world was there to be found a purpose-built sound recording studio before the Thirties. But it was EMI's technical department and artists' manager, Osmund Williams who rectified matters when he convinced his chairman, Alfred Clark that a £16,500 investment in a nine-bedroomed, detached house at 3 Abbey Road, St John's Wood, London NW8 would provide an ideal, practical base for an expandable studio and attract the finest musicians in the world. The purchase was formalised on 3 December, 1929 and plans to build what is now the large Studio One were drawn up immediately. Further cash was pumped into the enterprise when the adjacent building and garden was also purchased to allow the provision of offices, two additional studios, transfer and mastering rooms, and technical workshops. Williams, however, did not live to see his great quest reach its fruition. A few months before Sir Edward Elgar opened EMI Studios (as it would officially be named for more than forty years) on 12 November, 1931 with the London Symphony orchestra's historic recording of his 'Falstaff' composition, Williams died of a brain tumour. But "London's Latest Wonder", as the studio was heralded by EMI, will never forget his battling vision.

Classical music sessions were the dominant feature of Abbey Road's studio diary during the pre-war years, although it was also common for music hall celebrities such as George Formby, Gracie Fields, Bud Flanagan and Chesney Allen, Stanley Holloway and big band leaders including Joe Loss to record there regularly, while it also became a stop-off point for visiting international artists – Fats Waller and Paul Robeson among them. EMI decided to avoid paying royalties to American electrical recording system pioneer, Western Electric, by inventing its own moving coil microphone system. This was the first in a long line of EMI initiatives which included the manufacture of its own magnetic tape and recording machines (such as the BTR – British Tape Recorder – Series). Many such inventions were the brainchild of the company's in-house wizard, Alan Blumlein, who took out a patent for stereophonic recording and disc cutting only one month after the opening of Abbey Road, and was part of the R&D team which developed the studio's early multitrack recording facilities, in conjunction with Siemens Telefunken.

On a cold November morning in 1950, a twenty-four-year-old ex-Fleet Air Arm lieutenant braved the elements to start work at Abbey Road as the assistant to Oscar Pruess, the head of EMI's light orchestral and jazz/pop label, Parlophone Records. His name was George Martin and he would quickly play an influential part in transferring some of the company's emphasis on classical music into the pop field, in his later role as the label's Head of A&R. A former piano and oboe student at London's Guildhall School of Music, Martin and his colleagues Norman Newell, Norrie Paramor and Wally Ridley so impressed EMI's new chairman with their ideas, Sir Joseph Lockwood that he promoted these "sergeants" to A&R "generals" and was rewarded by a string of successes with new signings Ruby Murray, Max Bygraves, Alma Cogan and trumpeter Eddie Calvert, whose 'Oh Mein Papa' was the first Abbey Road recording to lay claim to the Number One single spot (in January 1954). For some years, Martin and Parlophone remained EMI's poor relations, in the shadows of HMV and Columbia's performance in the pop chart. His sense of humour was a driving force behind his passion for recording comedy acts, and none was finer than The Goons and, in particular, Peter Sellers. Working with the zany talents of Sellers, Spike Milligan and Harry Secombe provided Martin with an insight into sound effects and the creative use of tape, and the concept of the studio as a sonic workshop began to implant itself as a seed in Martin's mind. Meanwhile, by the late Fifties when groups were in vogue, Paramor had signed Cliff Richard And The Shadows, and Martin (who had already turned down Tommy Steele) was on the lookout to develop a similar rock 'n' roll or pop act. Then, in May 1962, just as it appeared to many people that Parlophone was on the verge of drawing its last breaths, Martin received a visit from a well-mannered artist manager named Brian Epstein who badgered the producer into listening to some demos recorded by a young Liverpool band at a failed Decca audition in the January of that year.

"There wasn't anything special about their songs or the way they were sung," says Martin of his first hearing of The Beatles, who then featured Pete Best as drummer. "But their sound was different. Different enough to organise a recording audition." Which he did on 6 June, 1962 when he met the group for the first time. "Cliff and The Shadows were a kind of template for British pop groups at the time, so when I saw The Beatles I was trying to decide who would be the front person. Would it be John? Paul? George? No, it suddenly dawned on me that their personalities were so intertwining that they should be seen as one unit. John had discovered that I'd done all the Goons records which intrigued him. Actually, I don't think we would have hit it off as well as we did unless I had already made those comedy records. They knew the Peter Sellers album and the *Beyond The Fringe* albums that I'd done with Dudley Moore and Jonathan Miller and people, so they were prepared to like me. They appealed to me straight away, they were bright, full of energy and I was very pleased that they seemed to like me too, which I would not normally be bothered about. In 1962, no one would have given tuppence for the future of The Beatles. I was practically laughed out of court when I presented their first recording to the EMI sales staff because they thought it was another one of my jokes."

Martin noted that John Lennon and Paul McCartney wrote their own songs which was an unusual talent among bands of their genre, and engineer Norman Smith alerted him to one such number, 'Love Me Do'. Thinking he had little to lose, he offered The Beatles a recording contract with Parlophone and set 4 September, 1962 as their first studio date. The previous month, however, saw the group replace Pete Best with a friend from the Liverpool circuit, Ringo Starr. In Martin's mind, Starr's drumming lacked what it needed and a session man, Andy White was hired to provide the backbeat for 'Love Me Do' on a subsequent session – produced by Ron Richards of The Hollies fame on September 11. Contrary to popular belief (though clarified by Mark Lewisohn in his fascinating diary, *The Complete Beatles Recording Sessions*), it was the 4 September version, with Starr on drums, which was actually released as the original single on 5 October, 1962, achieving a peak chart position of Number Seventeen. Twelve months later, Beatlemania began to thrill the world like no other pop phenomenon before or since, and almost every one of their releases was assured Number One status. Martin's success as a producer of other acts was no less impressive. Working also with the likes of Brian Epstein's other Liverpool signings, Cilla Black and Gerry And The Pacemakers, the records produced by Martin at Abbey Road during 1963 alone occupied the Number One chart position for a staggering thirty-two weeks.

No Such Word As "Can't"

The studio technology at Abbey Road during the first year of The Beatles' recording career was still extremely basic. Neumann and AKG microphones were the norm while in the control room of Studio Two, the home of almost every Beatles recording, a grey-coloured EMI REDD 37 mixing console took pride of place with its ten inputs and four outputs, linked to a BTR machine. Two-track recording was the norm – four-track was considered an outlandish facility for pop until October 1963 when 'I Want To Hold Your Hand' became The Beatles' first recording to use the format. But "basic" was not a description which could be allied to their work for long. While the group's approach to songwriting redefined pop music several times over in their relatively short career, it was their steadfast unwillingness to accept the words "it can't be done" and a hunger for manipulating "normal" sounds that magically transformed the recording studio from a simple vehicle for capturing straight performances on tape in 1962 into a playhouse for boundless creativity within four fast-paced years. In doing so, they shaped the future of record production and their influence and techniques continue to be as relevant in today's rock and pop world as they were thirty or more years ago, especially when one compares their mid to late Sixties canon with contemporary BritPop bands like Oasis and Cast.

The Beatles' early period as recording artists was notable for their spirited performances, unique vocal blend and George Martin's often vital arrangement skills. The direction began to change in 1965 when Paul McCartney played a new song to Martin called 'Yesterday', now the most recorded title in pop history. It was obvious to Martin that, subconsciously, McCartney was paying more homage to Elgar than Little Richard and that a Stradivarius would be far more suitable than a Stratocaster. "Not that Mantovani rubbish! This is a rock group!"

protested McCartney, then twenty-two. Although hard to imagine now as the recent composer of the *Liverpool Oratorio*, McCartney hated this threat against his rocker image. But once Martin promised to minimise the string vibrato effect that was so abhorrent to the composer, McCartney was forever sold on the use of orchestration. And so it came to pass that a "serious" score for a string quartet would be used to enhance what was essentially a solo voice and acoustic guitar pop ballad. Admittedly, pizzicato strings had adorned some of Adam Faith's early Sixties hits and lush orchestrations were part and parcel of Phil Spector's massive Wall of Sound. But with 'Yesterday', the marriage of classical and pop took on a whole new guise.

Ever crucial to The Beatles' appreciation of this new, highbrow world was Martin who, like a benevolent father-figure, would often smile authoritatively as "his boys" brought ideas for new songs to him like apples to a teacher. Devoid of any form of orthodox musical training, Lennon and McCartney would sit at a piano, humming or playing their tuneful brainwaves, while Martin suggested modifications and wrote out the dots. From then on, where orchestration was required, Martin took on the task to communicate in musical terms the group's requirements to classical session players. "I can't read or write music on paper and I don't want to learn to," says McCartney. "It's almost a superstition; it's too serious – like homework. So it's always been good for me to have someone around like George who actually knows music and is a brilliant arranger." In 1975, John Lennon said of The Beatles' relationship with Martin: "He [has] a very great musical knowledge and background, so he could translate for us and suggest a lot of amazing technical things...we'd be saying we want it to go, 'Ooh-ooh!' and 'Ee-ee!', and he'd say, 'Well, look chaps, I thought of this...' and we'd say, 'Oh, great! Great! Put it on here!' It's hard to say who did what. He taught us a lot and I'm sure we taught him a lot by our primitive musical ability."

As The Beatles grew up musically in the mid-Sixties, every new track was a fresh experience. Their inventiveness as writers and musical explorers extended far beyond the boundaries of two guitars, bass and drums, and their use of non-rock 'n' roll instrumentation, such as the introduction of George Harrison's Indian sitar on 'Norwegian Wood (This Bird Has Flown)' from 1965's *Rubber Soul*, was inevitable. If not apparent before, it became patently obvious by the time of *Revolver* that only Martin possessed the qualifications to make the most of The Beatles' increasingly outrageous sonic dreams – his experience of creating "sound pictures" for Peter Sellers and The Goons proving more vital than ever. "I introduced The Beatles to different tape speeds and reversing tapes, all that kind of thing," he says. "They didn't know anything about that and as soon as I showed them something new and weird, they would get enormously enthusiastic about it. I remember explaining to them how you could make a piano sound different and that got them very excited. You could almost see their minds working overtime and thinking, 'How can we apply this to our recordings?' But it was Paul's idea to use tape loops on 'Tomorrow Never Knows' and it was a very good idea too. They loved doing anything that was different and from quite early on actually it was a constant search for new sounds and new instruments. Their recording career amounted to a series of massive quantum leaps."

Revolver, the sessions for which began in April 1966, coincided with a change of personnel in the Studio Two control room: Martin's former right-hand man, engineer Norman Smith left the party and was replaced by the fresh-faced Geoff Emerick who had first made himself known to Martin as his sixteen-year-old second engineer on Rolf Harris's 'Sun Arise' in 1962. He made his debut in The Beatles' camp as the tape operator-cum-assistant engineer on an Abbey Road Studio One session on 20 February, 1963, when Martin overdubbed various keyboard parts on tracks for the group's debut album, *Please Please Me*. Emerick went on to assist on a small number of Beatles sessions over the following eighteen months, but his presence was mostly insignificant before *Revolver*. "Geoff and I have known each other for more years than we care to remember," recalls Martin. "Norman Smith wanted to become a producer and work with another group, but he also wanted to continue working with me and The Beatles. I thought he was right to look towards a career as a producer and I would help him out in any way I could, but I told him it wouldn't work out to also carry on as my engineer. The person who works as my engineer has to give me absolute priority over everything and I won't accept anything less than 100%. Norman understood and he left the team. So I had to look around for his replacement and I remembered Geoff being very bright, with a good ear for sound, so I chucked him in the deep end. In fact, 'Tomorrow Never Knows' was the first Beatles session he worked on as my engineer [on 6 April, 1966]."

"I was far from being a total novice because I had already engineered the 'Pretty Flamingo' hit for Manfred Mann, with John Burgess producing," says Emerick. "I got called into the office one day and was asked if I wanted the job with George. I was playing mind games with it for a while but eventually went for it. When I joined EMI at sixteen, there was no way that you would become a recording engineer until you were forty. So the changes that were happening at Abbey Road were quite drastic." Emerick and Martin quickly cultivated an almost psychic understanding of each other, to the point where even a wink or a glance from the producer would provoke the engineer into tailoring the desired sounds at the console. "Having worked with George for so long I can normally read his mind," says Emerick. "So we've tended not to talk to each other much at sessions." "We've obviously got to know each other pretty much inside out," agrees Martin. "Geoff fundamentally knew what I wanted in the way of sound and I used to like what he did in getting it. We have always been a very good team."

Nothing could have prepared Emerick for the swift change of gear in The Beatles' recording habits that was to accompany his debut as their engineer. "But I did have some ideas that appealed to them," he insists. "I was listening to some American records that impressed me and I didn't really know how they got those sounds. But I tried to change the miking technique that I was taught at Abbey Road, thinking that was what it took to achieve a certain sound. I started moving a lot closer with the mics and we started taking the front skin off the bass drum. There was a rule here that you couldn't place the mic closer than eighteen inches from the bass drum because the air pressure would damage the diaphragm. So I had to get a letter from the management which gave me permission to go in closer with the mics on Beatles sessions. I then went about completely changing the miking techniques and began to over-compress and limited things heavily. *Revolver* was the first time we put the drums through Fairchild limiters and that was just one example of the things that the other Abbey Road engineers used to hate because they had done it a certain way for so many years, so why change it? But The Beatles were screaming out for change. They didn't want the piano to sound like a piano anymore, or a guitar to sound like a guitar. I just had to screw around with what we had."

New-fangled Abbey Road inventions by the studio's general manager, Ken Townsend (who joined in 1954) which were to evolve during *Revolver* included ADT – Artificial Double Tracking – and its sister, flanging. "ADT happened as a result of John asking why he had to sing a part twice to double-track it," says Emerick. "Ken realised that if we took the information off of the sync head of the multitrack machine as we were mixing, we could advance it before the replay head on to a quarter-inch machine and use varispeed to create a ghost image on top of the original sound. We would often move the distance between the two signals by altering the oscillators and that was what we called flanging." The term "flanging" came about when Lennon asked Martin for an explanation of how ADT worked. "There was no way John was going to really understand it," says Martin, "so I made something up and said, 'We feed your voice through this and that and treat it with a double bifurcated sploshing flange which then doubles up your voice.' Of course, it meant nothing to him but he loved the effect and on almost every song on *Revolver*, John would say, 'Can you flange my voice on this one?' The word soon got around the recording business and 'flanger' is now well-known among guitarists as the name of a type of effects box. The name stuck!"

The classical influence came to the fore again on 'Eleanor Rigby' in a more dramatic style than 'Yesterday'. Inspired by Bernard Herrmann's score for the film *Fahrenheit 451*, Martin composed the arrangement after McCartney wanted the strings to play with a strident, rhythmic feel. The secret of the string sound, however, was down to the microphone technique employed by Emerick. One of the two cellists on that Abbey Road session in April 1966 was Norman Jones. "The first thing I noticed was how the microphone was positioned very close to my cello, almost touching the strings, and this made me wonder about what kind of sound they were looking for," he says. "Most of the players were quite horrified by this as it was very unusual. George Martin asked us to play the arrangement through once with vibrato, then once without. But Paul McCartney couldn't tell the difference!"

The Beatles completed their summer 1966 tour of North America at the end of that August and vowed never to hit the road again. In the *Anthology* television series – The Beatles' own account of their career which was screened internationally during late 1995 – Ringo Starr said that in contrast to the tight, pre-fame Hamburg and Cavern days, the group's musicianship had been affected by the constant screaming of the fans which was so loud that neither the audiences nor the group themselves could hear the music. By now, the recorded repertoire had become so intricate that it was impossible to recreate it live as a four-piece, and therefore they were forced to continue playing old hits, such as 'I Feel Fine', which had no bearing on the colourful new sounds being cultivated in the studio – the only place that now mattered. After August 1966, it was the only place in which The Beatles would *exist*.

With the slate wiped clean, 24 November, 1966 was a red letter day in The Beatles' diary. The four newly-moustachioed members arrived at Abbey Road that cold evening without a real game plan, although knowing that they would start work on a new album – hopefully one which would improve upon the techniques put in place on *Revolver*. The first song to be recorded was a dreamy, psychedelic Lennon composition called 'Strawberry Fields Forever' – one he had written two months earlier in Spain during his involvement in Richard Lester's film, *How I Won The War*. But the released version bore little similarity to the rendition Martin originally heard. "The whole format of the first take was different to the finished version in that it had no introduction and started with the verse instead of the chorus hook," he says. "But even that wasn't the way I saw it originally, it was still heavier than I imagined it to be. The first time I heard the song was when I listened to John singing and playing it on an acoustic guitar. John was very Dylanish in many ways but, of course, he had that lovely voice which I think was much better than Dylan's. Just to hear his voice with a simple guitar backing was absolutely delightful, and I wish we had been able to record a version like that – the way I first heard it."

Lennon was in love with his new Mellotron and saw 'Strawberry Fields' as the perfect vehicle for his first recorded use of the instrument, but it was McCartney who both constructed and played the soft flute-like Mellotron introduction on the backing track (Lennon added the downward swoops), while Harrison picked at his Epiphone Casino guitar and Starr drummed. As the four-track tape filled up with various overdubs including bass, maracas, piano and the Indian table harp, known as a swarmandel, the band, in Martin and Emerick's absence one evening, took the opportunity to add a bizarre range of percussion, which is clearly in evidence towards the end of the track. The cacophony caused by everyone hammering out of time to each other for several bars gave every good reason for the fade out/fade in ending.

Abbey Road engineer, Dave Harries, who later worked for many years as Martin's studio manager at AIR Studios, remembers the session well. "Mal Evans, Neil Aspinall [then roadie, now Head of Apple] and everybody was playing on that, all at the same time." he recalls. "We did the first track which was drums and cymbals, then we reversed them and played along on timpani, bongos and tambourine, after which we built up the basic track. All the shouting and hollering you hear at the end of the record came from the boys while they were playing the percussion, and it's all on the same track. I shouldn't really have been recording them while George and Geoff were away at the cinema, because it wasn't the done thing, but they were hot and insisted I do it, so I hit the red light and got on with it. It was a bit of a laugh really. Then when George and Geoff returned later on, I dived out the door." Martin recalls coming back to witness a virtual riot. "I just stood there wide-eyed, listening to what sounded like wild jungle music!" he says. Accompanying this Amazonian racket was a manic sequence of Mellotron notes, accessed by Lennon, which was a standard demonstration "programme" on the instrument, while McCartney also added his stinging lead guitar inserts for good measure. Harrison was not the group's only expert guitar soloist.

By the end of 15 December, 'Strawberry Fields' had become an altogether different animal than planned three weeks earlier. Martin had written a distinctive brass and string arrangement for four trumpets and three cellos, and it was assumed that, apart from a reworked lead vocal, the track was ready for mixing. But nothing was going to be that simple. Three days before Christmas, Lennon hit Martin with one mighty technical challenge. "John's ideas often flew in the face of our capabilities, but this one really had me worrying," he admits. "He told me he liked the second half of the take which included the orchestration, and the first half of another take without it, and could we edit those bits together? Unfortunately, those two takes were in entirely different keys [one tone apart] and the tempo also varied between them. I added sarcastically, 'Apart from that it shouldn't be a problem.' But John just looked at me and replied, 'Well, I'm sure you can fix it,' and walked off. He was serious, and really expected me to get a result. I was very sceptical at first but by the grace of God we did it. With some technical assistance from Ken Townsend we were able to slow down the faster orchestra take to almost match the pitch of the slower non-orchestral track at a pre-determined edit point, which I decided would be exactly one minute into the song. The only way the two would be able to meet was if we gradually decreased the speed of the first half during the run up to the edit point, and then married them together. To our disbelief but endless joy, it worked, even though that edit sticks out like a sore thumb every time I hear it. John just accepted it as all in a day's work for us."

While The Beatles worked throughout the early months of 1967 on their as yet untitled new album, EMI became impatient for a single. Reluctantly, 'Strawberry Fields Forever' was released on 17 February as a double A-side with McCartney's 'Penny Lane', to provide what many still regard as the greatest coupling ever, despite being the group's first single since early 1963 to fail to reach Number One (thanks to Engelbert Humperdinck!). 'Penny Lane' featured session musician David Mason's now world-famous piccolo trumpet *obbligato*, its inspired use coming after McCartney caught Mason's televised performance with the English Chamber Orchestra of Bach's *Brandenburg Concerto Number Two In F Major* and became intrigued by the clear, high tones of the instrument. Mason, a regular face at Abbey Road during that peak psychedelic year, recalls the 17 January session: "When I arrived at EMI, there was no one in the studio and it was almost in darkness, so I just sat down and waited...and waited. When they finally arrived, I thought they must have come off a film set or something because they were wearing some quite outrageous clothes, like candy-striped trousers and loud ties. They also had moustaches which they'd never had before. So I asked them about this and John said, 'We always dress like this, mate!'

"There was no part written for me to play at that point which I thought was unusual, though not for The Beatles, I understood. Paul sang some notes and George Martin sat at the piano writing them down for me. This took quite some time to do. I had brought with me quite a selection of trumpets and after trying out some ideas on a few of them, we eventually chose my piccolo A trumpet and the highest note of the solo was the top G on that instrument. It was difficult because I am not a screecher, I am a symphonic player. Once all this was out of the way, I recorded my parts in two takes but I must admit that I wasn't very impressed with their first backing track. It was quite bad, but they knew that. The final one was so much better. After I had done my bit, I went and had a listen and told Paul that it was probably the catchiest tune I'd heard them come up with and asked if it was going to be a single. He replied, 'Well, it's actually going to be the B-side of a new song called "Strawberry Fields Forever".' And they played that song for me. I thought it was interesting but I told Paul that 'Penny Lane' was much better. John overheard this and said, 'Thanks *very* much!' Then I suggested that they issue it as a double A-side but no more was said about the idea that evening. So I don't know if I was the catalyst, but the single did come out a month later as a double A-side."

Five months passed and Mason appeared on the live satellite television broadcast, *Our World*, where he once again played his piccolo A trumpet on The Beatles' 'All You Need Is Love'. "It was later sold at auction at a grossly inflated price," says Mason of his instrument. "After the inevitable success of 'Penny Lane', my popularity went up and suddenly there were quite a few pop records featuring high pitched trumpet parts, but then all the other groups latched on to The Beatles' gimmicks one way or another. Funnily enough, although I have performed all over the world with fantastic orchestras, like the New Philharmonia, it is 'Penny Lane' for which I am most famous."

Hippy Symphony Number One

The sessions which started with 'Strawberry Fields Forever' in November 1966 continued until the following April to produce the world's most famous, if not best, album: *Sergeant Pepper's Lonely Hearts Club Band*, so called after McCartney's whim to base an album around a fictitious group. "We just dropped the idea that we were The Beatles, so that if we came out with some really far-out music we could say, 'Oh, but this is Sgt Pepper's band,'" says McCartney. From the opening audience murmurs which preceded the title track, to the mournful, dying embers of the piano chord climax of 'A Day In The Life', the album was a technical masterstroke both in terms of the way it was recorded and the relationships between traditional and exotic instruments. It was the soundtrack to the summer of love and a million acid trips.

No song characterised the experimentalism of the album better than 'A Day In The Life' which was formed of two completely separate numbers, one of Lennon's and one of McCartney's, and linked by a freaked-out orchestral orgasm. "I saw *Sgt Pepper* as a classical/rock crossover that tore down the snobbery-sodden barriers that existed between the two types," says Martin. "I always found it ridiculous that people would refuse to listen to rock music because it was considered 'unworthy', somehow not as 'good' as classical music." The original backing track for 'A Day In The Life' (working title: 'In The Life Of...') was started on 19 January, 1967 and recorded in a standard manner on one four-track machine, then bounced down with additional Beatle overdubs. In the middle of the song, between Lennon's verse and McCartney's "Woke up, fell out of bed" section, a long twenty-four-bar void was marked out by McCartney's four to the bar piano prodding while Mal Evans counted out the bars for reference (heard more clearly on the mono LP version) and aptly set off an alarm clock to indicate the end of the passage. *Something* would fill that space later, though quite what they had in mind would not become concrete until 10 February when forty seasoned orchestra professionals arrived at Abbey Road Studio One (the large orchestral room) to engage in the most bizarre session of their collective careers. McCartney, with guidance from Martin, had decided to plug the gap by writing a score which would have each member of the orchestra play the lowest note possible on their instrument and over the course of the twenty-four bars rise in pitch before ending on an E major chord (which would be repeated at the end of the song). Violin leader, Erich Gruenberg was among the confused musicians that evening. "Paul McCartney explained that the number had two empty spaces in which he wanted the orchestra to generate some excitement, but there was no score," says Gruenberg, who studied at the Guildhall School of Music with Martin. "After experimenting with different approaches it was decided we would all start on our lowest note and finish on top E on the twenty-first bar. The 'A Day In The Life' session was quite a party. We were all handed bits of costumes, like wigs, red clown noses, and I was given a furry, clawed glove to wear. The studio was quite full with lots of girls and hangers-on, and The Beatles were wandering around with cine cameras, pointing them at people. Everyone entered into the spirit.

"About six weeks later, we did George Harrison's Indian song, 'Within You Without You'. Long before then, and even more so today, I took an interest in worldwide musical culture, so playing this number did not seem so strange to me as one might imagine. Unlike 'A Day In The Life', this was already pre-scored, but we had to develop how to phrase the music – bending the notes, playing quarter notes and authentically reproduce the Indian flavour."

At the orchestral session for 'A Day In The Life', Abbey Road's ambiophonics system (which used 100 loudspeakers around Studio One to feed delayed signals of the orchestra into the studio and back into the control room console) was used to simulate a larger sound. But this effect was multiplied when a new experiment was undertaken by Martin. "I decided to run two four-track machines in sync for the first time," he says. "We didn't have the luxury of SMPTE code with which to precisely lock the machines together, so I asked Ken Townsend to come up with a solution. He devised a scheme to feed a fifty-cycle tone from a track on the first machine and increase the voltage to run the motor of the second machine, and it worked...sort of. This enabled us to have the group's backing track occupying the whole of one four-track machine, and use the second to record four takes of the orchestra and effectively build up a huge performance of four forty-piece orchestras."

Another highlight of 'A Day In The Life' was Lennon's vocal sound which was plied with a twittering echo effect, care of Abbey Road's echo technique invention: STEED (Send Tape Echo Echo Delay). "The process involved us delaying the signal into the echo chamber via a tape machine," Emerick explains. "It was effectively delayed as a send. The signal which was to be echoed was sent to the quarter-inch machine, and we would take the signal from the replay head, send it to one speaker in the chamber with two condenser mics picking up the sound and then return it to the console. It's not an obvious echo. It's odd because you could put a bit of it around vocals and you'd get used to it, thinking that there wasn't any echo on there at all. But when you removed the effect you could really hear the difference."

McCartney's bass sound took on a new life during 1966 and 1967 after he put his usual Hofner "violin" bass into semi-retirement in favour of his new Rickenbacker 4001S. Suddenly a whole new world of melody was accessed as his bass lines competed with guitar solos for prominence. "The Rickenbacker was very nice, it recorded better than the Hofner," says McCartney. "It has a sort of fatter neck and it was much more stable. It didn't go out of tune as easily. Also, it stayed in tune right up the neck; the Hofner had problems when you got right up near the top so I hardly ever went up there. The bass line to 'Michelle' had a classical feel to it, a kind of Bizet influence that made the song a little more special. I was really proud of 'Penny Lane' and the bass lines on 'Lucy In The Sky', 'With A Little Help From My Friends' and 'Lovely Rita' which were pretty fluid, pretty cool. We had been listening to Motown and soul records in the clubs that were a lot more bass heavy than maybe we had done, and we would go back to Abbey Road and get them to break their rules about how to mike up the bass and get a better sound. We gave them a hard time but, you know, you don't get anywhere without breaking a few rules."

"We never really got anywhere with DI-ing the bass," says Emerick. "On *Sgt Pepper* particularly, we would always reserve one track of the four-track tape for Paul's bass overdubs. He used to stay behind some nights with me just for that purpose. We would put his bass amp in the middle of Studio Two and mike it from about eight feet away with an old valve C12, and sometimes use a second mike even further away and mix the two signals together. You can hear that on some of the *Pepper* tracks where there is a slightly different quality about the bass. The original four-track masters were one-inch, so every track was a quarter-inch wide and there was no noise. The quality of the bass on those numbers was outstanding."

History was quietly made on 17 March, 1967, when harpist Sheila Bromberg became the first and only female instrumental soloist ever to appear on a recording by The Beatles: McCartney's emotional *Sgt Pepper* track, 'She's Leaving Home'. Bromberg, whose distinctive harp playing is most dominant on the song's introduction, has vivid memories of the session. "I got to Abbey Road Studio Two and thought, 'This is nine till twelve at night.' It was all I needed having had a full day. And I had to get there earlier than anyone else to tune up my harp. So I was busy tuning away and I could see some figures moving around in the control room but I didn't know who they were. Then I looked at the music and it appeared difficult. It was just the fingering that was a bit awkward, so I thought it was just as well I arrived early to give me some time to sort it all out. I then became aware of a figure standing beside me and I was playing this piece through when this figure said, 'Well, what yer got on the dots then?' I looked around and said in my plummiest accent, 'I beg your pardon.' And it was Paul McCartney. He said, 'What yer got on the dots, luv?' So I played it and he said, 'Nah, I don't want that, I want something er..." I played it a little bit differently and tried to improvise around the actual notation, but he still wasn't having any of it. He kept saying, 'No, I want it to sound something like er...' And this went on for over half an hour, by which time I was going cross-eyed and sparks and steam were coming out of my ears! Paul was going on endlessly that he wanted it to sound different to how I was playing it, but he couldn't actually explain what it was he wanted to hear. At the same time, George Harrison was in the studio playing his sitar and I'm wondering what the hell I'm going to do with this tune! Ringo was wafting in and out but John wasn't there. I was quietly going berserk and had a real twitch going on. Suddenly George Martin came into the studio and I just collared him and said, 'George, what do you want me to play?' He said, 'Just play exactly what's written.' So that's what I did but it took until about a quarter past midnight, by which time a double chamber orchestra was in the studio, a double string section led by Erich Gruenberg.

"It was all straight in the studio with George Martin conducting us and we weren't playing behind a song. They put the voices on after. It was just the string orchestra and the harp. Then it became very late and Erich just stood up and said, 'Now ve haff to finish because tomorrow ve are verking!' So he just put his fiddle away and Paul McCartney said from the control box, 'Well I suppose that's that then!' Click. That was the end of the session and we all went home. The next thing I knew, everybody was talking about the *Sgt Pepper* album but a bigger shambles of how to achieve it as far as the studio was concerned, you couldn't imagine."

Two years later, Bromberg found herself playing on yet another session for Paul McCartney, this time for a record he was producing by the Welsh pop newcomer, Mary Hopkin. "My friend and I were complaining bitterly about having to record this awful music for £4 10s and I think I got the porterage fee up to thirty bob," she recalls. "So I said, 'Look, we're still going to get £6 for this.' But she was still blabbering on about this whole situation. Unknown to us, the mics were open and Paul could hear every word we had been saying from the control room. Finally, he trotted down the stairs and put his hands on our music stands, peered over the top and said, 'Fifty quid a piece do yer?' We must have looked very wide eyed and wide mouthed! I said, 'Put it there and we'll play it for you!'"

Still active as a musician, Gruenberg says, "On a personal level, I found The Beatles very sincere, kind people who were always further ahead than their contemporaries in every sense. It was always a joy to work with them. Before The Beatles, I had worked on a number of pop sessions including Norrie Paramor's sessions for The Shadows, also Shirley Bassey and Cilla Black with George Martin. The standard fee for a violin leader in those days was £11. But serious orchestration on pop records was quite rare until The Beatles. Other producers seemed to latch on to the idea that orchestration gave a recording more glamour. But, of course, it meant more work for people like me."

Today, George Martin remains disappointed by the omission of 'Strawberry Fields Forever' and 'Penny Lane' from the final track listing of *Sgt Pepper*, a decision he took after the pairing was issued as a single. "We always wanted to give value for money and the view was that we would have been cheating to include something that people had already bought," he says. "Nonetheless it was a super album." For Emerick, it was his proudest moment. "It was a very personal project for all involved and I have very good memories about the whole thing. When I came to sift through the old session tapes for the *Anthology* albums, the little bits of studio chat between the group brought it all home to me and I couldn't believe it was nearly thirty years ago." It was an album which was to drive future Beatles assistant engineer, Alan Parsons to a career behind the mixing console. "I was already working in audio, in the EMI tape duplication plant at Hayes which was outputting EMI's and other companies' product on quarter-inch reel to reel tapes," he says. "One of my jobs was making transfers from original masters. As a result of that job I became one of the first people outside of The Beatles to hear *Sgt Pepper* because I received the master for duplication only a couple of days after it was mixed. I was just overwhelmed to hear such a great piece of work. I was literally open-mouthed listening to it for the first time, and I knew then that I wanted to discover for myself the processes that went into making records. I rang the personnel department and requested a transfer to Abbey Road Studios, and it was all arranged."

Jeff Jarratt, later the respected producer of the London Symphony Orchestra's *Classic Rock* series of albums, amongst many other best-selling recordings, assisted the engineering of several Beatles tracks including 'Your Mother Should Know' after joining the studio in August 1966. Then debating whether to go to university or become involved with music as a career, Jarratt applied for a trainee position at Abbey Road in 1966 and was delighted to be invited to an interview with assistant studio manager, Barry Waite. "It seemed to go well, because at the end he said, 'Well, Mr Jarratt, we would love to have you working with us, but even if you do a degree and come back to work here in three years time, you will still have to start off making the tea.' It just so happened that I could start in two weeks' time and start making the tea. So they made my mind up for me. I had no idea of what happened in recording studios. I'd played in a band at school and one of the guys had a portable tape recorder, but that was all. I really didn't know what a record producer or a tape op actually did. I just wanted to be in a place where music was being made. When the people at Abbey Road felt you were ready or when they needed somebody you would then get wheeled into doing sessions as an assistant engineer and that would carry on until the main engineer didn't turn up for work one day, for whatever reason, then you would get a crack at doing it on your own. I was very fortunate because there was a change of management at Abbey Road and that allowed a lot of new blood in to take up engineering roles. The technical guys were all still wearing their white coats and on every session there would always be one of them sitting there in the control room, just in case anything went wrong.

"There was a tremendous buzz around the place. In fact, during the first week I was there, The Easybeats were recording 'Friday On My Mind' which, for me, remains one of the greatest pop singles. Being new, I couldn't just go into the control room and watch the session. So I hung around outside the door, listening to that great guitar riff. I know that in every field, people look back at the past and say how great it was. But in my experience, it was definitely great fun at Abbey Road in those days."

A few years later, another new starter at Abbey Road was John Leckie, a fan of early electronic music whose original ambitions lay in the movie world. After completing a two-year course in film and television at Ravensbourne College of Art, Leckie turned down opportunities with the BBC and the newly-launched London Weekend Television to spend five months making obscure 16mm films at a small Wardour Street film company. In 1969, already familiar with the basics of putting sound on tape through his experience with film, Leckie decided to blanket the London recording industry with applications for non-existent jobs. He struck gold when EMI was the only company to reply. "I was offered an interview and got shown around Abbey Road, then three months later I received a letter asking me to start as a tape op the following Monday," he says. "Like every other new starter, I spent the first couple of weeks sitting around watching what the engineers did on a session and suddenly the guy wasn't there anymore, so I was asked to take over. It was 100% practical experience and exactly what I wanted."

From the A&R department's booking of a session to the final mastering of a new record, Leckie saw it all, and when he was not directly involved in a session, he would find various essential tasks to fill his hours. "White label test pressings were always approved here, and checking their quality was often a good way of generating overtime money," he recalls. "You'd have a pile waiting for you which were identified by a catalogue number, not by an artist's name, and you would listen out for excessive noise, pops, clicks or jumps, and reject them if necessary. Another little job we had to do was the banding of fifteen ips quarter-inch tape copies which came to us from Capitol or overseas subsidiaries like the Russian label Melodia or ABC Dunhill [once famed for Steely Dan]. They would arrive without white leader tape between tracks, so in breaks from sessions, I would spend an hour or two putting leader tape in the right places, and then top and tail it with white leader at the front of the tape and red at the end. If you were quick and did it in half an hour you could knock off early and go down the pub!"

Even thirty years on, there are some aspects of working at Abbey Road which remain the same, such as the wide range of musical disciplines faced by the staff engineers. "Because of the huge range of music recorded here, engineers have always had the opportunity to work with different styles and become acquainted with the various demands of each type of session," Leckie says. "When I was on the staff in the early Seventies, it was expected that even though you might have stayed up half the night with Pink Floyd, you had to be in the next day to prepare the studio for a German opera singer. Even now, a young assistant engineer might find himself working on a four-week Oasis project and then go straight into recording a solo piano concerto. Abbey Road is one of the few studios in the world where you can gain that breadth of experience."

One of the first hard lessons learned by Leckie was that he and all of his young colleagues were dispensable. A session would always continue in his absence and should things go critically wrong, there would always be another wide-eyed, aspiring engineer ready to fill his shoes. He also discovered that accidentally erasing an in-progress tape could be dangerous to one's health! "When it's no one's fault but yours because you pressed the red button, you just want to die," he admits. "It only takes the once and you don't wipe anything for six months or so because you double-check everything."

The tape operator's role was well defined in the era which pre-dated the use of the multitrack remote controller, and much responsibility was placed on the shoulders of the young Leckie as he nervously activated the controls of the tape machine. "It was always someone's very specific job to start, stop, rewind and fast-forward the tape. That was the tape op's first priority because at any time the producer said, 'Run the tape,' or, 'Go back to the second verse,' the whole focus had to be on being able to act on his instruction as quickly as possible. It was down to you to record the tracks, do all the drop-ins and take care of the headphone sync mix, while the engineer positioned the microphones and made the balance on the desk. Invariably you had to be one step ahead of what everyone else on the session was thinking, but also be ready to go one step back."

Apple Scruffs

In July 1968, The Beatles began work on a new single, 'Hey Jude' (their first on the Apple label), which was notable not only for its length (7:11 mins), but also for its use of eight-track recording at a studio other than Abbey Road. Unknown to The Beatles, eight-track was in the process of being tested at Abbey Road for later introduction as a standard, but recent visits to Trident Studios in Soho by McCartney and Harrison (to produce Mary Hopkin and Jackie Lomax respectively) had introduced them to this exciting new prospect of being able to do even more overdubbing. Then a regular Trident customer, Gus Dudgeon remembers, "The Beatles weren't supposed to record anywhere other than at Abbey Road. But they recorded 'Hey Jude' there and the multitrack machine had an incorrectly sized capstan wheel which made the machine run at twelve and a half ips instead of the standard fifteen ips. So when EMI found out about the session and insisted that they take it back to Abbey Road to mix it, the tape was running too fast and no one could figure out why. Trident had experienced some similar problems with other clients' tapes, and The Beatles were forced to return to Trident to remix it. But my suspicion is that their tape machine was deliberately set up to record slower, in order that they got repeat business for exactly those reasons!"

Gerry Bron also became a victim of Trident's unorthodox tape speed when he worked on Manfred Mann's 1968 single, 'My Name Is Jack'. "We had been doing a lot of sessions at Olympic but this was recorded at Trident with a very young Alan O'Duffy engineering," he says. "I wasn't at all pleased with the mix I had done there and told Barry Sheffield that I wanted to take the tape back to Olympic to re-mix. But he told me I couldn't. I said, 'What do you mean I can't? It's my bloody tape, I've paid for it!' But he explained that they had an American machine with a sixty cycle motor which ran the tape at twelve and a half ips, which meant that I wouldn't be able to mix it anywhere else unless I could live with the track playing quite a bit faster. At which point I hit the roof!"

Sold on the idea of using eight-track after the 'Hey Jude' session, The Beatles demanded they have access to the technology for the remainder of their *White Album* sessions, which had been running since the previous May. Harrison's 'While My Guitar Gently Weeps' was the first Beatles song at Abbey Road to use the studio's "secret" 3M machine, thanks to Dave Harries' intervention. "When I first worked at Abbey Road there were only four-track Telefunken machines and the Studer J37s," says Harries. "The Beatles were always ones for innovation and I suppose that if they knew about something, they would want to use it. And they found out about the eight-track and used it from halfway through the *White Album*. I got into trouble for giving them the machine in the first place, because it was still undergoing tests with Francis Thompson but they still wanted to use it so I borrowed it and got bollocked for it the next day. If they'd have known it existed and not been able to use it, it would have been extremely frustrating. And if you have a band in the studio who were making such an enormous profit for EMI, you can't really hold them back. The problem was that we only had four-track beforehand so if you wanted to continuously overdub, you had to copy tapes and we didn't have noise reduction. So the machines had to be really well lined up and kept in top condition. You also had to limit the sound so that you could cut it for disc. If you had too much bass on a mix and it wasn't in the centre or out of phase, it was a problem for the disc pressers. So they were always compromised in some way though not held back. We used to try different things for them if they wanted an outrageous sound but we used to get in trouble.

"There wasn't a rule book as such. But we had D20 mics on the bass drum that were always going wrong and they didn't sound very good anyway. So I got an old speaker and wired it up to act as a microphone, then I put that in front of the bass drum and it sounded great. But then we were told we weren't allowed to use that because it wasn't a real microphone. That was just *one* incident. I don't think we were very restricted, it was just us giving the powers-that-be the impression that we were being unprofessional. But the band were developing musical concepts and they did what they wanted to do with George Martin. If they were held back, then it was at the right time, so that by the time they could create *Pepper*, the technology was in place to help them do it. If they had tried to make *Pepper* earlier, maybe it wouldn't have been quite the same album."

Today, most record producers and engineers operate on a totally independent, freelance basis, benefiting from the freedom to work with whom they like, whenever and wherever they prefer. It is a far cry from the early Sixties when the vast majority were dictated by the rules and conditions of their record company employers, and given staff salaries, without any share of royalties from record sales. Such a scenario would horrify the hit-makers of the Nineties, but up until three years before the *White Album*, George Martin was earning a mere £3,000 a year, while his "boys" were cleaning up big time. Understandably alarmed, Martin wasted no time in handing in his resignation and made plans to establish his own independent production company, Associated Independent Recording (London) Limited, otherwise known as AIR. In his book, *Summer Of Love*, Martin wrote, "EMI never paid me a bonus, despite having a Number One record for thirty-seven weeks. In 1965, I tried to renegotiate my contract. I discovered that Parlophone had made EMI a profit of £2,200,000. And I saw none of it – even under the new terms they were offering. So I defected and set up AIR."

This he did with fellow EMI producers, John Burgess (Manfred Mann, Freddie & The Dreamers) and Ron Richards (Hollies, P J Proby), along with Decca's top pop producer, Peter Sullivan (Tom Jones, Engelbert Humperdinck). To the outside world, nothing much had changed as Martin continued his pioneering work with The Beatles and others, as did his three colleagues with their own successful acts. But behind the scenes at the company's offices at 108, Park Street, London, AIR was negotiating highly favourable deals with EMI and Decca. As well as marketing their own services as producers, the four AIR men were keen to develop new production and engineering talent, and one young man who succeeded under the company's wing was Chris Thomas, who originally wrote to Martin in 1965 asking for a job. "George did try to set something up for me but it all fell through," says Thomas. "So by the time I left school, I had got another job and I was playing in a band and writing stuff for about two years. Then it got to the end of 1967 and all I could think of doing was working in a studio, producing lots of different bands, even though that job hardly existed. So I wrote another letter to George and asked if he remembered me. By this time he had set up AIR London and in March 1968 he gave me a job on six months' trial."

Thomas's training amounted to little more than sitting in the corners of control rooms, watching over the shoulders of Martin and his three partners as they worked on their various sessions. They included the early dates for the *White Album* in May 1968. "The first time I was ever allowed in the studio control room on my own was the time I came back from holiday that September and George Martin had just gone away on his holiday, leaving a note for me saying, 'Go down to The Beatles' sessions.' The band had already been at it for about three months and I automatically assumed that I'd go down there as normal, sit in the corner and not really do anything. But no! Paul walked in and asked me what I was doing there. I thought that there was no way George would have landed me in it. He must have warned them of what was happening. So I said, 'George told me to come down, didn't you know?' Paul just looked me in the eye and said, 'Oh well, if you want to produce us, fine, and if you don't, we'll just tell you to fuck off.' And he walked out! I don't think I said a word for ages after that. I just froze because they all sort of rolled up.

"Ken Scott had taken over because Geoff Emerick couldn't stand the atmosphere any longer and didn't want to continue with it. So I sat down next to Ken and they started doing a take of 'Helter Skelter'. They were saying, 'What do you reckon, Ken?' I was getting completely blanked by them. Then later, they were chatting about firing some people at Apple, but I was convinced John was talking about me. And I thought, 'Christ, not only am I going to get elbowed and told not to come back after tonight, but that's also going to reflect on my job with George.' So I just jumped in at the deep end from the moment they started working again. For the previous five hours or so, they had been completely ignoring me and I froze. Then they were doing a take and somebody made a little cock-up so I pressed the button which was like a klaxon – brrrrrrr! I said, 'Something went wrong there.' They said, 'No they didn't!' But they all came up the stairs to listen and agreed. I just took the bull by the horns and cracked the whip. It sounds extraordinary but it was only out of total fear that I did it, not anything else. We had started at about two-thirty in the afternoon and finished at two-thirty in the morning, and by the end of the evening, I said to Paul, 'What happens about tomorrow?' He said, 'If you want to come down it's all right.' I thought, 'He didn't say piss off. Wow!' So I came back the next day and they did another wind up. They were doing the backing vocals on 'Helter Skelter', those 'aaaahs' that you hear. That was four tracks of backing vocals. It was John, George and Paul doing a three-part harmony, then they double-tracked it twice to get twelve voices. On the last time, they flicked one of the mics around so it only picked up two on one side and one on the other, And I said, 'That sounds great, come up and have a listen.' Paul said, 'Hang on a minute, the mic sounds like it's switched off on this side.' I said, 'Well it sounds all right, because you can't tell the difference between eleven and twelve voices.' It was little things like that that were designed to test me. I was definitely being severely wound up! It was like, you know, are we going to let this imposter in?"

Eventually, Thomas won the confidence of the band and even found himself playing on the album, no doubt instilling pride in his mentor, George Martin. "It was great how it ended up because they were sticking me on everything and saying, 'Oh that's all right, he's here, he can play that, we'll just sit around for a while,'" Thomas recalls. "It got to the point where if there was a keyboard part, they'd get me to do it so they could go upstairs, hang around and get stoned! I'd be sitting there thumping away, you know. I played harpsichord on 'Piggies', piano on 'Long Long Long', organ on 'Savoy Truffle' and the mandolin and trombone sounds from the Mellotron on 'Bungalow Bill'."

His appearance on 'The Continuing Story Of Bungalow Bill', live in Studio Two with the four Beatles, coincided with Martin's return. "That was something else, playing with The Beatles with George Martin producing," he says. "Crazy! And while Paul was working on an overdub in Studio Two, John and I would go to another part of Abbey Road to track down some sound effects, which we did for 'Blackbird'." Several of

Thomas's suggestions were warmly embraced by The Beatles, such as his idea to introduce the harpsichord on Harrison's 'Piggies'. "The harpsichord was set up in Number One for a classical session and I almost got into trouble over this. I went in there and I was playing away thinking how good it sounded. I knew we were going to do 'Piggies' and I went in to see George Harrison and said, 'There's a harpsichord in there, do you fancy using it on your song?' So he sat down with me and started playing me another song called 'Something' and I said, 'That's fantastic, why don't you do that instead?' He said, 'Do you really like it? I'll give it to Jackie Lomax as a single then.' I thought, 'Oh dear!' So we continued to do 'Piggies' and we started to push the harpsichord out of Number One and into Number Two. Ken Scott looked horrified. He said, 'What the hell are you doing?!' I hadn't realised what they did in Number One with recordings of classical sonatas. They'd have a session one day, the harpsichord would be left absolutely in situ and tuned up perfectly the next morning before the session when they'd continue the recording. So you weren't allowed to move this thing at all and there's Ken quietly going berserk because I'd moved it. What we did in the end was to move it back into Number One, as close to where I'd found it and move everyone in there to record it."

Aside from his musicianly contributions to the *White Album*, Thomas found himself assisting Ken Scott on a number of the album's mixes. "I had the wonderful job of wobbling the bloody oscillator for Eric Clapton's guitar track on 'While My Guitar Gently Weeps', while it was being mixed," he recalls. "Apparently Eric had insisted that his guitar should sound a bit different to the normal Clapton. That keyboard sound was a flanged organ – very whiny and slightly out of tune. There were loads of things like that and I fell in love with that experimental side of the records. Consequently, I learned such a lot from those sessions in terms of adding detail and also how you could just play with stuff without taking the tracking side too seriously. You'd take it more seriously later and pay attention on the mix. It was almost like being a child with The Beatles. That innocent feeling of trying out loads of different things to see what worked and throwing ideas in the air and seeing what happened without sticking to a rigid plan. I certainly learned that you had to abuse the equipment you had to achieve a certain sound. There were no boxes around to do it for you."

The Beatles' only double set, the *White Album* contained the most diverse range of musical styles ever assembled by the group, its kaleidoscopic effect determined by the fragmented efforts of the members effectively serving as each other's backing musicians for most tracks. In 1968, future Elton John and Chris Rea engineer, Stuart Epps, was working as a disc cutter for Dick James Music, then the owner of Beatles music publisher Northern Songs, when he received a privileged preview of the album. "It was just unbelievable," he says. "When that came through the door, I had to do a tape copy for our music engraver and I put the word out among some of our staff that we had it. There were ten of us congregated in my little room, including Elton John [a DJM writer] and we all sat and listened to this new Beatles album. We were just dying really with each new track. It wasn't like just listening to new songs, it was listening to new technology. You'd hear a new guitar sound and think, 'How the hell did they do that? What is that?' The harmonies were incredibly well recorded with really tight double-tracking. I felt it was an honour to be working there and hear all this new stuff."

Earlier in 1968, the cartoon movie *Yellow Submarine*, inspired by The Beatles' *Revolver* track, was released to cinemas around the globe and attracted widespread praise from all, it seemed, apart from The Beatles themselves who were none too pleased with their wacky cartoon caricatures. The Apple soundtrack album, released in January 1969, cobbled together existing tracks such as 'All You Need Is Love' along with 'Only A Northern Song', 'Hey Bulldog', 'All Together Now' and 'It's All Too Much' – all of which had been recorded between the *Pepper* sessions of 1967 and early 1968.

The soundtrack gave George Martin the opportunity to break out of his producer's role and apply his composition and orchestral arrangement skills in the movie world. "I was involved in the film from the start and it was the first time I became known for being a film writer," he says. (He would later compose the score for the James Bond classic *Live And Let Die*.) "I got to know the director George Dunning very well and we had very little time to work. We actually did that cartoon film in a year, from beginning to end, which meant that I had to write all the background score as it was being made and I worked at home. I had a cut of the movie, I made my own measurements and scored an hour's worth of music as he was cartooning. Out of that came several themes. The opening theme is 'Pepperland' which is where you have this lovely beautiful old fashioned countryside, which is like a paradise before the Blue Meanies [the film's baddies!] get to it, and the old fashioned-sounding, slightly delicate 'Pepperland' theme suggests this. Then the Blue Meanies come along, and we have the 'March Of The Meanies' which is where they really run over the place and devastate the land. 'Sea Of Monsters' was another theme which was written for the part of the film where the heroes in the film come along to try and save the place."

Meanwhile, as the cartoon's soundtrack hit the streets in January 1969, distinct cracks in The Beatles' relationship were beginning to appear when the group began filming at Twickenham Film Studios for what would become the fly-on-the-wall documentary movie, *Let It Be*. The group made the decision to forsake the experimental bias of their last three years' work and "get back" to basic rock 'n' roll sensibilities, recording a new album at their own Apple Studios in the basement of their Apple offices in Savile Row. Planned the previous year and built immediately after the November 1968 release of the *White Album*, the studio was put in the hands of Alexis "Magic Alex" Mardas, a Greek electronics expert and good friend of Lennon's, who promised The Beatles the first sixteen-track studio in the world – one which would be centrally-heated and feature a log fire. Not only that, his further miracles would include sonic force fields to acoustically separate the drum kit and amplification. But things did not quite work out that way. "It was just a complete joke and a miracle that any kind of sound would pass through the console," says Alan Parsons. "Alex's idea was to have one monitor for each track, all lined up horizontally in the studio. Glyn Johns who was engineering couldn't believe what was going on. Alex said something like, 'Here's the console, but I'm still working on the machine, so we'll just work with eight-track for now.' It only took about twelve hours to realise that Magic Alex's invention was not quite what it had been cracked up to be and then some panicky phone calls were made to Abbey Road to borrow some four-track consoles so that things could proceed. They didn't have any staff at Apple, so I jumped in for a while."

Dave Harries remembers that, despite its cosmetic shortcomings, the desk did actually work. "We took a machine down there but unfortunately the desk was a bit of a lash-up," he says. "He used a cathode ray oscilloscope with eight traces for the meters, but that tended to cause a bit of a hum going into the desk. The gain structures weren't quite right on the desk and it was a bit thrown together, made from bits of wood and aluminium. It looked a bit like the control deck of a B52 bomber and he didn't buffer the monitors, so that if you were listening to tracks one and two on the left, and three and four on the right, and you pressed those buttons on the desk, because the monitor wasn't buffered, you also had that going on to the tape machine. So we actually had to buffer the desk by using power amps feeding into the speakers, so that you could switch anything you liked to anywhere without affecting the tracks going to the tape machine.

"It wasn't particularly well thought out but I got the tape machine, lined up to the desk as well as I could and got it all working then let the band do a session on it. I said, 'There you are, that's the best I can do with it.' And so they did their session but there was a lot of hum and hissing. We even took the scope out and left it down in the bottom of the desk to try and get rid of this noise. Finally, the band took one listen to the playback and just walked out. Then we got a phone call the next morning asking us to take one of our EMI mobile desks over there. It was all a bit sad."

Abbey Road: The Last Hurrah

With the drab and lifeless *Let It Be* tapes in the can and awaiting mixdown, The Beatles set to work on their final album, *Abbey Road*, in April 1969, with the subconscious belief that it would be their last as a group. Although a handful of the sessions in May were recorded at Olympic Studios, most others were rightly held in the group's traditional Abbey Road Studio Two venue.

For George Martin, *Abbey Road* was the group's greatest musical achievement and the work of which he is most fond. "It's very dear to my heart because after all the trauma of *Let It Be* we really got it together," he says. "When we did *Let It Be* I just thought it was the end and what a sad way it would have been to have gone like that because from *Sgt Pepper* I thought we were pointing the way to a new style of recording. We were establishing a trend and I wanted to follow it up, but *Let It Be* was recorded in a quite different way. When I was asked to come back and produce another album, I didn't believe that it would work out. I told Paul that I wasn't very sure that I wanted to do it. I said, 'I'll only do it if I'm really allowed to do it the way we used to.' He assured me that everybody was very keen and I went along with it.

"*Abbey Road* was the development of my own idea to establish something of a classical form in rock 'n' roll music, and I urged John and Paul to think of their songs as subjects in a symphony, using them more than once in different keys, have them in counterpart with each other and make up a longer work. One of my favourite pieces is the 'Golden Slumbers'/'Carry That Weight'/'The End' section which still sounds fantastic to me nearly thirty years later. It's a wonderful example of rock and classical music coming together very effectively. Of course, one side of of the album does reflect that approach. The other side doesn't but it was a good compromise, I thought."

With the exception of the *Let It Be* sessions, right up until their demise, The Beatles constantly searched for a new instrument to use on their recordings, like children with their toys. And on the *Abbey Road* sessions, they made interesting use of Dr Robert Moog's new monophonic synthesiser, which sufficiently interested Harrison for him to purchase one and use on his earlier *Electronic Sounds* album. "The early Moog was a pretty sizeable instrument with a two-tiered keyboard and masses of wires hanging out of it, and they had one set up in a room adjacent to Studio Three," Alan Parsons explains. "They had lines running from there into the control rooms, all plugging in around the building which you could do back then at Abbey Road. It was all done through communication lines. Mike Vickers from Manfred Mann brought the first model into the UK and I believe he was there to help out as a consultant. Most of the time was taken up with trying to get more out of the instrument than mere gurgles and buzzing, but it was very striking. I remember being told that the synthesiser was going to be the final musical instrument, that it would be the ultimate all-encompassing instrument, capable of producing any sound on earth. If you were to listen to it now, you wouldn't think it possible, but at the time it was very impressive, it was revolutionary. But it was monophonic and not really that capable of delivering much in the way of sounding like another musical instrument. One thing I do remember about The Beatles' use of the Moog was on the solo for 'Maxwell's Silver Hammer', when instead of playing the keyboard Paul used a ribbon to go up and down the scale. I think he was holding down one note on the keyboard to act as a switch for the sound, but it was his finger moving up and down the ribbon that produced the notes, as if it were a violin. There were no marks to tell you where the notes were, it just required a good ear."

The surprise addition of 'Her Majesty' at the end of the album was, Parsons explains, an accident. It was originally intended that it would appear between 'Mean Mr Mustard' and 'Polythene Pam' as part of the medley on side two until McCartney vetoed its inclusion. It was spliced out but mistakenly edited on to the end of the album's master reel. The crossfades on the medley, referred to during the sessions as "The Long One", saw Parsons taking care of the cues between tape machines. "The medley was actually compiled on the eight-track master and there weren't really that many crossfades because most of the songs were played from one to the other," he says.

Jeff Jarratt, who was second engineer on several of the album's early sessions for 'Something', 'Oh Darling', 'I Want You (She's So Heavy)' and 'Octopus's Garden', describes the situation as very technically demanding. "They were at the height of their creativity, so absolutely everything we did was carefully analysed because they had very definite ideas about how the tracks should sound," he says. "There certainly wasn't any evidence at the time that *Abbey Road* was going to be the band's last album together. But then I was probably enjoying myself so much in the control room that I wouldn't have noticed any peripheral tension between them!"

"The great irony of *Abbey Road* is that although it sounds like four great friends making joyous music, they were very close to breaking up," admits George Martin. "They really did work well together and the disharmony of their private and business lives was put aside. I think that maybe they all knew that it was to be their last album so there was a drive to make it a really good one. My memories of the sessions are all happy ones. 'Here Comes the Sun' is still one of George's best-ever songs, along with 'Something' – another *Abbey Road* highlight. It was the first time I really took notice of George's writing to be honest, but he went on to write some great songs afterwards. Because John and Paul were so high profile as songwriters within The Beatles, George rarely got a look in and that, we have all come to realise, was a big loss."

It was the end of an era, but one from which everybody in the recording industry learned, and is still learning, huge lessons. Alan Parsons, who after a long and successful career as a freelance producer and recording artist returned to Abbey Road in 1997 as Vice President of the EMI Studios Group (but resigned the following year), comments, "Recording studios became musical instruments in their hands and The Beatles' career was largely about them learning what could be achieved in the studio, learning about production techniques, learning that if you broke the rules you would get a better result. And the reason for the huge leaps and bounds in which technology has advanced over the last twenty-five or so years is because The Beatles demanded eight-track, demanded bigger consoles, and so on. There is absolutely no doubt in my mind that if not for The Beatles, eight-track would probably still be the recording industry standard."

Being For The Benefit Of Mr Martin

As The Beatles ground to a halt, George Martin had several things on his mind to prevent him from grieving over his estranged boys. Things were looking up for his AIR organisation and by 1969, he and his partners thought it wise to invest their enviable profits in a studio of their own, having spent the previous five years hiring the likes of Abbey Road at a premium. After combing the West End for some time without luck, they eventually found a large space on the fourth floor of the Peter Robinson building in Oxford Circus, originally the Peter Robinson banqueting hall. Being close to the local amenities of Oxford Street and Regent Street, and with plenty of natural light and attractive marble columns, it seemed like a perfect setting, although the escalating commotion of Central London was later to prove frustrating. Even the rent was very reasonable, at only £1 10s per square foot.

Plans got underway to build AIR Studios with Ken Shearer and EMI's Keith Slaughter, later AIR's first studio manager, in charge of the hard graft. It was decided to build a large room of about sixty by thirty feet for orchestral film soundtrack recording and scoring, with another thirty-square-foot room designed as a rock 'n' roll studio. Dave Harries, who moved from AIR to Decca in 1995, joined the AIR team from Abbey Road in 1970 while the studio was still being built. He says, "George Martin's original slogan for AIR Studios was 'Built by producers for producers'. We thought we would go into film dubbing, so we also built a dubbing theatre and mixing room. The four rooms were all equipped with Neve desks, the oldest being an 827, which was quite an early one. We installed Number One first, the largest of the studios, and when it was completed we had a huge launch party on 6 October, 1970 with about 400 bottles of champagne! The first albums we did there were with The Climax Blues Band and Procol Harum, while Studio Two was under construction."

Chris Thomas is sufficient living evidence of AIR's major goal to encourage fresh engineer and producer talent under the watchful eyes of the company's experienced professionals. "As the studio developed, a lot of our tape ops rose through the ranks to become producers in their own right," says Harries. "Eventually, AIR had quite a stable of its own producers who were ex-AIR engineers, like Steve Churchyard, Jon Kelly, John Punter, Bill Price, Colin Fairley and Steve Jackson. They were all managed very successfully by John Burgess for many, many years."

For many years, Martin had wanted to build a studio in a picturesque, remote location where artists could relax and record away from the city hubbub. His original idea was to build a permanent studio on a boat after hearing of colleague Geoff Emerick's adventures in the Virgin Islands with Paul McCartney during the recording of Wings' *London Town*. Eventually he had the idea to build a place on the small West Indian island of Montserrat. "There were certain tax advantages in going there, the communications, telephones, were all excellent, plus it was a stable British colony, and the locals were very friendly," says Harries. "So it was felt that it was the right place for us. We went out there to buy a water works called Sturge's Farm on about thirty acres of land where we built the studio in 1978. The studio actually opened for business in January 1979, again coincidentally for a Climax Blues Band album, of which I have some very happy memories. Of course, over the years, it earned a fabulous track record for albums, like Dire Straits' *Brothers In Arms*, Sting's *Dream Of The Blue Turtles* and many others."

Montserrat was obviously a place where AIR employees looked forward to being seconded. "Naturally," says Harries. "We used to staff Montserrat with a maintenance guy and tape ops and engineers from Oxford Circus on a kind of rota basis. But I think after a while it gets on top of you. You were very trapped out there and if you were doing a long project, you did actually look forward to coming back. Mind you, we used to laugh because you'd look out of the window at Montserrat and see the beautiful Caribbean Sea, whereas back at AIR in Oxford Circus, you'd look out of the window and see the side entrance of British Home Stores."

The Montserrat development opened something of a can of worms when choosing the ideal console. "MCI equipment, the tape machines and desks, were all the rage in the late Seventies," Harries explains. "But we preferred Neve desks because we were more used to them than anything else. We also felt that being in the middle of nowhere we should have something very reliable. Especially as there was a big 200kW medium wave and short wave transmitter on the island near the South American coastline, and we were a bit worried about RF breakthrough, so we wanted to make sure that the equipment would be good. But Geoff Emerick didn't want this, he wanted MCI. So we told Rupert Neve we wanted a desk but not a standard model because Geoff didn't like the transformer sound. Rupert said, 'What if I were to build you a desk with these figures?' The distortion was in two noughts and the 3dB point was 160kHz, so it was obvious that it would perform like nothing else on earth.

"We ordered the desk and everyone including Geoff was so pleased with its sound that we had a duplicate installed into Studio Two at Oxford Circus. It had a thirty-two-track monitor because at the time MCI were developing a three-inch tape machine with thirty-two tracks, although it never actually got off the ground. The thirty-two-track monitoring wasn't in-line – we had a separate desk with 8078 type modules. This console had a split 15V rail power supply so you could get the headroom without having to use transformers. You could get a very wide band width, low distortion and a beautifully clean sound. It gained a great reputation but because Montserrat was a single studio throughout the Eighties, we really had to have an SSL [Solid State Logic] desk. SSL came out with a lovely product in 1977 which was really a spin-off from the MCI desk design. It proved to be a worldbeater so with that Neve on Montserrat we tended to get a bit left behind. Although we got an SSL, we asked Rupert Neve [then at Focusrite] to build twelve extra channels on the end to give us the best of both worlds. We later put together a desk on which you could either have a forty-eight-input desk with a couple of tracks of monitoring, or you could have twenty-four inputs and twenty-four-track monitoring."

In 1982, after six weeks at AIR in London, Ultravox jetted off to the sunshine of Montserrat to complete and mix its *Quartet* album with Martin and Emerick. But as Midge Ure recalls, the exotic environment proved more of a distraction to the creative process. "It's such a gorgeous place and I even ended up buying a house there," he says. "Everyone was more interested in lying by the pool, although I think the incentive to work was that the studio was air-conditioned, so when it got too hot outside, you had to go back to work to cool down. George wanted to work in Montserrat and we obviously weren't complaining about it. It was a fun thing to do and we had a great time, as well as getting a lot of work done. Working on the Neve without any computerised mixing, it was all very hands-on with five of us sat at the desk in charge of ten faders each. You know, ducking under someone's elbow because you needed to turn the echo pan-pot at the end of the chorus or whatever. It was great."

Today, both AIR's Montserrat and Oxford Circus studios are no more. The former suffered badly in the storms of Hurricane Hugo in 1989, while the latter was superseded in 1992 by a brand new AIR operation at Lyndhurst Hall in Hampstead (see Chapter 11).

1995 And All That

In February 1994, twenty-four years after they last recorded together and a little more than thirteen years following the tragic fatal shooting of John Lennon, the incredible happened when McCartney, Harrison and Starr reunited at McCartney's East Sussex studio (Hog Hill, aka The Mill) to record new music to coincide with the making of the group's ultimate career story: *The Beatles' Anthology*. At first, the three were lukewarm about the prospect of making music without Lennon. It is to McCartney's credit that he – the one who became the main motivator after the death of Brian Epstein in 1967 – persuaded Starr and the normally reticent Harrison to come together once more. But, in an ironic twist of fate, it was Yoko Ono, often credited as the woman responsible for the band's break-up, who more than anyone engineered the reunion. In January 1994 when McCartney met Yoko Ono in New York for Lennon's induction into the Rock 'N' Roll Hall Of Fame, she handed him some of her late husband's unfinished demos with the suggestion that they be added to by his old Beatle pals.

Jeff Lynne, the ex-Electric Light Orchestra frontman-turned-producer and regular Harrison collaborator, was immediately given the task of "cleaning up" Lennon's crudely recorded mono cassettes and using technological wizardry to put the performance in perfect time to allow a backing track overdub. The following month, Lynne, together with Emerick and the three Beatles gathered to make history all over again. The first song they tackled was 'Free As A Bird', a song Lennon wrote in 1977 for an unrealised musical about the Lennons' loony life in the late Sixties, which was released by Apple in November 1995. The second song, issued the following March, was 'Real Love', a song with similar origins but overdubbed in February 1995 with the same studio personnel – a line-up which did not include George Martin. "I wasn't invited," he said.

Starr said at the time of 'Free As A Bird', "The only trouble with the tapes was that it was John singing along to a piano and recorded in mono. Firstly, the recording wasn't that wonderful and it wasn't like you could pull a fader and change each of the voice and piano levels. All we had to work with was what we heard and it wasn't in time either." For Jeff Lynne it presented an extraordinarily difficult task. "It was very difficult and one of the hardest jobs I've ever had to do, because of the nature of the source material," he says. "They were very primitive-sounding to say the least. I spent about a week at my own studio cleaning up both the tracks on my computer, with a friend of mine, Marc Mann, who is a great engineer, musician and computer expert. We tried out a new noise reduction system and it really worked. The problem I had with 'Real Love' was that not only was there a sixty cycles mains hum going on, there was also a terrible amount of hiss because it had been recorded at a low level. I don't know how many generations down this copy was, but it sounded like at least a couple. So I had to get rid of the hiss and the mains hum, and then there were clicks all the way through it. When we saw the graph of it on the computer, there were all these spikes happening at random intervals throughout the whole song. There must have been about 100 of them. We'd spend a day on it then listen back and still find loads more things wrong. But we would magnify them, grab them and wipe them out. It didn't have any effect on John's voice because we were just dealing with the air surrounding him in between phrases. So that took about a week to clean up before it was even usable and transferable to a DAT master. Putting fresh music to it was the easy part! 'Free As A Bird', however, wasn't a quarter as noisy as 'Real Love' and only a bit of EQ was needed to cure most problems."

When Lynne took the "treated" Lennon DATs to McCartney's studio for the overdub sessions, all concerned were adamant that analogue equipment and die-hard techniques should be used wherever possible. With McCartney's studio not surprisingly well stocked with a Neve console, generous vintage outboard and Neumann U47s for vocals, the only specialised item of equipment needed to be brought in from the outside world was an Oberheim OBX-8 analogue keyboard for what Lynne describes as "a soft, synthesised pad sound, played by Paul. What we were trying to do was create a record that was timeless, so we steered away from using state of the art gear. We didn't want to make it fashionable. It's just making the statement that they are all here playing together after all these years. So while it sounds fresh and new, it wouldn't have been out of place on the *White Album*."

Rumours abounded for some time about whether The Beatles would work on a third "new" track for inclusion on the third *Anthology* collection of rarities in the autumn of 1996. Although the three members did begin work on yet another incomplete Lennon song in February 1995, it was deemed unworkable in its raw state and in late February 1996 a final message came from McCartney's office that any plans had been scrapped. Asked whether he believes this signified the ultimate chapter in The Beatles' story, Sir George Martin replies, "Probably." Only time will tell.

chapter five

the art school dance goes on forever

"It was just the right time to get all serious."   **Manfred Mann**

The sound canvas which had been stained with the day-glo imagery of the Sixties was suddenly wiped clean in 1970. Innocence had long been lost, man finally reached the moon in the previous July and The Beatles had dissolved in a cloud of sibling polarity. The dynamic live sound which defined most Sixties recordings and was borne of groups performing together in large studio spaces was now being replaced by a more controlled means of recording. Rock bands were even beginning to turn their backs on the singles chart and the "hit song" in favour of creating extended pieces of music to showcase their musical proficiency and blow the listener's mind. With the availability of more tracks on which to record in the studio (increasing in Britain from eight to sixteen in 1971 and sixteen to twenty-four in 1973), bands and their producers could plan more lavish works and incorporate the use of newer instruments such as the Moog synthesiser. Books and films were often the inspiration for rock compositions of classical proportions, while some albums were tied to mythology and other-worldly conceptual themes. It was loud, pompous, high brow stuff – the kind of intellectual craftsmanship to wow duffle-coated university students but alienate more down to earth types who just wanted something to tap their feet to.

Few bands managed to exploit both markets, but Genesis came

closer than most with their tight, highly sharpened instrumental skills and a keen sense of melody. David Hentschel began working with Genesis in the summer of 1971, initially in a pure engineering role for the band's album, *Nursery Cryme*. Hentschel was then a staff engineer at Trident Studios – a place to which many top engineers eventually gravitated from major studios such as Decca and Abbey Road – and soon progressed to production after proving his worth on albums by Van Der Graaf Generator, Genesis, Wings and Harry Nilsson. He remembers Trident as being one of the most technically precocious studios in London at that time. "It was a case of anything goes and if anyone had an idea it got tried out and we used to abuse all the equipment," he says. "Trident had installed an eight-track machine just before I started at the age of seventeen in 1969, although we were still doing some four-track sessions for about another year. Then in 1971 we got a 3M sixteen-track machine which was the first in Europe. It was extraordinary to suddenly be able to record drums in stereo which we had never been able to do before. You might have done a stereo spread of the whole rhythm track, but the eight-track recording tended to feature mono drums, mono bass and guitars. With sixteen tracks, we could have stereo drums, and sometimes three tracks of drums which was pretty extravagant then. We might record the bass drum on one track and have a stereo mix of the rest of the kit."

The 'additional flexibility given to engineers through the use of sixteen-track machines explains the sudden clarity of rhythm tracks, particularly drums, which came to fruition in the early Seventies – a period when strict close miking was the order of the day and little or no room ambience would creep into the mix. With backing track sessions still essentially recorded live, musicians and their amplifiers were screened off from each other to achieve isolation, as paranoia over separation mounted in the control room. Even with the increased multitracking facilities, engineers were schooled to balance backing tracks perfectly at the point of recording. But the advent of twenty-four-track recording changed everything. "We had become so settled with sixteen-track that when the Studer twenty-four-track came along two years later, we didn't know what to do with it at first and it took us quite a while before we started making the most of it," Hentschel says. "Most of the time, whatever was being recorded was being done in stereo, even a set of congas. Because of that, mixes started getting boring with everything panned left or right. It was a while before people used twenty-four tracks for an arrangement by splitting things up and making things easier to mix by having certain things on different tracks."

The sessions for *Nursery Cryme* coincided with the studio's changeover to sixteen-track, which meant that many songs were started on eight, then completed with additional overdubs on sixteen tracks. In order to keep firm control over certain sections of a song's instrumentation in complex arrangements, up to five instruments would occupy one track of the master. "There were only four guys playing so there were lots of little overdubs," Hentschel says. "One track would have loads of stuff on it and it would make the mix very difficult, because in those days the desks were quite small. You didn't have enough faders to split one track between four or five faders in the mix, so you had to manually change the settings on each track as you mixed. It got the adrenalin going if nothing else! Mixing was a real fun experience then and a lot more creative than today. It was almost like a performance in itself. In an artistic sense I think it's a shame that automation has happened, although we all use those tools and probably couldn't do without them now. But there was something exciting about doing a mix without it. Occasionally you would get a moment of magic that might come from going out on a limb or just cocking up. Those create instances that you wouldn't plan normally, whereas the whole emphasis on the use of computers is to achieve the perfect result. But it's rarely the perfect result that makes for a great record."

The experience accumulated by Hentschel while at Trident was so intense and varied that rarely would he feel insecure about working with any type of artist. Trident actively encouraged engineers to specialise in certain areas of music, such as rock, MOR pop or classical. "Although we did specialise, any of us at any time could be thrown into a different kind of session which meant that you got a very broad grounding in how to record different types of music and different instruments," he says. "And it's only experience that tells you how to judge the placing of mics, by looking at the room and gauging the acoustics. You sure as hell don't learn it by plugging eight outputs from a drum machine into a console and sticking some reverb on it!"

If they were to divulge their true feelings, a number of producers who worked with bands during the early progressive rock period would admit that they were rather pushed to shed any new light on the omnipresent musical complexities coming into the studio from the rehearsal room. Even Gerry Bron, who after working with Manfred Mann in the late Sixties moved on to produce Uriah Heep, found it difficult to justify his presence at times. "Someone was always hanging around calling themselves the producer but they just let the band get on with it," he says. "I think the musicians were creating the records as much as the producers. The first real sign that Uriah Heep was going in any direction was with a track called 'Gypsy', and that was recorded just the way they rehearsed it. We probably embellished it, but we didn't change it much, so I think a lot of that was coming from the band." The same could be said of Genesis's early music, although David Hentschel's production expertise would prove vital to their later projects, after the departure of lead singer, Peter Gabriel.

Tricks In The Tale

With five years' invaluable experience at Trident under his belt, Hentschel turned freelance in 1974 as a producer, engineer and synthesiser player although he would often return to the studio for selective projects. One of which was the milestone Genesis album, *A Trick Of The Tail*, which marked Phil Collins' debut as the band's lead vocalist. Hentschel describes the making of the album in 1975 as "a good buzz. It started off with us going into the studio without a singer and we had just about got all the tracks down on tape. It seemed that lorry loads of cassette demos were arriving from singers who wanted to audition for the band after Peter Gabriel left. We got two or three guys down to Trident to audition to the tracks we had already cut, but they just didn't find the right person. Then Phil mentioned that he fancied having a crack at one of the songs and he did a bloody good job of it basically. From there on it was him. A lot of people used to say that his and Peter's voice sounded quite similar, and on some songs they did. But Phil was secretly dying to do it, there's no doubt about that. Once he got the shot it was hard to hold him back. On some albums you just know that there's something special about them, just in the way they develop and the sessions were really happening. Because Phil was new to the vocals, he was full of beans and that enthusiasm rubbed off on everyone around. When it came out it got rave reviews, and that was a real turning point in their career."

Rhythm tracks and vocals for the 1976 follow-up album, *Wind And Wuthering*, were recorded in two weeks at Relight Studios in Holland where, unlike many London studios at the time, it boasted a large live room with ample space for Tony Banks' massive keyboard selection and Collins' three drum kits. "I've done quite a lot of albums in residential studios but two weeks is long enough, especially if you are working quite intensely which you do with a band more so than with a solo artist," says Hentschel. "When you are a producer or an engineer, you are working flat out all the time. Once you have cut the tracks, all the members of the band want to do their overdubs so they are queuing up in the studio to get their bit done. But the poor old producer and engineer don't get a break at all, they're at it hammer and tongs! Also, living in a confined space, you start to get on each other's nerves, but that album worked out really well. We returned to Trident to finish off the overdubs and backing vocals, and do the mix. The guys were very well rehearsed, having spent a month getting difficult arrangements together like 'One For The Vine' and 'Eleventh Earl Of Mar', so by the time that we got to Holland, pretty much everything was in the right place. We never got into the situation where the band would be writing in the studio, not while I was working with them anyway!"

In 1978, with the band reduced to a trio following guitarist Steve Hackett's solo career move, Genesis began the first phase of their shift towards a more commercial approach to their music, which was heralded by the international hit singles, 'Follow You Follow Me' and 'Many Too Many'. Many of the tracks contained on the parent album, *And Then There Were Three*, continued the technoflash flavour so dominant on previous albums, but there were subtle differences, as Hentschel explains: "There was a conscious decision to try and do some more tracks that were radio-friendly, and if not three minutes long, then maybe four and a bit. They had an awareness that it was necessary for them to do it, but I think they would have been just as happy to carry on the way they were before. Of course, they became even more commercially aware after Phil's solo success. Even on the last album I did with them, *Duke*, there were a couple of his numbers on there which were more song-orientated than big arrangements. He was always into Motown and that went way back to when I first worked with him and he was about eighteen or nineteen. That's where his heart was really. He was always slightly frustrated because Tony and Mike were such prolific songwriters in Genesis and always had been. But *Duke* was the first opportunity for him to contribute two or three songs of his own. Then after the monster success of 'In The Air Tonight', I think Genesis just had to lean a little that way."

In fact, Genesis continued to embrace those commercial values with increased flair on later albums such as *Genesis* and *Invisible Touch* – right up until Collins' departure from the band in 1997, after which ex-Stiltskin vocalist Ray Wilson took his place for the album *Calling All Stations*. Although a poor international seller in comparison to previous works, this release managed to merge the pastoral acoustic moments and intricate arrangements of the Gabriel years and the band's later pop sensibilities in a manner which, on reflection, has great appeal – an opinion justified by the reaction to Genesis's 1998 live dates. Whether the band will be able to survive such a radical personnel change for more than one album remains to be seen.

Closer To The Edge

Much of Yes's conceptualism was apparent before the music was placed on the turntable: from 1971, progressive rock art king, Roger Dean assumed their designer's role and concocted potent, mysterious images of faraway landscapes on their album sleeves – the favoured accessory upon which to "roll a number" while "digging" the "vibes" contained within. Guitarist Steve Howe joined the band in the spring of 1970, replacing Peter Banks, and quickly became embroiled in sessions at London's Advision Studios for *The Yes Album* – the band's third. Making his debut as co-producer was Eddie Offord, who had engineered their previous album, *Time And A Word*. It marked the beginning of a long-running relationship between the band and Offord which would extend for many years. "I think it was luck and good timing that made the collaboration with Eddie last for as many albums as it did," says Steve Howe. "We could see quite quickly in his work that he was very in tune with us and could understand us even though we were playing a lot of busy stuff together.

"There were different lines he could focus on and get the sounds and pull the thing together, and we were very pleased about this. He had a terrific effect on our sound as a group and although he always had a musical opinion, he would never interfere musically. I think he sensed that there were plenty of other people taking care of that! But what he did was bring in a logical engineering perspective into it, saying, 'You can't do that, but you can do this,' or 'If you want to do that, it has to be done this way,' and so on. So we were doing things we thought had never been done before, transplanting music from one part to another, and doing crazy things like whirling microphones around in the studio and miking up amps that were on the floor, pointing up at the ceiling. We had used a Leslie speaker on my guitar and we wanted a kind of Leslie-ish, rotating sound so we did that one day. In fact, Michael Tait, who was working with Yes for a long time [and would later form his internationally-successful staging company Tait Towers], had the wonderful job of hurling the mic around. We just experimented within our own comparatively limited resources and we attempted to make something sound different. I don't think we realised just how different it was until we finished *The Yes Album* and heard what an almost peculiar-sounding record it was, yet it sounded so good."

Common to all recordings in the Yes canon was, and still is, the mighty bass sound of Chris Squire – surely a reference point for all aficionados of the instrument. His sense of melody, rhythm and uncompromising power was in evidence from the band's 1969 debut, although it was through Eddie Offord's production skills that its presence was brought to the foreground, especially on key numbers such as 'Roundabout' (from 1971's *Fragile*) – a song which began life in 1970 as a Howe guitar instrumental. Essentially a composite bass track, Squire doubled his trademark Rickenbacker 4001S with an acoustically-miked Gibson jazz guitar from Howe's extensive collection. Whereas Sunn amps regularly played a part in Squire's studio sound at this time, it was a vintage Marshall which gave this bass track its spiky edge. Offord has informed that the "secret" of the percussive "click" bass sound lay in boosting the treble on the amp, keeping a workable level of distortion, and rolling off the bass end. The lack of low frequencies delivered by the amp at this stage was compensated by mixing in a DI feed which introduced the bottom end. This approach to recording Squire's bass became a constant feature of Yes sessions for many years.

In hindsight, it might seem that the computer-assisted mixdown technology prevalent today was born for mixing the long and highly complex tracks for which Yes became famous. Yet all they and Offord could rely on was the editing block and a razor blade. "When we mixed, sometimes the same section would get mixed on its own because it had a different style of orchestration," Offord recalls. "So if you had something quite heavy going on in one section, followed by an acoustic passage, then you might think to mix the two sections separately. But the art was in perfecting the overlap on the edit. So when we finished a section, everyone would say, 'Right, now don't move a thing on the desk, because if you do, the next section won't work!' Then we would sit there for the next hour trying to get the next section right but, of course, somewhere in there you were bound to move something. You'd stick the two bits together and then realise, 'Oh, the hi-hat's dropped in volume.' So you have to mix that section again! But really you only had to mix the last two bars to make sure the hi-hat transferred well over the edit point. With an edit section, we would have to decide early on that a piece of music was going to stay that length, otherwise it could mean two edit sections, which in turn might result in something like fourteen separate small edits. That's not to say it was a crime or anything, it's just that we were trying to keep it to a minimum. Certainly we had to record with edits in mind."

David Hentschel was just as quick off the mark to adopt multitrack editing in his work with Genesis, especially, he says, on the longer tracks, of which there were many – too many. "We would tend to record those in sections, especially if a track was quite demanding," he says. "Occasionally with some that they would play right the way through, we would edit parts of two takes together. We might have done a really good take, but thought we'd do one more for luck. That might have had a really good middle section that we would chop in and build a master from the two performances."

But nothing that Hentschel did with an editing block ever matched the ruthless appetite for the razor blade which American producer, Richard Perry displayed when Hentschel engineered Carly Simon's *No Secrets* sessions for him at Trident. "He was a fucking nightmare!" he says. "He would drive the session musicians to distraction because it would not be uncommon to do sixty or seventy takes on one number. 'You're So Vain' was one of them and it seemed that for every song, he would do takes forever. The guy had a photographic memory and he would remember every single bar of every single take. So once there were seventy takes in the can he would spend God knows how long editing the best sections together until he got what he wanted, sometimes only one or two bars long. He used to use people like Barry Morgan and Herbie Flowers who were great players, very amenable and very hard to upset. But these poor guys, they'd come into the control room and the looks on their faces were unbelievable. They'd be pleading with him, 'Please, not another take!' They had peaked a long way back and had completely lost it. They didn't know what they were playing anymore."

As well as using considerable editing to weave together a seamless work of extravagance, Yes were not averse to attempting complete, blade-less mixes, even though it often resulted in frustration and sweaty brows. One such occasion was the mix of the title track of *Going For The One* in 1977, where the band and engineers John Timperley and Dave Richards (of Queen fame) mixed it twenty-seven times before all agreed on the definitive version. "What we were trying to do was get the ultimate mix all in one hit," Steve Howe explains. "We didn't want to edit this and edit that, because there were about five or six of us at the desk, moving faders and knobs around and so the music kept on changing. But it was me who said, 'I know which mix is the best.' They were each saying things like, 'I think twenty-five is the best', 'No, seventeen was better.' I said, 'Number two. We got it right the second time round.' We had been going on and on with all these mixes, trying to make it perfect, not knowing that we'd done the job so early on. And we might have come to that conclusion without me having remembered it, but it really stuck out in my mind. And that's what teamwork is all about, people noticing things that might not be directly to do with their job. Drummers often come up with good ideas for guitarists. That's a good collaboration."

Based on the Shastric scriptures, the 1973 double set, *Tales Of Topographic Oceans*, promised everything as a concept but it still could not match the success of the ultimate Yes classic – *Close To The Edge*. "I think the production ideas were at their strongest on *Close To The Edge* in the way that we used the music to steer us towards weird ways of using sound," Howe says. "The parts were becoming so refined and intricate yet every part was getting its own sound. It started more with *Fragile*, then *Close To The Edge* followed where there are only three tracks, one of which takes up a whole side. 'Siberian Khatru' was very much in the Yes rock vein, like 'South Side Of The Sky' and 'Starship Trooper'. A very playable, straight ahead kind of song. But as well as having that rock element, there were certain aspects of our musicality and orchestration that were always bubbling along and setting us on a course for great things.

"Eddie was having a tremendous effect on our sound but also in our lives as a person, and he hadn't yet got burned out by the touring [Offord was also the band's live sound engineer]. So Eddie was clear-minded, the group had put together the first concept that we could hang our hat on and it was a marvellously creative time. What we wanted to do on that album were things we'd never done before. We'd never played anything that long before, used sound effects or intricate timings. We had effects and bits of music flying in from tapes that we had recorded separately, such as a church organ that Rick played in a London church which was recorded and flown in to the sixteen-track tape for overdubs."

After personnel crises and an inevitable break which saw Rick Wakeman record spectacular solo albums including *The Six Wives Of Henry VIII*, *Journey To The Centre Of The Earth* and *The Myths And Legends Of King Arthur And The Knights Of The Round Table*, Yes regrouped in Montreux, Switzerland in late 1976 to begin work on *Going For The One*, which again featured the remote recording of Wakeman and a church organ for the track, 'Parallels' – but this time linked to the band via the telephone system. "Rick was playing in a church, live with us down at the studio in Montreux," Howe says. "He was about ten kilometres up the road and connected to the studio by telephone cables. We had rented these two telephone lines to give us stereo signals for the left and right organ, then on another telephone line we sent him the signal of us playing in mono. We must have spent about two hours getting the monitoring right before we started playing. That album was very good in terms of production, particularly 'Turn Of The Century' which is one of my all-time Yes favourites."

Towards the end of the most successful Yes line-up (Jon Anderson, Chris Squire, Rick Wakeman, Alan White and Howe), it is widely regarded that the band lost its way a little in terms of production. Matters were not made easy on 1978's *Tormato* by Wakeman's extensive use of the Polymoog synthesiser which failed to blend with Howe's guitar. "*Tormato* had a lot of detail and the mixes were very time-consuming and perfectionistic, but it didn't have the character of sound that some of others had, mainly I suppose because we were producing ourselves and there was no one else at the steering wheel," explains the guitarist. "It was also very difficult for me to settle down on some of those tracks. But most of what Rick was playing was great for me, in that he was multi-keyboard and I was a multi-guitarist in the sense that I was playing steel guitar and other instruments in the guitar family. Rick was operating in a similar way, but if anything I was being led on by those opportunities. I had always played a lot of different guitars on stage to add colour. In the studio there were no barriers for me. I could be using a Gibson stereo guitar with a delay on one side or two sitar guitars. The impossible was possible and that meant that on stage I was having to find a way to simulate those records, and it was constantly stretching me."

With the end of the Seventies came the news that both Anderson and Wakeman had quit the band and, even more shocking, they had been replaced by two newcomers – Buggles vocalist Trevor Horn and keyboard player Geoff Downes – who had recently spent time at Number One in the singles chart with 'Video Killed The Radio Star'. Confusion reigned: had the remaining Yes members lost their marbles? These were *pop stars* after all. Howe explains: "While a split was happening in the band, Chris, Alan and myself were rehearsing and preparing music that hopefully Jon and Rick were going to like and build around whatever they had. It wasn't possible at that time, but we had been talking about what would happen if there was a split and Chris was raving about the Buggles album, which the rest of us also liked. Chris suggested we ask them to join and although they didn't say yes immediately, they came over to spend a few days trying out some ideas to see if they would work and we saw that they had some really good music of their own. So we said to them that if they wanted to join, we would pool all the ideas, all the music and make it a genuine collaboration. The responsibility of filling the space left by Jon and Rick would have been a pretty huge and difficult one without us accommodating it."

The recording of *Drama* at the Townhouse saw a brief reunion with Eddie Offord who produced several backing tracks, but Howe says that most of the technical and production assistance came from engineer, Hugh Padgham and Horn, who within four years would become the most sought-after producer in Britain. "Being in the vocal position and not being short of production opinions, Trevor was able to guide us through some ideas and it became a real team again," Howe says. "In fact, *Drama* was mixed by Trevor and myself with Gary Langan and Julian Mendelsohn at SARM East in Whitechapel."

Pressure to complete the album in time for a tour was so great that holidays had to be cancelled, while Howe booked Gerry Bron's Roundhouse Studios in Chalk Farm to work for two weeks on guitar overdubs. "I was receiving the tapes of backing tracks that I'd played on every couple of days and I would simply concentrate on recording these guitar tracks on my own and finishing the songs," he recalls. "We were very behind. It was a very big project to take on in the timeframe we had allowed for it because something like 'Machine Messiah' was an involved track. We could have remixed that again really and brought it even more to the fore, but I am quite happy with that album."

Drama included the re-working of a Buggles song, 'I Am A Camera', which with the input of Yes became 'Into The Lens'. "Yes put all the dramatic stuff around it, like the intros and some other ideas," Howe says. "That wasn't the case on every number, in fact there are some numbers that Trevor and Geoff didn't write very much of. 'Tempus Fugit' and 'Does It Really Happen?' were written by Chris, Alan and myself in essence. But the whole album was split five ways because overall the collaboration was a very equal balance. 'Into The Lens' was probably the best example of what Trevor and Geoff did but

'Machine Messiah' was the biggest collaboration."

Manning The Workhouse

Although Manfred Mann – the band – became known to the public throughout the Sixties as purveyors of fine pop, Manfred Mann (real name: Michael Lubowitz) – the musician – made the decision in November 1969 to develop his other, more abstract talents with the formation of Manfred Mann Chapter Three as Vertigo recording artists. In hindsight, Mann now looks upon Chapter Three as "a mistake and an over-reaction to the past" – one which lasted all of eleven months. "It was just the right time to get all serious," he says. "Mike Hugg and I set ourselves certain parameters, like we wouldn't have a guitar player. So there was a rule there for a start. Then we were going to write our own songs, but I'm not much of a writer. There came a point where I realised that I couldn't just do anything I pleased because of our structure. We had done two albums and a third which was never released, and I just thought it was time to start again."

Mann got it right next time around with his Earth Band, formed in 1972 with Mick Rogers on vocals and guitar. For the first time in his career, Mann was now working without any preconceptions or a master plan, but such factors contributed to the natural evolvement of a new, classically-biased sound for the Seventies. He admits, however, that the earliest Earth Band line-up performed less convincingly on record than on stage. "I don't think the records were as good as they later became," he says. "I think that's a common paradox in the business, that a lot of bands who make good records can't seem to translate them well live, and vice versa."

Despite their progressive album stance, Manfred Mann's Earth Band took a leap into the singles chart in October 1973 with 'Joybringer', which was based on 'Jupiter' from Gustav Holst's *The Planets* suite, and recorded at Mann's own South London studio, the Workhouse, on twenty-four-track. Mann states that it was Mick Rogers who brought the idea into the fold. "Mick had been playing it with a band in Australia, using that theme," he says. "But they had called it 'Make Your Stash', and it was about drugs and all kinds of stuff that we avoid writing about these days! But it was a great tune. So I got hold of a record of Holst's *Planets* Suite and heard 'Jupiter', the bringer of joy, and it really did sound joyous so we cobbled together some appropriate lyrics. But I had to stretch the timing of the middle section to make it 4/4, rather than Holst's original 3/4 tempo. I was surprised at how successful it was, but it had a nice spirit and received a lot of airplay."

Like Genesis and Yes, the Earth Band's music relied heavily on editing. But unlike the aforementioned bands, the purpose was to ruthlessly reconstruct album tracks as more concise versions for singles. Prime examples were the band's 1976 cover of Bruce Springsteen's 'Blinded By The Light' and Robbie Robertson's 'Davy's On The Road Again' from 1978, which both featured the unmistakable, golden vocal tones of Chris Thompson. "We arranged and rehearsed 'Blinded By The Light' in one room at the Workhouse and recorded it mostly live in the downstairs studio, but only after we had done it for the album (*The Roaring Silence*) did we realise that there was some commercial magic buried within it," Mann says. "But the single was done in a much more complicated way compared to anything on the album. This was in the days before editing and crossfading between multitrack machines became easy, and originally there were all different bits and pieces of music that you don't even hear because they were all cut out. Sections were changing tempo and going into half time and double time, but within it was the germ of what 'Blinded By The Light' was to become.

"It was the most difficult track to make that one could ever imagine, because having played it and recorded it, we had to somehow make it into something coherent and it took months of crossfading before we even started to approximate what was released. The 'She broke down…' line originally occurred at the end of every chorus until it all got edited. When we finished the final mix, I wasn't sure whether we'd made a single or not because the whole process had been so mechanical that I was confused. But in relation to the total recording, I was happy with the edits and it was a miracle how we managed to achieve a result at all. 'Davy's On The Road Again' was the same kind of thing. The magic of that was in the first minute, so to find a way to somehow get back to that first minute I constructed a little moody, insignificant passage for the middle section."

At the time of my meeting with Mann, at the Workhouse in the spring of 1994, he was many months into the making of an album which finally saw the light of day two years later. According to those who have worked with him, such long lead times are not unusual for the native South African, whose indecisiveness in the studio is the stuff of legend. He is also quick to point out what he sees are his shortcomings. "I don't think I'm much of a record producer even though I'm still producing now," he admits. "The only thing I have going for me is a sense of dissatisfaction and I don't settle for things that other people will let slip by. I just keep going until I end up with something that pleases me. Sometimes I go on too long and it can take me years to make an album. The only time I am convinced about something is when I say it's wrong. The biggest problem with the Earth Band was maintaining consistency."

While Mann's tendency to question everything he does as a musician originally came to Gerry Bron's attention on the 'Ha Ha Said The Clown' session, Bron was in for even more frustration when he invited Mann to contribute a keyboard overdub on 'July Morning' from Uriah Heep's album, *Look At Yourself.* "It is one thing being a perfectionist, but a perfectionist who cannot make up his mind is another," says Bron of Mann. "'July Morning' had a very long ending with the same repeated chord sequence and nothing much really happening, and I told the band that we couldn't release it like that. Ken Hensley didn't really want to change anything, but I made the suggestion of getting Manfred in to play a solo on the Moog that he had been getting into. Manfred heard the track and commented, 'Gerry, I can't play anything on that, it's just the same chords going on again and again, and it's a terrible piece of music, what do you expect me to do?' After a lot of arm-twisting, I finally got him behind the Moog but he wasn't at all happy about the way he'd played, despite it sounding fantastic to me. He said, 'Well, if you think that was fantastic, I can do much better.' He went on to record about ten solos, all brilliant and all completely different to each other, but he still wasn't happy. Thankfully, I had saved five of the takes and put together a composite solo track from the best chunks."

Bron was far from being the only producer to endure frustration at the hands of a musician in this way, and dissatisfaction with performances in the studio continues to be a common phenomenon, especially among the more talented players. Even Jeff Beck. When the legendary guitarist worked with George Martin at AIR Studios on his 1975 album, *Blow By Blow*, he would take rough mixes home with him on a regular basis, only to be constantly displeased by his guitar playing. After replacing one particular solo on countless occasions, Beck remained silent for more than a month. He allegedly called Martin, saying that having lived with this solo for some time he still was unhappy, and could he go back and record it one more time. Martin's reply was, "But Jeff, the album's already in the shops."

Cultural Fusion

With his pride more than a little wounded by the escape of Fleetwood Mac from his Blue Horizon label, Mike Vernon turned his attention on developing the eclectic blend of music emanating from Dutch rock band, Focus, in 1971. Signed to New York-based Sire Records through Belgium's RTM Music, Focus was introduced to Vernon by Seymour Stein, then an American partner in Blue Horizon. But because of his loyalty to the blues, Vernon very nearly passed on the band for his label. "Seymour thought that Focus would be a band I'd like to produce although the whole idea of this band didn't really appeal to me, and they certainly didn't seem right for Blue Horizon," Vernon says. "Seymour drew my attention to the fact that if they ended up selling loads of records for Blue Horizon, it would be no bad thing. I didn't subscribe to that view at the time, but it's very easy to be blinkered and follow only one particular avenue. Nevertheless, Seymour persuaded me to see the band in Holland and, sure enough, they were the most incredible live band I had ever seen. The power of Jan Akkerman and Thijs Van Leer alone was enough to give you heart palpitations and I couldn't stop talking or thinking about them. When we came to make the *Moving Waves* album, it was like a dream although it wasn't the easiest album to make."

The sessions for *Moving Waves* and the unexpected hit, 'Hocus Pocus' – no doubt the first rock instrumental single ever to feature yodelling – were held at Chelsea's Sound Techniques and engineered by Jerry Boys who is now to be found running Livingstone Studios.

Vernon had already recorded there as the producer of Mighty Baby, a break away band from The Action. But the Focus sessions were an entirely different breed. "Sound Techniques was a real ramshackle place but it had character, especially in Jerry's capable hands," Vernon says. "The control room was quite poky and situated above the studio which was very light with lots of windows. The band pretty much played the tracks together and although there were obviously some overdubs, there weren't too many considering the sound of 'Hocus Pocus'. There were two Revoxes which were perpetually loaded with quarter-inch tape and whizzed around at different speeds to create various lengths of delays and reverbs, which was all very Heath Robinson. But in a way that's what was so good about it because there was this great feel about the sound. I used to use a lot of tape delay, especially as Jerry was so good with it and it was quite a challenge to come up with an album of that quality in such a crappy studio."

Work on 'Hocus Pocus' took Vernon and the band way past midnight on most sessions, and Vernon grins when he recalls Thijs Van Leer's manic yodelling overdubs. "It used to look more painful than it was in reality, because it was quite easy for him to do it," he says. "He was bright red by the time he'd finished yodelling the high bit! When Thijs got to work he became so energised, especially when he played flute." Vernon describes Van Leer and Akkerman as academical opposites who were constantly battling to be top dog. "Thijs was very fluent in music notation but Jan couldn't read or write a note, and I even doubted he knew what the notes were in any given chord. The tension which came from this was what made Focus what it was." The band later recorded at Chipping Norton Studios – Vernon's second home in the Seventies – where their producer witnessed the gradual breakdown between the two leading members. "It was probably the worst ten days I've ever spent in a studio," says Vernon. "The creative tension that was so apparent before had evolved into friction, to the point where Thijs couldn't be in the same room with Jan, and vice versa, and the tracks we worked on were pretty much individual efforts. The others in the band would play with Thijs, and then Jan would come in and record his guitar parts at midnight. When you listen to the later music it doesn't feel right and it's not surprising."

Horslips may not have become a household name in Britain, but in the Seventies they were outselling every major international act in the record shops of their native Ireland. Formed in 1970, Horslips virtually invented Celtic rock – a fusion of traditional Irish folk tunes and mystical themes with the contemporary rock styles of the day – and set the template for Big Country, Clannad, Runrig and, to a large extent, U2. The band's five ex-members – bassist, Barry Devlin, fiddle and mandolin player, Charles O'Connor, guitarist, John Fean, flute and keyboard player, Jim Lockhart and drummer, Eamon Carr – believe that part of the reason for their lack of commercial success in Britain was due to a political backlash against their country following the horrific Bloody Sunday massacre in Northern Ireland in January 1972. Not that this appeared to affect Phil Lynott and Thin Lizzy, who borrowed much from the Horslips melting pot.

The release of Horslips' debut album, *Happy To Meet, Sorry To Part* (Ireland's fastest-selling album of the Seventies), was heralded in England with a support slot on a Steeleye Span tour where a cult status was nurtured. The album was recorded on location at Longfield House in Tipperary with producer and engineer, Alan O'Duffy at the controls of the Rolling Stones Mobile. "It was a wonderful environment in which to make an album, and very cheap too," says O'Connor. Subsequently mixed at Olympic in London and released in November 1972, the album marked the first time a twenty-four-track studio had ever operated on Irish soil and national media reaction bordered on hysteria.

"Everything we did was the genuine article – tunes that had been passed down through the generations," Lockhart says. "No one had ever given Irish music this treatment – we wanted to take the melodies that were inherently Irish or Celtic and put them into a different form of music."

It was Horslips' next album which contained all the elements which would truly define Celtic rock. *The Tain*, from September 1973, was a musical documentation of the Tain Bo Cuailgne, or the Cattle Raid of Cooley, the 500 BC Ulster conflict between the men of Conaught and the possessive Queen Maeve, and O'Connor agrees that its unusual formula successfully captured the true essence of Horslips. "When we were planning our first album, we thought about doing a conceptual piece although it didn't happen until *The Tain*," he says. "Barry and Jimmy were into pop/rock, Johnny and I were interested in the traditional elements and Eamon was the poet. We found that in organising a conceptual album, every band member had a job to fulfil. Apart from me designing the record sleeve and Eamon writing poetic liner notes, it was a way of pulling five people together and getting more work out of them than just a set of songs. It was Eamon's idea to use that Irish saga as the theme of the album and at one time there was even a possibility of using the music in a stage show by the Abbey Theatre."

In Carr's mind, his band's embracing of Ancient Irish mythology was a meaningful way of establishing a unique image. "Before *The Tain* there was no clear definition of young Ireland," he says. "Musically, Ireland was probably best known in America for The Clancy Brothers and in Britain for The Dubliners. Yet we felt betrayed and it was important to express oneself in a way that helped establish an identity. I had been a Mod and my musical background was a standard one of R&B and soul, but my grandfather had a brilliant ceilidh band and I had no problem with that stuff either. So there was always an element of schizophrenia, that on one hand I would be into this traditional roots music, then on the other I'd be into Motown and Stax.

"Coming from County Meath, where there is Newgrange and all the mythological sites, I was very conscious of Ancient Ireland. But allied with that, I was into reading Marvel comics and Stan Lee was a huge influence. And I was very much aware of all the traditional Irish mythological superheroes. The merging of those two cultures was the kind of stuff you used to see in Oz and it only took a simple leap of imagination to visualise how these legendary tales might be placed into a musical format. The parallel was there between the Celtic and the Marvel comic heroes. But it wasn't a glib thing and you couldn't treat it lightly, otherwise it would have come out like Hawkwind. It had to be approached properly and fortunately I had studied Old Irish at college, so it was a case of delving back into these subjects and doing a lot of research, like I was preparing a thesis. Getting deeper into the story behind *The Tain*, I began to discover things that they never taught us at school. There had been elements of Eastern philosophy infiltrating into rock 'n' roll, possibly through George Harrison's interest in the Maharishi, but now I was examining Western mystery traditions and it was taking Horslips on a new journey."

Again with Alan O'Duffy producing, backing tracks for *The Tain* were recorded at Escape Studios in Kent, while the remaining music was assembled at Richard Branson and Virgin's newly-acquired residential studio, the Manor. The album's last track, 'Time To Kill', included an eerie reversed vocal refrain which sounded as if the band had disturbed the ghost of Cu Chulainn. "Someone had edited a piece of tape backwards on to the end of 'Time To Kill' by accident," Carr explains. "We were lounging around the floor of the studio and heard this, and thought, 'Hang on, this sounds really neat, we'll keep it in!'"

Devlin, who after the group's demise in 1980 went on to direct promo videos for U2 and become a leading screenplay writer, comments, "With the additional folk instruments we had a massive range of sound textures at our disposal which wasn't available to a regular rock line-up. But the melodies were always there and even during the times when we got into the heavyweight concepts, we still believed in the power of the three-minute song. There was a lot of sweat involved in trying to get the backing tracks really tight and swinging. In those days, you always knew that you had to get the backing tracks done within a week, the overdubs done within another week, then your vocals and the mix would take another week or so. There was always a very tight schedule."

To The Manor Born

Encouraged by the exciting and adventurous image that recording studios had acquired through the experimental work of the mid to late Sixties, and the lucrative benefits of being in this newly-thriving business, several new influential and independent studios sprang up all over Britain in the Seventies. In 1974, The Moody Blues took over Decca's Studio One and producer Tony Clarke, along with a specialist crew from Westlake Audio of Los Angeles, set about building Threshold Studio there while the band was away on a nine-month world tour. Understandably reluctant to allow Decca's precious studio to be tampered with, chairman Sir Edward Lewis was eventually persuaded by Clarke to part with considerable funds with which to build what became the world's first quadrophonic studio for the company's then flagship progressive rock act.

"It was worth the fight with Sir Edward because it had been very dull and basic, with green and cream decor, and unfriendly lighting," says Clarke. "The amplifiers and speakers were quite inferior for the times, and we wanted a more conducive environment. In the end we gutted the control room and it was a tedious process because we had to raise the roof and lower the floor, which involved two massive steel girders. It took six weeks of demolition work, followed by a further six weeks for building, and we installed four Tom Hidley monitors for Quad mixing, Crown amps, a large MCI desk and several tons of Cotswold stone for baffling. Almost immediately, Justin Hayward and John Lodge went in and recorded the *Blue Jays* album without any testing. I mixed a lot of records in Quad and they all got sent to King Records in Japan for release. We were told that Quad was going to be the next big thing and so we had to do those records. But, of course, Quad never took off as expected."

The Manor was one of the biggest success stories of the decade. During their stay there in 1973, Horslips were treated to a rare preview of an all-time classic. By day, the band worked on *The Tain*, while in the evening as they relaxed and reviewed their progress, an introverted, nineteen-year-old multi-instrumentalist from Reading called Mike Oldfield was assembling both his and Virgin Records' debut album – one which would sell in excess of fifteen million copies worldwide: *Tubular Bells*. "He kept playing bits of it to us every night by a log fire," Charles O'Connor recalls. "He'd already been working on it for many months when we arrived to do our album and I think he was pleased to play what he'd done to fresh ears because I got the impression that everyone else at the Manor had grown a little sick of Mike's album by then!"

The Manor, which while under EMI's control sadly closed in the spring of 1995, was Britain's first commercially-run residential recording studio, financed by young entrepreneur, Richard Branson and built in the stables of a run-down country manor house in Shipton-on-Cherwell, Oxfordshire by engineers, Tom Newman and Simon Heyworth during 1971, with electronics assistance from Phil Newell and Dave Hughes. While still in the construction phase, with only an Ampex 300 Series four-track machine and limited hardware as temporary equipment, the Manor hosted its first demo session with local rock musicians, The Arthur Lewis Band, whose number included bassist, Mike Oldfield, fresh from Kevin Ayers And The Whole Wide World. Heyworth, now senior engineer at one of London's top music duplication operations, Chop 'Em Out, recalls that the session was little more than "a shambles" and produced music of no real value, although it did bring to the Manor's attention Oldfield's raw but impressive talents on a variety of acoustic and electric instruments. Newman immediately took a liking to the shy teenager who played him some home demos of his own unique-sounding instrumental material, recorded on a borrowed Bang & Olufson tape deck, on which he overdubbed by covering the erase head with Sellotape. The next year saw the Manor officially open for business with The Bonzo Dog Doo-Dah Band as its first clients. As the studio upgraded to an Ampex sixteen-track machine and two-inch tape, Oldfield was by now a familiar face, having become involved with the continued building work and part-time engineering. In between client sessions (on which he worked as a tape operator and occasionally guested as a guitarist), Oldfield used the downtime to begin work on *Tubular Bells* in February 1973. The first side of which was recorded in one week; the second side took even longer!

"It was new territory for all of us," says Heyworth. "None of us had accumulated much experience with multitracking and working with sixteen tracks was altogether different than the four tracks Mike had been used to in his demos. The separate little musical themes that formed the whole album were fairly arranged in Mike's mind by this time, but it was how we were going to layer all the instrumental parts that was the problem, especially as it all seemed rather rushed. It wasn't a case of him playing a piano part all the way through the record, because piano wasn't always required. So we had to record and allow for drop-outs where, say, a guitar would take over on the same track, taking care not to erase the head or tail of anything. And I was the person who would have to count Mike in and out of a drop-in." Viv Stanshall's famous introduction sequence during the finale at the end of side one was a last minute Oldfield idea which was submitted to tape just prior to a Bonzos session. "Mike brought him in and stood him in front of the mic, asking him to dramatically announce the name of any instrument he pointed to or wrote down. It was all done very quickly."

The album was mixed on a new twenty-channel console, designed and built for the Manor by Audio Developments of Staffordshire. "*Tubular Bells* was one of the most difficult albums ever to mix – a typical case of all hands on deck, but made worse by the amount of different sounds occupying each track," Heyworth says. "You'd pull up a fader with a guitar on it and it would suddenly turn into a mandolin or Farfisa organ, and all these things interweaved to make the music as a whole. So there would be Mike, Tom, myself and anyone else who happened to be around, all assigned with certain duties, and there would be points where someone had the specific task to either raise the organ fader or put echo on the acoustic guitar, or whatever. But because of all the wear that the multitrack tape had been subjected to over the course of repeated overdubbing, there was a noticeable loss of the higher frequencies but we coped in the end. The actual tubular bells themselves caused a few tense moments in the mix because Mike was adamant that they should be blaring out in the mix from the point of entry, but no matter how we tried we couldn't transfer that kind of level on the cut. Eventually, and to Richard Branson's credit, the album was pressed on heavier than standard virgin (no pun intended) vinyl, the sort normally reserved for classical records, which was able to accept higher volume signals." Interestingly, it was not Branson but his colleague, Simon Draper who saw sufficient value in *Tubular Bells* to issue the album as the Virgin label's launch product. Nineteen years later, after becoming the most successful independent label in recording history, Branson sold Virgin Records to EMI for the princely sum of £560 million.

Almost twenty years to the day after the May 1973 release of the album, Mike Oldfield returned to its formula to produce *Tubular Bells II* – a virtual re-working of the original which benefited greatly from the new generation of digital synthesisers and sampling, and the trusty production skills of Trevor Horn. Going one stage further, Oldfield's *Tubular Bells III* was due for release in 1998. Now that's what I call milking a good idea for all it's worth!

Seven years after the worldwide acclaim that followed the original *Tubular Bells*, not least due to its inclusion in the movie, *The Exorcist*,

Oldfield began work with collaborator and producer, David Hentschel on *QE2* – an album which, like Genesis's *And Then There Were Three*, kept one eye on the charts while retaining key characteristics. The album was recorded at Oldfield's Denham home in 1980 and Hentschel recalls that while working with Oldfield was a thrill, the sessions were not without their fair share of lip-biting frustration. "Mike basically had everything set up at his home," he says. "We went through a certain amount of pre-production and he had some idea of the songs he wanted to do, so we spent a few weeks during which I would go down every day and work out parts for the two of us to play. Ideas were tried out with him playing guitar and me playing synths, along to a drum machine, thrashing out some arrangements. We approached the recording as an extension of the rehearsals, so it wasn't the case of suddenly going into a studio, because we were just carrying on the way we had been working. The only thing was that at some stage, we hit the record button and built the tracks up gradually. There wasn't really a control room when we were recording. He had built a mixing room by the time we came to mix the album, but up until then he had a mixer on the floor and an Ampex tape machine in the corner, and everything was in the same room. We were just wearing headphones and playing back off the speakers.

"The frustration came in really when I would come in the next morning after a positive day's work and he'd been up all night, erasing the work we had done the day before. He suddenly decided that he didn't like it and wanted to do it completely different. So to my complete surprise, everything that we had worked on had gone! I suppose that's what happens when you're working with a reputed genius. He was probably the person I learned most from about capturing a performance. When you are producing, you have to understand when to let mistakes go. Some bum notes can actually be good and contribute to the overall picture. When a performance is communicating you don't worry at the time that something might be out of tune or out of time if you have captured some magic. And Mike was very good at that I have to say; if he's played his bollocks off but made a small mistake, that performance will stay."

chapter six

lunar legacy

"All the way through the making of it we thought that we were on to something that was going to do better than anything we had previously done. Then, with the record cover at the end, we were all pretty excited because it was the first time that the music, the lyrics and the visual design all came together."
David Gilmour on *The Dark Side Of The Moon*

Pink Floyd's lyrics have traditionally carried references to failed communication, madness, the horrors of drugs and alienation: subjects which have ironically played their part in the band's personal and professional lives. Initially the offspring of one man's eccentric musical vision, Pink Floyd has graduated from a bunch of space cadet art rockers into a universally-respected, multi-million dollar music empire, yet not without its fair share of bruised egos and shattered relationships. But as a recording outfit, seldom has the band failed to deliver anything short of sonic perfection, breaking down perceived market barriers to penetrate the imaginations of all generations.

Formed in Cambridge in 1965 by a group of well-heeled art and architecture students, within two years (The) Pink Floyd would become the darlings of London's burgeoning underground scene at venues including the Marquee and UFO at the 100 Club. Often accompanied by psychedelic oil slide backdrops and light shows, the quartet's live performances were largely unrehearsed, featuring "free-form", jazz-inspired, "freak-outs" such as the underground anthem, 'Interstellar Overdrive', which often lasted one hour, based around a single riff or chord. In many ways, the band's original leader, singer/songwriter/guitarist, Keith "Syd" Barrett was Swinging London's answer to Brian Wilson – a brilliant visionary whose career eventually suffered from an acute LSD appetite. The early Floyd sound relied heavily on Barrett's bottleneck and echo treatments to achieve his unusual and unworldly blend of guitar effects, and Rick Wright's floating keyboard riffs, while bassist Roger Waters and drummer Nick Mason fought to keep up the audio-verité momentum.

The band soon attracted the interest of Joe Boyd, the folk and blues producer who had recently taken The Incredible String Band to Elektra, and in January 1967 invited the Floyd to record their first single with him at Sound Techniques Studios in Chelsea. A deal was secured with EMI's Columbia label for the March release of 'Arnold Layne', which was launched with a press release describing the band as "musical spokesmen for a new movement which involves experimentation in all the arts". The catch, however, was that only an EMI staff producer would be allowed to work with the band. Boyd, to the band's despair, was dropped and ex-Beatles engineer-turned-producer, Norman Smith was drafted in, though it has to be said that Smith worked wonders in translating the band's live characteristics to disc. In Brian Southall's 1982 book, *Abbey Road*, Smith said of his introduction to the Floyd, "I was still into creating and developing new electronic sounds in the control room and Pink Floyd, I could see, were exactly into the same thing, it was a perfect marriage."

'Arnold Layne' was an instant smash and its vaguely Eastern hue, provided by Wright's reverberant organ, typified the new era of psychedelic England. Recorded in Abbey Road's Studio Three as The Beatles added finishing touches to *Sgt Pepper* next door in Studio Two, 'See Emily Play' was chosen as Floyd's next single. Featuring a manic keyboard solo by Wright, recorded at half speed, it paved the way for the band's debut album, *The Piper At The Gates Of Dawn*, for which Smith would pull out a stream of production tricks picked up through working with George Martin on Beatles albums up to and including *Rubber Soul*. Echo delay was used like an instrument, and guitars and vocals were recorded at non-standard speeds with liberal double tracking, while sound effects were applied to conjure an outer space atmosphere on tracks such as 'Astronomy Domine', on which manager Peter Jenner was heard through a megaphone, announcing the names of planets and stars. This was *the* seminal English underground album and Barrett's peak as an artist.

Assisting Smith was a youthful Jeff Jarratt. "My first session as a tape op was for Pink Floyd on the *Piper At The Gates Of Dawn* sessions, which was very exciting," he recalls. "I was told that I would be working on these sessions and I'd heard that they were playing at the London Polytechnic in Regent Street. So I thought it was a good idea to go and see them play to get an idea of what they were all about. It was really intriguing and I remember being quite amazed at hearing this very different sound. There may have been other groups around doing something similar but they were the first I had come across. Then they came into the studios and it was astonishing to be a part of the creative process and all the strange tape effects we used. Syd was an incredibly innovative, creative guy and great fun to work with. It still is one of my favourite albums to listen to."

Ever the adventurer, Barrett began to ingest copious amounts of LSD which took its toll drastically on the previously gentle artist. By the end of their successful first year as a recording act, Barrett had finally "lost it" as he succumbed to the drug's brain cell-withering effects. Waters, Mason and Wright began a search for a surrogate guitarist, retaining Barrett as their reclusive songwriter, in a bid to rescue the band. Initially, fellow Columbia artist, Jeff Beck was considered as a frontman, only his vocals were not his strongest asset. Then their eyes turned towards Barrett's former busking partner, David Gilmour, and on 27 January, 1968, he officially joined the band on a £7 per week wage. As an experiment, a five-man Floyd existed for as many weeks, with Gilmour supporting Barrett's rapidly declining talents on stage. On 2 March, Barrett was forced to quit.

"I'd only seen the band a few times before when they were an art school band playing 'Bo Diddley'," Gilmour says. "I quite liked the songs on their first album but I wasn't keen on them live. Quite frankly what they were doing wasn't a great turn on for me. I think probably anyone coming into a fairly well-known band and having to follow in someone else's shoes is quite hard to do. We did a few gigs with both

Syd and I in the band together and he seemed to cheer up a little when I was there. But it became obvious that it wasn't going to continue for very long like that. One day we just never picked him up. Someone said, 'Shall we pick up Syd?' and someone else said, 'No, let's not bother.' And that was the end. I feel a debt to Syd."

A *Saucerful Of Secrets*, released in June 1968, was the album which signified the dawn of the Gilmour era. Of its seven tracks, three were recorded with Barrett before the end of 1967, with the remainder performed entirely by the new regime. The only recorded example of the fated quintet is 'Set The Controls For The Heart Of The Sun', on which Gilmour was required to add a guitar overdub to Barrett's part. The album's title track, although an eerie, rambling voyage into tape and echoed slide guitar effects which one would hardly call easy listening, awkwardly indicated a new direction. Floyd's freaky approach to composition attracted the attention of the film world as directors such as Michaelangelo Antonioni and Barbet Schroeder commissioned soundtracks from the band – an area in which they were to excel over the course of the next four years. After a year or more largely spent reproducing his predecessor's riffs on stage, Gilmour's guitar was finding its own voice by the end of 1969, the year of *Ummagumma*, the double set which featured one live album and an odd collection of solo pieces, including Waters' bizarre 'Several Species Of Small Furry Animals Gathered Together In A Cave And Grooving With A Pict' and Gilmour's 'The Narrow Way'. Recording alone for the first time, Gilmour set about capturing virtually every possible sound he could squeeze from his guitar, both electronically and acoustically – "a badly recorded experiment," he says.

Throughout the next twelve months, Floyd fought for a new identity which they hoped to achieve with their 1970 album, *Atom Heart Mother* (their first Number One) recorded in collaboration with electronic music composer, Ron Geesin. "The main theme came out of a little chord sequence I'd written, which I called 'Theme From An Imaginary Western', because it sounded like The Magnificent Seven to me," Gilmour says. "Its disjointed feel happened because we recorded the group first and put the brass and choir on afterwards. We should have done the whole thing in one take. Some of it strikes me as absolute crap." But *Meddle* was the album which, after months of arduous noodling at Morgan and AIR Studios during 1971, finally set the band on its feet. Its opening track, 'One Of These Days', a kind of heavyweight answer to the *Doctor Who* TV theme, featured Waters' Binson Echorec-laden bass pulse underpinning a glorious example of Gilmour's overdriven slide work. Meanwhile the album's equal highlight, 'Echoes', was significant for its lengthy, contrasting passages, merging an infectious guitar riff with the band's first convincing use of sound effects.

"We had mostly recorded at Abbey Road up to that point but they had made the decision to stay with eight-track, while everyone else in London was moving forward," Gilmour explains. "Although we did some things at Morgan, most of *Meddle* was done at AIR where George Martin had made the sensible decision to upgrade from eight- to sixteen-track just in time for our sessions, and it was there that the album kind of fell into place. 'Echoes' was nearly twenty-five minutes long and went through all sorts of different moments, all of which are really good. It was leading the way to *Dark Side Of The Moon*. When we started work on 'Echoes' we just recorded loads of different ideas which were absolute rubbish. Then we noticed what Rick's piano sounded like when we put it through the Leslie, especially when he played a particular single note, and the piece developed from there." The foundation had been set for one of the most successful albums in rock history.

The Dark Side Of The Moon

Recorded under the working title of "Eclipse – A Piece For Assorted Lunatics", *The Dark Side Of The Moon* catapulted Pink Floyd from cult band status to a world phenomenon. Released in March 1973, it set a new precedent in record production techniques and album packaging – two qualities upon which Floyd have continued to build. In his lyrics, Waters had by now emerged as an eloquent builder of conceptual themes, namely lunacy, death, greed and alienation, while as a guitarist Gilmour was fast becoming a hero, not surprisingly as a result of his stunning lead work on 'Time' and 'Money'. Where Waters made people think, Gilmour made the listener enjoy; his spacey sound generated largely from his own guitar equipment, rather than excessive post-production console tweaking.

Abbey Road staff engineer, Alan Parsons had already worked with Floyd on *Atom Heart Mother*, and like Norman "Hurricane" Smith had also worked in the control room of Studio Two on Beatles sessions (both interestingly became best-selling recording artists in their own right). Now that the studio had finally invested in sixteen-track equipment as standard, the band were lured back to their previous recording home. The band had been preparing for the recording of the album for more than six months before they began work at Abbey Road in June 1972, and skeletal live versions performed on the road that year served as evidence that *The Dark Side Of The Moon* was always intended to be a whole conceptual piece, rather than a group of individual songs, although it did not contain a sustained narrative.

At the outset of the project, Abbey Road's staff were blissfully unaware of the eventual significance of the sessions, which produced the most important album recorded there since *Sgt Pepper*. "Pink Floyd were obviously very well-known around the building," Parsons says. "They had recorded practically everything there since *Piper At The Gates Of Dawn*. Strangely, although *Dark Side* has that big sound, there was nothing that markedly different in the way it was recorded compared to what they had done immediately before, but this time we were using two generations of sixteen tracks, recording non-Dolby on the first sixteen and with Dolby on the second sixteen. There weren't many engineers who were not appreciative of the many qualities of the band. But I must say that when I first heard their music, I was not terribly impressed. I was working at Hayes and the *Piper At The Gates Of Dawn* album had come to me for duplication, and I was thinking that if this was to be the music of the future, then I wasn't going to be looking forward to it! But then like a lot of stuff, you get to like bits of it over the course of a long period. I was very impressed with *Atom Heart Mother*. I think it was a good move and a good opportunity for me to get involved with Floyd and do that kind of thing."

Setting the mood for the music which was to follow was an introductory "heartbeat", formed by a bass drum loop and made more effective by the use of one of the early Kepex noise gates. "One thing I did which I think gave the album a certain sound was that I Kepexed everything, not only going from the first sixteen-track to the second, but also on the mix," Parsons says. "They were quite revolutionary at the time and had a very individual sound. On the heartbeats, you hear the noise being modulated by a noise gate which is an integral part of that sound. Nick Mason originally played the bass drum to a click track, then we just chose the best few bars and looped them." An overwhelming use of synthesisers, especially the Peter Zinovieff-designed Electronic Music Systems (EMS) VCS-3 and Synthi A (a suitcased synthesiser with on-board keyboard and sequencer), provided a new range of sounds, none more sinister than on the instrumental 'On The Run', for which the EMS sequencer provided the timing reference. "Everything you hear on that track, apart from the sound effects, was done live by the Synthi A," Parsons continues. "Even the hi-hat over the top of it was done on that synth. There was no means of synchronising any two performances, that's why the whole thing was live, including the modulation. Even on the road, before a show, they would have to punch in the notes of the sequence manually, very slow, then speed it up on playback to give the fast sequenced effect you hear on the record."

One of Parsons' sonic imports was the recording of clocks which he had previously made in an antiques shop as a Quad demo, and was later used as the alarming opening of 'Time'. The clocks give way to steady ticking (actually muted, picked bass strings played by Waters on his Precision bass) and the distant, ambient strikes of Mason's rototoms, which had to be re-tuned and dropped in for each chord change.

This song featured a superb drumming performance by Mason who, Parsons says, appeared to treat his engineering skills with an element of suspicion at the start of the sessions. "On day one, we found ourselves spending a long time getting the drum sounds to sound right on the console, then they carried on recording a track," he says. "But then for the next song, they went through the whole process of getting the drums to sound right yet again. In between the sessions for *Dark Side Of The Moon* [which lasted, on and off, for eight months], Nick's kit had been packed away in cases, gone away on tour and played in different environments, and of course drums go out of tune. But I'm happy that the drum sounds on each track are reasonably consistent. With Floyd, though, it always seemed to come together very quickly and, anyway, I've never really changed my overall miking set-up for drums, apart from a difference of snare mic here and there. I've mostly used either a Neumann 84 or an 87, an AKG D20 on the bass drum, Coles 4038 ribbon mics for overhead, and 84s or 86s on the toms. But I never used compression; it's just a pet hate of mine and I think it kills a lot of natural sound, especially on drums."

Among the best-known highlights of the album was Rick Wright's haunting piano instrumental, 'The Great Gig In The Sky', featuring – at Parsons' own suggestion – the soaring, orgasmic vocals of Clare Torry. "They said, 'Who shall we get to sing this?' And I put my hand up and said, 'Well, I know of a great singer who can do it!' I had heard of her through an album of hit cover versions she had done, the type that proliferated in the early Seventies and was always recorded in a day, and I was very impressed with her. I had worked with Liza Strike, Doris Troy and Barry St John, the very gifted session singers who sang on the album, but I had never seen this girl before. She just came out of nowhere with this great voice and I just told them to give this girl a call. They didn't really know at that point what they wanted to hear in terms of the vocals. It was very much down to Clare and what she wanted to put down, although there was a bit of direction being given. They said, 'Sorry, we've got no words, no melody line, just a chord sequence, so see what you can do with it.' She was only there for a couple of hours and I think there were two or three takes, from which we assembled the best bits for a master version. But somewhere in the archives there are the bits we didn't use and I'm sure it would make for an interesting remix one day."

With sampling still a full decade away, Waters relied on a pair of Revox tape machines and two Beyer mics to record the sound of a cash register in his garden shed, then edit the sounds and form a tape loop to provide a percussive, rhythmic backing upon which to write his infectious 7/4 bass riff for 'Money' (which, allegedly, Gilmour actually played on the record). Like 'Time', 'Money' was notable for Gilmour's exquisite guitar solos. "Dave was inclined to record his guitar tracks with his effects already there, from his amp," Chris Thomas comments. "He had one of the first kind of guitar processors – a Hi-Fly which was made by the same guy [Peter Zinovieff, formerly a BBC Radiophonic Workshop engineer] who designed the VCS-3 – and he used that all over the album. So his sound was pretty big anyway and he would naturally want to go for that. On 'Money', the one thing I remember about that was I got him to double-track the descending riff at the end of the solo section to make that bigger and make a difference before it goes back to sounding quite small for the last verse. I always thought that part of the guitar riff didn't sound big enough, it had to be *really* big, you know! It's a very big guitar sound that he gets. Effects were thin on the ground and most were based on tape delay, EMT reverb plates and the live chamber. There was also the big green curve bender, as EMI called it. It was actually a parametric EQ which looked a bit like Cyclops because of all the horrible giant knobs!"

Sound effects had always loomed large in Floyd's music but they were never more important than on *The Dark Side Of The Moon*. Even on the earliest live performances of 'Money', a sound effects loop was in evidence. The one which features on the final album was compiled by Parsons to Waters' exact requirements. "We put this loop together in Studio Two," says Parsons. "It was a very well-thought out sequence of the sound of a cash register, a bag of coins dropped on to the studio floor, paper being torn and a telephone exchange Uni selector which we found on an Abbey Road archive tape. The whole thing acted as a click track for the band [Floyd played to the loop in their headphones] because it was exactly timed to seven-beats-to-the-bar, the time signature of the bass riff which Roger had written and built his song around. We had great fun measuring each piece of tape with a ruler to ensure everything was accurately timed, but even then if you listen closely the loop and the band wander away from each other, tempo-wise, occasionally."

It is doubtful that the amount of spoken word interjections which featured on the finished album was originally anticipated, although they are now among its highlights. Waters had the idea to bring random individuals into the studio – including road manager Peter Watts (and wife Patricia) and crew members Roger the Hat and Chris Adamson (the latter's pet phrase "You can have it any colour you like" providing the title for the album's side two jam) – and record their responses to a series of questions, and if anything interesting was said, it would be tried out in passages on the album. "No one really knew what people would say in response to the question cards," Parsons says. "It was only formal in that people were sent into the studio to sit in a chair, in front of a microphone, and I had to be the first! But my response was thoroughly uninteresting and boring, so they didn't use it!" (Parsons was in good company – Paul McCartney's contribution was another to be shelved.) Chris Thomas was also party to the Floyd's cosmic quiz. "Before Roger asked the questions, he said 'Don't say yes or no, but say how you feel,'" he recalls. "'Or say nothing if you don't want to.' And all these questions were pertinent to various parts of the record. Questions like, 'When did you last hit somebody?' and 'Were you in the right?'. Henry McCullough [then lead guitarist with Wings] responded to that one saying, 'I was certainly in the right, it was too much Guinness.' Those answers and anecdotes were flown in to the master from quarter-inch tape during the mixing stage."

One of Waters' questions was, 'What is the dark side of the moon?', and in response, Abbey Road's Irish doorman, Jerry Driscoll became a most unlikely star. "Jerry answered, 'There's no dark side of the moon really, as a matter of fact it's all dark,'" Thomas says. "We just said, 'Wow! We've got to finish off the album with that.' And we did." But Parsons also recalls, "After that he said, 'The only thing that makes it look alight is the sun.' That's the bit you don't hear because the band were too overjoyed with his first line and it would have been an anti-climax to continue."

The tracks were seamlessly crossfaded from one to the next by cueing two stereo source machines, yet without the aid of timecode. It has been reported that Gilmour and Waters conflicted over the sound of the mix, something which Thomas, who was brought in at the end of the project as Mixing Supervisor and to oversee the final overdub sessions, confirms. "When they were playing *The Wall* shows in New York in 1980, Dave was really sweet and said to me, '*Dark Side* would never have sounded like that if it hadn't been for your input,'" he says. "I said, 'What do you mean? I never really felt that I did an incredible amount.' He said, 'Roger wanted it to sound really dry.' [John Lennon's *Plastic Ono Band* album was allegedly Waters' reference point for dryness.] Dave was the one who wanted it to sound big and spacey, and, yes, I suppose it did sound quite a bit different to how they imagined it would." Parsons, on the other hand, does not recall any such difference of opinion. "The overall sound was pretty much dictated by what was on the multitracks and I don't think the mix necessarily revolutionised what was on the multitrack. If you were to play the multitrack tape now and put the faders up, it would sound like the *Dark Side Of The Moon* we all know. So, no, I wasn't aware of any conflict of that kind," he says.

"But the positive side of Chris's presence was that he helped to solve any problems between the band at the time of mixing. He was like a mentor, a guiding light and intermediary. It was a bit of a frustration for me that I didn't get all the engineering credit because of Chris's involvement, although I admire his work enormously and overall I think he helped out a great deal, but ultimately his ideas on the mix were different from mine. I had been working on the album for a year and I obviously knew it inside out by the mixing stage. Chris wasn't that familiar with it, so I suppose there was a little bit of disappointment from my side. However, there were times when I thought Chris was wrong, particularly about the use of limiting and compression on the mix, which I have never been a fan of. But, of course, he was the boss."

Thomas explains why, despite having a skilful engineer in Parsons, Pink Floyd hired him to finish the album. "The band said they wanted someone to come in and mix it, but I'd heard that they had sent the tapes off to four different people to mix, so they could choose their favourite mix," he says. "I thought this was a weird idea, especially as they had worked on it for such a long time and had been producing it themselves. I understood that they wanted someone to give opinions on whether something worked or not. But to take the tapes away and mix it? I said, 'Oh I definitely don't want to do that.' So in the end, they finally came in and we mixed it all together at Abbey Road. A lot of the tracks had already been bounced down and completed by the time I got involved. There were only two or three tracks of drums when we came to mixing it. They had already constructed the drum tracks and bounced it all down to that. It was quite simple by the stage I came in. Depending on the song, there would be one or two tracks of guitar, and these would include the solo and the rhythm guitar parts. One track for keyboard, one for bass and one or two sound effects tracks. They and Alan had been very, very efficient in the way they'd worked."

The Dark Side Of The Moon was one of the very first mainstream rock albums to be planned for both stereo and quadrophonic format releases, and Quad gave Parsons the opportunity to mix the album exactly how he imagined it. "All the effects on 'Money' and other tracks were recorded on four-track, so that they could be heard in true Quad on the final record," he insists. "But by the time the mix stage was upon us, Quad hadn't really taken off as a medium in the way it was expected to, so it was a little bit of an anti-climax. As far as the discrete four-channel mix was concerned, it was all fairly simple. You just used a four-track tape machine and bussed out of channels one and two to go to the front two speakers, and three and four to go to the back speakers. There were some joystick pan-pots and dual concentric faders that sent from front to back, and left to right. But in order to accommodate the encoding systems like QS and SQ [Quad to Stereo/Stereo to Quad], you had to steer away from panning anything into the middle of the room or phasing problems would occur. You had to leave a kind of hole between the middle of the room and the centre of the back of the room. You would find that anywhere in the front of the room or at the extremes of the room would be okay, but if you panned anything between the left back and right back, you had to move fairly swiftly. But as we know, the whole thing died a death. The encoded version is still out there as far as I know, but the one I am looking forward to hearing again someday is the discrete four-track version where everything is where it is supposed to be. The encoding systems were always a bit of a compromise." In 1998, three years after his original interview for this book, Parsons was awaiting a reply from his bosses at EMI regarding his wish to mix a special version of *The Dark Side Of The Moon* for a surround sound release.

In many ways, the subtle textures and use of sound imaging on *The Dark Side Of The Moon* have influenced a whole sphere of music and provided a number of producers with a basis upon which to create effective, non-commercial recordings. A project which was occupying the mind of Paul Staveley O'Duffy during 1995 and 1996 was a largely instrumental collage, an album provisionally titled *A Natural High* which combines world music styles with the powers of hypnotic language and subliminal frequency to create an aural experience designed to positively alter the listener's consciousness. The music was being recorded using 3D audio technology and joining forces with

O'Duffy was stage hypnotist, Paul McKenna whose narrative passages interweave with the music to take the listener on a seamless, relaxation-cultivating journey through a number of audio-simulated "scenes".

"The individual pieces of music are followed by interludes where a 3D audio image places you, for example, outside a pub by a stream, while a story is being narrated – a bit like *Black Beauty*," explains O'Duffy. "When I realised that story-telling would be a vital ingredient, I hit upon the idea of a hypnotist because they have great powers of persuasion. Paul was also thinking along similar lines and we teamed up with Michael Breen, an American neuro-linguistic expert, to assist us with the narrative script." McKenna himself says, "I had been making self-help tapes with some degree of success for about six years when Paul suggested we combine those psychological qualities with Zen stories, contemporary music and effects to create an album that works on a very deep level." The album was still awaiting release in mid-1998.

The Dark Side Of The Moon was performed live by the band, without Waters, for the first time in almost twenty years on Floyd's 1994 world tour, a recording of which surfaced on 1995's impressively designed *Pulse* live set. It has spent more weeks on the American chart than any other album and it is estimated that a copy can be found in one out of every five British households. "With *Dark Side*, all of our objectives were suddenly achieved," comments David Gilmour. "All the way through the making of it we thought that we were on to something that was going to do better than anything we had previously done. Then, with the record cover at the end, we were all pretty excited because it was the first time that the music, the lyrics and the visual design all came together. Roger was the main driving force behind what was happening at that point. I listened to *Dark Side* around the time of the release of our *Shine On* boxed set [1992] and I felt that it was pretty timeless."

But *The Dark Side Of The Moon* was not the only example of the band's productivity in 1973. Later that year, Gilmour was introduced through a mutual friend to an enchanting fifteen-year-old songwriter from Kent, named Catherine Bush. Attracted by her precocious talents and wishing to help her progress in the the music business, he invited her to his home studio near Harlow in Essex where he produced, engineered and played guitar on her first demo recordings. Five years later, Kate Bush became an international star (with a typically Floydian contempt for publicity) and Gilmour remains to this day a background, and occasionally guesting, figure in her career.

Building The Wall

Excessive touring in support of *The Dark Side Of The Moon* prevented any new release in 1974, although the band briefly attempted making an album with Alan Parsons called *Household Objects*, using non-musical instruments such as aerosol sprays, wine bottles and rubber bands. Then, during rehearsals that summer, Floyd sketched out ideas for three new pieces of music. One of which, an elegy for Syd Barrett, 'Shine On You Crazy Diamond', was later to appear on their September 1975 album, *Wish You Were Here*, the band's last to be wholly recorded at Abbey Road. "'Shine On' came out of the little guitar arpeggio figure which fell out of my guitar in a rehearsal studio," comments Gilmour. "When something does that you sort of repeat it over and over to see why it's attractive to you and where you should take it. That set Roger off and he loved it. That's what got the ball rolling. The best of our moments were when the best of Roger and his lyric writing, ideas and driving force came together with some of my more melodic, emotional moments that sort of fall out of my guitar once in a while. Certainly the *Wish You Were Here* album and 'Shine On You Crazy Diamond' are sublime moments for me. We did the basic track of 'Shine On' from the beginning where the first guitar solo starts, right through the sax break and on to the reprise that appears towards the end of the album. That was in all twenty minutes long and at one time it was going to be one whole side of the album. But as we worked on it and extended it and extracted things, we came to the decision that we would work on new stuff to slot in the middle of what effectively became two parts."

Pink Floyd had for some time used a converted chapel in Britannia Row, North London as a storage base for its considerable lighting and sound equipment when off the road, as well as offices and a convenient place for impromptu rehearsals. Now wishing to record their next album whenever it suited their diaries, and not Abbey Road's, they designated Britannia Row a recording zone and hired engineers Brian Humphries and Nick Griffiths to oversee the installation of its MCI equipment during the summer of 1976. The first Pink product to come out of Brit Row was *Animals* which was released in January 1977. Although not as broad in appeal as its two predecessors, it is still rated highly by Gilmour and like much of *Wish You Were Here*, its origins lay in Floyd's productive summer 1974 rehearsals during which they wrote the basic ingredients of 'Dogs' (sketched as 'You Gotta Be Crazy') and Sheep ('Raving And Drooling'). *Animals* is notable for the striking interplay between Gilmour's guitars and Wright's atmospheric synth and electric piano work, especially on the lyrically complex 'Dogs' which contained mood swings with every new passage and also featured Waters's chilling Vocoder passages in which he recited a bastardised version of 'The Lord Is My Shepherd'. 'Sheep', on the other hand, contained some of the band's most electrifying rock 'n' roll musicianship to date. Session guitarist, Snowy White was fresh from touring with Steve Harley And Cockney Rebel and Al Stewart when he received a telephone call from Floyd's manager, Steve O'Rourke, asking if he would be interested in supporting Gilmour on the subsequent 1977 In The Flesh tour, then unwittingly found himself recording with the band. "O'Rourke took me down to Britannia Row where they recording *Animals* and Roger Waters said, 'Now that you're here, you might as well play something,'" White recalls. "He'd come up with an idea for a gentle acoustic song, 'Pigs On The Wing', and I just played a guitar solo on it. They later decided not to put the song on the album, although my guitar piece ended up on the eight-track cartridge version which I never heard again until I came to assembling a retrospective album of my session work in 1995." (The eight-track cartridge was a favoured in-car format which temporarily rivalled the cassette in popularity until it disappeared in the late Seventies. The only commercial release of the full version of 'Pigs On The Wing' available today is on White's *Gold Top – Sessions & Groups* album on RPM Records.)

Never the best of friends, a struggle for power between Gilmour and Waters was beginning to materialise during the recording of *Animals*, although Gilmour claims to have been the major force behind the album's musical content. In 1978, Floyd escaped to the

South of France as tax exiles, where they commenced work on their next project. Co-produced by Bob Ezrin, of Alice Cooper's *Welcome To My Nightmare* fame, and Waters and Gilmour, *The Wall* began as a double album, released in November 1979, and grew into an epic which generated one of the most ambitiously theatrical concert productions of the last fifteen years, and an equally grandiose Alan Parker movie. While the band recorded at Superbear Studios in France with engineer James Guthrie, Nick Griffiths was assigned the task of assembling a collection of explosions and other sound effects back at Brit Row, before the band moved to the Producers' Workshop in Los Angeles to complete the album. "Roger demoed the whole thing and it was excruciating to listen to, but you could tell instantly that there was a great idea in there," says Gilmour. "It took Roger and Bob a bit of time to get the story line straight. At the time I bought it all but since then I have to say that my reappraisal of it is that it's rather a whinge. *The Wall* is a conceptually brilliant album with some very good music in it, although frankly I think the rest of us felt some of it wasn't quite up to standard. But we'd had disagreements like that before and I think some of the best of Roger's stuff on the album came as a result of being pressurised by some of us to come up with better material."

Produced in an atmosphere of personal turmoil (as befitted the album's subject matter), *The Wall* included what many consider to be some of Gilmour's finest moments as a guitarist on 'Comfortably Numb', 'Run Like Hell' and 'Another Brick In The Wall (Part II)', the latter having had the distinction of being the last Number One single of the Seventies and the first of the Eighties. While Gilmour's solo on the single, played on his 1955 Les Paul Gold Top, was a spontaneous gem, recorded directly through the mixing console with the sound fed through a Fender Twin amp to capture a mix of two different signals, the 'Comfortably Numb' solo was formed in a patchwork manner. "Roger and I had a number of bitter arguments about how 'Comfortably Numb' should be recorded," he says, "and we did in fact record two versions, editing the best sections of each together. The solo, as with a lot of my things, was mixed together from several different takes because I am liable to drop a clanger or two when I start getting wild. If I play safe, I tend to hold something back. So I like to work through a number of solos then take the best elements to construct a perfect track, making sure it's mistake-free, of course! Sometimes a solo will happen in one take, but I always want to have a reason for playing the notes I play."

The Final Cut, issued in March 1983, proved to be a prophetic title and, as Gilmour says, "was torture to make". At Waters' insistence, Rick Wright had quit the band during the making of *The Wall*, but returned as a salaried musician for the 1980-1 concerts. Now he was completely absent from *The Final Cut*, essentially a Waters solo album featuring songs previously shelved from *The Wall* and, it would seem, salvaged in desperation. Gilmour took a sideman's role to Waters' increasingly inflated ego and was eventually taken off the production credits. Mayfair Studios' John Hudson oversaw a number of the *Final Cut* sessions engineered by James Guthrie. "James had worked as my assistant engineer in the Seventies and it was he who recommended Mayfair to Pink Floyd," Hudson says, "but I think Alan Parsons had also put a word in about the studio, that it had some nice rooms and during the eleven months they stayed here we completely re-tailored the place for them. James was freelancing then and I helped him out on setting up mixes. He would spend a couple of days on a mix before the others came in to have a listen, and Roger had this amazing way of approaching things. On one occasion, after James had set up a great mix, Roger came in and killed all the faders which rather shocked James and everyone else. Then, one by one, he pulled up the faders gradually as if he was playing a musical instrument and put together a totally different mix which sounded brilliant. But Roger could be very strange. He came to me one day and said quite seriously, 'John, we really like it here, but there is just one thing...' and my heart absolutely dropped. He said, 'Everyone is a bit too jolly.'"

A new name in the Floyd camp during the project was engineer Andy Jackson, who began his studio career as a tape operator at Utopia Studios in 1976 and later worked with producers Phil Wainman and Richard James Burgess on hits by The Boomtown Rats (including the 1979 Number One 'I Don't Like Mondays') and Landscape. He was led into Floydian territory by former Utopia colleague, Guthrie, in 1982 and has remained a key player ever since. "Working with James taught me how to be a good engineer and I learned a lot about subtractive EQ which few others seemed to be into," he says. "It's about getting rid of the stuff you don't want, rather than gradually adding loads of top and bottom, and you start instead by decreasing the amount of middle. James has phenomenal ears. There's something called echoic memory which is the aural equivalent of photographic memory and I'm sure he has it. He can remember mixes and will instantly tell you if something has changed. There have even been occasions when no one has understood what he meant and they've brought in the technical boys to take something apart, and sure enough they find something. Then when they change it, you can tell it sounds better. He also did a mix once for Ambrosia, an offshoot band from The Alan Parsons Project. He had already done one mix and without referring to that first mix, he was able to completely duplicate it in a different studio, using a different desk and monitors, because he has this aural memory. The final version was an edit between the two mixes and no one could tell the difference!"

When *The Wall* metamorphosised into the Parker movie, Guthrie hired Jackson's engineering skills to assist his soundtrack tasks. "We remixed the album in the Pinewood dubbing theatre on fairly mundane equipment and we were using Maglink which was the pre-SMPTE synchronising tool," Jackson says. "It was a monstrous system and I was looking after all that side of it. That led me to do *The Final Cut* which was originally going to be a soundtrack album for the movie, featuring different versions of the songs from *The Wall*, such as 'Mother', 'Another Brick In The Wall (Part III)' and 'Empty Spaces', plus what Roger called 'Spare Bricks' – *Wall*-esque songs left over from the original album. Halfway through this we discovered that we weren't going to do a soundtrack album after all, but we carried on anyway, which probably explains how *Wall*-like *The Final Cut* turned out to be. It was an unfortunate time to start getting involved because the pressure of working with Dave and Roger who were both at each other's throats was intolerable. Dave didn't have much to do with the album, although he played on a lot of stuff. He didn't want to know and it became very much Roger's baby."

The Final Cut was notable for the use of a new 3D sound system called holophonics, invented by physiologist Hugo Zuccarelli who had developed the system while conducting research into hearing in blind people. "No one really understood it apart from Hugo who approached us when we were in the studio working on the album," Jackson explains. "He told us he had something we might be interested in so we said, 'Okay, let's see it.' It was amazing and in some ways it's the best 3D sound system of its kind there's ever been. Particularly his first one. It's essentially a microphone which looks like a dummy head, rather than a post-record processor, so you have to record *with* it. Hugo discovered that the conventional wisdom about the way hearing works was wrong and he ended up building this dummy head thing. We recorded various sound effects with the system, but some things were recorded non-holophonically then played through some speakers and recorded again to achieve a feeling of space. *The Pros And Cons Of Hitch-Hiking* [Waters' 1984 solo album] used holophonics for bits of ambient sound. It worked very well and even on a budget hi-fi you do get the feeling that there's another dimension to the music. But it works best on headphones. The best example of holophonics was Hugo's first demo of sounds like haircuts and doors opening, where you recognised distance. Other people took his ideas and went on to develop similar things, like Spherical Sound which we used on *A Momentary Lapse Of Reason*, but it wasn't as good."

Welcome To The New Machine

Jackson found himself in the difficult position of appeasing both Waters and Gilmour as a floating engineer for their respective solo albums and tours in the dormant Floyd years of 1984-6. During his time with Gilmour for the recording of his *About Face* album, he took note of the guitarist's production know-how: skills which would soon become more vital than ever. "Dave's very technical and he has very good ears too," he says. "He's kind of lost track a bit as technology has progressed, but you can sit him in front of a desk and a machine and he'll do it all himself, as he did when he was demoing for *About Face*. His demos have always sounded very reasonable, although he would never claim to be a real engineer at all. It's the same with his live guitar rig which is immensely complex, but the gist of it is a development from what he put together in the first place."

The inevitable split with Roger Waters came in December 1985.

Gilmour, having invested too much of his life in Pink Floyd, decided to continue with Mason and Wright under the Floyd banner, and by the summer of 1986 was already working on a new album with Bob Ezrin. Waters, however, was clearly having none of this and took out legal proceedings to prevent his ex-colleagues from using the name "Pink Floyd" – a case settled out of court in late 1987, mostly in Gilmour's favour. Financed by Gilmour and Mason, *A Momentary Lapse Of Reason* (released in September 1987) was, in part, a return to form, even if it did rely heavily on session players like bassist Tony Levin and drummer Carmine Appice to lend a cohesive edge.

Andy Jackson found the recording of *A Momentary Lapse Of Reason* hard work. "Dave was under a lot of pressure and his marriage was breaking up," he reveals. "He had something to prove, working without Roger. All things combined, in retrospect, it was maybe a positive force. Nick and Rick had very little involvement and the band had effectively disintegrated. It wasn't a fun album to record by any means. We spent a long time on it, about a year, whereas *About Face* came together fairly quickly with a four-piece rhythm section and it was very relaxed. But *Momentary Lapse* was a construction job from the word go and I got very fried on those sessions because of the intensity. The demos had drum machines on them and sequencers, and we'd end up with sixth generation demos until we had something approaching a song which was a separate process. Loads of extra songs didn't make it. Then having got to that point, the demos were highly refined. They weren't really demos anymore, more like templates and we'd use those to build the masters. We would then overdub real drums and bass. Dave would say, 'That guitar's okay, that one isn't so let's re-record that part.'"

The lack of effort on Mason and Wright's part might have led one to regard it as Gilmour's third solo album, even though typical Floyd characteristics – the 'Echoes'/'Shine On'-like sound effects, keyboard and picked guitar intro of 'Signs Of Life' – justified the band name. His guitar track on 'Sorrow' was recorded, at great expense one imagines, through a concert PA system at Los Angeles Sports Arena, although most of the album was crafted at Gilmour's newly-acquired houseboat studio, the Astoria in Hampton. "Dave's guitar was originally recorded on the boat using a Fender Twin amp," says Jackson. "But he wanted to get a 3D effect, so he went over to Los Angeles and used a mobile with someone else because we were double shifting and I was in another Los Angeles studio with Bob Ezrin working on another part of the album. Dave hired the LA Sports Arena and a PA system, and played stuff out through the PA and recorded the stadium sound. It was kind of reprocessed with the stadium."

Jackson agrees that Pink Floyd has traditionally been a technology-driven band, a description which certainly fitted the approach to *A Momentary Lapse Of Reason*, but less so for the band's acclaimed March 1994 release, *The Division Bell*, which, with considerably increased input from Mason and Wright, was a more unified Floyd effort than anything since *Wish You Were Here*. After several jam sessions with bassist Guy Pratt and Bob Ezrin at Brit Row and the Astoria, the band sketched more than sixty musical ideas which were worked into an impressive album. At last, Gilmour felt he was in a real band again, instead of "shaping" music with a bunch of associates. "On the boat for that album we had ATC monitors and a DDA AMR24 desk which we replaced halfway through with an AMEK Hendrix, although it has since been refitted with a seventy-two-channel Neve VR desk with flying faders," says Jackson. "There were two twenty-four-track machines – an Otari MTR100 and a Studer A80 which is actually quite a nice-sounding machine. There is always a massive range of outboard equipment, particularly classic vintage gear like Fairchilds and Pultecs, and a great valve mic selection. It's an extremely well-equipped studio, probably my favourite, and I've worked more there than anywhere else now.

"*The Division Bell* was great fun and pretty much all recorded on the Astoria, apart from a few odds and ends where we went somewhere else to record a Hammond because we can't get one through the door on the boat. There was the idea of tracking something at Olympic with Guy Pratt, Gary Wallis and Jon Carin from the live band, but it didn't work out very well and we preferred the sound of the boat. The boat is very small and we were able to get a very tight, dense drum sound which, looking back, is very Pink Floyd anyway. I don't think we ever got a drum machine out of the cupboard! Even the demos were done with real drums. We had a permanent set-up on Dave's boat whereby Nick would fancy doing something on the drums and I'd already have the sound set up."

Obviously pleased with *The Division Bell*, David Gilmour said upon its release, "What was really nice about the recording of this record was that myself, Rick and Nick came together and worked well as a unit in a way that we hadn't done for many, many years. We used less sequencing than the previous album and played more music in real time. The elements that made Pink Floyd what it was, whatever these pinch of salt fragments they may be, three of the four who have been part of it for the last [thirty] years are still in there contributing. It feels like there are better things to come." With the next Floyd album expected in 1999, and underway aboard the Astoria as this book's second edition went to press, those "better things" are eagerly anticipated.

chapter seven

just one more galileo

"I woke up one morning in late 1975 to the sound of Queen's 'Bohemian Rhapsody' coming from my alarm clock radio. I just laid there absolutely spellbound by this incredible piece of music. It was an amazing experience to hear something so different, so beautiful and powerful. It was wonderfully crafted as a song and a recording – a potent combination of rock and classical qualities. I don't remember where I was when Kennedy was shot, but I will always remember about the first time I heard 'Bohemian Rhapsody'."

Jeff Jarratt

As Queen, Freddie Mercury, Brian May, Roger Taylor and John Deacon brought a previously unheard melange of sound to the fore when most of their tired rock contemporaries in the mid-Seventies were playing it safe as they rested on their laurels. Queen's prowess at layered vocal harmonies, dominated by Mercury's soaring operatics, was second to none, while Brian May's multitracked guitar orchestrations were arguably the most creative contributions to the instrument since Jimi Hendrix's feedback-drenched sounds in the Sixties. In the studio, the band embraced the innovative breakthroughs laid down during the psychedelic and progressive eras, and took them to another plain. While they relied on a simple instrumental line-up of guitar, bass, piano and drums, they played them like they were new inventions and in doing so, delivered a genuinely new, epic slant on rock. Launched into the age of glitter, it was no surprise when Queen's flamboyance earned them a glam rocker tag. As soon as 'Killer Queen' regaled the airwaves in late 1974, however, many realised this band had what it took to survive any fashion. Yet for all their glories, Queen never took themselves seriously and even in their most intense musical moments, one could still detect a glimmer of humour which, in the ever fickle world of pop, was probably their saving grace.

At the helm of Queen's integration of sound between 1972 and 1978 was producer Roy Thomas Baker who, while at Decca and Trident Studios, had gained vast experience in rock, opera and classical music. Baker had already produced Queen's first three albums (*Queen*, *Queen II* and *Sheer Heart Attack*) by the time Mercury casually previewed a new song called 'Bohemian Rhapsody'. Little did the producer realise that every ounce of his acquired expertise would be called upon in moulding this epic. Baker served his "audio apprenticeship" at Decca in the mid-Sixties, starting as a tea boy-cum-second engineer and quickly progressing to an engineer's role. Then, in early 1969, Baker joined Trident as a staff engineer where he would work with the finest American and British artists of the day, from Zappa to Santana, and T-Rex to Free. "It was," he says, "a great stepping stone."

In friendly competition with George Martin's AIR production company, Trident started its own independent initiative, Trident Audio Productions, after luring some of the country's best engineer talent, including EMI's Ken Scott and Robin Cable from Saga. "The people at Trident weren't too happy about starting a production company as they felt they would be competing against their clients for studio time, but they realised there was a lot of talent out there which needed an outlet," says Baker who met Queen in 1972 while on an inspection tour of Wembley's De Lane Lea studio complex, when the band was still using the name Smile. "Queen were recording free of charge while the engineers tested," he says. "I didn't know of the band then and I was more concerned with going over to see what this big, new studio was like. That's when I ran into the guys and heard the demos, and they were working on a song called 'Keep Yourself Alive' which immediately sounded like a hit to me. I just thought that here was a band doing something new and fresh. You could tell Queen were so good just by listening to the musical content at that stage and sitting down and chatting to Freddie Mercury."

After signing to Trident Audio Productions, Queen began work on their debut album with Baker and engineer John Anthony during downtime at its Soho studios, often working from two am through to the following lunchtime. Brian May's idea for lush, multi-layered guitar parts was already in place by the time of Baker's arrival. As an astrology student and a high academic achiever, May was always going to approach the guitar differently to any other player. He built his unique-sounding "Red Special" guitar with his father at the age of seventeen for just £8, and despite being assembled from an unlikely range of domestic objects is still in use more than thirty years later, sounding as masterful as ever and needing little maintenance attention. Even before Queen had made its first demo, he imagined a role for his instrument which extended far beyond traditional rhythm backing and soloing. He had a vision of using the guitar in an orchestral manner, interweaving phrases and counter melodies around vocals. But, in practice, he was not able to fully experiment with this approach until Queen began working in the recording studio, using extensive multitrack overdubbing to create a string section effect.

Although studio technology played a vital part in the stunning results, what must not be overlooked is the unique tone of May's homemade guitar, his vibrato technique and the use at all times of a silver sixpence in place of a plectrum. "Brian was already on to something different in terms of trying to orchestrate his guitars in a different way to how most people would approach it," Baker says. "I had quite a bit of an orchestral background through working on classical music at Decca and that helped with structuring the phrasing of the guitar parts. We never thought of Brian's guitar as a raunchy instrument like most guitarists do, it was an orchestral instrument. Brian's great strength was in phrasing a part then double-tracking or harmonising very accurately and quickly."

In looped form, May's orchestrations gave the 1976 album, *A*

Day At The Races its surging, regal introduction, often compared to the work of a synthesiser – hence the qualifying statement on all of the band's Seventies albums, "No synths". The general record buying public took it as a reaction against the growing use of electronic instrumentation, although the band were never against the use of synths, as their later work would show. Prompted by Radio One DJ John Peel's inaccurate comments about the guitar and synthesiser work on 'Keep Yourself Alive', May in particular wanted to make it abundantly clear that the lush sounds were all care of his Red Special. Baker was no less frustrated and says, "We would spend four days multilayering a guitar solo and some imbecile from the record company would come in and say, 'I like that synth!'"

Roger Taylor's legendary gong made its debut on the experimental 1974 *Queen II* album. "It became a trademark which started with us pissing around during that second album," Baker says. "We were experimenting with ideas, both musically for themselves and technically for me. Freddie said to me, 'If there are any ideas that you've had that you can't use with boring, human-type bands, we'll try them out on this.' A lot of it was backward cymbals, backward gongs and backward tom fills. Anything that Queen ever did was encompassed in that second album. *Queen II* was like the kitchen sink of every known Queen effect. Musically, there were the ballads, the heavy bits and complex arrangements and it all came from there. Phasing too, and everything had to be done by hand because, of course, there was no other available means. We had to get tapes and run them around the room by hand just to get phasing."

Moving closer to the zenith of their creativity, backing tracks for Queen's third album, *Sheer Heart Attack*, got under way at Rockfield Studios in June 1974, although the main bulk of the work began at Trident in mid-July. The sessions were hampered by May's periodic ill-health and his inability to venture outside of his bed. When he returned to the studio, he found that the band had continued to work on backing tracks without him and spent the next two weeks, virtually on his own, adding the sheer weight of vocal and guitar harmonies which would lend the album its awe-inspiring power. One of May's greatest contributions, both as a guitarist and songwriter, was 'Brighton Rock', the album's opening track. Many bands had previously achieved exciting results with the use of delay, but with this one track, Queen surpassed them all with May's stereophonic guitar sweeping triumphantly, from channel to channel. The precise guitar parts on 'Killer Queen', meanwhile, took several days for May to complete, with a total of twelve separate overdubs required before being bounced down to four distinct stereo tracks. But while this track in particular showed the band was a cut above the rest, no one had the faintest clue about what lay in store exactly twelve months later...

'Bohemian Rhapsody'

Released on 31 October, 1975, 'Bohemian Rhapsody' was a production beyond comparison, residing at the top of the UK chart for nine weeks and honoured in 1977 by the BPI as The Best Single Of The Last Twenty-Five Years. It even returned to the top of the chart in December 1991, after the bitter news of Mercury's death from an AIDS-related illness. Metamorphosing from wistful ballad to an operatic pastiche with a fiery rock climax, all within six short minutes, 'Bohemian Rhapsody' was greeted like manna from heaven in the largely barren musical ground of the mid-Seventies. Recording began at Rockfield Studio One in Monmouth, Wales on 24 August, 1975 after a three-week rehearsal period in Herefordshire. During the making of the track, however, a further four studios – SARM East, Scorpion, Wessex and Roundhouse – were used. At the time it was the most expensive single ever made and guitarist Brian May was to later refer to the track's parent album, *A Night At The Opera*, as "our *Sgt Pepper*". A brave claim, but one which May was able to stand by.

Producer Baker recalls his first hearing of the song: "We were going out to dinner one night and I met Freddie at his apartment in Kensington. He sat down at his piano and said, 'I'd like to play you a song that I'm working on at the moment.' So he played the first part and said, 'This is the chord sequence,' followed by the interim part and although he didn't have all the lyrics together yet,

I could tell it was going to be a ballady number. He played a bit further through the song and then stopped suddenly, saying, 'This is where the opera section comes in.' We both just burst out laughing. I had worked with the D'Oyly Carte Opera Company at Decca so I learned a lot about vocals and the way vocals are stressed, so I was probably one of the few people in the whole world who knew exactly what he was talking about.

"It was the first time that an opera section had been incorporated into a pop record, let alone a Number One. It was obviously very unusual and we originally planned to have just a couple of 'Galileos'. But things often have a habit of evolving differently once you're inside the studio and it did get longer and bigger...and bigger still. The beginning section was pretty spot on and the end section was fairly similar, although we obviously embellished it with guitars and lots of overdubs. But the opera section ended up nothing like the original concept because we kept changing it and adding things to it."

Baker and Queen recorded the basic backing track at Kingsley Ward's Rockfield Studios in three sections, later transferring to Scorpion Studios in North London and SARM for work on the guitar overdubs and extensive vocals. Looking into the studio from the control room window during the backing track sessions, Taylor positioned himself and his kit at the live area end of the studio, Deacon stood by his Marshall bass stack against a wall to the right and May hid himself away in a portable isolation booth, while Mercury sat at the piano, close to the window. "The first half or ballad section was done with piano, drums and bass, the normal routine," Baker says. "We never really started the opera section at that point. We just left a thirty second strip of tape on the reel for later use, not knowing that we would ever overrun it. Then the end rock section was recorded as a separate song, in the way that we would normally record a loud rock number of that period. The thing that made it difficult was that even the end had lots of vocals on it – the 'Ooh yeah, ooh yeah' part – so we had to record the basic backing track of drums, bass, guitar and piano, then do the background vocals without having the lead vocal on first. That wasn't the regular way of doing things because the lead vocal would normally dictate the phrasing of the background vocals. But we wouldn't have had enough tracks left for the rich backing vocals if we hadn't gone this route.

"The opera bit was getting longer, and so we kept splicing huge lengths of tape on to the reel. Every time Freddie came up with another Galileo, I would add another piece of tape to the reel which was beginning to look like a zebra crossing whizzing by. This went on over a three or four day period while we decided on the length of the section. That section alone took about three weeks to record which in 1975 was the average time spent on a whole album. We formed a three-part harmony by recording one harmony at a time and bouncing. So we did three tracks of the first part and bounced it to one track, three of the second and three of the third. We would then double bounce to one section so that particular phrase would have a three-part harmony just on one track. We would do this to each background vocal part across the song and ended up with fourth generation dupes on just one of the parts. By the time we mixed two of the other parts together, the first part was up to eight generations. This was before we wore out the master and began making twenty-four-track to twenty-four-track tape transfers. Once that had happened, the distortion factor on those vocals was very, very high." Although a project of this magnitude would understandably cause anxiety among many in Baker's position, the technical restraints of the era did not alarm him. "If something had to be longer, we would just add extra tape," he says. "If we needed more tracks, we would track bounce to free some more room on the tape. The making of 'Bohemian Rhapsody' was basically one continuous track bounce!"

Due to the complex nature of the recording, it is not surprising that the occasional vocal *faux pas* was noted by Baker's keen ears. He was not militaristic, however. "There were a few harmonies that were a little dissident, such as two notes next to each other which weren't quite spot on in passing phrases," he admits. "We left those there because they weren't classed as mistakes. In classical music they are allowable whereas in rock music, they normally are not. But in passing phrases it seems to work okay. If there was anything we heard at the time which we thought we wouldn't get away with, we would just wipe it and re-record it. So everything you hear was planned, albeit disjointedly planned, the way it should be."

Of the miking regime, Baker says, "We weren't into multiple snare miking back then, so there was just a single mic on the snare. We tended to use mostly condenser mics at that time and generally Neumann U67s or U87s on the toms and overhead. The transformation between U67s or U87s was going on at that point and studios usually had one or the other. An AKG D12 was used on the bass drum. They were the days before the [AKG] D112, which seems to be the standard now. John Deacon's bass was DI'd. Studios tended to make up their own DI boxes then because no manufacturers appeared to be making them. They weren't active DI boxes either; people would make them with a transformer sticking out of the end with wires going all over the place. There was always a slight sound loss when you plugged them into the amp so we had to compensate for that. We also used an Electrovoice 666 and sometimes a Neumann U67 condenser on his cabinet to pick up a bit of air. Freddie's piano was miked with two Neumann U67s and we also set up a Shure mic for his guide vocal. He didn't sing all the way through the backing track takes, just the first couple of words of each line as a reference for the band."

But, as ever, much experimentation was undertaken before May's guitar sound was perfected. "We used to have a few different types of mics set up, from which we would choose or blend signals for any one given sound, and it's a technique that I still use today," Baker reveals. "Brian's Vox amps were backless, so we also set up some mics behind them and near the wall to capture some ambience and the full spectrum of the guitar sound. There was always a lot of experimentation going on during our sessions. Brian generally used Vox AC30s but John had also thrown together something like a Tandy Radio Shack speaker with a three-watt amplifier and we tried that with a treble booster. We tried putting microphones down metal and concrete tubes to get more of a honky sound, and it all seemed to work. It certainly all stands up today when I hear it all again."

While the first three Queen albums had been made on sixteen-track equipment, 'Bohemian Rhapsody' benefited from twenty-four-track technology, although not without a few problems. "We found that the different twenty-four-track machines we used had different formats but we managed to compensate for that," Baker says. "We just used the one machine because there was no synching available to us. We started off at Rockfield on the Studer 24 which looked like a huge fish fryer. Then we did the vocal overdubs at Scorpion Studios where they had a Telefunken machine. Telefunken had this great idea to make their edge tracks [one and twenty-four] wider than the inside tracks, because they claimed there would be a higher risk of drop-outs on the edges but it made their machine totally incompatible with others. Unfortunately, Telefunken's attitude was: 'We invented the tape machine, we can do what the fuck we want!' So we threw that machine out and used a variety of machines from there onwards, including an Ampex which sounded phenomenally good but had transport tension problems. A track would play at a different speed by the end of the reel. The only contemporary machine we never tried was a Stephens."

Along with engineers Mike Stone, Gary Lyons and Geoff Workman, Baker took control at the sessions on a variety of consoles, including a custom-built board at Rockfield, a Cadac at the Roundhouse and "an old blue Neve with big knobs on it" at Wessex. When Baker and Queen retreated to SARM East Studios for the mixing sessions, they were treated to a Trident B console. "That console was the second B range model that Trident delivered from Malcolm Toft," he says. "It was a great board with such a unique sound, although I couldn't say why. I noticed that when it was re-sold, it was described as the board used to mix 'Bohemian Rhapsody', and I think they got more money than they originally paid for it. We used an MCI machine at SARM which we called Munchy, Crunchy and Intermittent because it was always falling apart!"

Now famous for his work with The Art Of Noise and Trevor Horn, and productions for Spandau Ballet and T'Pau, Gary Langan was a fresh-faced, eighteen-year-old assistant engineer at Sarm, when he came to work alongside Baker, Stone and Lyons on the 'Bohemian Rhapsody' mix. SARM started life at the beginning of the

Seventies as a tape copying facility with two Revox machines, trading in Osborn Street, Whitechapel as Sound And Recording Mobiles. Encouraged by his session musician father, Langan joined SARM straight from school. "Gary Lyons and Mike Stone taught me everything I knew about engineering," he says. "There isn't anybody like those two guys these days. Compared with many of today's engineers, they had a different, better level of technical skill." Langan initially became involved with Queen when Baker brought two songs from the *Sheer Heart Attack* album to SARM for re-mixing. "After working at SARM on a few projects, it seemed that Queen didn't want to mix anywhere else for some time. So I ended up working on all of their 'Marx Brothers' albums – *A Night At The Opera, A Day At The Races* and *News Of The World*. The only band with whom I'd worked was Queen; I didn't know about how other bands recorded. So spending weeks doing guitar solos with Brian and even more weeks doing vocals seemed like the norm to me. My job was really to learn and look after the band. To be seen but not heard was the task in those days, but I became really good friends with all of them."

His first task on 'Bohemian Rhapsody' was to put together a composite multitrack master from the three distinct sections of the song. "Nobody really knew how it was going to sound as a whole six-minute song until it was put together," he says. "I was standing at the back of the control room and you just knew that you were listening for the first time to a big page in history. Something inside me told me that this was a red letter day, and it really was."

One new item of equipment which was installed at SARM only days before the 'Bohemian Rhapsody' mix was the Alison computerised mixing system. Gary Langan has cause to snigger. "It was the first automated system in the world but it was ridiculous because it never worked properly!" he laughs. "You had to store data on two tracks, so you'd end up with no more than twenty-two tracks of music on your tape, to provide room for the data."

"It was an old VCA system which was responsible for the distortion at the end of the opera section," Baker adds. "If you listen to the record closely you'll notice it. But there wasn't a single thing we could do about it. It was a combination of the extra track bouncing and the use of the old VCA technology that was employed for the computerisation. When it got to that stage, the meters were so pinned that the VCAs in the board would not take any more volume. So we had to turn it off and the end rock section of 'Bohemian Rhapsody' was actually mixed by hand in the traditional way, where we each had control over a fader or group of faders."

It was planned that the highly pronounced snare beat at the beginning of the heavy rock section would be a distinct edit point, its crashing velocity a by-product of the manual mixing. "That was the point at which the VCAs were turned off but I did also push it there," informs Baker. "You hear a marked difference on the end section where it totally cleans up; it's crystal clean and loud. It wasn't planned that way; it was purely an error because we couldn't get rid of that distortion. It didn't worry me too much though because one of the trademarks of Queen was the heavily saturated sound. On *Queen II* and some of the big Queen themes, especially 'Bohemian Rhapsody', the generation copies caused so much distortion on Roger Taylor's drum tracks that it became a sound in itself which people have since tried to copy with outboard equipment. Even today, people are still trying to recreate that in-your-face distortion with machinery! So by accident we started a trend without even knowing it, in the same way that with an electric guitar, if you turn it up to ten, you'll hear distortion. But that became the band's sound."

With a band whose four individuals could all hold their own as songwriters and creative leaders, one of Baker's major tasks was to singularly encourage them to work as a concise unit while keeping the distinctive Queen sound. "It was a more difficult situation than working with a band with one songwriter, because they were all so good," he says. "But it didn't matter who had written the song; it still had to sound like a Queen record. They were great to work with, although like most bands there was an element of internal bickering. I always told them that it was too embarrassing for them to have an argument in front of everyone in the studio. So I would always make a room available for them to go to and argue in private. I think most of their arguments were about who had the B-side, that royalty thing. I remember Roger moping about because he really wanted his song, 'I'm In Love With My Car', on the B-side of 'Bohemian Rhapsody'. He locked himself in the tape closet at SARM and said he wouldn't come out until they agreed to put it on!"

The trend-setting Bruce Gowers-directed video which was made to promote the single cost just £4,000, which considering how it helped to launch the concept of the modern promo video was a minor expense. Information regarding the total cost of the audio recording, however, seems to have disappeared. "It must have been very expensive, but it wasn't something that worried me because it didn't seem to be my department and, as always, I was out to make the best record possible," Baker says. "I was just given a start date and a deadline for the whole album. We were still mixing one of the songs for the album during the press playback at the Roundhouse, so the press heard one track as a rough mix. We never worried about budgets at that time, but it was cheaper to record then."

Baker and Queen were united in the belief that 'Bohemian Rhapsody' should be a single, even though he song's six-minute length gave EMI's decision-makers cause for concern. "It was, after all, breaking all the rules," Baker says. "So we rang EMI and told them we had a single, inviting them down to have a listen. We told them how long the track was and before they had even heard it, the comment was, 'Oh, I don't know, I don't think we'll be able to get any radio play with a song that long.' We said, 'But you haven't heard it yet.' They said, 'Well, just going by what the current formula is, if it's longer than three and a half minutes, they won't play it.' The way I rationalised it was that there had previously been Richard Harris's 'MacArthur Park' and Barry Ryan's 'Eloise' [both 1968] which were very long, and that justified to me that it was probably the right time to release a long song and get away with it. We thought we'd better get some outside advice and around the corner to Scorpion Studios was Capital Radio where Kenny Everett worked. We invited him over for his professional opinion and his response was very animated. He said, 'I love this song, it's so fucking good. This is so good, they'll have to invent a new chart position. Instead of it being Number One, it'll be Number Half!' It was the oddest thing I'd ever heard! So we all went out for an

Indian and Ev asked for a copy. We had a reel-to-reel copy but we told him he could only have it if he promised not to play it. 'I won't play it,' he said, winking.

"On his show the following morning he played the beginning of it, saying, 'Oh, I can't play anymore, 'cause I promised.' Then he played a bit more later. Eventually, he played the track fourteen times over the course of the weekend. By Monday, there were hordes of fans going to the record stores to buy 'Bohemian Rhapsody', only to be told it wasn't out. There was a huge backlash to our end from EMI's promotion department who told us we were undermining them by giving Capital Radio a copy. But they said that we had no option because they told us that nobody would want to play it. In the meantime, John Reid [Queen's then new manager] had got together with the MD at EMI Records and they just went ahead and started to press the single. During the same weekend that Ev was playing the song, there was a guy called Paul Drew who ran the RKO stations in the States who happened to be in London and heard it on the radio. He managed to get a copy of the tape and started to play it in the States which forced the hand of Queen's USA label, Elektra. It was a strange situation where radio on both sides of the Atlantic was breaking a record that the record companies said would never get airplay."

Unfortunately, there are no rough mixes around to audibly demonstrate how 'Bohemian Rhapsody' was created in stages. This can be attributed to Queen's paranoia of having unfinished recordings lying around the studio. "We never did a rough mix because we all had Philips dictaphones that we'd stick near the studio monitors and record a mix for listening to privately," Baker says. "We'd attempt some rough mixes ourselves for other songs just to see if edits would work, but rough mixes had a habit of getting into the record company's hands prematurely. So if we ever did any, we would hide them or disguise them. Once, at Trident Studios, Billy Cobham was working next door and so we hid our tapes in that control room, labelling them 'Cilly Bobham'. If it had been labelled 'Queen', we knew that EMI would have a copy the next day."

More than twenty years on from the original release of

'Bohemian Rhapsody', Baker rightly believes that the song still deserves attention as a creative monument. "I listen to it now and it's a great piece of art, although I didn't realise at the time we had made a classic," he says. "It was the first combination of opera and rock, and the summit of everything we were doing before recording and mixing became automated. If we hadn't produced certain effects by hand, nobody would have bothered to invent the box that did it automatically and I'd like to think that a lot of the stuff we were doing in the Seventies started trends and got copied later by machines."

After working on *A Night At The Opera*, Baker took a break from the Queen camp and concentrated his activities on American bands like The Cars, only to be coaxed back by Roger Taylor for one more album (*Jazz*) in 1978. "'Bohemian Rhapsody' is definitely one of several of my pinnacles, but I saw a backlash against over-production so I changed," Baker says. "One of the ways was to get involved with The Cars because I could use all my production techniques as a way of under-producing. The punk thing was bubbling under and bands were trying to get through with a more raw, understated sound, and I really enjoyed making sparse records with The Cars and Alice Cooper. I could see the backlash coming, just as I could see it happening in the Eighties and out of that came Pearl Jam and Nirvana. There are times I can clearly recall where I have made a conscious move to change my direction, and 'Bohemian Rhapsody' was the pinnacle of my over-indulgence as a producer."

Jeff Jarratt regards 'Bohemian Rhapsody' as an important classical work, on a par with the traditions of the so-called "serious" composers like Beethoven and Mozart. It was the Queen record which directly inspired his and partner, Don Reedman's successful *Classic Rock* series of albums with the London Philharmonic Orchestra. "I think that many contemporary composers in the rock and pop world should receive the same acclaim as Beethoven," he says. "If you look at the way in which some of Queen's songs and recordings were crafted, they are musical masterpieces that are comparable with some of the work that the serious composers have done. When Mozart was composing, he was using the contemporary instruments of his day as the medium of performance, just as Queen did in 1975 for 'Bohemian Rhapsody'."

After tolerating life in the earthquake, fire and riot-stricken zone of Los Angeles for many years, Baker moved out to Lake Havasu, on the California-Arizona border, where he set up his home and luxurious studio complex. "In Los Angeles, it got to the stage that we had armed guards shooting people from the studio roof," he recalls. "There was also the North Ridge earthquake disaster, the fires and all kinds of bullshit going on. I thought, 'That's enough, I'm gonna build a studio in Lake Havasu and have done with all of this!' We have a nice estate surrounded by beautiful mountains, there's fresh air and you can see all the stars at night. In the middle of the desert there's a great seventy-two-track recording studio which everyone loves!"

Baker's studio is almost totally based around retro technology with an architecturally designed, variable format "classic console", comprising a rebuilt Seventies classic Neve mixing board, a TL Audio valve board and Summit and TL Audio valve input equaliser modules. The control room monitoring system features re-coned 1962 Tannoy Big Reds, powered by Hafler amps and fed by a sixty-two-channel Mackie console. The tape machine is an analogue forty-track Stephens with Dolby SR which can be linked to four Tascam digital recorders to provide an extra thirty-two tracks. "I often record discretely on the analogue and transfer over to the digital so that I can take it anywhere I like for overdubs," he reveals.

There is also a Sixties Fender Rhodes piano built into the back end of the console, as well as a vintage 1949 Hammond B3 organ with Leslie rotary speakers and, taking pride of place, an internally-miked bright red Schaffer grand piano. "The ceiling has stainless steel bass traps and there are plate glass windows and sliding doors separating the control rooms and studios," Baker says. "There are concrete pillars and floors, and fifteen foot high ceilings. The guitar/piano room has concrete walls and it has the greatest sound I've ever heard, with a boost at 600 cycles which I love. There's also a formidable art collection on display and I'd imagine I've spent more money on art than most people spend on equipment!"

Baker, who worked on two albums by IRS signing Mozart before their split, is constantly surprised by the interest shown in his Seventies achievements by young bands. "I work with teenage bands and they are always referring to the Queen and Cars records, almost like they want to live vicariously through my life. They seem so preoccupied by the Seventies and early Eighties, maybe because there isn't as much of a scene anymore."

chapter eight

stack heels to safety pins

"Chris Spedding phoned me one night and said that they were on at the Screen On The Green at about one in the morning. So I went up there, met Chris and saw the Pistols, and it was totally incredible."
Chris Thomas

Not so long ago, the Seventies stood accused of being the pop era's soulless decade, filled with tacky artists and impotent records. More recently, however, the media has had good cause to favourably reappraise the period, the general consensus being that, if one can ignore the dreadful fashions, the music was actually quite good, sometimes glorious. Naturally, music had a lot to live up to after the Sixties revolution and in retrospect, the psychedelic hangover which appeared to affect the business laid an intangible barrier which, for most artists, was difficult to overcome. In spite of the originality of The Beatles, The Rolling Stones and The Who, all of whom wrote their own brilliant material, most pop acts in the Seventies who favoured a singles chart direction were forced to rely on the efforts of Tin Pan Alley "bubblegum" songsmiths – from the London equivalent of New York's Brill Building stable – who churned out hit after hit, with the ease of an East End sweatshop. Pop music was in desperate need of a personality fix.

By the end of 1971, the next big thing had arrived: glam rock. With Marc Bolan and T-Rex, David Bowie, Slade, Gary Glitter and The Sweet heading the cast, the music was all about loud guitars, resonant drums, satin suits and (in some cases) defying the barriers of gender. The glam craze peaked in 1973 just as a new breed of disco music from America threatened to topple British stars from their platform soles. After a brief no man's land period in which pop music became detached from real social issues and fans looked in vain for new heroes, the anti-establishment brigade of The Sex Pistols, The Clash and The Damned brought the music business to its knees with their riotous new sounds and anarchistic attitude. Only Elvis and the Fabs had a more profound impact on youth culture as punk blew like a hurricane with a sneer and its obligatory two-finger salute. Of the old guard of rock and pop artists, a mere few survived as punk sorted the wheat from the chaff and gave conceited old rockers with their tired concepts the news that they were no longer relevant. It was clean-up time and with the formation of a wealth of new independent labels set up to market the punk product that majors wouldn't dare touch or even understand, it was arguably the healthiest period in British music for fifteen years.

Musical fashions come and go, and technology will always provide a means to develop new styles, but the power of the song and its effective presentation will always transcend the decades. The late Sixties and early Seventies saw the emergence of a number of quality singer-songwriters, both in Britain and abroad. Carly Simon, Billy Joel, Harry Nilsson, Gilbert O'Sullivan and Cat Stevens were fine examples but none can boast the international success and longevity of Elton John.

John's career began in 1961 under his real name, Reg Dwight, as the pianist and occasional songwriter with R&B outfit, Bluesology. After a failed 1967 audition for Liberty Records, he was put in contact with Lincolnshire lyricist, Bernie Taupin and immediately set up a songwriting partnership, even though they did not meet each other in person until they had completed more than twenty songs together, by post. In 1968, John and Taupin signed to Dick James Music as staff writers on a wage of £10 per week each, and in the March of that year, John's first single, 'I've Been Loving You Too Long' was the first of two singles released by Philips which failed to chart.

Working at DJM's demo recording studio in 1968 was John's now long-time associate, Stuart Epps who recalls the environment of the singer-songwriter's formative steps towards eventual fame. "The studio was used by all of DJM's songwriters, like Roger Cook and Roger Greenaway who would come in and demo six to eight tracks, fairly live, with Herbie Flowers on bass and the line-up which became Blue Mink," he says. "A couple of months later, all these songs would be in the charts, recorded by Dusty Springfield, Gene Pitney and many others. After 'I've Been Loving You Too Long', Elton did his subsequent recordings at DJM when I was still the office boy. Steve Brown, who still works for Elton, had been working at EMI then moved to DJM, and Elton brought him into the cutting room where I was working to listen to the album that Elton had made with Caleb Quaye [ex-Bluesology guitarist] producing. It was quite *Sgt Pepper*-ish, thinking back. But Steve said he didn't think it was very good. We were saying, 'Bloody cheek, who does he think he is?' He thought it was too poppy, so we didn't like him! But then he got very friendly with Elton and Bernie, and produced a single called 'Lady Samantha' [the second and last of John's Philips releases] which got a lot of airplay although hardly anyone bought it, despite it being a great record. After that, Elton signed to DJM's new record label and he and Steve went into the demo studio and did the first album, *Empty Sky* with Roger Pope and Nigel Olsson on drums, and Dee Murray on bass. Although I didn't engineer it, I got credited with guarding the studio because I stood in reception making sure people didn't come in while they were recording! When it came to making the second album, Steve started thinking that he wasn't doing Elton much justice as a producer, so he was looking around for another producer and it was him that got in touch with Gus Dudgeon, having heard the good job he did on David Bowie's 'Space Oddity'."

Dudgeon regards the *Elton John* album, better known as the *Black Album*, as the most important record of John's career and it set the singer/piano man style which others would attempt to emulate but seldom equal. But, Dudgeon says, the *Black Album* was not originally made with a commercial market in mind. With few people in the industry convinced that John had the necessary physical attributes to become a pop star (glasses, build and general looks conceived as obstacles), the album was recorded as a glamorous demo album of his songs, in an attempt to gain cover versions by the famous. "I received a series of demos from Elton which really constituted the eventual album and I don't think we introduced another song to the project," Dudgeon says. "I was very used to working as an engineer with rhythm sections and orchestras, but most of the orchestrations I had recorded to date tended to be twee, as if they were there only for sweetening. Elton's songs demanded something different and more adventurous. Songs like 'First Episode At Hienton' sounded complex and classical in some ways, and certainly not what was happening in the charts, so I asked DJM for a carte blanche budget to allow me to take some time over creating a production style around these beautiful, new-sounding songs. To my amazement it was approved and it allowed me to think as big as I wanted. I already knew Paul Buckmaster who had done such a great job on other sessions such as 'Space Oddity' and whose orchestral arrangements leaned towards the classical. It was really through Buckmaster that I got the gig, because they originally wanted George Martin, not unsurprisingly. I could just sense that Elton's songs, his piano style and delivery, combined with Paul's orchestration would work so well."

Although Dudgeon was still a largely untested producer, DJM agreed to place him with John and a string of sessions was booked at Trident Studios in early 1970. Thanks to Dudgeon's intricate planning, the *Black Album* took only one week to record and mix with engineer Robin Cable, and cost only £6,000 (including the sleeve design). "'Space Oddity' was something I planned to the last detail and it worked brilliantly, and so I thought I had better apply the same tactics with Elton's album, which accounts for why it was cut so fast," Dudgeon says. "It was one of the most enjoyable weeks of my entire life and it set a pattern for the next five or six years. We would go to the pub at the end of every session and all that Elton, Bernie, Paul, Robin and I did was smirk at how amazing the music was sounding."

The *Black Album* was a style template which John adhered to for several years, on albums such as *Tumbleweed Connection*, *Madman Across The Water*, *Honky Chateau*, *Goodbye Yellow Brick Road* and *Caribou*. Dudgeon cites Billy Joel as being but one stellar artist who gained much from John's influence. "Billy's first album, *Piano Man*, was smothered with Elton influences and even the sleeve bore a striking resemblance to Elton's," he says. "But it's an area of music that no one seems too bothered with anymore. I was trying to marry rock 'n' roll rhythm sections with great orchestrations, where the orchestration was equally as important as the rock element and I hand-picked every musician to guarantee that we did what we set out to do."

Four years and ten UK hit singles into his working relationship with Elton John, Dudgeon had accumulated no mean fortune from his producer royalties and was advised by his (then) accountant, Keith Moore to consider starting a sideline business to offset the colossal levels of tax he was paying. And so one of Britain's great rural studio legends, the Mill, was born. "We thought of all kinds of things like car hire companies until the idea of a studio arose," Dudgeon says. "I knew I wanted somewhere with a view because in most studios, you can work for a week and not actually see any sunshine, and it turned out that Keith's secretary's uncle had the ideal property and was thinking of selling."

Stuart Epps (who took over Alvin Lee's rural Wheeler End Studios in 1996) had just returned from an American tour with Elton John and Kiki Dee in 1974 when Dudgeon told him of his purchase of a property in Cookham, near Maidenhead in Berkshire. "The place looked great and the project seemed like a really good one," says Epps. "Gus had used an MCI desk at the Marquee and it was his favourite desk, so he went over to MCI in Florida and talked to them about having a desk custom-made. But when they listened to all of Gus's ideas, they decided to incorporate them into a new forty-two-channel desk they were building, and our one came in custom colours. The Mill was designed by Gus's main engineer at that time, Phil Dunne, and it was about two years before it was really finished because it got a lot more complicated than it was supposed to have been. So we started recording around 1976 and the first album we did was with Solution, a Dutch band that Gus was producing."

Most of the early projects at The Mill were Dudgeon productions with new artists, such as Shooting Star and Voyager who scored a sizeable hit with their single, 'Halfway Hotel'. But of Dudgeon's newer talent, the most successful was Chris Rea, who signed with Magnet Records in 1977 and made his first two albums, *Whatever Happened*

To Benny Santini and *Deltics* with Dudgeon, who became accused of attempting to mould Rea into the new Elton John (even though the same critics claimed he was doing similarly with Joan Armatrading!).

In an ironic twist of fate, 1995 saw Rea's purchase of Dudgeon's old studio. "When I first met Chris he was very nervous and shy, and he had no opinions of his own that he would share with me about his music," says the producer. "So someone had to make some decisions and I took the reins. He did have a problem with using session musicians because he would have preferred to use some pals from the North, but the A&R guy at Magnet was totally into what I wanted to do. Chris's songs had great potential for orchestration but he wasn't too sure whether we should be using strings or not. 'Fool (If You Think It's Over)' was written during the course of the album and I had already agreed to the album on the basis of all the other songs. Then, when he came to me with this about a week into recording, I just knew that it would be a big hit. The same thing happened when I worked with Lindisfarne and they came up with 'Run For Home'. But usually, the first time you discover whether you really stand a good chance of having a hit is when you hear your track on the radio for the first time, amongst everyone else's records. "

In spite of Rea's subsequent European success, 'Fool' remains his only major American hit, and Dudgeon repeated the winning formula (same arrangement, rhythm box and edits) some years later for Elkie Brooks' cover of the song. "Chris was making a big song and dance over the fact that I'd put strings on his single," Dudgeon says. "Then it looked like being big in America [Number Two] and I said to him, 'Are you now going to run around and say that it shouldn't have had strings?' He said, 'Oh no, I'll keep that to myself.' I advised him that it would be the wisest thing to do, rather than shoot himself in the foot. For someone who wasn't keen on session musicians in the beginning, he has made a meal of it in more recent years, both on albums and for tours because he now realises their commercial worth."

One Elton John session at the Mill which Epps and John's co-producer, Clive Franks remember for all the wrong reasons was for 'Song For Guy', an instrumental track from the 1978 *A Single Man* album. "It was one Sunday afternoon when Elton came in looking really down and sad," says Franks. "He told us that one of our messenger bikers from Rocket Records [John's own label] called Guy had been in a road accident the previous day and was killed. Guy was a really sweet kid and everybody liked him. So the tone of the day was very sad. [Percussionist] Ray Cooper and the rest of the band started arriving and we were all talking in the control room when Elton just disappeared into the studio area to play piano. After what must have been a hour, he called me in and asked me to listen to this glorious tune. He played it all the way through and I was so moved that I was shaking and tingling. I told him that we had to get this recorded straight away. Stuart was engineering with me and we put a reel of tape on the multitrack that looked like it had a good five or six minutes left on it."

Epps takes up the rest of the story: "For me, it was the scariest moment in recording history! Elton went out and played a bit to the Roland rhythm box and we got a good piano sound, so we put the machine into record and he started playing this thing. He'd get to about thirty seconds of the way through and make a mistake, so we'd stop the machine and start again. But he kept making these little mistakes and we could see that he was getting tired and pissed off. It was only meant to take five minutes and already an hour had gone by. It was quite a complex piece so you can see why he was making these mistakes. Then it all seemed to come together and we were about two minutes in and he's roaring, he hadn't made a mistake or stopped yet. Suddenly I've looked round at the twenty-four-track machine and there was not a hell of a lot of tape left on the reel. There was a fair bit but we hadn't bothered to put a full reel on because we thought it was just going to be this little piano idea. We thought we'd still be okay. By now, he was three minutes into it and still going, and we're looking at the tape machine and beginning to get edgy. We're thinking, 'Christ, if he gets to the end of this and we run out of tape, he's going to go mad, he'll just kill us.' He's someone who has a terrible temper when he goes for it. We thought it wouldn't take much longer. So I was standing by this tape machine and Clive was looking at him to see if he was about to finish. But he was still roaring and we were mentally willing this tune to finish, sweating, because there was only a tiny bit of tape left. We really thought we were fucked. But just as he finished playing the last note or chord and it died away completely, the tape came off the reel and we couldn't believe our luck. Our lives were spared the wrath of Elton! And I still don't think he's aware of what was happening all that time."

All That Glitters

John Hudson commands universal respect from producers and artists alike for his Midas touch at the mixing desk. Now the owner of London's Mayfair Studio (which he and his wife Kate rescued from oblivion in 1978), he began his audio career at the BBC in the Sixties before becoming a balance engineer at Spot Studios, a four-track demo facility in South Molton Street which was renamed Mayfair in 1974 – but not before this engineer carved his name all over the early Seventies glam rock sound. "It was in 1971 that I saw an ad in *Melody Maker* – 'Balance Engineer required for a small West End studio' – and went along for an interview," Hudson says. "I had never seen a recording studio, and it was such a fantastic vibe. So I was knocked out when the guy offered me the job straight away, mainly because of my BBC experience. Within the first year I was recording Gary Glitter and The Bay City Rollers whose writers used the place for demos with real session musicians! If you wanted to do five demos, you booked the musos and three hours in the studio. You made five backing tracks and in the afternoon you put the voices on, then mixed it."

Songwriter Phil Coulter, who was then signed to Leeds Music, was a regular Spot Studios client along with arranger, Mike Leander, and after working with Hudson at the controls for six months it was agreed that he would be the chosen engineer for a set of master sessions. The singer on those dates was Paul Gadd, and Hudson was an eye witness to his metamorphosis as Gary Glitter. ("He nearly ended up being called Terry Tinsel.") Back in 1971, the formative Glitter stomp sounded like the extra-terrestrial bastard son of Fifties Americana and Spector's Wall of Sound. In short, nothing like it had ever been heard before.

Hudson reveals the background to the formula. "Studio time was very cheap compared with how much you would make out of selling the record, so you could afford to write in the studio," he says. "So when Mike Leander was writing the songs he was literally making a demo and the master at the same time. He would hire a drum kit, come in and bash around, and play some piano, and I would be in the control room recording everything on to quarter-inch. The bass drum was on one track, the snare on another and the cymbals would just break through a little on to both tracks. Mike would play for hours, until he was completely knackered and covered in sweat. Once he was happy with a certain section of the drumming, he would ask me to make a two-bar loop, then relay it to a speaker by the piano so that he could write a song. By 1972 we had an eight-track and we would copy the loop onto two tracks of the quarter-inch and then record the piano onto the third track while he got the song vaguely together. After a while we wouldn't need the drum loop anymore and Mike would start to lay down the rest of the instrumentation down for the master on his own, although I remember playing bass myself on at least a couple of Gary's tracks."

Despite giving the impression of being heavily delayed, à la Spector, Hudson insists that the drums on Glitter's early hits ('Rock And Roll Parts 1 & 2', 'I Didn't Know I Loved You Till I Saw You Rock And Roll', etc) were not delayed at all. "That was a big secret at the time, although if you listen really carefully you can hear what it is," he says. "It was the toms and the claps which suggested that sort of sound, but the actual basic drum loop was very dry. There were a lot of overdubs. The basic drum track was just snare and bass drum, but Mike would then record at least two more tracks of drums, playing all the way through the song and dropping in for certain parts." The infectious riffs played over the top of the drum tracks were courtesy of Leander's unorthodox guitar tuning. "The strings were tuned in octaves and fifths, so the top E was A, the A string was probably back down to E, the D string would be tuned up to E, the G was probably up to B, while the next two [B and E] would remain as standard," Hudson continues. "It produced such a strange droning sound and we knew we were on to something different. Mike used a full-size jack plug and sometimes a cigarette lighter as a slide, playing the guitar through a tiny Futurama amp with a ten-inch speaker, and I miked it with a couple of AKG C12s. We would often track the guitar as many as fifteen times, bouncing between two tracks at a time, Mike's theory being that as well as sounding big it would hide any mistakes!"

The large, thirty-channel custom-made Spot mixing desk proved to be problematic and Hudson often had cause to conduct major repair work between – and sometimes in the middle of – sessions. The desk featured an eight-track monitor section, thirty inputs, two post-fade fixed effects sends and two pre-fade fixed cue sends, all patchable. The EQ was simply treble and bass boost and cut, with a boost-only mid of 1kHz and 4kHz. In addition, the Spot control room used a pair of original blue Pultec EQ units and four transistorised outboard EQ units offering a range of selectable frequencies, as well as two Fairchild compressors and an EMT reverb plate. At the time of Hudson's arrival in 1971, the studio employed two Philips quarter-inch tape machines for mixdown – one mono, one stereo (later replaced by a Scully) – and an Ampex A440 four-track for multitracking. "The Ampex deck was in a huge stainless steel box and the amps were in a rack of four," Hudson comments. "The machine was classic, because there was obviously no remote control for it and the deck wasn't automated, so if you rewound the tape you couldn't even press play until the tape had stopped, otherwise you'd snap the tape. So you had to be very much on the ball. The control room was very small with three speakers at the front – two for playback and one to monitor recording – and there was no such thing as subtle panning. The sound was either placed extreme left, extreme right or in the middle. When we did all the Gary Glitter stuff, we used to play the track back through the left and right speakers, and whatever we were over-dubbing we would monitor on the centre speaker, and it was pretty loud for those days."

When Spot took the decision to upgrade to eight-track, it invested not in the industry standard Ampex brand, but (to Hudson's endless dismay) an English Leevers Rich machine. "It was quite flash," he recalls. "The deck was fairly automated and it had a locater in it, a very simple rewind to zero-type locater. But the main flaw in the design was that you couldn't drop in without there being a huge delay and a click. I demonstrated the problem to the manufacturer's engineers and they told me that I wasn't supposed to drop in, and that I had to record from the beginning of the song. They obviously had no idea about the realities of recording, but they did end up modifying the machine for me after a few heated exchanges."

At the time of Spot's change of name to Mayfair Studios ("Spot was always a dodgy name"), he had risen to chief engineer status and set about persuading the owners to upgrade further, from eight to sixteen-track. "Everything was advancing so fast," he says. "One minute you were eight-track and the next minute you were sixteen. But by the time they got around to buying the machine, there was already a hint of twenty-four-track. But that was the thing about the Seventies – no one could move fast enough, and these switches from eight- to sixteen- to twenty-four-track all happened within about three years."

In 1974, Leander and Coulter had become so successful with Glitter, The Bay City Rollers, Alvin Stardust and Hello that their tax situation demanded they record most of their work overseas. Being Mayfair's top clients, this adversely affected the studio's revenue and it also led to Hudson leaving the staff to turn freelance and join the duo wherever they needed his engineering skills. It was also during this period that Hudson met his future wife and business partner, Kate, who was then working as Coulter's assistant. "Suddenly, I was going to Los Angeles and Paris which was good for me because I could work in all these different studios, although some of them were horrific!" he says.

While Hudson was away, a new talent was emerging on his old stamping ground. Being the first professional recording studio he ever worked in, Mayfair played a significant part in Midge Ure's early career when he drove to London from Glasgow with his band, Slik to make his debut record, the Number One 'Forever And Ever' in late 1975. The band had been signed to Bell Records by producer and songwriter, Bill Martin, with whom Coulter had written much of The Bay City Rollers' repertoire. Previously known as Salvation, Slik provided Martin with another opportunity to exploit the talents and dreams of yet another bunch of Scottish hopefuls. Ure arrived at the studio expecting his band to record the track themselves, but he was in for a shock. "We heard this really bad Bay City Rollers-sounding backing track coming out of the control room and we just sniggered, thinking it was another Rollers record in the making," he recalls. "But then we were informed quite abruptly by the producers that this was our track and they had already recorded the backing before we arrived. I got very protective and said, 'Look, I'm a musician and I don't want to just put my voice on someone else's backing track.' I was subsequently hauled out of the studio into South Molton Street for a swift bollocking!

"For a kid, that was quite a daunting prospect, standing there with Bill Martin, who was a very successful industry figure then. He was screaming abuse at me in the middle of the street, saying I was a complete amateur, a tosser, and I should just get back in the studio and sing the bloody song! Of course, that's what I did. It was ultimately our choice. Bill just said, 'Do you want a hit record or would you prefer to be obscure for the rest of your life?' And in that particular genre, in that teenybop market, I suppose it's no different these days. We still have groups of young, pretty boys and girls who sing songs written by forty-year-olds for fourteen-year-olds. That still exists and it probably will *ad infinitum*. But that's only one side of the music business."

Eventually and much to his better judgement, Martin relented and allowed Slik the luxury of performing on their own records, possibly in the belief that the band was going to be the last "pretty boy" act he would discover for a long time. "The main difference with Slik was that we had actually been in existence for three or four years before that first single," Ure says. "We had been a regular pull on the Scottish live circuit and were quite a good band for our age. That made all the difference and so when we were doing the Slik concerts after our Number One, we did retain some credibility because we were able to play live, without backing tapes. We were also writing, but like any aspiring writer you tend to emulate whoever you're into at the time. So if you took a cross section of our songs from that period, you'd find one that sounded like Queen, one like Roxy Music, Ziggy Stardust – they were all very much our fledgling footsteps.

"I knew that Martin and Coulter were going to write the songs and that they'd be fairly dodgy. But being young, green and naive, we just thought we'd go along with it and do a couple of their songs. We believed that if we were successful, they would come around to our way of thinking, so we could start getting into the studio to do what we wanted to do. Which is what eventually happened, but the bubble had burst by then."

After four years largely spent outside of Britain, the success of

Leander and Coulter began to diminish. Glam rock had petered out and Hudson moved back to London. Mayfair, meanwhile, had not sustained business in the interim period and was on the verge of collapse. Hudson was forced to pick up the pieces. "Everything had changed and Mayfair was in a bit of a sorry state," he remembers. "The opportunity arose for my wife Kate and I to take over the running of Mayfair, as the respective studio manager and chief engineer. Twenty-four-track was standard by 1978 and I knew that would have to be the first consideration, but there was also a lot of deadwood to be thrown out. Most of the staff were drongos sitting around reading the paper. It was hard work, but we very quickly built it up from a business that was about to go bust to being fully booked."

The Most Of RAK

The Animals' 'House Of The Rising Sun' in 1964 sparked a lucrative production career for Mickie Most as he spent the rest of that decade building his profile with an astonishing range of hits for Herman's Hermits, Donovan, Jeff Beck and Lulu. By the early Seventies he had formed his own record label, RAK, as the marketing arm for a whole new roster of best-selling acts, including Hot Chocolate, CCS and Kenny.

Legendary drummer, Cozy Powell became known to Most as a member of The Jeff Beck Group after joining in late 1969 and he went on to regularly play on sessions for the producer and a wide range of his artists. In 1970, Powell, Beck and Most travelled to Motown Studios in Detroit with a view to cutting an album of instrumental Motown covers. Unfortunately, the album never saw the light of day, although it gave Powell a fascinating insight into both the American way of recording and Beck's musical mentality. "The sessions were just centred around Jeff and I playing with a lot of the great Motown house session players like James Jamerson on bass," he told me in 1996. "The Motown staff wouldn't even let me near their house kit, let alone play it! It was a very small room with a wooden ceiling and Jamerson's Ampeg bass stack was right by the door, the kit was in the corner and you weren't allowed to move anything. So I found some space and set my double kit up in there.

"We recorded about nine tracks but the album was never released because Jeff wasn't ever happy with it, even though some of the playing on it was fantastic, as you can imagine. But Jeff was going through a period where he wasn't sure of what he wanted to do and he was very confused about his direction. Part of him wanted to have a rock band, another was into jazz and another part of him was very influenced by what Stevie Wonder was doing at the time, which is why one of the tracks was 'Superstition', recorded way before Stevie released his own version."

It was while in Detroit that Most discovered a pint-sized female singer and bassist who would soon bolster the already considerable fortunes of his new label. "Someone said there was an all-girl band called Cradle playing down the road, so we got tanked up and went to see them at this theatre," remembered Powell. "Sure enough, there was Suzi Quatro and her sisters, and they were really good. Mickie saw something in Suzi and decided to bring her back to England and make her a star, it was as simple as that. Mickie had a bunch of songs prepared for her, some of which I played on. I would be on call and he'd ring me to see if I was free to do a session, but you never knew what you were going to play. It could have been anything for anyone and it was an unknown quantity until you got to the studio. Sometimes he would change his plans during a session and I'd suddenly end up playing on a different song."

The majority of Most's early Seventies productions were recorded at Morgan Studios before he invested in his own impressive RAK Studios in St John's Wood. During Powell's session phase with Most he recorded three of his own solo singles, as a glam rock answer to Fifties drumming legend, Sandy Nelson. Powell's big hit over the winter 1973-4 period was the thunderous 'Dance With The Devil'. "Mickie jokingly came up with the idea of me recording a drum solo and it was all very light-hearted," he said. "We had a riff that sounded like Jimi Hendrix's 'Third Stone From The Sun', but in actual fact it came from the end of a Ronnie Hawkins track called 'Bo Diddley'. We put this idea together with a few arrangers then about a month later it was released and went into the charts.

"Although Mickie kept me informed of its progress I didn't really keep much of an eye on it until I was told I had to do *Top Of The Pops*, then suddenly it dawned on me how successful this thing had become. The record had been played once an hour, every hour for a week on Radio Luxembourg and all of a sudden it was huge. It was the Christmas period and not only do people buy more records at Christmas, but the records stay in the charts longer. I got to Number One in one chart, Number Two in another and Number Three in two others. Being Christmas there was a massive amount of TV exposure and I did *Top Of The Pops* with Pan's People dancing in front of me. I was the envy of every musician I knew!

"Mickie had a great ear and he always managed to record and mix things incredibly quickly. Although people used to criticise him because of his success, Mickie knew exactly what he was doing as he proved with RAK. If somebody had talent he would really home in there and get the best out of them. Everyone else went by the wayside."

It was with great sadness and extreme shock that I learned of Powell's death in April 1998, the result of an horrific car crash on the M4 motorway in his Saab – the same car in which I had shared a journey with the legendary drummer only a few months before. The shock was multiplied when I remembered speaking to Cozy forty-eight hours before the tragedy about a future project which would include "some heavy friends". Quite what that would have been we may never know.

Visconti, Bolan And Bowie

It was during the late Sixties as Denny Cordell's assistant that Tony Visconti first met and discovered the full potential of Marc Bolan and David Bowie. Both were operating as acoustic, folk-orientated acts at the time, but with Visconti's encouragement, both found their classic electric rock formula which typified the early Seventies glam sound. Visconti says that Bolan, in particular (who had previously played in rock band, John's Children) had ambitions to be an electric guitarist, although he did not own anything other than a beaten-up acoustic. "All Marc could afford at this point was a second-hand six-string acoustic guitar which had a broken G-string peg, so he always carried a pair of pliers around with him to help tune the thing," comments Visconti. "It was that £12 guitar which he used for the three years we were making the Tyrannosaurus Rex albums. And, of course, his partner, Steve Peregrine Took was playing all these strange little percussion instruments he found in Woolworth's or junk shops. Little clay drums from Morocco that he picked up for next to nothing. There was also something he called a pixiephone which was actually a one-stringed bowed instrument with a gramophone bell on the end. That was quite well featured on the first album."

Visconti first laid eyes on Bolan and Tyrannosaurus Rex at London's UFO Club in the autumn of 1967 when Cordell suggested the time was ripe for his assistant to find a new act of his own to produce. "There was a little buzz at that time about them, I'd heard they were good," he says. "So I went down to the UFO and listened to the set, and I was mesmerised along with about 300 other people. Unlike the normal rock thing, the audience didn't scream and clap. They didn't utter a sound until the song was over, then they went crazy with this thunderous applause. And I was so impressed with Marc that afterwards I introduced myself, gave him my business card and Marc was full of himself. He said, 'Oh you're the eighth producer who has been in here this week. Maybe I'll give you a call. John Lennon wants to produce us.' It was all a lie, of course. The next day Marc called me and seemed very interested, so he and Steve came down and auditioned for us right there on the floor. They put down a little carpet and did the whole set in front of Denny and I. There was a £400 budget for the first album and not much more for the second, maybe £600. So for economical reasons, we had to do the first two albums [*My People Were Fair And Had Sky In Their Hair, But Now They're Content To Wear Stars On Their Brow* and *Prophets, Seers And Sages, The Angels Of The Ages*] non-electric with that acoustic guitar."

As the recording of *Prophets, Seers And Sages* reached its climax, Bolan introduced a new song, 'Elemental Child', which featured the first instance of an electric guitar on a Tyrannosaurus Rex record. "It was my guitar, it was borrowed," claims Visconti. "Marc had been coming to my flat along with David Bowie. I was a few years older than them and out of all the people they knew, I was the only person who had a stereo gramophone, so we could listen to The Beach Boys and The Beatles in stereo. I was also the only person they knew who had an electric bass and electric guitar. So both of them were playing my instruments, and some nights we would all be together, jamming. We were all secret Beach Boys fans and on Marc's albums such as *Unicorn*, when we finally had a little money and the electric guitar came along, we tried to get a big Phil Spector or Beach Boys kind of snare drum sound, but again, the only drum kit they could afford was a Chad Valley kids' kit from Woolworth's! That actually had a great sound to it and it was the first record which featured a drum kit along with the other electric instruments. The electric influence was directly from me and we always loved rock records. Maybe the closest we ever got to a folk connection was Marc's interest in The Incredible String Band."

Again for economical reasons, Bowie remained a highly portable acoustic act towards the end of the Sixties and was so financially strapped, Visconti reveals, that he even had to borrow the twelve-string guitar which helped him on his way to the top. "When it came to making the first album with him at the end of 1969, it was clear that we couldn't make a folk record and he did actually want to go electric," Visconti says. "So I used a band that I was producing at the time called Junior's Eyes which included Mick Wayne, who played guitar on *Space Oddity* and John Cambridge on drums. Mick didn't join us permanently but John did and it was he who brought Mick Ronson in. Mick was the one who really made the electric connection. When we heard Mick play we just knew we had to make that kind of an album. He was one of the first heavy metal guitarists. I was actually playing bass in Bowie's band and it was Mick who influenced me to get more electric and bigger-sounding. He sat me down and made me listen to Jack Bruce over and over again, saying, 'Tony, you have to play like this because I play like Clapton!'"

By now recording under the abbreviated band name, T-Rex, October 1970 saw the release of Bolan's 'Ride A White Swan' as he expanded his band line-up to a quartet. A major hit, the single climbed to Number Two in the British chart and was followed the next spring by the first T-Rex Number One, 'Hot Love'. It would be fair to state, however, that glam rock truly began with the band's second chart-topper, 'Get It On' and its parent album, *Electric Warrior*, both of which launching Bolan as a pop icon in his native Britain and America.

"'Get It On' was recorded in three different studios around April 1971. It was the first time I could afford to go back to America for a holiday!" says Visconti. "'Hot Love' had been recorded at AIR Studios and was massive, and I met up with Marc and the band in New York while I was on holiday and they were on tour. I said, 'Why don't we make some records?' So we hired a studio in Manhattan and we recorded 'Jeepster' and 'Monolith', then they flew to Los Angeles to play at the Whisky A Go-Go. We had already worked with Mark Volman and Howard Kaylan (The Turtles and Flo And Eddie fame), and while we were all in LA, we went down to Wally Heider's Studio to record three tracks together, one of which was 'Get It On'. We used the house engineer because at that time I wasn't engineering, I was mixing. I felt that as a producer, my main duty was to mind the music and leave all the sonic decisions to the engineer. So I wouldn't touch the board during a tracking session because there was just too much going on. The master backing track was the third of three takes, and everything you hear is the original bass, drums and guitar. Then Marc added a second electric guitar and Mark and Howard immediately did the backing vocals on the spot. At about two am, we ran out of brandy, vodka and drugs, so the session ended at about three. But we got three great tracks in the can from that trip and later on during the tour, when we got to Europe, we made some more recordings in France. When we got back to London we had to do a few more tracks for the album, like 'Mambo Sun', and some overdubs for 'Get It On'."

While it is known that King Crimson's Ian MacDonald played the saxophone parts on 'Get It On' at Advision Studios, to this day it is unclear whether it was Blue Weaver or Rick Wakeman who played piano – both strongly insist that they deserve the credit. Visconti believes it was Weaver, although he now has reason to doubt his memory. "I do recall Blue playing on 'Telegram Sam' but we are talking about something that happened a quarter of a century ago!" he admits. "I think it was Rick, but Blue told me that Rick doesn't do those glissandos, those ripples up the keyboard like Jerry Lee Lewis used to do. Blue said, 'I play that way and that's why I'm sure it was me!' What I am sure of is that the actual overdub was done in London at Trident Studios."

At the same Trident sessions, strings were planned for most tracks on *Electric Warrior*, but not 'Get It On'. "I looked at Marc a bit superstitiously and said, 'We've had strings on the first two hit singles, do you think we should stop now?' He said, 'I think you've got a point but did you write anything?' I hadn't but I knew what to do. It was in the key of E and on the spot I just arranged something around the chord changes in the chorus. They were G, then A minor and E. All I did with the strings was to get the cellos, violas and violins to just play the root notes of the chorus – G, A, E – G, A, E. That was it. I wrote those notes out but I didn't even write a full score, I just counted in the string section one bar before the chorus. '1-2-3-4...G...A...E.' We put the strings in the mix of that third single and it was another Number One in Britain and a Number Ten in the States. Marc was an instant superstar."

'Heroes'

Before Germany became unified once again in 1989, Hansa TonStudios by the Berlin Wall was noted for its intimidating exterior. From the control room, the gun turrets on the West German side and the Red Guards in East Germany could be plainly seen, while music was the only thing on the minds of those occupying one of the most beautiful studios on the European continent. In 1976, David Bowie had emerged from a low point in his life and was now at his creative peak. Writing a song as uplifting and optimistic as 'Heroes' came naturally. Lyrically, it was inspired by Bowie's observations of Visconti's affair with backing singer, Antonia Maas – the couple who were "standing by the wall" as they "kissed but nothing shot over [their] heads". Set against a synthesised wall of its own, care of Brian Eno's unique treatments, 'Heroes' signified yet another phase in Bowie's chameleon-like career, with a vaguely industrial flavour which would be developed on later albums, including *Lodger* and *Scary Monsters*.

"Like most Bowie records, we had already laid down the backing track and we used Hansa Studio One which was mainly used for classical recordings," explains Visconti. "It had a little stage where you could put a percussion section and in the remainder of this room you could probably fit in about 120 musicians. So we put Dennis Davis, the drummer, up on this stage, George Murray's bass amp in one corner, Carlos Alomar's guitar amp in the other, and the rhythm track was recorded as a three-piece. We also applied a trick I began to use on *Low* which involved using a harmoniser on the snare drum and playing the end signal back through Dennis's headphones. The harmoniser was tuned just below pitch and with the feedback knob on, so when Dennis hit his snare drum, it would go 'byyyooooww' and drop in pitch. In the mix it sounds more fixed, but when the drummer hears it in his cans, the harder he hits it, the longer the pitch will drop.

So Dennis was hearing that effect in his headphones and was quite literally 'playing' that sound. Also, we were using room mics because it was one enormous live room which gave us a big drum sound."

The main hall at Hansa, once a Nazi banqueting venue before and during World War II, was also used for Bowie's impressive vocal recording, aided in no minor way by Visconti's ingenious miking technique. "We were connected in the control room to that big room by CCTV, so I had to watch the band and Bowie on a TV monitor," he says. "I took great advantage of the size of the room for Bowie's vocals because he is capable of great dynamics. I had one mic right in front of him with a pop shield, and I said, 'When you're singing softly this mic is going to pick you up.' Then I put a mic about five metres away from him, and said, 'When you sing louder, this mic is going to pick that up because I'm going to put some gain on it.' I then put another mic at the back of the room, about fifteen metres away, and told him, 'When you sing really loudly, this mic will open up and the acoustics of the entire room will be heard on this track.' And he was really cool about that idea and experimented with how loud he had to sing to open up each of these mics, before we even did a take. So a lot of the ambience you hear from the vocals on that record was created that way, especially on the third verse when it gets into his higher register vocals. At that point, the back mic is picking him up and you can hear the hall's acoustics. It was the first time I'd used that technique and I've never used it since because you don't often find rooms that big."

Finding the right microphone for such a stylised vocalist was a difficult task for Visconti when the pair began making records together. Although Visconti is a Neumann aficionado and initially believed the classic Neumann U47 valve microphone would bring out all the right inflections in Bowie's voice, he was surprised that the solution was to be found elsewhere. "I went through my collection until I found a Beyer M160 double ribbon microphone, a real hi-fi mic that gets used for classical string sections, and it really brought out the low end of his vocal range," he says. "At the time, his voice had a real nasal quality and he was always asking me how he could make his voice sound deep and resonant. David always liked double-tracking his vocals and it was our joint idea. We wrote a lot of the arrangements together and when Eno was along for the ride, he would come up with

The Who's *bassmeister*, John Entwistle, reminiscing at home in Gloucestershire

Raymond Douglas Davies: The Kinks' main man, on stage in 1994

Fleetwood Mac in 1969, the year the band parted from producer Mike Vernon

Pictured at a recording session are Mick Vernon, Hu
Sumlin and Neil Slaven.

26k

Recording the Feb. '96

'blues'

IN 1963, 21 year old **Mick Vernon** brought out the first issue of his rhythm and blues magazine, "R and B Monthly," which he reeled off on a hand press at his home in Godstone Road, Kenley.

the blues enthusiasts a serv making rare records. Thes be issued once every two m each record being produce 75 times and sold at 8s. 6d

But the first of the Horizon records has been re by Mr. Vernon himself on a able tape recorder in his be The artist is guitarist **Huber**

Local Surrey newspaper article from February 1965, announcing the launch of Mike Vernon's Blue Horizon

Eric Clapton and Ginger Baker listening to a playback during the Tom Dowd-engineered sessions at Atlantic Studios for *Wheels Of Fire* in 1968

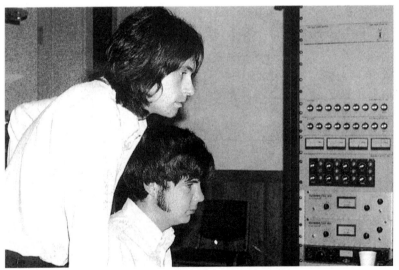

Mike Vernon (left) and engineer mixing Jimmy Dawkins' *Transatlantic 707* album at

Jack Bruce tries his hand at a bowed string part for Cream's *Wheels Of Fire* album

The Moody Blues listen to a playback of *To Our Children's Children*, July 1969

Abbey Road's famous echo chamber – reinstated in 1995 at George Martin's request

George Martin listens as The Beatles run through songs for 1967's *Sergeant Pepper's Lonely Hearts Club Band*

"The Threetles" back together in 1995 with George Martin

An aerial view of an Abbey Road Studio Two Beatles recording session in February 1968, taken from the control room window

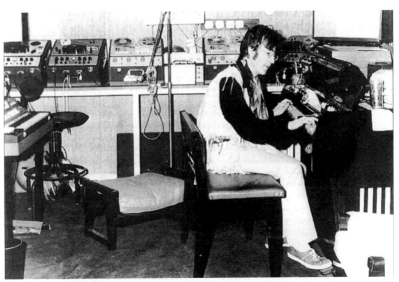

John Lennon experimenting with the Mellotron in his home recording studio, Weybridge, Surrey, during the summer of 1967

Abbey Road's retired general manager, Ken Townsend, in 1980 with the Mellotron used on 'Strawberry Fields Forever' and the 'I Want To Hold Your Hand' Studer J37

The master tape box containing 'Strawberry Fields Forever' and 'When I'm Sixty

Violin leader, Erich Gruenberg, who featured on 'A Day In The Life', 'I Am The Walrus' and 'Within You Without You' among several orchestrated Beatles classics

'Penny Lane' was notable for David Mason's distinctive piccolo trumpet flourishes

Sheila Bromberg made history in March 1967, becoming the first female instrumental soloist to perform on a Beatles record, contributing to 'She's Leaving Home'

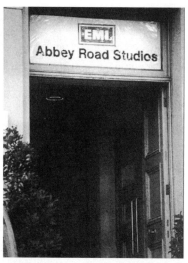

Abbey Road job offer which launched Jeff Jarratt's career. His freelance projects have since sold 35m units

The most famous recording studio entrance in the world

Jeff Jarratt in his Barnet, Hertfordshire, home studio with the ex-Abbey Road EMI TG Series Mark II 24/8/2 valve mixer he loaned to The Beatles' *Anthology* project for the remixing of archive rarities at Abbey Road's Penthouse Suite during 1995 and 1996

Grammy award-winning Beatles engineer Geoff Emerick at AIR Studios with Gallagher and Lyle, 1975

Steve Howe recording a guitar part during the Montreux sessions for Yes's *Going For The One* album in early 1977

Pioneers of Celtic rock, Horslips. (L-r) Eamon Carr, John Fean, Charles O'Connor, Barry Devlin and Jim Lockhart

Manfred Mann and Uriah Heep producer and Bronze Records founder, Gerry Bron, pictured at his Roundhouse Studios which relocated to London EC1 in 1995

The Manor's original mixing console. An early transistor model, handbuilt by engineer Phil Newell

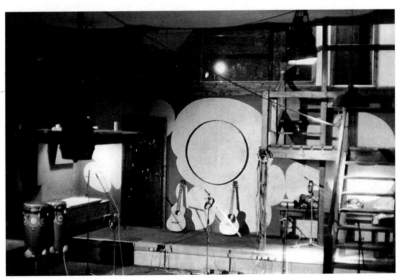

The completed studio at the Manor, where Mike Oldfield's *Tubular Bells* was recorded

David Hentschel helped to mould the early music of Genesis, post Peter Gabriel

Alan Parsons in his own Parsonics Studio, East Sussex. Engineer of *Atom Heart Mother* and *The Dark Side Of The Moon*, his Project gave him solo

Andy Jackson, a Floyd engineering mainstay since 1992

The Dark Side Of The Moon: the 1973 album which propelled Pink Floyd to the premier league of rock artists

Darlings of the psychedelic underground scene: The Pink Floyd in 1967

(L-r) Rick Wright, David Gilmour and Nick Mason, 1994 – the cosmic elder statesmen of British rock

The original single of 'Bohemian Rhapsody'

A classic Queen still from the 1975 promotional video for 'Bohemian Rhapsody'

Queen producer Roy Thomas Baker: "'Bohemian Rhapsody' was the pinnacle of my over-indulgence!"

After working with Queen in the Seventies, engineer/producer Gary Langan became Trevor Horn's right hand man and scored hits of his own as part of The Art Of Noise

Roy Thomas Baker's RTB Studios in Arizona – a retro studio for the Nineties

Chris Thomas: a producer for all seasons

Master of the Glitter mix, engineer John Hudson in his Mayfair studios

Elton John and Chris Rea associate, engineer/producer Stuart Epps in Studio Two at the Mill

The majestic hall at Hansa Ton Studios in Berlin – the venue of *Heroes*

some abstract things. But for the real pragmatic, practical backing vocals, strings or guitar parts, that would be either me or Bowie, or both of us collaborating. With vocals, we'd start out with one vocal line, work out an obvious harmony to that, then a harmony to that one, and so on."

Visconti also recorded the tambourine in the large hall, along with another item of percussion which appeared to be a cowbell, playing on the beat in 4/4. But Visconti explains, "It's actually the flange of a ten-inch reel of tape to which we took a drumstick and beat the hell out of it! We didn't have a cowbell in the studio so we just used whatever was lying around. Of course, once we'd used this tape reel, it was all bent and misshapen so it could never be used to hold tape again after that session!"

At the overdub stage, Brian Eno was around to add a little trademark weirdness to the proceedings with his faithful synth-in-a-suitcase rig. Robert Fripp had arrived in the control room to lend his lead guitar work to the track while plugged directly into Eno's synthesiser. All the guitar effects achieved on the striking introduction were achieved in this way. "I was sending the guitar to a ring modulator and doubling the frequency of it, pulsing it, filtering it, and all those kinds of things," Eno says. "Fripp himself is very sonically aware, so not everything you hear originates from me, but we had worked together previously and so we were very happy with the arrangement whereby he would plug into my little synthesiser and I would play around with his sound.

"Ring modulation is a whole subject on its own and people don't use it that much, but I find it fascinating. To be able to pulse something is very interesting. If you put a low frequency oscillator in one side of the ring modulator and the instrument in the other, the effect is a pulsing effect. If you change the wave form of the pulse that's going in and you make it a square wave, it's a very sharp pulse. If you make it a sine wave, it's softer. Changing the speed creates another effect and it all adds up to a peculiar, non-musical sound. A filter is a way of either exaggerating or diminishing one area of the sound spectrum, and most filters enable you to alter what is called the Q, which is the sharpness of the notch that you're working on in the sound. If you have a very high Q, the filter starts to oscillate and becomes a sound source in itself, but one that is in some way linked to the instrument sound that's being fed in to it."

Always on the look out for a social distraction, Bowie lived life to the full when he was recording in Berlin during 1976 and 1977 and outpoured the flavour of the environment in his writing. Eno says that, although the city's atmosphere itself did not influence him in any way, working with Visconti on *Low* and *Heroes* was, as usual, a great thrill. "Tony creates such a very good feeling in the studio," he says. "We also had a fine band and the basic rhythm section were such nice people. But the ambience of Berlin made no difference itself. It was an interesting place to be because it was so inflated by government money to make it look like an advertisement for capitalism. Culturally, it was very alive, but I hardly ever left the studio to see it first hand!"

Mr Blue Sky

Jeff Lynne is the first to admit that the vocal and orchestral qualities in arrangements for songs like The Electric Light Orchestra's 'Mr Blue Sky', 'Livin' Thing' and 'Telephone Line' are direct reflections of his adoration for The Beatles. When he wrote those numbers in the mid-Seventies, he could not possibly have imagined in his wildest dreams that not only would his idols reunite twenty years later, but he would also be their co-producer. His vision for a band which built on the marriage of classical and rock 'n' roll largely established by George Martin was initially put in motion by ELO's founder and Lynne's former colleague, Roy Wood. But it was Lynne who took the ELO theme to its commercial limits and in doing so, captured the attention of such notables as George Harrison, Brian Wilson, Tom Petty and Dave Edmunds, all of whom achieved huge success in the Eighties with Lynne at the console.

Lynne's first professional band was Birmingham's Idle Race, whom he joined as a replacement for Wood who left to form The Move in 1966. His talent for crafting a highly individual sound in the studio dates precedes Idle Race's first recordings for Liberty Records in 1967. "To be honest," he says, "I had always secretly been a producer in my own mind. I had just got a Bang & Olufson 2000 Deluxe tape recorder which was only a little machine but very advanced for its time, and I started making demos of my own songs. It enabled me to record a guitar on the left channel, then bounce it across to the right along with another instrument. So you would end up with two sounds on the one channel and you could then bounce those with yet another instrument over to the left again. I used to keep bouncing until I had something like ten instruments on the tape and that taught me the principle of making records, before I started working in the big studios. It taught me how to be an arranger and a producer at the same time.

"Then the record company booked the group into Advision Studios where we were working with two engineers who produced the first album. We would do gigs during the week and leave Sundays free to record, so it took months to finish it. We'd drive down from Birmingham in the van, record for about four hours and then drive back. After we did that album, the record company were really pleased and asked us to do another. That's when they asked, 'Who's the producer?' and I replied, 'I am.' Having done all these home recordings I thought I knew all about it. I played some of my recordings to the guys at Liberty and they said they wanted to sign me as a songwriter. So not only did I become a songwriter, I became a producer too. Being as I wrote the songs, I kind of thought that I was the best person to dictate how they should sound, in a protective more than a big-headed way. I could hear them in my mind. I found that the atmosphere on the demos was often better than on the masters. There was a charm missing on the polished versions and, not knowing much about the gear, I always thought it was the clinical environment of the studio to blame. When I reproduced the same song in the studio on the eight-track Scully, it sounded too hard and brittle, whereas I was getting tons of compression and distortion from my little machine which added to the warmth of it. But I persevered and finished the album which was okay."

Although Lynne had little difficulty in communicating with experienced engineers on their level, he became a prime target for prankery. "The engineers would take advantage of my technical ignorance by playing tricks on me," he recalls. "Not evil tricks, just good-natured, silly things. I might ask them to put a bit more bass on something and they'd turn a knob that wasn't actually doing anything.

I'd say, 'That's it, great,' and they'd say, 'We haven't done anything!' I was just a mere lad of about twenty then so I suppose they must have wondered who the hell I thought I was, wandering into the studio and calling myself a producer. But I was still learning about EQ and stuff like that, and watching them all the time, even though I was in charge. But even now I don't have much of a clue about the patch bay."

After being asked to join Roy Wood in The Move several times during the late Sixties, Lynne finally agreed in October 1970, lured by Wood's preoccupation with an idea for an "electric orchestra". "Roy and I had become good friends and we used to talk about the idea of having strings as an integral part of a group," Lynne says. "It began as a fantasy thing really and we later found out that it wasn't very easy to do. My whole reason for joining The Move was so that we would be in the same group and try this idea. We had a few months of practising and learning how to be a group with strings, and hired some guys from London who were classically-orientated. We were using a British Legion hall in Birmingham and started introducing live strings on some numbers, but we had good reason to worry about how we could pull it off in front of an audience because it sounded like shit! It was mainly feedback and a few farting noises." After several false starts, The Electric Light Orchestra made its live debut at the Greyhound pub in Croydon on 16 April, 1972 – an experience which haunts Lynne. "The guitar amps were much too loud and you couldn't hear the cellos that much unless they were feeding back," he admits. "So it was a big problem. Finally, we got hold of some Barcus Berry contact pick-ups for the bridges of the cellos and that seemed to completely cure the problem. So after a few months of struggling with miked-up cellos we suddenly sounded like a good band."

Key to ELO's definitive albums of the mid to late Seventies, including *Eldorado*, *A New World Record*, *Out Of The Blue* and *Discovery*, was orchestra and choral arranger, Louis Clark, originally a fellow Brummie band musician. "Lou did the unthinkable and left to go to college in Leeds to learn music properly," Lynne says. "As I knew that he had done that and I was into using a big orchestra on the *Eldorado* album, I thought I'd see if he could help. I had all the concept and songs worked out, then got Lou over and played him all the pieces. I gave him a rough idea of the tunes I wanted playing and he wrote down all the chords and notes in the proper dot format. When it got to the more intricate riffs, I would play them in the way I wanted them to be heard, and he'd write them down and play them back to me so that I could tell if the inflections were right. Then it came to the big day and we went into De Lane Lea in Wembley with forty string players. I was standing there thinking how scary the whole event was because I'd written it all and it was costing us a fortune to have all these guys! But when they struck up with the introduction piece, the *Eldorado* overture, I was just bowled over and kept saying, 'This is fantastic, bloody fantastic!' So any nervousness I may have felt about it possibly all being a waste of time completely disappeared and I was simply elated."

Although in the Nineties, Lynne favours a minimalistic approach to recording vocals and is often satisfied with just one double-tracked voice, this contrasts with the days of 'Shine A Little Love' and 'Turn To Stone'. "I went through a long phase where I had to have everything sounding like a choir and double-tracked everything at least four times so it became nice and thick," he says. "I very rarely used echo although I often used slapback, but not reverb. If I'm known for anything I suppose it's for making dry records. I just prefer to have a close-up vocal with no echo. I have made some wettish-sounding tracks in the past but certainly over the last six to eight years the records I have made have sounded pretty natural, except when I come to mix them."

Another Lynne trademark is his use of EQ as a vocal effect. "I have always been a fan of 1kHz as a frequency," he explains. "I will start with a big, fat slab of backing vocals and then thin them right out, like I did to my intro vocal on 'Telephone Line'. But that was a naughty one because I did that at the mastering stage. I had the opportunity to be in on the mastering of *A New World Record* and that idea came to me at the very last minute in the mastering room, so I did all the EQ modifications on the spot. I applied that drastic 1kHz EQ, a kind of telephone-sounding filter, right down on the cut. People don't normally do that sort of thing. As you can hear, the EQ gradually backs off as it meets the end of the first verse. Of course, it affected the whole of the beginning of the track and I thought it was a really cool thing, because it all sounded like it was coming down the telephone. So that started my love affair with 1kHz and I use it from time to time, sometimes on guitars, just to make things jump out at you rather than make everything blend into each other."

Most Jeff Lynne productions are quick, spontaneous affairs. It is clearly the way he prefers to work, nevertheless a short timespan has never prevented him from delivering a highly personalised sound. Artists and producers who maintain a distinctive sound throughout long periods in their careers are often criticised for creating, albeit unknowingly, pastiches of their own hallmarks. But Lynne is not losing any sleep. "The way I sound is natural to me and I don't have any disciplines as such," he insists. "There is only so much I can do within my own personal taste. And I'm still trying to fathom out just exactly *what* it is I do."

Vocals, or rather the extreme overdubbing of them, formed the rich textures which made 10cc's 'I'm Not In Love' one of the most inventive productions of 1975. Originally written as a Latin-flavoured, bossa nova number, work on 'I'm Not In Love' commenced at the band's own Strawberry Studios in Stockport in late 1974 with singer/guitarist, Eric Stewart sharing his regular engineer's role with Peter Tattersall. The record featured a staggering 240 separate voices, delivered by colleagues Graham Gouldman, Lol Creme and Kevin Godley. It was Godley's suggestion to use a thick bank of voices in the place of a normal instrumental backing, but Stewart came up with the technical foresight to achieve the dense wall behind his own lead vocal performance. Godley, the drummer who left 10cc in 1976 and is now a world-renowned video director, says, "'I'm Not In Love' never worked in its original format although we knew that the basic song was very good, so every now and then while we were working on the album, *The Original Soundtrack*, we'd go back to it and try to pick up the loose threads. It was then that I came up with this vocal brainwave."

Employing Les Paul's original technique of bouncing tracks together *ad infinitum* became the backbone of Stewart's approach. "We worked out that if we kept the rest of the backing, the bass drum [played by a Moog synth] and the electric piano, to a minimum we would free enough tracks on the sixteen-track machine to build up a really lush vocal sound by making each of the remaining tracks really huge-sounding," he says. "Almost endlessly it seemed, Eric got the three of us to double track and triple track our 'aahs', until there was a total of 240 individual voices melting together. Part of the secret was in the notes we actually sang which formed a chromatic scale over a group of tracks, and each fader on the desk represented a chord made up of our individual voices. It was brilliant fun and also a little bit scary to mix, because we all took control of groups of faders, and we moved them up and down like we were jointly playing a keyboard, shifting the voices around within the mix. It was very hypnotic and beautiful to listen to, and we remained gob-smacked for ages."

May 1974 saw something quite different hit the British singles chart. American brothers Russell and Ron Mael had already been recording together for four years when Muff Winwood produced Sparks' breakthrough Island album, *Kimono My House* and Number Two hit, 'This Town Ain't Big Enough For Both Of Us'. Flashes of The Who could be heard in the power of Sparks' music, but at the forefront of the sound was the keyboard playing of Ron Mael (a dead ringer for Adolf Hitler's slightly more deranged-looking brother) which gestured towards to the electronic pop music which would dominate the charts at the turn of the Eighties, and in which Sparks themselves would play a part.

Sparks were always different, even when they *tried* to be a normal rock band. "We used guitars and live drums but we never fitted in with the real definition of a rock band," Ron Mael says. "Early on we really liked The Who and that was the sound we were aiming for but the keyboard took things the other way. A lot of people today take it for granted that the keyboard part on 'This Town...' was sequenced, but there were no sequencers back in 1974. It was all down to my very strict, stiff playing. At that time we were using electronic, technological sounds but having to invent them in a way because they didn't otherwise exist. The sound I got was from an RMI keyboard that I bought when Russell and I moved to London at the end of 1973. It sounded so terrible to me that I bought an Echoplex and that combination became my sound for the next three albums. I still have the RMI in LA and when we recently decided to go on tour we had to sample that keyboard. Part of its sound is due to it being slightly out of tune all the time."

By 1976, the Maels' star had begun to wane but with their eyes firmly set on the increasingly synthesiser-charged dance world, it would be only three years until they were back in the charts with the Giorgio Moroder-produced 'Number One Song In Heaven'. Ironically, the synth bands of the early Eighties who emulated Sparks, like Depeche Mode and The Human League, later discovered guitars. Whereas, with Sparks, it has been the reverse situation and for many years, many people in the UK perceived Sparks as a novelty act. "If we are a novelty act then we're one of the longest-standing novelty acts in history!" laughs Ron Mael. "That's one area of the British music industry that we like in a detached way, that things happen very quickly. What we were doing in the beginning was so stylised, with our off-beat image and everything, and there were people who thought we were a one-line joke. There is some humour attached to our music but we never considered it one-dimensional because we always like to have different layers beneath the obvious humour."

Waterloo Sunrise

The same month which saw the British chart debut of Sparks also bore witness to Abba's first Number One single, 'Waterloo', the Swedish winning entry of the 1974 Eurovision Song Contest. Traditionally, Eurovision victors have tended to enjoy all of two weeks of fame before disappearing into terminal obscurity, but Abba became one of the best-selling acts of the Seventies and by 1977 had become a world phenomenon with their American chart-topping single, 'Dancing Queen' and a handful of British Number Ones. Abba's ability to merge brilliantly-crafted songs and superb quality vocal harmonies with a polished, creative production style gave critics every reason to compare them with the likes of The Beatles and The Beach Boys. Their sales, at least, were comparable.

Abba's engineer, Michael B Tretow had worked for the group members (Anni-Frid Lyngstad, Benny Andersson, Bjorn Ulvaeus and Agnetha Faltskog) individually, before Abba was formed in 1972, and stayed with the group until its demise in 1983. The group's own studio, Polar Studios, was completed in May 1978 but before that time, Tretow and Abba recorded virtually every track at either Stockholm's Metronome, Marcus or Glen studios. When Polar opened in 1978 it was equipped with a twenty-four-track MCI tape machine and a Harrison console. But within only a few years, Polar became one of the first studios in the world to install the 3M digital thirty-two-track machine, using it for the first time on the 1981 album, *The Visitors*.

With songwriters and producers, Andersson and Ulvaeus bereft of any technical knowledge, it was left almost entirely to Tretow to deliver the distinctive Abba sound. "It was not really until the *Super Trouper* album that we had the sound together," he says. "And then soon after, we went digital and the sound changed again. None of the mics sounded the same anymore, nothing sounded the same. In fact, all of the things I had learned in the past were wasted when digital came along. Sounds did not transfer in the same way. The first big sound we achieved was when we got the sixteen-track tape recorder at Metronome. Before that we'd been using eight-track. When the sixteen-track arrived it was equipped with a varispeed facility. Because of that we were able to de-tune instruments a little and double-track them at different speeds. It hadn't been possible to do it quite like that before then. We overdubbed the whole band using varispeed and couldn't get enough of it! We recorded the drums, bass, piano, guitars, everything twice, most of the time, pairing the tracks in stereo with the de-tuned varispeed track on one of the channels. That goes for the vocals as well. We used to record them at different speeds to get different harmonic effects when they were replayed at the correct speed. 'Dancing Queen' was a classic example of a piano recorded with varispeed to give a subtle chorus effect. If you overstretched the varispeed distance, you would end up with a harsh, metallic piano sound, like a honky tonk piano."

As soon as synthesiser technology reached an advanced level of quality, Abba spared no time in incorporating the new sounds into their records. "At the start, there weren't really any synths worth using," he continues. "But we did eventually get a Mini-Moog and used it on things like 'SOS'. Then we got a Polymoog and Benny bought a Yamaha GX1, the big white synth. That was the heaviest, most bulky synth I'd ever seen but it had some great sounds. Some of the string sounds were better than the real thing, I thought." But to the rest of the team, real strings were irreplaceable and it was the group's resident bass player, Rutger Gunnarsson, who normally had the job of arranging for string sections. "Bjorn and Benny would come up with ideas for string parts, but it would be Rutger who would figure it all out and write the arrangements down," Tretow says. "Bjorn and Benny don't read music but they knew what they wanted."

Working with different equipment all the time until the advent of Polar Studios, there was no routine to follow from session to session, and every album was a new pioneering exercise. For the lush vocal sounds, Tretow chose an AKG 440 microphone as a standard from the time of *Arrival*. "Sometimes one mic would sound good on one song and on others it wouldn't sound good at all," he says. "But we found that the AKG 440 worked just about every time. We didn't use any special effects on the vocals until the digital delay from Eventide came out. On the first two albums, around 1972 and 1973, you still couldn't even buy a chorus unit."

One of the most striking, and much imitated, qualities of Abba's production style lay in the sound of the acoustic guitars. It was a sound which eluded Tretow and Abba for some time but it was initially inspired by what they were hearing from American bands like The Eagles. "You had to choose the right guitars to use for a start and we found the best ones to record were Martins," Tretow says. "So we got a couple of Martin guitars and I had a lot of mics around them. We had one close mic right up next to the strings, near the sound hole, and we had a pair of ambient mics up in the air away from the guitars, routed through the MXR flanger, but not in the flange mode. We just wanted it to sound slightly de-tuned, but without a chorus effect. We tried just about every different possible way of recording those guitars, like recording with Dolby and playing back without.

"I think we probably approached the recording of the acoustic guitars in a similar way each time, but we might be distracted halfway through and alter the procedure. Sometimes we just wanted a different sound or tuning. We normally recorded the guitars in stereo pairs: one guy on the left, the other on the right. But I would make a stereo mix of them rather than having them as two individuals placed on each stereo channel. A stereo pair where both guitars had an ambient sound, where you can hear both guitars rather than isolate them on each track. On some tracks, like 'The Name Of The Game', we would get the guitars to sound just right and then use heavy limiting and compression."

Still many years before advances in synthesiser technology made the use of large bands of studio musicians uneconomical (in many producers' eyes), the availability of session work reached an all-time height in the Seventies. For musicians seeking to earn a living in this area, like bass player Mo Foster, it was a matter of firstly proving their worth whenever the occasion arose, then strengthening contacts with session fixers, contractors and producers in an environment which was still dictated by Tin Pan Alley mentality. Without a regular band, Foster placed a "Bass Player Available" ad in *Melody Maker*, expecting little or no response. But then...

"The producer, Chris Demetriou rang me out of the blue and told me he was looking for musicians to work with ex-Manfred Mann singer, Mike d'Abo," says Foster. "After touring in America and the UK with Mike, my name got around the business, and on one occasion in late 1971 I was hired to cover for someone on a Barry Ryan session for a Russ Ballard song, 'Can't Let You Go', at Lansdowne Studios. I knew nothing about sessions and turned up with a flask and sandwiches because I didn't know how long I'd be there for. There was Clem Cattini on drums, Ray Cooper on percussion, Mike Moran on keyboards, Ray Fenwick on guitar – all fine players and nice guys who must have thought my naivety was amusing! That was the beginning of a word of mouth situation which gradually mushroomed."

Among the key sessions Foster played on during the early Seventies was for Jimmy Helms's 1973 single, 'Gonna Make You An Offer You Can't Refuse', and within a few years, his bass skills were in high demand for the growing European disco market which became renowned for a rash of faceless dance tracks, including Cerrone's 1978 international hit, 'Supernature'. "A lot of those disco sessions were recorded at Trident Studios where the arrangers used to write out the whole chart for three guitars, bass, drums and percussion," says Foster. "Every note was written down for us and it was always 120 beats per minute, and you'd end up walking around at 120bpm all day! But it was the springboard for a lot of really enjoyable gigs."

Bass players began to discover a use for the fuzz boxes and wah-wah pedals which guitarists had exploited during the previous decade, and in 1974, Foster became one of the first in the UK to apply MXR phaser and distortion pedals to his sound. "Then," he says, "the Mu-Tron Envelope Follower came out and it enabled bass players to copy the emergent synth bass lines, as heard on Herbie Hancock's 'Headhunters'. A lot of bass players were trying in vain to emulate this but the Mu-Tron helped you achieve a pretty good facsimile of that sound.

"An amusing by-product of all this was that those of us using pedals could charge a doubling fee. Because of a Musicians' Union loophole, a pedal was considered another instrument, so as soon as your foot hit the button, you were on to another twenty-five per cent. That was precisely the reason why the use of effects proliferated so much in the mid-Seventies. A lot of us session guys became wise to the financial possibilities and I ended up with a dummy black box (dubbed the "DFA") which did absolutely nothing. I used to put my foot down and ask, 'Does that sound better?' and producers would say, 'Yeah, great, we'll use that.' The fools deserved being taken for a ride!"

Project Leader

Despite his acclaimed engineering work on Pink Floyd's *The Dark Side Of The Moon* and many other landmark recordings, by the mid-Seventies, Alan Parsons was experiencing dire financial troubles. As a result of a chance meeting in the Abbey Road Studios' canteen, he met his manager and future collaborator, Eric Woolfson and the time soon arrived for him to not only break free of his employment with EMI but also become a recording artist in his own right, as the founder of The Alan Parsons Project. But not before he achieved the rare notoriety of producing two consecutive Number One singles for EMI in February 1975 with Pilot ('January') and Steve Harley And Cockney Rebel ('Make Me Smile'). It appeared at the time that Parsons was attempting to tailor a whole new production style around Pilot, especially with the percussive hooks of 'Magic', 'January' and 'Just A Smile'.

"They were handclaps actually," he reveals. "Handclaps that went through a Dolby in the wrong direction and got expanded. It was a little hook between each record. But although I should take credit for the overall sound, the claps weren't my idea as it was already a part of the composition before I worked on it. Pilot were discovered by three guys who were working for EMI in Manchester Square. It was a strange situation to have three EMI employees all managing the same band. They had the backing of the Head of A&R at the time but when the first whiff of success came, they all left the company to work with Pilot full-time." No one was more surprised than Parsons when another of his productions was responsible for knocking Pilot's 'January' off the top spot. "I was skiing in Kitsbuhel at the time and got very drunk after I learned about Steve Harley getting to Number One," he recalls. "I couldn't believe it – one Number One single being taken over by another. It was quite an achievement and I had lots of people in the industry congratulating me."

The following year saw Parsons working with John Miles on the symphonic 'Music', but it was Al Stewart's glorious 1977 hit, 'Year Of The Cat', that arguably remains one of Parsons' finest production moments. Like 'Make Me Smile', which featured the madrigal flourishes of Jim Cregan, its acoustic guitar solo is one of the track's highlights. "On 'Year Of The Cat', Peter White played the acoustic solo, followed by Tim Renwick who played the electric part," Parsons says. "But an acoustic solo is quite different in itself and I've always gone for a heavily compressed acoustic sound. I don't think it was my idea to have an acoustic solo on 'Year Of The Cat', but it was on 'Make Me Smile'. The role of a good producer is always to make the artist think that he is the one responsible for these brilliant ideas, even if he isn't. I've never been one to fuss over who should take credit for things, because at the end of the day it is the end result that matters most."

Miles's 'Music', with its changing tempo and moods, appeared on the surface to be a complex work, although Parsons insists that if one was to remove the orchestral arrangement, it would reveal a simple song with basic instrumentation. "It was relatively easy to work on," he says. "The first take to be recorded just had piano, bass and drums, and the orchestral arrangement had already been pretty much pre-arranged by John, but interestingly we had to change one note of the string riff slightly because it was an exact copy of 'Nights In White Satin'. It was conducted by Andrew Powell who continues to work with me today. Steve Harley discovered Andrew. He worked on 'Sebastian' and some of the arrangements for the first Cockney Rebel album which I wasn't involved with. Then EMI's A&R department put my name forward as the producer for their second album, and that's how I met Andrew. They had an enormous cult following as the band of the moment, but they didn't really have any real success until 'Judy Teen' came out [in May 1974]."

It was Woolfson who encouraged Parsons to consider his own musical talents and launch himself as a recording artist. "Eric reassured me that everyone was aware I'd engineered *The Dark Side Of The Moon*, and instead of producing everybody else's records, I could be making my own which turned out to be *Tales Of Mystery And Imagination*," he says. "But at that time I didn't know that it was going to be as involved as it was. I just thought it was going to be just a bunch of songs. It seemed to come together very well though, however, working by myself it took a long time to finish. It was frustrating to break off from time to time to produce other artists, but it did allow me to sit back and look at what I was doing with some objectivity. In the old days, the Project albums were nearly always motivated by Eric Woolfson saying he had some songs. There was generally a long gap between albums and I would go off and produce other artists or take a long holiday."

Parsons realised early on that not only did Woolfson possess a thorough knowledge of music, but that he might also be in a position to assist him with his financial plight. "There I was with all the success but nothing in the bank," he recalls. "So Eric went to EMI and asked, 'Where's my boy's money?' I had just produced two Number Ones in a row for the company but I didn't have the nerve to ask, 'Please may I have some more money for this?'" It was agreed that even though Parsons was making his own records, he would remain on the EMI payroll until he eventually left the company some years later. "It was in everybody's best interests because I was still booking Abbey Road as it was the studio I knew and loved best. I would still have worked there whether they were paying me or not. So I was being paid on top of what I was getting as an independent producer for people like Al Stewart and John Miles."

While Parsons continued to produce their records, Pilot's four Scottish members (David Paton, Billy Lyall, Ian Bairnson and Stuart Tosh) moonlighted as the nucleus of The Alan Parsons Project. "It was a convenient arrangement," Parsons says. "They were good all-round musicians and I got on with them very well. To go with regular session men seemed a bit of a cop-out to me and, besides, they needed the work. They were, after all, only a one-hit wonder. Well, a two-hit wonder if you count 'Magic' as well as 'January'! We worked like an extension of their band and got used to playing together."

Another producer to break free from EMI and enjoy enormous success on his own terms was John Leckie. After surviving his experiences with Phil Spector in 1970, Leckie went on to work on a vast array of fascinating projects as an Abbey Road staffer during the following eight years, including Pink Floyd's *Meddle*, Be Bop Deluxe's *Sunburst Finish* and the early albums of Magazine and Simple Minds. By July 1978, however, he was faced with the choice of either remaining loyal to EMI or taking the huge leap into the world of the unknown as an independent producer/engineer.

"I had produced XTC's first album [*White Music*] at the Manor during my holiday in late 1977 and purposely didn't tell anyone at Abbey Road about it," he explains. "Although I had been working with Be Bop Deluxe in other studios, they were an EMI band so it was okay, and I could have recorded XTC at Abbey Road but not at a non-EMI studio. There had to be an EMI element and I was threatened with the sack if I stepped out of line. By the summer of 1978, XTC had become quite successful and were ready to do their next album [*Go 2*] at the Townhouse, so I felt compelled to explain my predicament to my studio manager. But he once again told me that I'd be fired if I worked with them at the Townhouse. EMI wouldn't hire my services out to Virgin so I had to leave."

Today, Leckie's success has been built entirely on a foundation of British artists, and he says that one of the great freedoms of being a freelancer is being able to turn down uninspiring projects. Whilst with EMI, he turned down a job with Capitol Records in Hollywood, preferring to stay in Britain where, he says, the harder-edged music had more appeal. This decision, made just over twenty years ago, ultimately steered him towards his landmark achievements in the Nineties. "Britain was a really exciting place for music but what was going on in America was The Eagles and a lot of what I'd call unadventurous, old-fashioned crap," he says. "I decided it was more happening in the UK and returned home.

"There are some great things in America, it's a land of extremes. You can always tell an American band from its attitude and the way they've learned to play which is very different from the British method. An American band in rehearsal will jam for three hours whereas an English band's idea will be to sit around and talk about it! I think there's more craziness and eccentricity here which leads to greater invention."

Lords Of The New Wave

Chris Thomas's arrival as a trainee at AIR in 1968 gave no suggestion that he would become one of the leading producers of his generation. In the Seventies alone, the energies he poured into The Climax Blues Band, Roxy Music, Bryan Ferry, The Sex Pistols and The Pretenders were paid back in dividends but it was still only the start of greater things. His work with Roxy Music began with their second album, *For Your Pleasure*, and followed through to 1976 with the live collection, *Viva! Roxy Music*. One year prior to the release of *Viva!*, Thomas took the band to AIR Studios to work on tracks for their *Siren* album, which featured 'Love Is The Drug', possibly *the* single which manages to capture the late night, lounge lizard essence of mid-Seventies Roxy. Thomas recalls the record being a typical example of an early take influencing the final result. "The song was written for a B-side, an Andy Mackay track that was heavy on saxophone, and it didn't have any bearing on what was to follow," he says. "It was like, 'Okay, let's do one of Andy's songs now, here are the chords.' It was a great tune for rowing to. We used to fool around in the studio and mime the Vikings rowing across the sea, invading! A lot of Roxy Music stuff started off with just some chords and a rhythm, then everyone would make it up as they went along, putting their own bits on. And two months later, Bryan would come in and sing a lyric over the top of it and it would all happen. 'Love Is The Drug' was one of these occasions. It had no lyric and no one had any idea of what the song was going to be about. So we made up this backing track, all live with Johnny Gustafson playing bass and a keyboard going down at the same time as a guide, and then Bryan came in and put down this vocal, and we just couldn't believe it. The whole thing was now completely transformed.

"At the beginning, I was wondering what we could do with anything that might be available. The first thing I thought of that was different was to tighten up Paul Thompson's snare drum skin very, very high, then take the snare itself off so there was no crack on it, and put that sound through a Leslie at the end of the studio. The funny thing though was that I never thought it was a great sound, but everybody says how brilliant it is. Martin Chambers [Pretenders drummer] told me he heard the song in a cinema advertisement and how wonderful the snare drum sounded. But that's the thing, you know, because if you've worked on something and you're that close to it, you can never be sure that what you're doing is good or not. There's nothing to judge it by and you know exactly what you've done, so there's no mystery involved."

Few producers could work with The Beatles, Procol Harum and Roxy Music before moving on to the high priests of punk, The Sex Pistols and still produce work of convincing brilliance, but then Thomas is no ordinary producer. Eighteen months before he first set foot inside a studio with the Pistols in October 1976, Thomas met entrepreneur, Malcolm McLaren who was hoping to manage The New York Dolls and discussed with Thomas the possibility of producing them. Thomas, however, was busy producing Roxy's *Siren* and the Sadistic Mika Band in addition to performing live on keyboards with John Cale, but unknown to him, McLaren was also managing a band calling themselves The Swankers who were about to recruit a new singer and rename themselves The Sex Pistols.

"I met Chris Spedding who was playing guitar on the John Cale tour and he was really championing the Pistols and saying, 'They're the best band I've ever seen,'" Thomas says. "He actually took them into RAK to do some demos with them, and he wanted to get involved with them. This might have something to do with the rumours that Chris played on the Pistols' album, but he definitely didn't do any of it. He phoned me up one night and said that they were on at the Screen On The Green at about one in the morning. I said, 'Ugh, where's that?' He said, 'Islington.' It was like the other side of the world to me! This was the same night in September 1976 that the Pistols did 'Anarchy In The UK' on *So It Goes*, their first ever TV appearance, and I watched it and I was amazed. I thought, 'Christ, we're definitely going out tonight!' So I went up there, met Chris and saw the Pistols, and it was totally incredible."

On the day after signing to EMI on 9 October, the Pistols began recording 'Anarchy In The UK' at Lansdowne Studios with producer Dave Goodman and engineer Hugh Padgham. It was intended as their debut single but all concerned were unhappy with the progress of the sessions. Four days later, another attempt to record the song at Lansdowne was made with EMI's staff producer, Mike Thorne but again – no luck. Finally, Thomas was contacted by McLaren and Thorne, and a meeting was set up between them and the band's Steve Jones, Glen Matlock and Paul Cook to find a way forward. But no Johnny Rotten? "Apparently, John hadn't been told about all this, which must have cheesed him off," says Thomas. "But they played me some demos of songs like 'Pretty Vacant' and I thought this was a great rock 'n' roll band. The reason they were interested in me producing them was not because of what I'd done with Roxy or anything successful, but a very obscure Kilburn And The High Roads thing called 'Rough Kids'. I'd got dumped on to do this for Pye and it came out one week and got deleted the next. But they all knew it and it was one of their favourite records. It's funny because you always get a job because someone has loved one of the records you've produced."

Although some sessions were held at AIR, most were conducted at Wessex Studios in Highbury New Park, the first on 17 October, and Thomas recalls with a wide grin the anxiety caused by attempting to derive any musical worth from the voice of Mr Rotten. "We did most of the backing tracks without John there and it was almost like this whole thing was going on without John knowing anything about it," he recalls. "Then when he came in to do the vocal, he started yelling and screaming, and I thought, 'What the hell are we going to do here?' So I went down to have a chat with him and he said, 'You're the one with the track record, you tell me what to do.' So they knew that I had a track record, but I'm not sure if they knew who with. That was the first time I had the idea of bringing in some PA speakers for the drums, because Wessex was a very dead studio. We fed the snare mic signal through the PA speakers. It was a nice, big room but it was carpeted everywhere. So I got the idea of making it sound kind of trashy, and I suppose I should have just gone to another studio but Bill Price had worked there and said he found it a good place."

Chris Thomas says that the main musical brains behind the Pistols' sound belonged to Steve Jones. "Steve's amazing guitar sound was a combination of his guitar and the Vox AC30 he used," he explains. "Bill Price found out that only one of the speakers actually worked, so we used that one speaker. I think he got the guitar off one of The New York Dolls and you only had to plug it in and play a barre chord, and it would play itself. It sounded like you'd just turned on a Hoover and the sound you hear on record is pretty much the natural sound. Steve also played all the bass parts when Glen Matlock left after we recorded 'God Save The Queen'. So he'd play the barre chord on the guitar, then play the bass root note underneath it, and that gave a tremendous amount of power. It was like playing a seven-string guitar with a huge low octave underneath it. The only other aspect to the sound was a truckload of compression, particularly on the guitars and drums. The limiters were absolutely leaping out of their skulls!"

Mixing under such circumstances was normally an easy task, although 'Holidays In The Sun' was a little more involved. "When we were mixing that, we each had a cue about every two seconds," Thomas laughs. "You had to really hope you got through okay and if you missed any bits, you'd have to chop them and stick them together. It was hard work in those days but the recordings were very natural on the Pistols' stuff. It became formularised because there wasn't an awful lot changing between the songs. The only one that did change was 'Holidays In The Sun' where we changed the structure of the song. We chopped that around because they'd written that in a bit of a funny way. It had the potential but it didn't have the right bits and sequences in the right places. As on many occasions, Bill Price was my safety net. He had such a lot of technical knowledge that if I were to say, 'I'd like to try this or that,' he would instantly know what to do and respond. I wanted to have goosesteps on the front of 'Holidays In The Sun', but I wanted them in time with the bass drum. Of course, goosesteps are very slow so Bill made up a tape loop of a goosestep and he triggered it off the bass drum. Of course, you wouldn't have a problem these days because you'd immediately think about using a sample. But Bill was always great at helping me achieve ideas, especially when I was stuck. It was in these situations where he was very thorough and because I didn't have to think about those things, it left me the space to get on with producing."

Working with The Sex Pistols did not come without its fair share of trauma and one night after a session at Wessex in June 1977, Thomas witnessed the adverse side effects of the band's notoriety when he became entangled in a pub brawl, no thanks to Rotten. "I had been working five days a week with Paul McCartney on the soundtrack to his *Wings Over America* film [*Rock Show*] and by the time I went down to Wessex on a Saturday to do something with the Pistols, I was completely shattered," he recalls. "It got to about six pm and Steve and Paul decided to go to a pub in Green Lanes. John, Bill and myself stayed on at the studio to finish something and joined them a bit later. I had about half a pint and was quite happy to leave it at that because Bill and I were both tired and we still had some work to do, or something like that and they said, 'Do you want another half?' I said, 'No, I won't be able to work properly.' Then someone said, 'Shall we just stay and have a drink and not work for just once in our lives?'

"We had a good drink and Steve and Paul left reasonably early, then John started talking about how some blokes in the bar were going to have a go at us. I said, 'Give it a rest, John, we're supposed to be having a drink, not have a go at people.' I phoned my girlfriend, Mika, to see if she wanted to come over in the car. So she parked it around the back of the pub. John wanted to go somewhere to watch a re-run of *The Prisoner* and seeing as Bill wanted to go back to the studio, he thought he'd go and watch it there. So we left the pub and were about to get in the car when we heard this noise, 'Oi!' We turned around and there was a huge bunch of blokes, like a football team, all with bottles, knives, everything. They jumped on me because I was the closest one to John, but it was obviously him they were after. Apparently someone went to stab me in the back but Bill pulled this guy off and I ended up with a cut through my jacket and shirt, and down my back. I got knocked to the ground and they started kicking me and poking me with a knife. But it was all over in a flash, a few seconds. Bill got quite nastily done over and given a fair old kicking by the guy he pulled off me. Then they all vanished, Mika went back to the pub to ask if she could use the phone and the guy wouldn't let her. I suppose the pub was probably behind it. I went back to work with McCartney on the

Monday and on the Tuesday morning it was the headline in the *Daily Mirror*. I think Paul must have phoned up just about every hospital in London to find out where I was. Then I rolled in and he looked all concerned, saying, 'Are you all right, you okay?' I didn't know what he meant. He said, 'Have you seen this paper?' I said, 'Nah, that was Saturday night!'"

Shortly before the end of the Seventies, Thomas took over the production duties from Nick Lowe for new band, The Pretenders, featuring Chrissie Hynde, Martin Chambers, the now late lamented guitarist Jimmy Honeyman-Scott and bass player Pete Farndon. Recorded during the summer of 1979 and released in January 1980 just as the single 'Brass In Pocket' reached the top of the charts, *Pretenders* ranks with one of the best debut albums by any rock band, itself becoming a Number One. 'Tattooed Love Boys', a live favourite, included one of Honeyman-Scott's greatest moments as a guitarist in which he constructed a solo with sections which each paid tribute to his favourite players. The staccato, machine gun effect at the end of the solo was, Thomas recalls, pure Pete Townshend.

"Jimmy played a Les Paul which had two pick-ups and two volume controls, and you can turn the volume off on one of the pick-ups and keep the other up full," he explains. "Then, with the toggle switch, you just rock it back and forth very fast and it cuts in and out, like a machine gun. Jimmy did that and slid his hand down the neck at the same time to get that descending sound. The first person to use that idea was Pete Townshend on 'Anyway, Anyhow, Anywhere'. Jimmy played that solo absolutely live. He was right down outside the window and he'd obviously worked the whole thing out and practised it thoroughly beforehand and it sounded like each two bars of the solo was one of his favourite guitarists. He just said, 'Right, I'll do a solo now,' and there it was, he played it all in one hit. We were speechless, we thought, 'Christ, that was fantastic!'"

While the omnipresent "dead" and clinical acoustic sounds prevalent among recordings in the Seventies was favoured by most producers, a small anti-movement began to gain force in New York around 1976, with the likes of Craig Leon, Richard Gottehrer, Lenny Kaye and Ed Stasium preferring a return to the more lively sounds of the Sixties. This was no mere retro stance, but a full-blooded attempt to regain an edge to music which had become lost over the previous ten years. "People were producing some incredibly lifeless records with a lot of close-miking and bass drums, snares and hi-hats recorded individually," Leon observes. "Probably the deadest-sounding studio in New York at that time was the old Record Plant. Tom Hidley was designing all the rooms at that point with live and dead areas, and the dead ends were very dead! There would be no live band feel on the record whatsoever. And the biggest culprits of that were bands like Steely Dan which was exactly what we were trying to fight against. Steely Dan had really great players and that was what they were showing off, rather than an overall production and, sonically, their records were extremely dull. They had no air around them at all and it gave the impression that there was a rug over everything! I think that was quite unique to that decade. But if you listen to some of the really great performance-orientated recordings from the Fifties and Sixties, like Miles Davis's records, the miking techniques were very ambient and live."

Along with Gottehrer during 1976 and 1977, Leon worked on the first two Blondie albums (*Blondie* and *Plastic Letters*) and The Ramones' debut release, using the limited techniques available to achieve a larger than life sound. "A lot of things you hear on those albums were sounds which became much more easy to achieve a few years later," he says, "such as having strict time while keeping it very live. That was still before all the digital effects came into place. So if you wanted a live room sound you had to have a live room. And those records were recorded on a very live sound stage at Plaza Sound in New York which was previously the recording home of the NBC Symphony Orchestra. The studio used to be the orchestra's rehearsal rooms, above Radio City Music Hall, and it was about the size of Abbey Road Studio One which is pretty huge! It was about sixty feet long by thirty feet high and it was a classic Thirties orchestral room. Because of the room's size we could get much liver drum sounds than anywhere else in town because all the other studios had drum booths the size of a toilet. So we took [Blondie drummer] Clem Burke and put him right in the middle of this big room because it was large enough to still get good separation on the guitars. Some of the tracks were done at Bell Sound, the studio where The Shangri-Las and The Four Seasons used to record. The New York punk producers and engineers like myself, Richard and John Cale from The Velvet Underground who produced Patti Smith preferred to use the older studios."

The equipment at Plaza Sound in 1976 included an API console and a 3M M79 multitrack machine with interchangeable sixteen or twenty-four-track heads. "There were a couple of limiters and some API compressors which were very savage," he continues, "but that was more or less it and it really dictated what your sound was, the rest of it being down to the musicians and what they were using. There wasn't much money around to throw into a recording budget because the record companies didn't have too much faith in Blondie and The Ramones at first. The budgets were minuscule but that helped the sound, I think. Things weren't radically different to what we're doing now in terms of live bands. Although in the Nineties, I am finding that some of the current BritPop bands are a little reminiscent of that style. Oasis are an exception, as they appear to epitomise the style of recording that we were trying to forge ahead with in the late Seventies."

Now acclaimed for his production and engineering work with U2, Depeche Mode, Nine Inch Nails and PJ Harvey, Flood (born Mark Ellis) started his career at Morgan Studios in Willesden at the height of the punk phenomenon of the late Seventies, working on and overseeing sessions by Siouxsie And The Banshees and The Cure. While at school, Flood worked as an occasional pirate radio DJ, then after spending a whole week telephoning London studios to find an opening as a tea boy, he got lucky. But the music he witnessed upon arrival at Morgan in 1978 was a far cry from the styles with which he is now synonymous.

"During the first week I was there, Thin Lizzy, Black Sabbath, some other dodgy heavy metal band from Birmingham called Money and Jack Bruce were all recording," he says. "The place had four studios and one week there might be a BBC orchestral session going on in one room and a heavy metal band in the next. There were lots of people around, lots of different kinds of music and it was a good, all round introduction for me. At the end of my first day, I was just sitting around at the back of a session just as a tea boy and it was about nine pm, but I hadn't realised it was that late because I was just fascinated by the whole process of what was going on and knew this was what I wanted to do. It's that fascination that still carries on today."

Morgan (which was founded by session drummer Barry Morgan and is now run as Battery) was a fine example of an independent London studio which bred many a future notable engineer and producer. "Some of the people I worked with at Morgan included Roger Quested, Gregg Jackman who went to work at RAK with bands like Yes, Jethro Tull engineer Robin Black, Mike Hedges who worked with The Cure and The Banshees, rock producer Chris Tsangarides and Robert Mutt Lange's right-hand man, Nigel Green...lots of talented people."

At an early age, Flood (who earned his tradename through his overeagerness to make tea) became interested in Faust, Tangerine Dream and the formative synth music of the decade. But at the age of fourteen in 1976, punk came along at just the right time. "I can remember at Morgan that within the first couple of months of me starting there, The Cure were in doing their first album, The Banshees too were in briefly," he says. "These were all bands that I had loved going to see and suddenly they were in the studio where I was working. It just made the whole thing seem even more like what I wanted to do. I think I was a bit too naive to know what was going on, because it takes a while before you can start to manipulate situations. Sessions didn't seem to take as long as they do now. All the backing tracks for the first Cure album [*Three Imaginary Boys*] were done in virtually three days. But then The Sex Pistols' album took most of a year to make using standard production techniques. So in terms of time and effort, as much went into that as some of the progressive rock bands of the mid-Seventies, but the point of focus at the end was very different. Bands like The Clash did their album inside a week and it had a very raw sound, but it might just have been that they didn't have enough money to spend any more time on it or they didn't want to fall for all the trappings that go with spending loads of time in a recording studio. The Pistols, however, were the opposite."

chapter nine

living in the plastic age

*"There was no point in being polite – I had to find a way of making
my records sound extreme to some degree because that was the
only way to get people's attention."*

Trevor Horn

The Eighties was the decade in which recording technology and
synthesised instruments progressed in such leaps and bounds
that, in the hands of some artists and producers, it became at least as
important as the song. In Britain, Thatcher's decade gave rise to
yuppiedom and an aura of elitism which, listening back, characterised
much of the music of the day. The dry, often clinical productions of the
Seventies had been overtaken in part by the liveliness of punk, but the
Eighties witnessed a veritable explosion in sound and ambient
processing which affected the whole of the pop/rock genre.

If there was a shared emphasis among the varied styles thrown into
the charts from the early to mid-Eighties it was one of unnatural
sounds, created electronically by sequencers, drum machines,
synthesisers and the advent of sampling which in itself caused an
uproar, especially from the stick-in-the-mud characters who were not
using such techniques. The ability to capture an existing sound on a
digital hard disk and replay it faithfully within a fresh piece of music
contributed to a revolution in the music world. Suddenly we were
listening to dance records which featured the drum tracks of Led

Zeppelin's John Bonham, originally recorded back in 1971. Sound effects which had taken the previous generation of artists many weeks, even months, to perfect through antiquated methods were "stolen", fed into samplers and applied to mostly unrelated new records. "Revolutionary!" was the cry from one side of the industry. "Sacrilege!" countered the opponents. Eventually, it became compulsory for artists to credit the origins of such samples and award a portion of their publishing royalties accordingly.

Rap, the black-originated, streetwise dance cousin of punk took pride of place in the hearts and minds of late Eighties youth, while a more "techno" approach gave birth to the acid house craze which reached its peak around 1989. Both forms of music were a mirror of the state-of-the-art technological developments. It was a time of great frustration for the traditional musician who had only his comparatively basic musical skills to offer as a drummer, guitarist and bassist, although most keyboard players rejoiced in their new-found freedom to enhance their talents with an ever-growing range of keyboard-based wonder toys. Unable to find session work in this environment, many highly skilled drummers threw in the towel, accepted defeat and traded their prized kits in for drum machines in favour of careers as programmers. It was a brave new world and only the forward-thinking would survive.

The most significant and long-lasting advance, however, was in the format of the actual records themselves. Until the early Eighties, the vinyl forty-five rpm single and thirty-three rpm album, along with the optional cassette, had enjoyed a long, healthy life. But on 17 May, 1978, the way of the near future was announced when Philips gave public notice of its intention to launch the Compact Disc using fully digital recording and replay systems. It would be a further four years before its first issue in Japan by CBS/Sony, and it finally reached Europe and the rest of the world in March 1983. The CD had a mighty impact not only on the record buyer, as the discs and the machines cost the proverbial arm and a leg to begin with (I certainly could not afford one until 1987!), but also on the way music was recorded.

Phil Ramone heard the shape of things to come when he visited Sony's Japanese headquarters in 1979 and received a preview of the new digital format. He went on to become an international ambassador for the digital medium, preaching its gospel wherever and whenever he could. "Sony asked me to talk to the business at large about this new medium, but because the industry was so vinyl-orientated and the cost of CDs and the players was so expensive to begin with, everyone thought we were out of our minds," he says. "At the beginning, we were labelled as not being interested in analogue anymore, but you don't lose interest in or outgrow your child, you re-adjust for their life and for yours, and it became an incredible change."

In tandem with the CD, and pre-empting it, digital studio recording was made possible with the launch of the Mitsubishi thirty-two-track digital recorder and its rival from 3M, but only the risktakers and the wealthiest of studios were able to invest for some time. Even now, sixteen or more years after the arrival of digital, the debate still rages in some quarters about whether digital or analogue is best and, depending on the nature of music being recorded, those on both sides of the fence are correct. Enthusiast Ramone persuaded Billy Joel to record *Songs From The Attic*, the world's first digitally-recorded live album, and its success prompted the digital re-mastering of Joel's 1977 best-selling album, *The Stranger*, which became the first-ever pop CD hit. "As we entered the Eighties," Ramone says, "it was obviously the new game in town." A game which of all the top artists in Britain, Dire Straits was to play to the full – its 1985 Phonogram CD album, *Brothers In Arms*, acting as the main catalyst for record sales of CD players in Britain that year.

Burgess A Go-Go

Musically light years away from Mark Knopfler at the opposite end of the early Eighties pop barometer was the pioneering electronic act, Landscape, co-formed by New Zealander, Richard James Burgess as a side career to his role as the drummer with the little-known late Seventies country rock band, Easy Street. Originally an instrumental band with a somewhat schizophrenic jazz-funk/punk repertoire, Landscape attempted to climb on the pub rock circuit, only to find landlords shaking their heads in confusion at the absence of a singer or lead guitarist. He may not have laid down any plans to become a producer, but the early Landscape gigs proved to be a valuable training ground for Burgess. With a Revox tape machine and a pair of microphones (along with used tape "borrowed" from the studios he worked at as a session player), Burgess recorded the band's occasional performances and released the best material on Landscape's own Event Horizon Records. Such was the reaction to this aggressive, distorted form of jazz, that these indie singles began to appear in the New Wave charts – one of them even becoming an underground best-seller as word spread around the major labels about this interesting new sound.

But Burgess was never one to sit still for long and was often involved in more than two bands simultaneously. With Easy Street now a distant memory, he formed yet another side project, Accord, with Landscape keyboard player, Chris Keaton and classical musician, Roger Cawkwell, as an avant garde electronic improvisation group. Accord performed on BBC Radio Three and later won a British Arts Council competition where they performed at the Purcell Room in London. Electronic music and its technology had fascinated Burgess since the early Seventies when he owned an EMS Synthi A synthesiser. At one point in 1977, he broke a finger while installing a studio in his house, preventing him from drumming on sessions for several months. But the time was not wasted. In fact, it shaped not only the beginning of a new-sounding Landscape but a whole section of the electro-pop and allied New Romantic revolution of the Eighties.

"John Walters [Landscape partner] and I had been talking about various musical ideas and the Roland MC-8 Microcomposer had just come out and the only person I knew that had one was Hans Zimmer," Burgess says. "It was very expensive – about £5,000 at the time – but Roland allowed us to check out this piece of kit at their offices while the staff were out of the building at their Christmas party. We were there all day, locked in, but by the end of the evening we had figured out that it was possible to seriously make music with this thing."

At the same time as this discovery, Burgess was also working with Dave Simmons on developing the Simmons SDSV drum synthesiser with a view to "bringing drummers into the late twentieth century". The eventual commercially-available product was to become a major sound source for the music of the early Eighties, as a bridge between the traditional drum kit and the advanced drum machines which arrived later in the decade. Burgess had previously written an article for *Sound International* magazine about the state of electronic drums, airing his disappointment in the Syndrum and Synnare which were only able to produce the most basic of synthesised signals. "I talked to all the different drum companies about this but no one was particularly interested apart from Dave Simmons," he says. "We wanted to develop something which was truly touch sensitive and at least performed the function of a drum, even if it didn't quite sound like one. Percussion is defined by an incredibly fast rise time and a hard attack, but none of the so-called electronic percussion of the time did that. But we managed to create that by cobbling all the sounds together on an ARP 2600 synth and Dave got to work packaging the whole thing electronically. The pads were touch sensitive and you could seriously approach it like a real drum. But when I started dabbling with the MC8 microcomposer I realised that by using the multiplex outputs you could actually trigger the drums from the computer. This started to really excite me because suddenly all the possibilities were opening up. At this time, the Linn Drum was still yet to happen – none of the really usable drum machines were out there yet."

Intrigued by his experimental tales, a number of artists and producers invited Burgess to bring his prototype electronic rig to sessions and it became apparent to all that he was truly breaking new ground. "People tended not to DI that much in those days, apart from maybe bass guitar," he recalls. "Not even synthesisers, because they were fed through regular backline stage amps and miked up. So it was quite revolutionary when I went in with my computer and the prototype SDSV [then simply a piece of wood with dangling wires and small jack connectors], then DI it and actually get a good sound. I had to teach the producers and engineers about all this but then I realised it was rather stupid and that I should be in the producer's role if I already knew about it."

But Burgess was already no slouch when it came to recording practices, having picked up several techniques during his days as a session drummer. "A whole race of brilliant engineers came out of Utopia, Trident and Mayfair," he says. "The Trident line led on to SARM before Trevor Horn got involved and the engineers who trained at

Mayfair tended to move on to Utopia. I worked at all of those studios during that period, and Mike Stone, who had just come off the Queen albums, took me to SARM to work with him on the Easy Street records with Gary Langan assisting. It was a great period for me in terms of learning about engineering because Mike would be talking to Gary a lot about different engineering techniques and I'd be all ears, having been a studio freak all my life."

Teaming up with Rusty Egan of the cult New Romantic London club, Blitz, was a smart move on Burgess's part. "Rusty's thing was to cobble together this whole electronic music scene out of records that were around," he explains, "like the *Midnight Express* soundtrack by Giorgio Moroder, Yellow Magic Orchestra, some Kraftwerk records and a few Bowie tracks which had an electronic sound to them. Landscape was fitting into that genre and we did some remixes of some of our stuff especially for Blitz and Hell, the other club which was important in establishing the New Romantic movement."

Egan and Burgess then "discovered" an act named Shock with whom they recorded an all electronic version of The Glitter Band's 1974 hit, 'Angel Face' at Mayfair Studios, appropriately with former Glitter engineer, John Hudson co-producing. "I believe that it was the first completely computer-generated record and probably the first time an electronic record had gelled so well. I suddenly saw the whole future in front of me and in my mind that was when Landscape changed from what it was to an electronic, computer-generated project."

Hudson, who also worked at this time with Burgess, Midge Ure and Egan's Blitz colleague, Steve Strange on Visage's 'Fade To Grey', comments, "I was thoroughly disenchanted with punk and welcomed the new electronic movement and the separation you could achieve with synths. From one point of view it was great to limit the amount of miked-up stuff, because you didn't have any spill. On the other hand, it made things sound very small and dry because there were no effects on them, so when you were mixing it prompted you to do things to make, say, a synth fit into a particular space. Now there are hundreds of digital effects you could use but even in 1980 we only had an Eventide harmoniser, one echo plate and about three tape machines for different delays. So you had to concoct a mixture of all those to give you a different effect."

Burgess's production career began in earnest with Landscape's album, *From The Tea Rooms Of Mars...To The Hell Holes Of Uranus*, for which he and Walters had originally written most of the material with a view to live performance. Noting the minor but significant success awarded in the indie charts to Landscape's previous incarnation, coupled with the effect Burgess's electronic leanings were having on the people around him, RCA stepped in with a major deal and was amply rewarded with the singles 'Einstein A Go-Go' and 'Norman Bates'. "Apart from two tracks which hung over from our original live approach, the rest of the album was completely electronic with the MC-8 and the Simmons SDSV, which still had not been released into the marketplace," says Burgess. "We recorded a lot of the album at Utopia and Mayfair, using about eleven different engineers, from Andy Jackson and Greg Walsh to John Hudson and Hugh Padgham. Everyone was young and fresh, and I'm sure they must have learned a hell of a lot doing it."

Experiments included the feeding of horns through octave dividers, distortion units and ring modulators, and the resulting album became a playlist regular at Blitz, where Burgess met a bunch of North London lads who became the next target for his arrow-sharp production values. "They told me they had a band called Spandau Ballet and they seemed interested in my ideas so I played them some stuff," he says. "About three weeks later, their manager Steve Dagger called me out of the blue and asked me if I wanted to produce their first album. I said yes, thinking that when they got their record deal I'd probably be blown out in favour of an established music business producer. But Chrysalis who eventually signed them wanted to keep me on, which was an unexpected thrill."

Burgess immediately took the band into the studio to record their debut single, 'To Cut A Long Story Short', a Top Five hit in December 1980, and followed it up with 'The Freeze' in advance of the band's first album, *Journeys To Glory*. While the band's sound had already become an established entity before his intervention, Burgess believes that Spandau Ballet was wrongly perceived as a strictly electronic band from the start, not least due to the Blitz link. "But," he says, "they did have the Yamaha CS-10 synth which we used for the main riff on 'To

Cut A Long Story Short'. It was a really horrible nasal-sounding synthesiser and we had to triple-track it to make it sound any good at all. But I was very keen to help create an individual sound for each band I worked with by distilling the essence of what they were about and then capturing that on record in a unique way. The first time you hear their first record, you should know that it's someone different. The second time you hear it, you should recognise that it was that interesting band you heard for the first time last week, or whenever. I'd seen a lot of their gigs and their line-up was two guitars, bass, drums and vocals. But pretty quickly Steve Norman stopped playing guitar and took up percussion, then saxophone."

Many new qualities were introduced to the band's musical style through working with Burgess, who in advance of their sessions planned his approach with academic flair. "I wrote a whole lot of notes on the band before I started working with them and analysed what I wanted to create," he reveals. "I really wanted that riff to be very distinctive; I didn't mind if it was nasal-sounding, as long as it was the synth answer to the guitar riff on 'Satisfaction'. Because we were aiming it all at this electronic club scene that was really happening, it was important to have a tight, in-your-face, disco bass drum, but not the same kind of snare sound. I didn't want it to sound like stuff that had gone before, like the late Seventies Euro disco stuff. Having played on a lot of those records as a drummer, I knew those sounds back to front so I knew what to avoid. I felt more inclined to get a more alien sound about the drums. The track was more or less recorded live as a band with some overdubs but I would record the drums and then take the ambience of the drums and gate it to the snare which gave it that strange ambient feel. Almost everything had to be created either in the room with different miking techniques or through the use of gates, compressors and EQ. I guess I did quite a lot to shape the recorded sound of the band, but it has never been my philosophy to go in and completely dictate what a band should sound like or indeed change their whole approach. I viewed my job as helping them be as comfortable as possible and capturing them at their best so that their records had a lot of impact."

A year before Burgess met the acquaintance of Spandau Ballet, while still involved with Accord, he was introduced to yet another new item of technology – the Fairlight CMI (Computer Musical Instrument) – which heralded the start of what is now termed "sampling". Burgess's interest was preceded by witnessing a series of computer-generated music concerts where the musicians created algorithms for real instruments and appeared to make the sounds of trumpets mutate into violins. Burgess was awe-struck. "This was all done on huge IBM mainframe computers which filled rooms and cost a sizeable fortune," he says. "They had to work through the night because they were sharing time on the computer with lots of other people and companies. I was informed that someone had invented this sampling device in Australia. Being from New Zealand I had been thinking about going out there anyway that Christmas, so I literally jumped on a plane and flew over there. I met the people who were behind the Fairlight and when I got back I started to become heavily involved in it."

After becoming one of the first two British-based Fairlight owners, (the other being Peter Gabriel) Burgess managed to recoup some of his large investment by conducting the Fairlight programming on Kate Bush's 1980 album, *Never For Ever*. "It was really exciting because Kate's one of these really open-minded people who when you walk in with a new device looks at it and immediately grasps its potential," he says. "The machine came with one disc which had a dog barking on it, a pizzicato bass, a gunshot and some other things. Instead of using the stock sounds which most people did, Kate had her brother Paddy bring in a load of ethnic instruments on which he could play one note very well. He played them all into the Fairlight and Kate and I created whole orchestrations around these sampled sounds. She wanted the sound of a rifle being cocked as part of the percussion track for 'Army Dreamers' so her older brother, John, brought in a massive collection of rifles, all of which we sampled and merged together. As far as I know it was the first time anything like that had been done."

Gradually in the early Eighties a new generation of studio technology began to emerge and Burgess used them to the full on later productions with, among many, Romford's finest dance act, Five Star. One highly prized effects unit to be used by him on such recordings was the Lexicon Primetime processor. "It was a revolution because you could suddenly start to dial up useful, interesting sounds instead of scrambling around to create them manually. It was equipment such as that which began to open the doors to a lot of real possibilities in the control room."

Heaven Sent

Hailing from the steel capital of England, Sheffield, The Human League was one of the bands which typified the new electronic movement of the early Eighties and whose 1981 album, *Dare*, was one of the most commercially successful of the era. But the band's history dates as far back as 1973 when Martyn Ware and Ian Craig Marsh each invested in a synthesiser, Marsh building his from a Maplin electronics kit. Their partnership began, as with most teenage novices, with them doodling with the strange sounds emanating from their new toys. At first, they had no intention of becoming professional musicians, let alone producers. But later, while employed as computer operators in their home city in 1977, they formed a synth band, The Dead Daughters, at a time when such music was out of phase with the punk environment. Within a few months, with the addition of vocalist Philip Oakey, they became The Human League and landed their first record deal with Edinburgh-based Fast Records in the summer of 1978.

Ware, now the sought-after producer of artists including Vince Clarke's Erasure, says that the band never expected to sign up with a label on the strength of their home-produced demos, as most record companies were then led by what they saw in a band's live attributes and the reaction of their audiences. "We were quite unusual in that we never did demos, certainly not as a means of trying to convince a record company that we were worth signing," he says. "We didn't even think it was vaguely possible. So we were only recording stuff for our own pleasure. We had a Sony two-track machine which we bounced to and from. Our first single, 'Being Boiled', was done by bouncing from track to track and adding a different instrument every time, without even having a mixing desk. If we did anything wrong while bouncing, we would have to go back and start the track from scratch. We weren't even planning the overdubs in advance. We just put a kick drum down which sounded half decent, then a snare, a hi-hat, a bass line, and so on in a completely haphazard manner until the thing came out as it did. 'Being Boiled' cost about £2.50 to record – the price of the tape. But we were doing it for fun and there was no mental pressure on us from record companies demanding a hit. So my skills and understanding of production, and having an ear for how different sounds fitted together, all started from there."

The early Human League design philosophy was based on a need for all sounds, apart from the human voice, to be synthetically created, as influenced by Kraftwerk, Walter (Wendy) Carlos and Giorgio Moroder (the producer of such classics as Donna Summer's 1977 seminal electro-dance track, 'I Feel Love'). "We didn't like to use the Dr Rhythm boxes that were the only drum machines around, but instead we had a hardware sequencer which ran the Roland System 100, the first modular synthesiser you could buy," Ware says. "We were also fans of straightforward pop which maybe gave us an accessible edge. In our book, there was never a distinction between production and performance, so it was as natural for us to produce our own records from the word go as it was to write them. Production was an integral part of the writing."

Touring in 1979 as the now Virgin-signed support band to Siouxsie And The Banshees, Iggy Pop and Pere Ubu may have given The Human League a useful grounding in presentation, but their remote-controlled entertainment concept (which included the use of film backdrops and a slide show) was costly. It also fell foul of Talking Heads' audience and the band was dropped from the December 1979 tour. "Playing live was not really essential to us," Ware admits. "It may have been fun, but we didn't achieve anything. In fact, it almost destroyed our record contract. By the spring of 1980 we had released two albums [*Reproduction* and *Travelogue*] that everybody now claims were very influential, but it must have been only the opinion leaders who were buying them, certainly not the general public. In today's world we would have been dropped like a stone."

Band members were becoming divided over musical policy by the autumn of 1980 and Ware and Marsh quit The Human League, leaving Oakey and Adrian Wright to pick up the pieces as a more straightforward pop act. Rather than form another group, Ware and Marsh developed the British Electric Foundation as a production umbrella for a variety of projects, including Heaven 17 which was fronted by photographer-turned-singer, Glenn Gregory. "We were incredibly arrogant, but all for the right reasons," says Ware. "We so enjoyed being in the studio recording and writing, and it came so naturally to us that we went to Virgin and suggested that instead of us forming another group when we left The Human League, they should sign us as a production unit. It was virtually unheard of at the time although it's now very common. In real terms, a lot of the currently successful Euro dance groups are production units who bring in vocalists to front a project. So I suppose we were quite influential in that respect, because we told Virgin that we wanted to find singers to perform on our productions, and we would present them with albums. But due to the structure of the contract, it was completely unrealistic because they could nail us down to giving them three albums per artist and we weren't ready for that. If it had all gone well and we'd have turned into Jimmy Jam and Terry Lewis [influential American dance producers], we'd have all been multi-millionaires now."

For the first Heaven 17 album, *Penthouse And Pavement*, and for BEF's *Music For Stowaways* (actually the *first* BEF album, but only a limited edition instrumental cassette release), Ware recorded on a simple Ampex eight-track machine which, alarmingly, had only six of its tracks functioning normally. Synchronisation between the machine and synthesisers was achieved not with a SMPTE generator but an unpredictable pilot tone, and the hardware sequencing was purely monophonic. Ware also purchased a monophonic Roland Jupiter 4 synth around this time. "Although those things sounded incredibly naive, they were also very attractive and sort of timeless," he says. "It's fundamentally because if you look at the constituent parts of an orchestra, most of the instruments are monophonic and if you are forced into a situation where you have to create the desired effect through monophonic instrumentation, you usually end up with something that is more pleasing to the ear."

Right up until the mid-Eighties, digital hard-disk samplers were still unheard of in Britain. Unless one could afford a five-figure sum to buy a Fairlight, one way of remotely triggering short bursts of sound at a given point was by the use of the AMS delay unit in which samples could be stored for instant replay at the touch of a button. Ware first tried this method for the mechanical effects on 'Crushed By The Wheels Of Industry', where the sound of two concrete paving slabs scraping together was miked and fed into the AMS. Varispeed was also used by Ware to create a false impression. "The second version of 'Being Boiled' which was on The Human League's 'Holiday 80' EP had a synthetic brass section which we recorded at half speed because I couldn't play that fast!" he says. "You don't get into that stuff in studios anymore because of sampling. I have actually worked with engineers who are absolutely dazzling on the programming side but if you ask them to turn the tape over and record reverse reverb on the piano, they'd look puzzled and say, 'Oh, that's an interesting concept.' But they use those sounds all the time on the sampler."

After *Penthouse And Pavement* became a Top Twenty success in October 1981, a manifesto for the BEF was established with its first major album project the following spring, *Music Of Quality And Distinction: Volume One*, featuring a range of high profile singers from the present and the past (including Sandie Shaw, Paul Jones, Gary Glitter, Glenn Gregory and The Associates' Billy Mackenzie) performing familiar cover versions against a backdrop of pure electronic music. "We perceived no barriers in the way the thing could work," says Ware. "It was a kind of emancipation. We had the power to make electronic music appeal to the masses and it almost became like a crusade. But by that stage we were already getting bored with the narrow-minded attitude that everything had to be electronic; it was like we were driving ourselves into a corner. Electronic reverbs and harmonisers were only just beginning to become popular, and this opened up a pathway to using the best expression of acoustic instruments and then electronically mutating them. That's when our design philosophy changed."

Although Ware admits that he never truly accomplished all his aims with the BEF, many lessons were learned as he enjoyed his image as a renegade on the periphery of the business. "Heaven 17 took off a lot faster than we anticipated," he reveals. "It was a lot easier and less messy to deal with the record company as Heaven 17, pop group, rather than keep explaining to them what BEF was all about. I did record another BEF album in 1992, *Music Of Quality And Distinction: Volume Two*, which was electronically-orientated soul music with an amazing line-up of people on it. I didn't think anyone had approached that properly before and I was very pleased with the result."

Hot on the heels of Heaven 17 singles 'Temptation', 'Come Live With Me' and 'Crushed By The Wheels Of Industry', the BEF was singularly responsible for returning Tina Turner back to her former glory after many years spent in virtual obscurity. "I had already done a backing track for 'Ball Of Confusion', the Temptations number, when we were looking for singers for the first BEF album," Ware explains. "It turned out really well and we had arranged for James Brown to record the lead vocal, which at the time was a ground-breaking idea. Then we received a telex from James Brown's lawyer telling us that he would do the track providing that he got all the points on it, and we got none. We may have had the greatest admiration for him but we couldn't possibly agree to it, because we weren't a charity organisation and we thought we deserved to make at least as much as him from the royalties. So the whole thing fell through and we tried to find Bowie to do it. But someone at Virgin told us they were going over to Los Angeles and one of their friends knew Tina Turner.

"I was a big fan of Tina's although no one would touch her with a barge pole back in 1983. I always loved 'River Deep, Mountain High' and we even did a cover of it with The Human League which never saw the light of day. We sent Tina a demo of the song and paid her air fare to come over, and Roger Davies had just taken over her management and was trying to get her a deal. She turned up at the studio and asked to hear the backing track. As far as she was concerned, the music might have come from Mars or somewhere because it was so alien-sounding to her. But she was brilliant and had obviously rehearsed it in advance, but it was obvious that although she must have heard of The Temptations, she didn't really know who they were! Everyone was knocked out with Tina's performance and the whole track, so much so that when it came for Tina to record her *Private Dancer* album, she came to us to do 'Let's Stay Together' with Greg Walsh. It was a very fortuitous affair because record companies are a lot more cynical now about matching certain producers with artists in order to attract a particular audience and level of success."

Ware's growing reputation led him into new territory when he donned an R&B producer's hat to work on Terence Trent D'Arby's debut album, *The Hardline According To...*, in 1987. "A real R&B producer has his bag of tricks, the contents of which change over the course of time, and they will get used," Ware says. "There is a certain palette of sounds which is familiar across the board in American R&B – a particular drum machine, certain types of keyboards. An American record company can ring an R&B producer and they know what they are going to get before the session's even booked. It's almost like going to buy an accessory for your car. The quality is consistent and the basic hallmarks are the same. Occasionally, someone will come up with a track or an album which is ten per cent better than the rest and everyone goes wild. Suddenly that producer is the flavour of the month." This is clearly a facet of the music industry which Ware cannot and will not concern himself with. Given the instruction to produce, for instance, a Bobby Brown record and incorporate the same characteristics at the fore of a previous hit, Ware will run a mile. "I cannot imitate people, it's not within my capabilities," he insists. "So if a label risks an R&B project with me, they know they are going to get a record that is unpredictable and quite unlike what a real R&B producer will deliver."

A founder member of Depeche Mode, Vince Clarke has remained at the forefront of electronic pop music for more than fifteen years, using a number of artist vehicles to display his musical flair. Yazoo (with Alison Moyet) and The Assembly (with Feargal Sharkey) were among his first forays after leaving Depeche Mode at the end of 1981, but his partnership with singer Andy Bell as Erasure has remained his career mainstay since 1985. Ware teamed up with Clarke and Bell to produce one of their most recent albums, *I Say, I Say, I Say*, and he provides an insight into the enigmatic songwriter's method of working. "Vince is a completely unique individual and the reason he likes an outside producer is because he can't be bothered with all the nuts and bolts of the final fifteen per cent of the job which makes it sound finished," he says. "He's interested in the putting together of tracks, the creative, musical side, and then he's quite happy to let someone else take care of the rest. He's never in the studio when Andy is doing the vocals. That's the producer's job as far as he's concerned and, in fact, he and Andy never record together at any one time. It's not that they can't work together because they are great pals, but Vince just prefers to work on his own.

"We did two or three tracks together and I would advise Vince on sounds. But that was crazy because he obviously knows his own machines better than I do and we write similarly, in that the writing formula is in the multitracking. He writes monophonically too, although under duress I got him to do a few pads here and there. It evolved to the stage where I'd just let him spend a day on his own knocking up a basic track, then I'd come over in the evening and might point out a few things which weren't working properly and we'd modify them. It helped that Vince had respect for my early work because we had a friendship thing going and it wasn't like the typical producer-artist scenario. The tracks would come together fairly quickly after that and we'd play the backing tracks to Andy who would go away and write some lyrics."

'Vienna'

Inspired by Roxy Music, Ultravox formed in 1973 as Tiger Lily and spent its formative years under the leadership of original lead singer and frontman, John Foxx. Its eponymously-titled debut album, produced by Brian Eno and released by Island in March 1977, was critically acclaimed and pointed the way forward to the electronic scene, even though its feet were then firmly entrenched in the burgeoning new wave culture. The following year saw Ultravox recording in Germany for the first time with producer, Conny Plank. Sales of *Systems Of Romance* disappointed Island and the band was unceremoniously dropped, but the subsequent replacement of Foxx with ex-Slik and Rich Kids vocalist/guitarist, James "Midge" Ure, and a new streamlined direction honed for the electro-pop movement, gave Chrysalis every reason to pick up Ultravox's contract in April 1980. The first album from the new regime, *Vienna*, included the rousing singles 'Sleepwalk' and 'Passing Strangers', but it was the title track which became a classic of its day (a Number Two, blocked only by Joe Dolce's 'Shaddap You Face' – enough said) and catapulted Ultravox to once elusive heights.

The basic tracks for *Vienna* were recorded during a three-week period in the spring of 1980 at Mickie Most's RAK Studios, after which the band retreated to Plank's German studio for ten days of overdubbing. "There was nothing particularly interesting about recording at RAK, it was a very sterile environment," Ure recalls. "But Conny's place was a big converted barn and much more atmospheric. Back at RAK, the equipment we used for that first album was incredibly basic although we had just bought a few new bits and pieces to work with. Warren Cann [drummer] had just bought a Roland CR-78 [the world's first programmable computer drum machine, housed in a wooden cube] but you could only programme two drum patterns at a time. It wouldn't hold anymore than that! So the 'Vienna' drum part was just two patterns, one of which was the half-time part on the verses, to which Warren added some synthesiser drum pads for those 'pi-cooooh' sounds. The second part was where it sped up for the middle solo in double time. But in order to do this section, we had to do a twenty-four-track edit. So we recorded the entire track right up to this middle part and then snipped the tape. We then recorded the new, faster section with the violin solo and did the same again with the slower piece for the ending. So there were three pieces of tape edited together because there was no time code or any device for locking the drum machine and the other instruments together. Nothing was there to automatically speed things up or slow them down for you. It was all done manually, by sticking pieces of tape together."

To precisely synchronise the drum machine and the Mini-Moog for various crucial parts on *Vienna*, which also included the synth bass-driven 'All Stood Still', the band used an electronic pulse which was picked up by a "spike" located in the back of the synth. "Chris Cross would stand there and play these parts live," Ure continues. "And if he fucked it up near the end of the song, we had to go back to the beginning and simultaneously lay the drum machine and the synth bass down again live. It sounds crazy now but we had to have everything well arranged in advance with good count-ins at the beginning of everything. You couldn't go back like you can now and just drop in on a track if you cocked up because the technology we needed just wasn't available then. For every piece of electronic equipment that Ultravox used, we had to have a duplicate because we'd had it adapted in some way. When we went out on tour, we had a wealth of equipment. Two of everything. If a Mini-Moog went down on us, we couldn't just go down the road and pick up a replacement from the nearest music store, because our one had been modified to take this spike for picking up the pulses. It was always a continuous daunting task, having to use all this gear, most of which was very flaky stuff. Mini-Moogs, in particular, were notorious for unreliable pitch. The oscillators would drift in and out all the time, making club gigs a nightmare! You had to constantly tune them up. Then there was the other problem that, because there was no memory or patches, you had all these knobs and switches to re-organise between each song. It was an incredibly basic set-up."

The glorious piano on 'Vienna' was, despite the electronic bias of the moment, a genuine acoustic piano and the idea to feature it so prominently in the track was all Plank's, who Ure rates as one of the best producers and engineers he has ever worked with. "Conny was more technically astute than actively creative in his direction," he says. "He left the arranging side to us in the belief that the musicians should handle the music and he would record the ideas and atmospheres on tape. On the 'Vienna' session we sat down and chatted about it. We'd already done the backing track and finished the overdubs out at his place, where he felt more comfortable with his own desk and toys that he liked to use. And before he recorded the piano, he listened to the song and said, 'I see this as a very sad song of a very sad man, alone in a big empty ballroom, and he's playing the piano, playing this refrain that he's played over and over again all his life, and he's tired of playing it. That's how I see the sound.' And that's exactly the sound he got – a very haunting, sad piano sound. He simply put some EQ and echo effects on the piano and suddenly there was this soulful, melancholic sound on tape. We were amazed!"

Although the violin had been used by Ultravox prior to Ure's arrival in the line-up, 'Vienna' marked the first occasion where it had been featured so heavily. Its use with the piano against a striking electronic backing track conjured the desolatory atmosphere. "When we were at RAK I remember we were experimenting quite a bit with the violin and it's where that part was recorded," he says. "We tried recording it in the studio's reception hall which was all marbled so it gave great resonance. It seemed a much better idea than sticking it in a soundproofed room. We did some drum tracks in there as well.

"We had no big master plan with Ultravox but what we did know was that we wanted to be different. We didn't want to repeat ourselves and that's why we didn't make *Vienna* Part Two, which would have been easy to do. There was a lot of pressure on us to do that. The follow-up album to *Vienna*, *Rage In Eden*, was written and recorded entirely at Conny's studio in three months which was a hideous thing to do. Looking back on it now, it was like a prison sentence. It was freezing cold, we couldn't speak the language, couldn't understand the TV or radio. It was a very intense time and very experimental. Very brave too. In a way the album shows that because it's depressing, but it was depressing to record it."

Trevor Horn: The Definitive Article

If there was one producer who defined the lavish sound of Eighties pop more than any other it was Trevor Horn. Through his work with Frankie Goes To Hollywood, Grace Jones, ABC, Dollar and Malcolm McLaren, he bridged the gap between electronic and naturally performed music, and delivered it in a slick, exaggerated package. It was the sound of decadence, the sculpting of a fresh, recognisable musical image from the very latest technology with productions appearing so expensive that one could even smell the money.

Horn's fascination for recording can be traced to his mid-teens in the Sixties when he would spend many hours after school tucked away in his bedroom, writing songs and recording them on a humble two-track machine, balancing the sounds with a small mixer he built and encased in a pencil box. In 1966, at the age of seventeen, he visited a small Kettering studio to make his first demo, playing bass, piano and singing, while noting how the engineer double-tracked elements of the recording. Although he says the music was "dead crap" (Horn was turned down by Island's Chris Blackwell at the age of nineteen), Horn became enthusiastic about the whole exciting process, but it was several years before he was able to seriously involve himself. His twenties were spent earning a solid living as a bass player on the cabaret circuit in nightclub house bands and he was eventually able to finance the equipping of his own studio in Leicester in 1975. "I was able to afford some good quality equipment, but there wasn't enough money left over to pay for the building of the studio, so myself and another guy built it with our own bare hands," he recalls. "It took us a whole year to finish because I would be playing every night and working on the studio during the day. I always liked microphones and the look of studios. I was also very drawn to photos of people working in studios, so it seemed inevitable that I would have one of my own one day."

The studio was built as a commercial operation, but business was slow to begin with until Horn had an idea which both brought about a stream of customers and gave him the necessary drive to investigate his potential as a producer. "I noticed that the TV show, *Opportunity Knocks* was having a song contest so we advertised that we could record quality demos of songs for entrants," he says. "People began turning up with crappy old songs and I basically tidied and tarted them up a bit as we recorded them. I wasn't thinking too much about it because it was just a job. One day, someone said to me, 'What you are doing is called record production.' It was like someone had lit a light bulb in my head and it was obvious to me that this was what I was going to do, even though it took a further six or so years before it really started to happen."

While playing bass for Tina Charles, who enjoyed a Number One success with 'I Love To Love' in 1976, Horn learned some important lessons from observing her producer Biddu's techniques. "I discovered just how precise records have got to be in terms of rhythm and also learned a lot from hearing his raw backing tracks because you very rarely get to hear a producer's raw tracks," he says. "I'd thought they sounded a bit dry and cold, but I understood what he was doing and I was pretty certain that 'I Love To Love' would be a big hit as soon as I heard it."

Around 1978, Horn made his first appearance at SARM East Studios while still working in Tina Charles's band. A side project he was involved with required forty-eight-track facilities and SARM was the first studio in London with two synchronised Studer twenty-four-track machines. SARM was owned by Gary Lyons and Barry Ainsworth, and financed by Lyons's uncle, David Sinclair whose daughter Jill Sinclair left a teaching post to run the company after Lyons moved to America to capitalise on the success he had enjoyed with the first Foreigner album. SARM engineer, Gary Langan met Horn on the very same day as Sinclair and all three struck up a formidable relationship which, in the case of Horn and Sinclair, led to wedding bells and the beginning of one of the most powerful music partnerships in the modern-day British music industry.

'Video Killed The Radio Star' introduced a new slant on pop production in the autumn of 1979 when, as half of The Buggles with Geoff Downes, Horn achieved his debut Number One. "The Buggles was an idea that Trevor had been playing around with and when Jill heard the demos she suggested the formation of a record company specifically for those records, the label which eventually became ZTT," Langan says. "Trevor thought that was a great idea but the next day, he walked into a meeting at Island Records and they offered him a deal which Jill couldn't match. So I think she said something like, 'Marry me and take the deal with Island!' That's when I started working with Trevor on The Buggles although some of the early backing tracks were done with Hugh Padgham at the Townhouse, only because SARM wasn't big enough then and Trevor wanted to use real drums."

Horn says that although he had a mild obsession with technology, more important was his desire to make records which were commercial, yet out of step with the sounds of the time. "I was finding the sound of records to be quite boring," he admits. "It was the second half of the Seventies, an album-orientated period when all the music was played manually and it all had a rich, rosy glow. I tried making those kinds of records but it really didn't work for me; I just couldn't get them to sound right. I figured that if I couldn't get records to sound like Elton John, which I couldn't because I couldn't figure out how they did it, then whatever I could do, I'd better exaggerate it. I was more interested in doing perverse things with sound, except that in 1978 and 1979, none of the equipment which would later allow me to do that was available. So I had to pre-date that technology by finding my own ways of achieving certain sounds. 'Video Killed The Radio Star' [and the album *The Age Of Plastic*] was made without any drum machines or sequencers, even though it sounds like that way. There was no point in being polite – I had to find a way of making my records sound extreme to some degree because that was the only way to get people's attention. Before you have a hit you always believe that no one is interested in you. You can walk into any record shop and there are thousands of records available to buy, so why should someone buy yours? The only reason would be because it stood out from the rest and it had something the others didn't. Originality is the most important thing and it doesn't matter how you made it as long as people are moved to buy it."

The advent of the programmable drum machine was the key to Horn's development as a producer, but even its absence did not prevent Horn from shaping a machine-like sound from human players. He was clearly thinking ahead. "In 1977, I got Paul Robinson to play his kit one drum at a time – the snare, bass drum and the hi-hat – and I recorded them on separate tracks, then used the sounds like a drum machine, punching him in and out on the desk," Horn says. "Paul said, 'That's sounds fucking awful, just like a machine.' I said, 'Great, that's exactly how I want it to sound!' I still use Paul today on some things, but back then he was a lot more surly because drummers ruled the roost until machines became so prevalent. I understand what his angle was but it was time for change." When sequencing hardware became available, despite its early crudity, Horn had a bespoke rig built for him with the help of Dave Simmons. "With Dollar and ABC I used a combination of a Roland TR-808 drum machine [one of the first to arrive in the UK] with triggers built into it by Dave Simmons," he says. "I had heard his drums on a record and I loved the sound of them because I loathed real drums. He enabled me to trigger his Simmons drums from the machine and it was a major step forward for me. I also had a terrible Roland sequencer to which you gave a list of notes and you could trigger it to play those notes endlessly. You might punch in four Ds, an E and an F sharp, and you could trigger it from the 808 and when it was synchronised with drums it was fantastic, a major breakthrough."

Buggles colleague, Geoff Downes had invested in a Fairlight just before the duo split up (Horn joining Yes, Downes joining Eighties rock supergroup, Asia) and after a long period when Horn poured his scepticism on this £20,000-plus system, he suddenly realised its potential. "I went out and bought one, much to my wife Jill's horror because they cost an extraordinary amount of money," he reveals. "Back then, producers didn't carry gear with them, not even a microphone pre-amp, so it was a serious move. But I knew I was right to buy the Fairlight even now. I used to say to people, 'Isn't this great, I've got one of these, I know how it works and I'm the only nutcase who owns one.' I wasn't the only Fairlight owner, of course, but nobody else was being as adventurous with theirs. I just thought, 'Boy, are we gonna have some fun with this.' And we did until Akai introduced the cheaper sampler and everyone twigged what was going on. But for a few years, we had it all sewn up and going around the world working with Malcolm McLaren put me in a very strong position for a considerable time."

Langan, who remained Horn's engineer throughout his early Eighties productions, comments, "Trevor was the first person I knew who had a great command of machines and he had this obsession about everything needing to be strictly in time. So he was hell bent on using all the new machinery that was coming out which enabled him to achieve that. There wasn't anything actually being played on Dollar's 'Hand Held In Black And White'; the drum sound was a mass of reverb combined with processing through the console. There were no rules as far as Trevor and I were concerned, we could do anything and you knew that everything we did was going to be good. Then came ABC's first album, *The Lexicon Of Love*..."

Criticism has been levelled at Horn by those who feel he too rigidly imposed his production ideas on certain acts, ignoring their natural qualities. But he insists that he would only take a production as far as the artists would let him. Nevertheless, there was very definitely a trademark accompanying all of Horn's records and ABC was just one successful band to reap the rewards. "When I first met ABC in 1982, they were young and hip, but I was in my Thirties and I'd been through the Seventies and played in Yes," Horn says. "I didn't know what to make of them at first because I could see that they were very bright and charming, but they wanted to play disco music. I didn't understand that because anyone who wanted to sell albums did not play disco music. ABC were playing songs about their lives, but they were kind of groovy. After I spent a bit of time with them, I realised that they were coming on like Bob Dylan meets disco. I knew about disco having played in all those terrible ballrooms and nightclubs but they had taken on a different feeling since ABC started to frequent them. I was more of a rock concert-goer when I was their age, but as soon as I understood what they were trying to do, it made things a lot more straightforward.

"The first track I did with them was 'Poison Arrow' at RAK Studios and like the first time you work with any band, you're always uncertain as to how far they want to go with the production, and it's easy to misunderstand each other. ABC wanted to compete with the Americans and didn't want to make an indie-sounding record, but they were a live group and, unfortunately, it sounded to me like an English indie band. I said, 'It's all right, it sounds okay but how far do you want to go? Do you want to make a great record or is this going to be good enough for you?' Martin Fry [singer] said, 'We want to make a fantastic record and beat the Americans at their own game.' I told them that if that's what they wanted to do we would all have to work hard and I would need to wheel in my rig and programme the whole song into the TR-808 with the bass on the sequencer. We were going to lay that down in perfect time and then the band members were to play on top of it. It was like drawing on tracing paper."

ABC were no slouches when it came to musicianship and in drummer David Palmer, who currently plays in Rod Stewart's band, Horn at last found someone who could play with the regimented feel of a machine. "A lot of American guys had already got this and they knew what that kind of feel was about," Langan observes. "Very few English guys really understood this. But Dave did and he was dynamite. The backing tracks for all the ABC stuff were recorded at Tony Visconti's studio, Good Earth, at the bottom of Wardour Street. David Bowie was in town during the making of the first album and because Bowie was an old friend of Tony's, he used to come and hang out at the sessions. Dave Palmer would memorise each song and play all the drum parts to nothing but a click track. Bowie sat there for hours giving it his blessing and saying it sounded fantastic. And it did."

Once ABC latched on to how Horn's plans and direction was going to work for them, they very quickly turned on to the use of electronics, but retained complete control of the record, allowing Horn to apply his techniques while on a tight rein. "It was never like they didn't know what was going on," he says. "They were very bright boys even though I would be the last one to deny that I did a good job, all of the lyrics and melodies were quite brilliant and I had nothing at all to do with the writing of them. Producers are only effective if they have great ideas. I did a lot of the arrangements and I remember changing the ending of 'Poison Arrow' but they came up with the idea of sound effects in the middle of it which I never suggested. After we did 'Poison Arrow' and they sussed out how the process worked, they started arriving with stuff already programmed. By that point they had already bought a Linn Drum and done all kinds of stuff so my job became much easier, because they were now really into it. I brought in Anne Dudley [who in 1998 won an Oscar for her soundtrack to *The Full Monty*] to play keyboards and she was brilliant. She also did the string arrangements because I thought if we were going this far, why not use real strings? They sounded much better than the phony ones that the Americans used."

Rarely does a record producer become a household name. Phil Spector and George Martin are exceptions to the rule, of course. But Trevor Horn was added to that small, elite club in 1984 through his and ZTT's image-shaping work with the outrageous Frankie Goes To Hollywood. The Liverpool band was discovered by Malcolm Gerrie of of the now sadly defunct Channel Four music show, *The Tube*. The Frankies were given a small budget by Gerrie with which to make a video for screening on the show. The song was 'Relax' and Horn saw its transmission while producing Yes's *90125* album at Battery Studios.

"We always used to have a break to watch *The Tube* on Friday evenings and this video came on with all these women chained up to a wall and a whole load of other kinky stuff going on," he says. "Chris Squire said, 'This band looks really interesting. Why don't you sign them up for your new label?' Jill and I had just started ZTT but I hadn't signed anyone. I thought they were pretty good even though there were some obvious faults to the track, but I didn't think too much more about them until I heard them again on David Jensen's radio show, doing a BBC session for 'Relax'. It was then that I realised just how fantastic the song was and I couldn't believe that Jensen didn't realise what the track was about [sex, incidentally]. I knew that song could be a hit so I said to Jill that we had to sign them, regardless of the cost. What we didn't know was that everyone had turned them down because they didn't know what to do with them and they were also on the verge of splitting up. But they had a great combination of rock music and Donna Summer dance music with this guy, Holly Johnson's magnificent voice. On the first album, *Welcome To The Pleasuredome*, he was singing at maximum throttle in a way that I'd never heard anyone sing. He had a unique voice and that is always the most important thing."

To say 'Relax' caused a stir would be to issue an understatement. DJ Mike Read saw fit to ban the record from his Radio One playlist, but that was playing right into ZTT's hands. Banned records are normally the source of enormous fascination among the record-buying audience and the ensuing controversy propelled the single to the very top. Further complaints came from the gay community who objected to the gross sound effects on the twelve-inch version made by samples of the band diving into a swimming pool and Horn dropping various objects into a bucket of water. What the listener judged these sounds to be was, of course, a subjective matter. As 'Relax' headed the singles chart in February 1984, Horn began to worry whether the band actually had a worthy song for a follow-up single. He originally persuaded them to record the future Grace Jones hit, 'Slave To The Rhythm' but they also had 'Two Tribes' up their sleeve. It didn't sound as instant as 'Relax' to Horn but he briefed the ZTT team that every measure should be taken to ensure that a hit, and a major one to boot, was created from its insignificant frame.

Of the actual creation of 'Two Tribes', Horn says, "The first thing I did was take the band into the a cheap recording studio called Producer's Workshop and have them play a live arrangement which had the same staccato bass part. We listened back to the recording and it sounded okay, although not a big hit so we had our work cut out. Steve Lipson was fairly new on the scene as an engineer and I suggested to him that we programme the bass part with a four on the floor, and that sounded really good. The backbone of the track was really a Linn 2 bass drum with a sample of a slapped E bass guitar string going across it. Bottom E is very sympathetic to a bass drum and it sounded huge on the radio. And Steve played a fantastic guitar part which I still regard as a classic piece of guitar playing. He also played on 'Relax' and 'Welcome To The Pleasuredome'. Nasher was a good player in a certain kind of way, but Frankie was always a combination of Nasher and Steve's interpretation of Nasher. Steve was even engaging in conversation with me at the same time as he did the 'Pleasuredome' solo! The only other guitar player who has turned me on as much was Trevor Rabin in Yes. Dave Gilmour's good but if you listen to the guitar solos on *Slave To The Rhythm*, I can point out where Dave finishes and Steve starts, and it's really something else."

Together with ZTT's journalist ally, Paul Morley, Horn cooked up the threatening nuclear attack atmosphere of the record, based on the band's original lyric. "Paul had got hold of a classified CND documentary tape which would be played on every TV and radio station in Britain if ever there was a nuclear attack," he says. "It was narrated by the actor Patrick Allen and it had all that stuff about what the public should do in the event of an emergency. Of course, this was in the early Eighties when there was still an element of threat from the Communist bloc. We talked about integrating this tape into 'Two Tribes' but, of course, I was very aware of the fact that we couldn't just use Patrick Allen's voice because he was a working actor and we'd be ripping him off. So we booked Patrick for £1,000 to come in and do a specific voice-over. We typed out exactly the entire transcript from the tape and gave it to him when he arrived. But he observed that when he originally did it he had to sign the Official Secrets Act and he didn't know whether he should be recording this for us in case he got into some serious trouble. I explained to him what we needed him for and the concept of 'Two Tribes', and to his credit, he said, 'Ah, what the hell, let's do it!' While he was behind the microphone he remembered that there was something that had been omitted from the original tape. It was a line that said, 'If your grandmother or anyone else should die whilst in the shelter, mark their bodies carefully and put them outside.' I thought this was fantastic and it just added to the extremity of it all. I had all this stuff on a quarter-inch reel of tape and couldn't wait to use it on the record. Then, when we did the twelve-inch, I got the guy from *Spitting Image* to impersonate Ronald Reagan because we couldn't use Reagan's actual voice for fear of being taken to the cleaners! Steve and I were on a roll and having a laugh, basically."

By the beginning of July 1984, Frankie occupied the Number One position with 'Two Tribes' and Number Two with 'Relax' at a time when the twelve-inch extended mix format was coming of age and rivalling the regular seven-inch for importance. The ZTT masterplan had worked and helped 1984 become one of the most successful years in terms of British record sales. "We sold twelve million twelve-inch copies of 'Relax' in England alone and that was unheard of at that point, so we knew we had a big market for twelve-inch mixes especially as ours were exciting," Horn says. "The music business is one of the last few in which if you do something good, people are automatically going to buy the product. It might be promoted in certain ways but at the end of the day it's about what you buy as opposed to how you buy it. When you feel you have captured an audience, you want to give them something that will stimulate them and give them enjoyment with value for money. We wanted the first twelve-inch of 'Two Tribes' to be great, the best we could do. In fact, we didn't want to let that record out until we had a great twelve-inch.

"There was a great outtake from 'Two Tribes' that started with 'Reagan' saying, 'Ladies and gentlemen, Frankie Goes To Hollywood. Probably the greatest thing this side of the world.' Then everything stopped and there was a huge belch. That was the original introduction but I took it away, thinking that I wouldn't want to hear this year after year. So we substituted it with Nasher saying, 'Oh yeah, well 'ard,' which I thought was much more in keeping with the Frankie humour. They were funny guys to be around and they definitely inspired the way we went about things."

Grace Jones's *Slave To The Rhythm* album was originally conceived as a single until Horn's dissatisfaction with the work in progress instigated a number of different versions of the song. This culminated in what he describes as "the ultimate twelve-inch mix", and one which was a reference point for all mainstream pop producers in the mid to late Eighties. "Grace is pretty off the wall anyway and how she presented herself suggested to me that she should be handled rather like an art object," he says. "I wanted to create something timeless so I got the writers to re-write the song over a Go-Go beat, as it eventually came out. But I still like the Germanic first version. Because we had two highly contrasting versions, we thought it might be worth going further with some other approaches to the same song. This was recorded at the commercial peak for twelve-inch mixes, so instead of having an album of different songs we could present an album which was really an overblown twelve-inch."

Horn acknowledges the huge input of colleague and programming expert, Steve Lipson, and explains that the eventual breakdown of their five-year partnership came as a result of two highly successful, charged up individuals sharing the same workspace. "It was a team," he says, "but then most hugely successful projects are not due to a single person. On *Slave To The Rhythm*, Steve was producing me being a producer, which is a weird concept but that's how it worked. You don't work with somebody night and day for five years in this game if they're not important to you. He is an incredible technician in terms of working equipment. Where other people could only cope with engineering, Steve would engineer with absolute ease, play guitar and bass like a demon, and programme creatively with brilliance. He was the first person that I ever saw running a computer with a sequencer locked to SMPTE in a control room on a day-to-day basis. I never saw that happen before. We had a computer locked to whatever track we were working on at any given time. But this was in 1985 which was very early for something like that."

ZTT's disjointed image was typified by the quirky Fairlight workouts of The Art Of Noise, a project (whose name was inspired by an Italian futurist manifesto) which gathered together Anne Dudley, JJ Jeczsalik and Gary Langan to create the most unlikely, though ultimately successful, chart music. Forming a group could not have been further from their minds but the idea originated during the nine months it took Horn to produce Yes's *90125* album, following Jon Anderson's return to the role Horn temporarily occupied in 1980. "After about seven months of working virtually every day of every week at a variety of studios, I was beginning to see green men climbing the walls,' Langan says. "We had been up at AIR in Oxford Circus to cut a track but it was scrapped. I kept the multitrack though because the drum sound on this track ['Leave It'] was just phenomenal. A month later, when the band had gone home one night, myself and JJ [Horn's assistant and Fairlight programmer] had the idea for putting the drums from this multitrack into the Fairlight as a complete sample. The idea wasn't to have separate samples of the bass drum, snare and hi-hat, like everyone else was beginning to do with AMSs, but have it as a composite sample of the whole kit. So that's where the drum sound on 'Close (To The Edit)' came from. JJ and I effectively recorded the first Art Of Noise single that night, although to us it was a demo. We just looped the drum sample and added a few other things on top.

"I kept a cassette of this for a while during the time that Trevor was being courted by Chris Blackwell and there was talk of ZTT being set up. One evening after another session when the band had gone home and things were getting quite depressing, I seized the moment to say, 'Well, shoot me or whatever, but I've done this and used one of the scrapped Yes drum tracks to do it.' I put on the cassette and he just went mad, thinking it was brilliant. He took it straight round to Blackwell the next morning and that was the start of ZTT, because Blackwell wanted us to be the first signed act. I had learned the piano from the age of seven but I gave up when I was kind of fourteen or fifteen because I got bored with it, so I wasn't an accomplished musician and we needed someone who could play keyboards. Anne was the natural choice because Trevor had always used her as a keyboard player and arranger. The fact that she was so straight and on the level was such an interesting contrast to someone like JJ who was completely crazy. He's a real eccentric guy who was originally a geography student who ended up being a Fairlight programmer. Figure that one out!"

The Art Of Noise revelled in the bizarre and no concept was ever more so than their collaboration with veteran American guitar picker, Duane Eddy for an electronically distressed re-vamp of his 'Peter Gunn Theme', recorded in the dining room of Dudley's Hertfordshire home. "Duane was picked up at the airport and stuck in a little Trust House Forte hotel somewhere near Luton, and he turned up at Anne's the next day," recalls Langan. "We had this Vox AC30 in the dining room with a couple of mics on it and Duane came in and played. It was weird because he just stood there playing his big guitar with 'Duane Eddy' written across it, wearing a huge sheepskin coat and a rhinestone guitar strap. There he was, this great guitar legend standing in the middle of Anne's dining room! When it was all over we all went down the road to the pub for dinner and that was it. I never discovered what Duane really thought of it all because we never had the time to work it out. It was so odd and he'd never made a record like this before in his life. But we got a great letter from Henry Mancini who wrote the tune."

The Hit Factory

Think of the names Mike Stock, Matt Aitken and Pete Waterman and a number of images immediately flash in the mind. Tacky pop? Maybe. Infectious, danceable tunes? Certainly. Serious listening? Definitely not. The South London-based production trio who made stars of Mel And Kim, Rick Astley, Jason Donovan and Kylie Minogue, among many of their boy/girl next door signings, easily rivalled Trevor Horn for chart success in the Eighties. Behind the cabaret gloss and lightweight facade, a genuine scientific approach went into forging a conveyor belt of hits, the volume of which had rarely been seen from a production house since the halcyon days of Holland-Dozier-Holland, Waterman's heroes.

Waterman started out in music as a club DJ which he says has always been a good vantage point for investigating public taste and what really makes them want to dance. A lack of good material from Motown in the late Sixties ("When Motown turned hippie," he says) caused a vacuum in his ballroom and it forced him to make his own instrumental records of Motown hits with local musicians to keep people on the dancefloor. He soon found himself working with bona-fide acts as a producer and by the time he met Stock and Aitken in 1984, his Loose End Productions had already notched up a handsome fifty chart placings with the likes of The Belle Stars, Matchbox and Musical Youth, the financial rewards being so great that he temporarily based himself in California to beat the English tax system. Contrary to the laddish, high-tech image his team nurtured at their late Eighties peak, Waterman considers himself a product of the old school where engineers were engineers, producers were producers, and never the twain would meet. "I'm the sort of guy who likes to bring in people around him, like a good musician and someone who takes care of the technical side," he says. "The sort who walks in with a clipboard and says, 'Okay lads, there's your four minutes. It's all over now!' That's the way I've always seen record production. I'm also a good talent spotter and a good judge of what will and won't sell, which is based on a lot of years in the business."

Shortly before he left to take exile in America, Waterman made what he calls "the worst record of my life...about CB radio" with the song's writer, Mike Stock. "It was so poor," laughs Waterman, "that we gave the record company their money back!" Upon his return to England, Waterman resumed contact with Stock and with Aitken it was decided to form a new production company. "We put pieces of paper on the table with our names on and pushed them around until the order sounded snappy, like Holland-Dozier-Holland. That was very much where our idea came from. You can make comparisons throughout the whole of our partnership to them, right through to our final demise," he says.

In the beginning, SAW established a lockout agreement with Marquee Studios where they produced their first releases. But by the end of their first year together, they had accumulated such a vast array of outboard equipment and keyboards that a large van was hired every time they moved into the studio to begin a project. It was beginning to dawn on them that the only necessary items they lacked were a mixing console, monitors and a tape machine, and having worked on SSL (Solid State Logic) desks elsewhere, they realised that the Marquee's comparatively substandard Harrison console was not meeting their increasing requirements, Waterman decided it was time to invest in his own studio and an SSL. He found the ideal place on the south side of London Bridge in the Borough, an old studio which was about to declare its bankruptcy, and took it over as PWL Studios (aka the Hit Factory) in January 1985.

"We were very technologically-minded and even today we probably have more equipment at PWL than any other studio in the UK," Waterman says. "If there's something new I want to hear it. In 1984, we were at the forefront of a new wave of technical producers and we were throwing away all the shackles which had been put on producers in the past. We didn't want drummers and would never entertain the thought of having a real, live drummer in our studio. So we were able to do things with drum patterns which a human couldn't physically do. Things with bass drums that no one had ever done before because it was possible to programme silly drum patterns on a machine. You could play triplets on a bass drum which drummers could not do for long. I had been working with Stevie Wonder in my previous partnership and I bought a Wave PPG and a Wave terminal which allowed us to really work on the sound and change it to our requirements. So when it came to doing the basses on our first records, we spent days working on the sound. What I had learned in the States was that if you could roll bass off a record, you got more volume on and it also by-passed radio stations' limiters. So you could make a record which was around 10dB louder than anyone else's on the playlist."

Waterman's preferred music at the time was what he terms "gay music", ie the Hi-NRG or Eurobeat electronic dance music favoured among the gay club culture, and he and his two partners set about designing a sound which would work in that environment. "The sound to light systems in those clubs worked on frequency response and this made us start looking at the records not in terms of sound but frequency," he says. "We started to put things in which affected the lights, particularly cowbells and handclaps. By writing certain patterns in you could make the lights go bloody crackers! There was no way the lighting jockeys, as they were then, could even work the lights as fast as our records could. You had a bass drum which had hardly any bottom in it and then took all the bottom out of the basses and made them really heavy at the middle frequencies. We added triplets on the handclaps and cowbells, and made them sound really screwed up so that they took your head off when played loud. There was no bass on the record at all, so when you played it loud like all kids love to, it sounded so fantastic. There was no extreme bass distorting the speaker on the bottom end and the speaker moved very little in real terms, and the clarity was such that it was like a lump of cotton wool had been removed from your ears because it was so sharp."

Knowing that SAW could not compete with the "quality" pop of Trevor Horn, who had fast become a legend with Frankie, Waterman looked to the gay market, thinking that it was one area which the major labels steered clear of and, therefore, there would be little competition. "We were quite happy to each work for £100 a week for a couple of years so that we could learn the job," he reveals. "Because I knew the gay scene very well and knew all the DJs, because it was the old Tamla Motown market, I knew there were potentially 15-20,000 buyers for any record you made in that vein. I hoped that I could push that to about 25,000 so that we would be safe and could earn about £200 a week each and not starve. That's why we became analytic about the way we approached everything. It wasn't for any reason other than we had to make a living and that was the only market in which we stood a chance of surviving."

Of the SAW team structure, Waterman comments, "It was a joint responsibility. Somebody would look after something one day and another one of us would look after something different the next. The only defined role was Mike Stock's as the tunesmith. We came up with some lyrics and maybe some banal tunes, but it was Mike's job to knock all of those elements into a good song. But all the records were finished by me. I was there at the start and end of everything, and I always mixed the tracks." By 1987, SAW had stockpiled so many hits that there were those in the media who were suggesting that a new singles chart be developed just for SAW artist releases. This popularity prompted the release of a greatest hits album, *The Hit Factory: The Best Of Stock-Aitken-Waterman*, which carried the subtitle, "Today's Sound/Tomorrow's Technology". "We were into phrases and it sounded just right at the time," Waterman explains. "We were the first to use samples on everything although I now laugh at the crudity of what we did. But we had 1.57 seconds of sampling which back then was like a year! So people came to us because we did things with technology that no one else was doing and we were the first to use new equipment like the Calrec microphone and Sony digital recording."

Inevitably, as is normally the case in Britain with any homegrown success story, SAW came under fire for apparently churning out the same music fronted by different faces. Waterman still refutes the claim that the trio had a set formula. "If you listen to Princess, it's nothing like Dead Or Alive," he states. "Kylie's records were nothing like Rick Astley or Jason Donovan. They are based on a completely different musical structure and come from a different area. If anything, our problem was that when we really became successful around 1988 we weren't adventurous enough which we had been two years earlier. In 1989, because of the success of Kylie, she had stymied us and tied our hands because we were making so much money from her records that we didn't have the bollocks to turn around and say we didn't want it.

"I never took the criticism seriously at the time and I still don't. My challenge was always to say to people, 'Well, here's the studio, it's £1,000 a day to hire, so why don't you come here and do better?' but no one took me up on it. Suddenly in the mid-Nineties, people are starting to dig up the old Mel And Kim records and realising how unbelievable they were. We had a fabulous time making records together but we never made them for the critics. I attended a lecture in about 1988 where it was said that rock 'n' roll wasn't exciting anymore and it had died. I got up and told them the reason was that they were too old, they had missed the point, and there was a rock 'n' roll revolution going on out there called Stock-Aitken-Waterman. Just because it didn't suit their tired old tastes, they couldn't see how outrageous it was! Their grandads probably had the same problem with The Rolling Stones."

The mid-Eighties was another landmark period for John Hudson when he teamed up with long-time colleague, producer and songwriter, Terry Britten, to work on Tina Turner's *Private Dancer* and *Break Every Rule*, earning two Grammy awards for his efforts. Another producer impressed with Hudson's mixing skills was Alan Tarney, and both collaborated on several A-ha projects at Mayfair, including the 1986 Number One epic, 'The Sun Always Shines On TV'. "When Alan and I worked on that track, I started the mix but he was kind of getting in the way, moving faders and stuff," says Hudson. "I must have offended him a little because at one point he said, 'I'll go for a walk, because I think you'll be happier if I just let you get on with it for a while,' and I was so relieved! The trouble is, I can be blunt in the studio, and if someone asks me if the bass drum sounds crap, I'll simply say, 'Yeah, it's really shit!' I'm never very polite. Most of the producers I have worked with like to do a little bit of twiddling on the desk. These days you can store everything and it's automated, so they can't make any fatal mistakes. As long as I have got past a certain point, I think it's fine. It's teamwork after all. And after I got things happening on the A-ha track, Alan returned to EQ the vocal and pick out a certain character within the voice, which is something he's very good at. After a while, he could see that we were on the right track and said, 'Okay, I'm not going to touch it anymore now.'"

Hudson's mix of 'The Sun Always Shines On TV' was checked by Tarney by listening to a cassette in his car, a method which, although not favoured by Hudson himself, remains a standard among many producers. "Alan was gone for ages and I got it into my mind that he thought it was terrible," he says. "When you have been working on something for about twelve hours, you sometimes wonder if you've lost it or if it's gone in the wrong direction. You think, 'Is this what A-ha are supposed to sound like?' But he came back raving about it, saying how he could hear everything and it sounded so huge, even at low volume."

'19'

Paul Hardcastle entered the music business in 1984, enjoying rapid success with his first minor UK hit single in the April of that year. Primarily a keyboard player/producer with his feet firmly in dance music, his next four singles (including one under a pseudonym) met with similar response in the lower reaches of the UK chart. Things picked up significantly over in the United States when 'Rain Forest' hit Number One in the specialist R&B listing. But Hardcastle's hypnotic aural documentary of the Vietnam war, '19', saw both him and the extensive use of sampling realise their full commercial potential.

Hardcastle explains the track's purely accidental origins: "I was watching and videoing a TV programme called *Vietnam Requiem*. I'd been thinking at the time that I wanted to make a different kind of record, so I set up a Revox reel to reel to record the dialogue. Just after the programme had finished, I went down to the studio in my place in Leytonstone and tried taking some of the sounds from the programme and experimenting with them. It started working quite well but what was missing was some way of getting across how old the kids were who died in Vietnam. So I was thinking in terms of putting that over in a chorus. I tried getting people to sing it, doing a rap, and tried loads of stuff, but it wasn't quite right. Then I got hold of an Emulator 1. It was one of the first samplers and I had hired it for the day for something else. I just started mucking about and recorded me saying, 'Nineteen.' I was fooling around and doing something rhythmic on one key with that sample, going, 'N-N-N-N' and thought this would be a good idea. So I did what I normally do when in search of inspiration and that's go and make a cup of tea! I left everything for about fifteen minutes and almost forgot what I'd done. But when I played it back, I thought, 'Shit! This is a different way of putting over a chorus,' and no one else had done it before. The further I progressed, I just got more and more into it and thought I might as well make the record as it's supposed to be. The main keyboard melody line came later. It was just something that just went behind what was going on in the chorus. That was after I knew the chorus was going to be '19'. The master tape still says 'Vietnam'."

A Roland TR-808 drum machine was used for the rhythm track; its repetitive pattern being a result of Hardcastle's self-confessed inability to programme. "I was concentrating on the main idea of the song and there was no time for fucking about!" he says. "So I put this rhythm down first, followed by a bass line which was all half-tone stuff, giving it an edgy *Jaws*-like feel. Then I started structuring the words around this rhythm track. There were other things on there, stuff about soldiers' brains being blown out. They made it on to the twelve-inch but understandably they were a little too heavy for the regular seven-inch single." Mixing was undertaken at Sound Suite Studio in Camden Town. "They had a bit more gear than me, a few more effects which came in useful. I worked on the mix with an engineer called Alvin Clark and we had a lot of fun with it. We filled that multitrack up with the remixes and it was one of those situations where what we were doing absolutely screamed out for Total Recall and computer-aided mixdown. We did the 'Destruction Mix' and 'The Final Story Mix' and we were literally overdubbing onto the tracks that already had stuff on them. It was a nightmare! We then did foreign language mixes with the narration in Spanish, French, Italian, German and Japanese."

Apart from Janice Hoyt's vocal lines and narrative sections, all of the voice tracks were Emulator samples derived from Hardcastle's original Revox tape of the *Vietnam Requiem* dialogue. Parts of that programme were later used in the spine-chilling '19' video. "I think the reason it worked was because it was real," he says. "We didn't use actors to recreate the stuff. We used an actor for the retrospective bits where he says, 'In 1965...' and so on. But the news clips were from the time, even though technically they sounded shitty. You can tell the guy is distressed about what he was saying. It was genuine and that's the reason it worked so well. It hit home." Not everyone shared Hardcastle's enthusiasm, especially his label, Chrysalis, who firmly requested that he tone down the gruesome details of the Vietnam apocalypse. "They told me that no one would play it," he reveals. "Then, all of a sudden, it had twenty-six plays in one week on Radio One. The label then said, 'We knew it would do well all along,' which taught me a lot about record companies!"

Most of the recording of '19' was carried out at Hardcastle's own studio, which was partly financed by a £10,000 insurance payout following a motor bike accident. "It enabled me to buy an ACES twenty-four-track tape machine and a desk. The machine must have been the worst piece of equipment on the market and it broke down every week. But as soon as I got it, the first thing I recorded on it was 'Rain Forest', which sold over 400,000 copies. [In the UK, it reached Number Forty-One on the mainstream singles chart.] And so that proved that making good music isn't all about equipment. Nowadays I use Synclaviers and things like that. But it was that piece of crap machinery that recorded 'Rain Forest', and then came '19'. So the gear paid for itself 5,000 times over in no time at all. Even with all the engineer call-outs."

'19' stayed at Number One in the UK for five weeks, entering the singles chart in May 1985 for a sixteen-week residence, and earned the Ivor Novello award for International Hit Of The Year, as well as being the best-selling single around the world in 1985. In the United States, where Vietnam is still a touch paper-sensitive subject, the controversial '19' made the Top Ten but generated a wide range of reactions. "Some of the newspapers got the wrong end of the stick, saying it was anti-American, but I didn't get any hassle," Hardcastle recalls. "In fact, I got letters from Vietnam vets, thanking me for making the record and every year they use it as their main theme tune for their annual march through Washington. I met lots of vets when I went over there and it meant a hell of a lot to them. I suppose it was just strange for them to see this little British guy doing it!"

Hardcastle has since achieved great success as a composer for television and although he appears to be absent from the UK charts he continues to enjoy healthy international sales. '19', however, will be hard to top. "It's a record I'll always be proud of," he admits. "Some people might say it's a bit gimmicky but I believed then and I believe now that it was an honest piece of music. The only gimmick was in the stuttered sample and, really, it took a lot of guts for me to put it out. I could have got crucified. The success of '19' set me up relatively early on in my career, so I didn't have to go to the record company, cap in hand, every time to ask them if I can make a particular type of record. One can only imagine the situation if I hadn't have had my own studio and gone to the A&R guy and said, 'Look, I've got a great idea for a new record. It's about Vietnam and it's gonna go "N-N-N-N-N-N-N-Nineteen".' I'd have been told, 'Get out, you're mentally ill!'"

Another young producer to come to the fore in the Eighties, through hits with Swing Out Sister, Was (Not Was) and Hipsway, was Paul Staveley-O'Duffy, whose family already boasted a gifted producer/engineer in his older brother Alan. Having won an RAF scholarship, his original career goal was to become a pilot, but it was not long before O'Duffy the younger caught the studio bug. "I used to go along with Alan to various sessions, like The Rolling Stones, Steve Marriott and Horslips just to see what happened and I was mesmerised by how effects were created," he says. "I eventually got a job as a tea boy at Marcus Music Studios and went from that to being an assistant, then graduated to engineering.

"I began doing remixes when it became in vogue during the early Eighties and went to live in America for a while where I also played bass in a band called Film At Eleven which was a disaster, although I only used that experience to further my production career. All through being an assistant and engineer, my real goal was to be a producer. I always had an overwhelming desire to discover what makes a song work and if it's not working, how do you fix that? I wanted to find out how I could keep a listener interested for three minutes."

While developing his craft in the States, O'Duffy's relationship with AMS paid off in huge dividends. "They used to send me anything I wanted, regardless of where I was working, so I got to know a lot about their equipment," he says. "I was recording at Sigma Sound in New York where they had an AMS delay, and at the time nobody knew you could lock sounds into it and trigger them off. But I was bonkers for doing this and triggering off all different drum sounds and weird things. I used this technique on 'Sex-O-Matic' by The Bar-Kays and I guess it must have sounded different to anything else then. I came back to England to start as a producer, but it was difficult at first because no one wants to use you if you have no track record. But a couple of the records I worked on in the States had started to do well in clubs over here and some of the A&R guys picked up on this. That's when I got the chance to produce Hipsway who were quite successful and did well in America especially with their biggest single, 'The Honeythief'. I had engineered lots of bands and been quite vocal in that department, helping with the production. I'd even played on some things and I thought production would be a similar experience, but the difference was quite dramatic. I became an engineering producer, working with an assistant. Instead of having to explain to another person what I wanted on the desk, I could do it myself."

After his initial success with Hipsway, Phonogram approached O'Duffy to work with another of the label's new signings, Swing Out Sister. "Their sound evolved from me listening to the group," he explains. "They were quite jazzy when I first heard them and I tried to pull them towards being pop. I suggested a proper orchestrated string arrangement in the background and a brass section because not many people were doing that. There were certain Sixties sensibilities that I wanted to include without making their records sound like they came from a different era. We were in the studio one day, working on the drum track for 'Breakout'. I got a Ludwig Black Beauty snare and sampled it into the Fairlight. We hit it on the rim and it sounded fantastic, miked up with some ambient mics. Every nuance was sampled so that the programme would sound like a real drummer. But I thought, 'Well, it just sounds like a good snare drum and everybody gets a good snare sound. What I should do is get a really bad snare sound!' So I rang the hire company and asked them to send me the shittiest snare they could find. I tuned it up very badly so that it was ringing horribly and we used that instead for 'Breakout'. You need things like that to grab attention and if something sounds smooth and bland, it'll just sink into the background."

O'Duffy was later called in by Phonogram to make sense of a collection of tracks by Was (Not Was), including 'Walk The Dinosaur', after sessions with Don Was at the helm did not meet the company's

A&R man, Dave Bates's approval. "I don't think Dave rated Don as a producer," O'Duffy says. "He certainly wasn't delivering a sound that was fashionable or of the moment. So Dave asked me if I'd be interested in producing them because he believed Don had taken the project as far as it would go. What Dave had heard was a much earthier version of what I ended up doing. I was given carte blanche to do anything I wanted; either re-record the songs, re-arrange them, do additional production or just different mixes. So I went over to the States and took my people with me. I felt the basic ingredients were okay but I needed to address it differently. We had a brass arrangement written and reworked the rhythm section so that they moved the right way at the right time to set up the chorus in a better way. I gave the track more punch and bite, and made the whole thing larger than life, whereas Don's version was considerably understated, but that's his style. It must have been quite difficult for Don with someone else coming in and taking over his show, although he never really made me feel like that. I was very focused on what I was doing, I wouldn't have been concerned with any bruised egos. Don would come down to the studio whenever I needed a hand, although it wasn't often. I think most people think that he produced 'Walk The Dinosaur', certainly a lot of American A&R people do."

Phonogram's Bates was also responsible for signing Scots idols, Wet Wet Wet. With their cover version of The Troggs's 'Love Is All Around' occupying the Number One position for a whole season and more during 1994, the Wets have matured into pop heroes for a discerning adult audience. But it is a far cry from their early days as bright-eyed white soul boys in the mid-Eighties with their 1987 debut album, *Popped In Souled Out*, produced by Michael Baker. Since then, bassist Graeme Clark has taken over the band's production and sees this as an area he will develop in later years.

The band's initial releases focused on delivering a modern interpretation of Motown-orientated soul and R&B music, tailored by state-of-the-art tools and principles. But *Popped In Souled Out* was not intended to be the band's first album. More than a year before its release, the Wets travelled to Memphis to record with veteran soul producer, Willie Mitchell (of Al Green fame), using a battery of vintage equipment that would have shocked techno heads beyond despair.

Clark still rates those June 1986 sessions among the band's best moments. "I loved that project," he states. "That was an album that was made like a proper album. We recorded a whole batch of songs in six weeks at the same studio with the same mics and with the same producer. That's why there's a real continuity all the way through and it was definitely a stepping stone to greater things, we thought.

"Willie Mitchell was great. It was 1-2-3-4, no click tracks, no time code, just a straight ahead performance on to tape. It was a breath of fresh air because we had been working with The Pet Shop Boys' producer, Stephen Hague earlier that year and become blinded by science and computers. Suddenly all the trappings of being in a modern recording studio were taken from under our feet. Willie was using a sixteen-track recorder, all the old mics that Al Green used and the same drum kit. It was like going back to the Memphis of the Sixties and, of course, it was the first time we'd been out of Glasgow, and only nineteen years old. To go from the cold West of Scotland to hot, humid Memphis was pretty wild. We learned an awful lot from that experience and apply it today. You should be able to write a song just with a piano or a guitar and make it sound good in that format."

But the fruits of the band's Memphis sojourn did not sit well with Phonogram's image of the band and the album sat on the back burner for several years before being issued as an album of "historical interest value". "It was a marketing decision which is an area I've never been comfortable with," Clark reveals. "But those guys do it every day so they must know better, or so they tell you. In my mind though, the *Memphis Sessions* album was our most successful album to date, not in commercial terms, but certainly musically. It immediately made us sound like we emerged from the early Seventies because it was all valve equipment which I've always believed to be far superior than the modern stuff."

The Genesis Of Hugh Padgham

Ambient, gated drum sounds proudly reigned throughout the Eighties to the point when artists and their producers stressed the importance of such qualities to almost obsessive levels. Possibly the first artist to achieve notoriety in this field was Phil Collins, whose explosive drum fill halfway through his 1981 classic, 'In The Air Tonight' gave others a benchmark to follow. The person responsible for this new approach to the recording of drums was Hugh Padgham who from the late Seventies fiercely crusaded against the dull acoustic treatment of music. It was Padgham who, with more than a little assistance from the new SSL desk and the live room at the Townhouse Studio, found industry fame as a result of his sonic experiments with Collins' drums.

Padgham's engineering career began as a trainee at Advision Studios in 1974 but he soon left to take a tape operator's post at Lansdowne Studios, the second oldest independent studio in London. Working under Adrian Kerridge, Padgham received what he describes as an excellent formal training and in the four years he remained on the staff he progressed from assistant to main engineer and worked a wide range of projects with producers Gerry Bron, Mike Batt and Jonathan King. However, disenchanted by the classical bias of Lansdowne, he left in 1978 and became part of the Virgin empire as a key player in the fortunes of the Townhouse. "I was living in Buckinghamshire and I got involved with a guy called Trevor Morais [ex-The Peddlers] who set up a rehearsal studio in Little Chalfont which was later to become Farmyard Studios," he explains. "It became the happening place to rehearse for bands and the Manor Mobile was regularly hired for recordings there. Virgin, of course, owned the Manor and when I heard of their plans to build the Townhouse, I wangled my way into getting a job there. Although I hadn't done an awful lot of engineering before I left Lansdowne, I waltzed into the Townhouse saying that I was an engineer and because there were so few of us I got lucky. That's when it all took off for me, towards the end of the punk era."

Recorded drums in the Seventies, Padgham says, never sounded remotely like those heard at live gigs, but the new wave artists were calling for a change and demanding that producers approximate their natural attributes. It was a timely crossroads. "I wanted to hear drums sounding more wide open and trashy, recorded in a large room as opposed to being in a booth and close-miked," he says. "But the first time that big drum sound appeared in an overblown way was on Peter Gabriel's third solo album, on his song 'The Intruder'. When the

Townhouse was built there were two studios there and we installed a big Helios desk in one of them, and the second studio was just going to be for demos. Then the owners took the decision to turn it into a proper twenty-four-track studio with a cheaper desk. This was just around the time that the American companies like Harrison and MCI were bringing out desks, and then there was also Oxford's Solid State Logic. They were all offering desks at about half the price of the Helios in Studio One. But we decided to buy British and go with this new company which, of course, went on to conquer the mixing desk market. [Solid State Logic was actually formed in 1969 but brought out its first mixing console in 1977.] This SSL desk was amazing because it was physically small, but it also had noise gates and compressors built into every channel. This meant that rather than having to patch things into the desk, there were Trevor channels which already had those elements built in. There was also a thing called reverse talkback. When you pressed the talkback button it opened up a microphone in the studio so you could hear what everybody was saying from the control room. The mic was an omni-directional and SSL had built into the desk a really vicious compressor on the talkback button. So I got the maintenance engineer to give me an output from this talkback compressor on to the patch bay so that I could plug it on to tape.

"I was experimenting with this during the making of the Gabriel album and Peter heard this sound and thought it was unbelievable! We did some of the sessions with Phil Collins and he was just playing his drums and I was giving him the foldback in his headphones. I put this talkback compressor mic into another channel on the desk and because of this noise gate and compressor being on every channel, I just turned the noise gate on for a laugh. Suddenly, when Phil played it produced a massive sound which shut off between the beats of the snare and bass drum because I had the release of the noise gate wound up very fast. Phil heard it in the headphones and started playing to the speed of the noise gate's release. We still didn't have any samplers then. Peter asked Phil to play to the release of the noise gate for five minutes and he wrote a complete song around the sound of the drums."

It was a session which Collins could hardly forget and the results transformed his way of thinking overnight. Impressed by Padgham's keen engineering abilities and sense of adventure, Collins invited him to work on his first solo album, *Face Value*, six months later. The sound achieved on 'In The Air Tonight' was a direct descendant of the Gabriel session, thanks to SSL and the live drum room at the Townhouse. "That stone room became quite famous but it was cheaper to leave that room like it was when it was being built," Padgham says. "Tom Hidley at Westlake Audio came down to handle all the acoustic design and it worked well in the control room but we were trying to get a live area as well for the musicians. We got a lot of stone brought over from the Manor and we faced the walls with this nice yellow Cotswold stone, and left it like that. Tom came in and told us we had to have some trapping put in to kill resonance in certain areas, but we just said, 'No, sod it, we'll leave it like it is!' So it was a combination of the console and the room acoustics, because you can't get the drums to really speak unless you can achieve a certain amount of room ambience."

The sound of Collins' kit was a result of a two-tier miking technique: the main sound originating from a room mic with its signal heavily compressed, while the close-miked signals from individual drums were added subtly in the overall mix to act as a pinpoint. "If you have one or two mics in an echoey room, at least twenty feet away from the kit, there would be no defined stereo image," Padgham says. "Also, it was good to introduce some crack from the snare drum but I would always start off with the room sound."

With his newly-found drum sound and a fresh dose of optimism, Collins retained Padgham's services for the recording of Genesis's 1981 *Abacab* album and the subsequent eponymous (or *Mama*) release in 1983. "With respect to David Hentschel who had worked with the band previously, I think Genesis wanted to get away from the Seventies and we built a stone room down at the Farm [Genesis's own studio base, built in 1980] which was a near replica of the one at the Townhouse so that we could recreate Phil's sound," he says. "They started writing differently because drum machines had come into fashion and polyphonic synthesisers had just arrived. They also had their own studio facility for the first time and did a lot of writing and experimentation which they had not developed so freely beforehand. Rather than come into the studio with songs, they would just go into the studio and jam for a couple of weeks. I would record everything for them to listen to and develop ideas around the jams. I think all of those influences had a big effect on the direction the band took from then on. Phil started to use Simmons drums on the *Mama* album, although I hate the bloody things now!"

Although Padgham began to make his mark in the recording business at the time when electronic music took over from punk as the flagbearer of British pop, he remained adamant that he wished to work with humans, as opposed to machine-orientated acts like Depeche Mode and The Human League, as he gradually drifted into production as a result of his fine work as engineer to producer, Steve Lillywhite. Eventually, he summoned up the confidence to leave the Townhouse and turn freelance. "Both the Gabriel and the Phil Collins albums were Number Ones in the UK, and I did two albums with XTC who realised I was doing a lot of the work," he says. "I was never one to just sit at the desk with the producer and not say anything, even though it wasn't my place to air my opinions. But Phil and XTC obviously saw that I was making sense of certain situations and they asked me to go ahead and produce them."

XTC's 1982 double album, *English Settlement*, was one of the biggest successes of Padgham's fledgling production career, recorded at the Manor after the band returned from a world tour in 1981. They were sessions which Padgham remembers with great fondness. "Andy Partridge was one of the funniest guys I ever knew and he complemented Colin Moulding who was one of the driest," he recalls. "We had just built a live room at the Manor which meant we were able to get that Townhouse sound. They always came in the studio raring to go and Andy had a good foresight as to what he wanted from a session, so it was quite easy for him to explain to me any ideas he had for particular sounds and we would talk them over until I could make it happen at the desk. Being stuck out in the middle of the countryside, we'd start to go barking mad every now and then, so we decided that every Saturday night we would go to the pub and get half pissed and play Space Invaders, then return to the Manor with a crate of beer so we could then get completely pissed! I'd then get the band playing and they'd come out with these unbelievably fantastic renditions of old Led Zeppelin and Jimi Hendrix numbers, and we'd rename the band The Jimmy Edwards Experience. Andy would sing all the lyrics in the style of Jimmy Edwards and it was just so hilarious. I recorded it all with two mics on the drums so that Terry Edwards sounded like Mitch Mitchell."

Through his laudable work on 'Senses Working Overtime' and other tracks from *English Settlement*, Padgham attracted the interest of The Police, with whom he co-produced *Ghost In The Machine* and the band's final studio album, *Synchronicity*. "Sting wanted to find someone new because they had done three albums with Nigel Gray and he fancied a change," he says. "While The Police were touring in South America with XTC, Andy Partridge suggested to Sting that they use me, saying, 'Oi've got a mate called Hugh and ee's bloody good is ee,' in his lovely West Country accent. I'd met Sting before at the Townhouse because he was signed to Virgin Music and he was producing another one of their songwriters. But I didn't even meet Andy Summers and Stewart Copeland until we got to the airport to fly out to AIR in Montserrat.

"Sting did his demos for the album at Le Studio in Quebec in the middle of nowhere and while he was there he got the French-Canadian pianist, Jean Roussel to play on a demo of 'Every Little Thing She Does Is Magic'. Sting really liked the demo and particularly Jean's piano part, so when we got the master back at AIR we got the band to record a new backing track and Sting's vocals while retaining the piano. I thought 'Invisible Sun' was brilliant and they had a few more synthesisers than was normal for them. Before then they were very content with working as a fairly straight three-piece unit with guitars. But Sting began writing more serious lyrics and the music was reflecting the mood of the subject matter. This song was about the troubles in Northern Ireland and the chords were quite dark and mournful. I had persuaded them to take a bunch of keyboards out with them, like the Oberheim and the Polymoog. Because nobody in the band could play keyboards very well, the phrasing of the keys was very simple. But my whole feeling towards production was that simplicity was the aim. I think simple records can sound so fantastic but they are the hardest to make, because what isn't there is just as important as what is there. I try to stress that to artists whenever I can."

Back in England, shortly after mixing The Police's *Synchronicity* album in Quebec, Padgham received a panicky telephone call from Virgin's Simon Draper, asking if he would step in to take over from Chris Thomas on the production of The Human League's difficult follow-up to *Dare*, *Hysteria*. "Chris had bailed out due to personal problems but I wasn't actually very keen because I was more into real bands and having had a fair bit of success as a producer by then I was a bit full of myself, so I initially turned him down," Padgham recalls. "I now had a manager and he got involved by increasing my price, but this didn't worry Simon who was willing to give me whatever I wanted within reason. It was a deal I couldn't refuse so I ended up doing it. Jo Callis who was formerly the guitarist in The Rezillos had joined as a synth player a couple of years beforehand and 'The Lebanon' was the first Human League song to feature distorted guitar chords, so Jo was in his element. When I turned up I was inheriting something that had been started at least a month before. But much to my surprise, I loved the sessions because Phil Oakey is such a brilliant bloke, the second funniest I've ever worked with after Andy Partridge. It didn't matter that the girls couldn't sing and that it took a whole day or sometimes two to get the backing vocals down for one song!"

Band Aid

Of all the masterful productions in the Eighties which took months of loving care and precise analysis before completion, the one which made the biggest impression on the world at large was mostly recorded in one day and it put into motion a new charitable consciousness among the rock elite. A news report from BBC Television journalist, Michael Buerk in the autumn of 1984 on the escalating famine in Ethiopia shocked and sickened Boomtown Rats frontman, Bob Geldof along with millions of other viewers. The difference being that it was *he* who was moved to construct Band Aid and invite the cream of contemporary pop music to appear on an all-star single, written by him and Midge Ure, with all proceeds going to a new fund set up to help those in dire need. Sunday, 25 November, 1984 was the day when U2's Bono, Sting, Boy George, Paul Young, Duran Duran, Spandau Ballet and fellow stars arrived at SARM West Studios in Notting Hill, London to record their en masse vocals for 'Do

They Know It's Christmas?' – now a seasonal classic in its own right – over a backing track which had been recorded well in advance.

"I recorded it at home in the first studio I built, in Chiswick," Midge Ure reveals. "I originally wanted Trevor Horn to produce it but we only had about three weeks to get this thing written, recorded and in the shops for Christmas. Trevor said he'd love to do it but it would take him six weeks or whatever. So I said to Geldof, 'Look, I've got my own facilities. Let's do it here.' So he came over to my studio and we recorded his bits of the song and tried to make some kind of sense of it all. I wrote some new bits for it like the theme at the end and I sat in the studio for four days recording a backing track and putting the thing together. In fact, I did all the instrumentation at home, except for Phil Collins' drums."

Ure also reveals that the groaning sound which introduced 'Do They Know It's Christmas?' was originated as a sampled guitar. "It had a kind of growl sound to it and I used the tremolo arm to bend the note," he says. "Then when I sampled it, I just slowed it down and used it like a sequence. I wanted the track to start off very mournful, atmospheric and slightly sad. There's also a lonely-sounding bell on the intro that was a Yamaha DX7 keyboard and the pad behind the intro is actually my voice. I'd recorded some choir-type voices with regular chord changes, a bit like Ultravox's 'Hymn' in a way, but not quite as grand." The introduction also featured a percussion sample sourced from the music of some absent friends. "Tears For Fears weren't actually on the session but I sampled the drum from the beginning of *The Hurting*," Ure admits. "It was a great drum sound, so I sampled that and used it at the beginning of the track, and they thought it was incredibly novel. They were very pleased to be on the record, even though they hadn't realised it at the time."

After the star vocalists completed their task, it was left to Phil Collins to overdub his distinctive drumming before mixdown. "Phil had been working on his solo stuff and it was his only day off, and he was kept hanging around for hours and hours," Ure continues. "He just sat there placidly and said, 'Am I on yet?' We said, 'Soon, soon!' By the time it came to recording his drums, it only took two takes. His drums were all set up and the sounds were all there. Phil just told the engineer what to do. We stuck up a pair of overhead Neumann mics very high above the drum kit and compressed the hell out of them, so as well as getting the dry sound coming through, you also heard all this sucking and blowing ambience. It just all came from the kit. It was tuned perfectly which I think is the key to a good sound to start with and it took us maybe ten minutes to tweak the sound, then we ran the track and he played the first take absolutely perfectly. He just thought he overplayed, so he asked us to run it again and that was it."

From its tear-jerking introduction, the song grew into a massive fists-in-the-air anthem complete with seasonal bells and a feeling that optimism was perhaps only a few million record sales away. "Considering we only had twenty-four hours in which to record all the vocals and Phil's kit, and do all the filming, I think it was a major achievement. It certainly deserved a knighthood!" says Ure, referring in jest to the royal reward Geldof received for his charitable efforts. But Ure does harbour a little resentment to a production credit which he feels was undeserved. "Trevor Horn came into the studio at one point and he couldn't keep his hands off it. He had an idea to do a madrigal-type thing with the vocals. So we spent about an hour and a half messing around with this idea but we just said, 'Hold on, you're killing it, just forget it!' He was credited as co-producer, but he shouldn't have been. I think that was a smart move on someone's part because forever in America it will be credited that Trevor Horn and Midge Ure produced the record which was annoying, especially after he turned it down."

chapter ten

the oblique strategist

"I think one of the brightest people around is Brian Eno...he's terrific."

Sir George Martin

It is always wise to expect the unexpected and open one's mind to impossibilities when working with Brian Eno. Even as far back as 1971 when he joined Roxy Music as its androgynous-looking synthesiser player, it was obvious that any musician he came into contact with would never think, play or sound quite the same again. And over the twenty-five years that have followed since his tentative steps into the professional music world, Eno, as a producer, guiding light and multimedia artist, has lifted experimental ambient music out of its previous cult status and integrated it and its philosophies into mainstream projects by David Bowie, U2, John Cale, Talking Heads, James and Bryan Ferry, steering such luminaries to the heights of their imagination.

Twice in the Nineties, in 1994 and 1996, and in the face of stiff opposition, Eno has been presented with the BRIT Award for "Best Producer". He is arguably the most consistently influential producer in Britain, in no small way due to his challenging views on studio etiquette and what have become mainstay approaches to writing and recording. Strangely, in listening to the way in which he discusses his work with artists, one is tempted to draw parallels with a psychoanalyst revealing details of his patient. It appears that Eno's productions depend more on an artist's interaction with other personalities than the arrangement of musical notes.

When he first became involved with Roxy Music, Eno described himself as a "non-musician" in an effort to distinguish between the classical idea of a trained and dextrous musical instrumentalist, and someone like himself, who uses music technology to form atmospheres. Today, mainly because of the success he has shared with best-selling artists, he is more likely to think of himself as a musician, but the word "standard" will never be a part of his vocabulary.

"I think I belong to a community of musicians who make music in a new way," he says. "That might involve playing an instrument well but it might just as easily mean playing a record deck well, as a lot of the DJ people do. Or being able to use a recording studio console or tape machine. These are all areas in which people have been musicians in the history of rock music. The distinction I am trying to make is that there is this new thing going on which should be called musical activity. In the early Seventies, there was a very clear distinction being made between the musicians, those being the instrument players, and the technicians who operated all the machinery. Somewhere in between was the producer, and it seemed obvious to me that these roles overlapped so much during the recording process that they were almost identical in many cases. All those people were increasingly involved in creative, rather than technical, jobs. So I was really just trying to spread the umbrella and say that all sorts of talents come under the category called musician, and I did that by drawing attention to my own limitations!"

Eno left Roxy Music in 1973 and began a wildly varied solo career with his album, *Here Come The Warm Jets*, which made heavy use of the EMS Synthi A suitcase synthesiser he had experimented with on *Roxy Music* and *For Your Pleasure*, as well as using it to "treat" Phil Manzanera's guitar and Andy Mackay's wind instruments live on stage. The same synth, in fact, used by Pink Floyd to colour *The Dark Side Of The Moon* (see Chapter 6). "I used it on everything at various times," Eno says. "I had a little mixer on stage which I designed and every one of the stage instruments came to my mixer, and I could then send them into the little EMS and a couple of tape recorders that I used for echoes and things. I did live on-stage producing, really. The first time anyone had done that, I believe, but it was quite easy to do. I just had an ordinary mixer that had sends on it. If I wasn't sending an instrument to any effect, it would just go straight through to the mixing desk, *au naturel*, albeit louder. But if I interrupted it and turned the send knob, I would divert it through all of my equipment and then I could start changing the sound, by putting it through a filter, distorting it, putting it through a ring modulator, pulsing it and all sorts of different things. From there, from those treatments as I called them, it would be sent back to the mixing desk. The engineer would be receiving the original instrument, plus whatever I had been doing to it, or if I wanted to, only my signal would go to the desk and totally by-pass the original sound. The same principle applied in the recording studio."

Unlike most instrumentalists whose playing skills are determined by a certain degree of formal or self-training, Eno approached his synthesisers, tape recorders and processing devices rather like a child in a toy shop, and his studio activities became similarly unorthodox. "I couldn't work in a normal way with normal instruments, so I just let these things do what they would do anyway and some kind of new music came out of it," he says. "I started coming to the studio with less and less worked out pieces, and I eventually came in with nothing at all. I would just start working with that thing, the studio, as the instrument. I'd say, 'Okay, let's start with anything – a drone or a single repeated piano note. What happens if I put an echo on that? What happens if I make that echo wobble by sending it through a tape recorder with a bent capstan?' That was something I used quite a lot at the time. As soon as I do that I start to get some feeling for the sound. It starts to become liquid or spreads out in a strange, non-recognisable way. Then I think about adding other sounds, piling on more layers and acting very much like an abstract painter with his canvas.

"To me, the image of the studio was rather like landscape painting, where you'd set the canvas up in front of the existing scene and the skill, in theory, was in getting the scene onto the canvas, just as the skill in old recording methods was in getting the song onto the record. What I was saying was that there was nothing outside of this process – this process called recording is the creative process. We don't have the canvas standing in front of any landscape, you are going to make the landscape here and now."

Working with pianist Harold Budd during the late Seventies and early Eighties, Eno began to examine the technique of subliminal mixing, essentially exploring the use and value of the different audio frequencies of the piano. "I would split his piano signal into four or five different frequency bands, so everything equivalent to the lower string of a bass guitar would be put onto one track of the tape," he explains, "then the next frequency band that is equal to the human voice range would be put onto another track. I would make up four or five tracks like this, so I could split the sound spectrum up into different regions and then I would work separately with these regions. Instead of putting echo on the piano as one might normally do, I'd spread that sound out, flange it or put it out of phase, but just on the bottom end. Then with the next band of sound, I'd leave it out completely or put it far back in the mix and over on the right hand side. I could then maybe put a repeat echo on the third band, and so on. I started to get really atomic about sound and analyse it carefully to see what could be sucked out of it, what could be found within an existing sound and made more of. I wanted to use the studio like a microscope for sound, which is what good engineers do. An engineer who really knows how to record drums, for example, is an absolute pleasure to watch. They're so careful at finding little aspects of the sound that they can do things with."

Eno's startling application of effects and processors has opened the doors of perception to many of his artists, and it is often the order in which effects are routed in relation to each other which has been the secret behind his sonic art. But the ingredients are forever changing. "I don't ever have effects in one order," he insists. "The order of effects is as variable to me as a melodic phrase might be. I'm always experimenting with things like that. It would be conventional perhaps to send a signal first to distortion and then to reverb. But it's actually very interesting to me to try the opposite. What happens if you distort a whole reverb? You get back a sheet of sound that has become kind of distressed. It's all deviations for me."

Whenever Eno works with an artist, new or old, his main contribution as producer is to drive the artist to think openly about what it is they wish to achieve, articulate those thoughts in sound and sharpen the direction in which it is travelling. And Eno works best when he is travelling to a place he has never been before. "My role in the studio is to become enthusiastic about certain possibilities, and keep harping on until people do the things to shut me up," he admits. "I get excited about new ideas and if I hear the beginning of a new idea, I only want to pursue that. I have no time for anything else that's going on, and there are other people around anyway to look after those other things. I want to keep hammering on about this new thing that I haven't heard before. So a lot of what I do is more conceptual than musical in that I create an atmosphere of innovation, if you like, and it doesn't matter if an idea gets tried out and ends up a mess. Just as much as it doesn't matter if a couple of hours are spent on something that results in nothing. What does it matter if something isn't nicely polished at the end of it? I try to keep asking those kinds of questions to get people excited about what they are doing."

Reminded of his 1981 project with David Byrne, *My Life In The Bush Of Ghosts*, Eno acknowledges the worth of reflecting artists back to their natural talents and automatic thought patterns. Eno also helped to shape Byrne's long-time band, Talking Heads, as a powerful international force, by producing possibly their most important albums, *More Songs About Buildings And Food*, *Fear Of Music* and *Remain In Light*, the latter spawning the classic 'Once In A Lifetime' single.

"People often play great things but don't really notice, or they notice but don't realise what they've done," he explains. "When you do something new and good yourself, you might think it's good, but you want a reaction from other people, you want someone to say, 'Hey, that is good.' I'm never insecure about my feelings for other people's ideas, in fact I have very strong opinions about them. So whenever there is a brilliant idea, I actively encourage the players to develop it further. I used to do this a lot with David Byrne where he would play or jam rhythm guitar parts and within something I might hear a four-bar pattern that was fantastic. I would learn it and because I can't play guitar, I would sing it to him over and over until he effectively re-learned what he had already been playing, but hadn't noticed. That's important and it's getting them to take seriously what they uniquely do.

"Quite often, the things that only you can do seem like mistakes because you haven't heard anybody else do them. So I'm telling the artist not to be ashamed of their own ideas. Most musicians when they go into sessions get applauded for sounding like someone else, or a slight variation on someone else's style. I hear this all the time from people who go into sessions and try something out that they think is exciting, and everyone looks a little unsure and thinks, 'What's that?' Then they go and play an old James Brown riff and everyone's saying, 'Wow! That's what we want!' So you have to realise that most of the time musicians are being encouraged to sound recognisable. But what I'm doing is encouraging them at the points when they're not and it's more about them finding confidence than bringing out their true personality."

Double Dealing

Instead of focusing on perfecting one album, when Eno recently undertook projects with David Bowie and the Manchester band, James, he instigated the plan to simultaneously record two quite different albums – in Bowie's case, it included the *Outside:1* set, while James recorded both the *Laid* album and the more free-form *Wah-Wah* during the same sessions at Peter Gabriel's Real World Studios.

"It certainly seems a unique way of working in retrospect, but at the time it was a very natural thing to do," former James guitarist, Larry Gott comments. "We never planned to record two albums, but Eno was so impressed when he overheard our jamming and improvisations during rehearsals that he just wanted to keep the twenty-four-track master tape rolling to capture everything. Eno has a very complex, problem-solving mind which can assess a situation quickly and work out the best way to utilise his time within it and get the most out of it. He had already heard a few demos of some songs we had worked on for *Laid* and he wanted to come down and rehearse with us for a few days before starting on the album. When he came into the rehearsal room, he discovered that what we did mainly was improvise and that's how we write songs. Most of the songs he had heard were improvisations that had just been played a few more times and refined slightly.

"He liked what we were doing so we just gave him a whole bag of tapes of jams from rehearsals over the previous twelve months or whatever, and he selected certain bits for us to work on as a kind of pressure valve release from what was going on with *Laid*. So he booked another room at Real World where we jammed straight to twenty-four-track and his assistant, Markus Dravs, mixed those jams while we worked in the other studio on *Laid*. There was a very moody song called 'Burn The Cat' which was all started by Eno at a keyboard where he was just tooting one note, suggesting that he was a lonely motor boat going across a lake at dusk. That was a scenario he created for us to work around. The Eno-esque influence was very much as a result of the territory in which we subconsciously ended up, by his guidance or by him just being there. His is quite a presence and we felt that with him in the room as an observer, our jamming took on a different character to when he wasn't around. Having an audience there creates a different kind of tension, and all the more so when it's Brian Eno."

Significant creative and ice-breaking benefits can be enjoyed by working in this way, believes Eno. "If you have a bunch of people sitting in one room and working on one piece of music, and getting lost and immersed in that piece of music, everyone's thinking that they should say something just to prove that they're still awake and paying attention because it's embarrassing to sit in a corner for four hours," he says. "It's much more important for people to genuinely feel they have something to contribute than just interject for the sake of it. If you have two studios running simultaneously, there are two pieces of music being worked on at once and this really does something for the social balance of events, because there are two places you can be. You have a choice and you can go to the studio and the music that is more interesting to you at that point in time. There is nothing worse than being stuck in a studio when you're not interested in the track or don't feel you have anything to offer. You just go into the other room.

"It's also a fantastic device for perspective because if you walk from one room into the other, there are some aspects about the newer music that become blindingly obvious to you. You walk in and say, 'The whole sound is too muddy, the drums are much too loud,' or, 'This chorus is pathetically weak.' You can have very clear impressions of something if you come in from something else. If you're all sitting around the desk, working on one piece of music for days, that clarity disappears. Also, having two records running simultaneously means you have two sites in which to locate things. Most people do not make just one kind of music, they have a lot of different ideas and I think a lot of records are ruined by people trying to half-heartedly squash them all in and mix them up in an unthought-out way. By this method, you can say, 'Okay, in this record we can have all of this kind of thing, and in this other record we can have all the other kinds of music.' Of course, they can overlap, but as a working tool you can take ideas as far as they can go without them starting to cancel out or fight with other ideas. One of the great luxuries of working with vinyl records was that you had two sides to work with, which we no longer do. You could say, 'That song belongs on side A, and that's more appropriate for side B.' A great tragedy with CDs is that you can't do that and the album is one long continuous programme. So I think my aim to make two different records is partly a response to missing A- and B-sides. We can't make two sides, but we can make two records."

Oblique Strategies

One of the most refreshing aspects of Eno's approach to music-making is his ongoing adoption of "Oblique Strategies" philosophies which can just as effectively be applied in life as inside the recording studio. These theories have their origins in Eno's earliest studio experiences when time was at a premium, yet the pressure to achieve interesting results was great. Beginning as a list of aphorisms, these Strategies emerged as a guide to back door session approaches.

"When you're working in a studio, because it's an expensive place to be and there's pressure to get a result, you can very easily lose the ability to step outside of the process and just think about what you're doing," he explains. "Thinking is not something that's done a lot in studios because it's a fast place, you have to keep going, the clock is ticking and the bill is mounting all the time. So I used to notice when I first started working with Roxy that we'd spend all day working away very hard, and on the way home I would suddenly realise that we could have solved a whole problem if only we had remembered such-and-such an idea. Those ideas that I thought we should have remembered weren't necessarily about melodies or rhythms, but things like, if we had thought about how something would have sounded through a little radio, that would have dissolved our problem. You might have spent two or three hours on some absurdly tiny detail which wouldn't even be noticed on a tiny radio, so maybe that shouldn't have occupied your time.

"Another important question to ask is, 'What wouldn't you do?' Imagine you're sitting there working, things are getting difficult, the situation reaches an impasse and nobody quite knows what to do. You keep trying things but they don't work, so it's at that point where you should ask yourself, 'What wouldn't I do? What are the things I wouldn't think of doing?' It's interesting because you've obviously thought already of the things that you thought would work, but they didn't. It's a little bit like when you've lost something and you go around the flat looking in all the obvious places where you might normally leave something. Clearly it isn't in any of those, so you then think about all the places you wouldn't usually think of looking. Chances are that you'll probably find the object."

Instructions in Eno's book to adhere to when at a creative cul-de-sac might include: change instrument roles. Take a break. Do something boring. Consult other sources, either promising or unpromising. Remove ambiguities and convert to specifics (or remove specifics and convert to ambiguities). Allow an easement, the abandonment of a stricture ("This thing has always been like this, but let's let it not be like that for a while and see what happens"). Emphasise repetition. Retrace your steps. Cut a vital connection... "Most pieces of music are based around some centre, like a drum track or a drone, which really holds everything together. Just try taking that element out of the music and see what happens. Suddenly, when you take it out you start to hear everything else that's there, and you start to realise that some of it is redundant, obsolete, stupid, unformed or, even more interesting, that some of it stands completely alone and is in fact another, new piece of music. A lot of my own work comes out of doing this by examining what happens when I take away the most important thing and find I'm left with something completely new that you can develop from there in another direction."

Eno also urges musicians to not be afraid of musical ideas which appear too basic and simple. "Sometimes the best thing you can do is do something simple and monotonous, like tap-tap-tap-tap-tap-tap, for five minutes without any embroidery or ornamentation," he suggests. "But there's a whole conspiracy of musicianship that says,

'Oh no, that's below you, you can't be as basic as that.' But that narrow-mindedness can be destructive."

Despite experimentation and improvisation being high on his priority list, Eno is surprisingly economical with studio time, sometimes to the chagrin of his often insecure clients. He believes that economy is vital to exciting music, and that huge budgets, by comparison, can only lead to problems caused by uncertainty.

"I'm one of the fastest people in the studio and I have a sort of rule when I produce to not spend too much time on a record," he says. "I come into the studio in spurts, like a week in every month, and it puts me in a position where I can hear things quite freshly and I can make some kind of an assessment about what's being done. It's nearly always the artists who are slowing things down, and I'm always telling them, 'Come on, come on, we've got to get this thing finished quickly!' Nearly always the effect of spending a lot of money is to make things more normal. Hollywood is the best example of that, where you have fifty-six lighting technicians and four camera gaffers, and you know that what they're all for is to make it look like every other film you've ever seen. If you really want to make original results, work quick and work cheap, because there's more of a chance that you'll get somewhere that nobody else did. Or you'll get nowhere at all. But you won't end up with this respectable, nice, professional result. And I have all sorts of strategies for making things fast."

In the studio environment where a labyrinth of technical possibilities can offer a million different time-consuming permutations for making records, one such strategy is to place enormous value on conceptual pre-production. "When people are low on inspiration, they choose to investigate these permutations to see if an idea evolves there," he says. "Sometimes it works, but very often it doesn't and it could take months. So I'm very concerned to try to clarify the vision as much as I can before going into the studio. And the main point of clarifying a vision is not to tie yourself to some kind of picture of what the final result will be, but simply to be able to say with conviction, 'I'm not interested in that, in that, in that or in that,' and cancel out some of the variety. The most useful thing you can do is to get rid of some of the options before you start. It's like going into a Chinese restaurant and being presented with a 322-page menu and thinking, 'God, I just want something to eat!'"

U2, Eno And Flood

This sensible, though rare and unusual, train of thought provided great appeal to U2 who, in 1984, were in just the right frame of mind to break free of previous working modes when they recorded *The Unforgettable Fire* at Slane Castle in County Dublin. But when first approached to produce the album, Eno felt that his influence might lead to a spoiling of their winning formula. "They had a big album with *War* and were coming up to the crest of a wave, and ready to break *very* big," he recalls. "But I thought that if I started working with them, they might end up with something arty and esoteric, and it might wreck them completely. So I was more than a bit worried about that, not that I thought we'd do bad work, but that their success graph that had been going ever upwards might soon plummet! So as insurance, I brought along Daniel Lanois who I had worked with a lot in Canada and who I think is a fantastic producer with a real talent for working with groups of musicians. I knew that even if it didn't work out with me, the record would be in his safe, inspired pair of hands. So I wasn't thinking that it was a difficult situation. In fact, because of working with Dan, I was allowed to be as far out as I wanted, so I could say, 'Why don't we try this? Why don't we try that?' And they wouldn't be left there thinking, 'God, what's going to happen to our record?' As it turned out they were completely receptive to my appeals to experiment and were very good at it as well. So a lot of these problems didn't actually arise anyway. And the combination of Dan and I was extremely good, and we worked very well together, covering different territories of the working out of the record. Our roles were complementary and just as indispensable as each other's, so there was no hierarchy in that respect. It was just a good locking together of territories."

A gifted, soulful musician and singer himself, Lanois's lack of enthusiasm for flashmanship and false, glossy production complemented Eno's desire to construct a more focused U2 sound. "Dan looks for things that really move him," Eno says. "I think his great talent in the studio is for creating a climate that encourages people and makes them think that anything is possible. One of the ways he does this is by putting a great deal of attention into anticipating things. If he's working with Edge, he will think, 'Right, he's playing this guitar at the moment, but at some point later he's probably going to want to try something on this other guitar, so I'd better prepare a channel on the desk, so that if he does, I'll be ready to record it.' And Dan and I spent a lot of time evolving ways of making the recording process a seamless one. The worst possible scenario in the studio is where the band are really fired up to go and excited and fresh, and some dumb idiot of a producer says, 'Can we hear the snare drum, please? Sorry, we haven't got that mic on yet.' All this is absolutely unprofessional, of course. But Dan is the reverse – he'll arrive at the studio very early to check all the headphone mixes and does everything possible to make sure that if a musician suddenly changes his mind and wants to play something else, the whole session doesn't grind to a halt. Now all of this is sort of invisible work in a way and people don't notice it because by definition it's meant to be unnoticeable, but it's absolutely invaluable, especially on sessions where you're relying a lot on improvisation which we were most of the time. Although some of these songs were written, most of them weren't and some of them were only sketched ideas that needed playing and working out."

On subsequent albums, such as *The Joshua Tree*, *Achtung Baby*, *Zooropa* and *Passengers*, the level of experimentation increased with every project, although Eno insists that even before his initial involvement in 1984, U2 preferred not to be overly dictated by a song's structure. "Part of the skill involved in this situation is being disciplined enough to ask ourselves, 'What kind of thought condition do we want to be in? What do we want to be thinking about? What sort of ideas, in an overall sense, make it easy for us to make a piece of work?' At the start of the sessions for *Zooropa*, they'd got out of the habit of improvising and for various reasons, they weren't doing it. So I said, 'We should just start improvising again and see what we get,' so I joined in and played with them. I said, 'What we should be doing is imagine we are making hypothetical film soundtracks, not making songs.' [Hence the progression to the 1995 *Passengers* project.] This is always a very liberating idea, because a film soundtrack doesn't have to have a centre – the film itself is the centre. It allows you to make music that is pure atmosphere and this really allowed some good things to come through in their case. In our relationship, Dan would deal with the functional landscape and I would deal with the conceptual one, and I'll tell you,

you can't have one without the other. You have to control both."

Of the many interesting sounds on *Zooropa*, the sequenced guitar on 'Lemon' witnessed the return of Eno's EMS suitcase synth. "That's actually a ring modulator treatment and it is basically Edge's guitar," he says. "Edge now has his own version of my synthesiser. In that synthesiser there's a little joystick and when you move that joystick you produce a voltage. If you send that voltage to one side of the ring modulator and the guitar to the other, and you start moving the joystick back and forth, it's exactly like bowing a string. So that way you can pulse something precisely in time to the track."

Working alongside Eno on *Achtung Baby* and *Zooropa* was Flood, whose work on creating "industrial" sounds for Trent Reznor and Nine Inch Nails was a reference, particularly on 'Daddy's Gonna Pay For Your Crashed Car'. "I was trying to push sounds as far as they would go and one area that always seemed sacrosanct to me was drums," Flood says. "People would always talk about nice stereo drum sounds and it didn't seem to be an area that you could get away with much experimentation. So gradually through working with people like Trent who tend to be programmed, I would change the sound of the drums from being big and overdone, to being small and dry, and adding over the top samples. Then on *Achtung Baby* we started asking questions like, 'Why can't we use a wah-wah pedal over the whole drum kit?' [In fact, Mickie Most had already used a wah-wah pedal on a set of congas for Hot Chocolate's 'You Sexy Thing' in 1975.] If you put a snare drum through an EQ to overload it, it sounds exciting and gives it an edge. So this has all evolved over a long period and I'm now at the point where I'm starting to re-address the issue, because it has become a bit of a trademark.

"The snare drum sound on 'Daddy's Gonna Pay For Your Crashed Car' was basically a certain pitch of snare drum played in the first place with heavy compression with some EQ and distortion. Within the context of the music it just makes everything sound very lively. There is a certain way that Larry Mullen Jr likes to hear his drums, but as with all the members of U2 he is completely open to trying anything different. And inevitably there will be a lot of to-ing and fro-ing of ideas; some work and some don't. In my role, if I bowl in and say something is absolutely brilliant and the artist is saying, 'Mmm, I don't really like it,' that's where I have to taper my enthusiasm and just store the idea for later use on another project.

For a real live drummer with an "organic" approach, it is surprising how warmly Larry Mullen Jr has embraced experimentations with drum samples, loops and machines. Although this use of technology began to infiltrate U2's music as early as 1984 ('Bad') and progressed with spectacular effect on 'God Part II' (from *Rattle And Hum*), it was not until the more recent *Achtung Baby* and *Zooropa* that it became an integral part of their sonic make-up. "My relationship with Flood has always been about taking basic ideas and making them special, using the technology available in the studio," Mullen Jr says. "As far as playing with samples and things like that is concerned, a lot of that is done during the construction of a song. There might be some sort of a pulse or rhythmic idea that's been used in constructing the melody, and when we get to playing on that it will be a question of maybe emphasising more of the machinery, and using less of the real drums. I believe the future will see more of a marriage between rock 'n' roll and technology. That is definitely the way forward. For me, it's not like I'm coming from a position of strength where I can say, 'Hey, I know better.'

"I'm open to anything that will make me sound better and machines do that, so I'm perfectly happy with that marriage. I actually get off on playing alongside machines and it has certainly improved my playing a hundred fold. There may have been a bit of resistance in the beginning because I think the expectations for what would happen between machine and drummer were very high. When you actually work through it, you find that it's not about one or the other – it's about the marriage of both elements to create a musical atmosphere in which the best work can come out. However, it has to be an equal marriage otherwise it's disastrous. There are some producers who prefer not to use drummers, letting the machines take over and concentrating on the musicians. But to many drummers that attitude is very offensive and a lack of diplomacy can lead to tension. It's important for producers to strike a balance."

Eno's involvement with both James and U2 continued in 1997 when he co-produced James's *Whiplash* with Stephen Hague and was also present for U2's *Pop* album sessions in Dublin.

chapter eleven

mothers of invention

"The world is going to open up into a whole new scene and the next ten years will witness a revolution in the way we record music because of the developments in communications technology. But I hope I will still continue to mic up drum kits!"

Hugh Padgham

And so the Nineties, or rather the effect that current musical principles and technology will have on record production in the future, as we shall examine in both this and the final chapter. In a way, this book is timely as it comes at a time when it is possible to draw a line between what can be termed the traditional view of recording and new standards which look set to remain in place for many years. The resistance to digital recording, even among many die-hard analogue fans, has been gradually diminishing as prices drop and improvements are made in miniaturisation, audio quality and user-friendliness. But it is not only the machinery that is becoming smaller.

The last ten years have seen some startling changes in the perception of master tape formats. For a long period, two-inch tape was considered the perfect vehicle for twenty-four-track analogue recordings, mixing down on to either quarter- or half-inch tape to produce the production master. Whether recording analogue or digitally, it is now a common standard to mix down on to DAT (Digital Audio Tape), the size of which is a little smaller than a regular cassette or Video 8 tape. More and more recording artists and producers, however, are turning their backs on tape in favour of hard-disk systems, and Sting's *Mercury Falling* and George Michael's *Older* were just two 1996 projects which utilised the format – countless more artists have fallen in love with the medium.

It has been estimated that by the year 2000, most major studios would have changed to this standard, while others would have at least integrated digital editing systems, such as Pro Tools or the Fairlight MFX-3. The introduction of ADAT bridged a gap between analogue tape and digital hard-disk recording, and the colossal numbers swayed by its merits either have moved or are considering moving to hard-disk. Even now, a number of manufacturers have ceased production of open-reel tape machines as they pour their resources into the way of the future.

One of the by-products of miniaturisation has been the availability of affordable professional-quality home recording systems which, in the hands of the professionals, have reduced the amount of time spent in major commercial studios because the extensive pre-production work which can be conducted more economically outside of that environment. The compact cassette multitrack recorder, generically known as the Portastudio (launched by Tascam in 1979), made it possible in the Eighties for bedroom-based musicians to record adequate four-track demos without the need to leave their home. Today, digital hard-disk versions of the Portastudio, such as the Roland VS880 and Fostex DMT-8, deliver a quality of sound that was only attainable in a major studio a few years beforehand. But it is generally believed that the commercial studio, although partly threatened by the rapid increase in artists recording at their private bases, will continue to be as relevant as ever especially for mixing – or so say the studio managers.

In no small way, new technology has aided the rise of DJ producers, who have been able to produce fresh-sounding remixes for club audiences (shades of Pete Waterman's past) and by doing so are among the most significant contributors to modern-day British and international music culture. Among these remix producers are Paul Oakenfold and ex-Housemartin Norman Cook – the latter responsible for turning hits such as Cornershop's 'Brimful Of Asha' into Number One successes, by applying more of a club-orientated dance feel to what was a basic pop track.

Musically, the cyclical nature of trends and fashion became more apparent at the beginning of the Nineties, when the influence of underground dance music on wider musical disciplines was patently obvious. No sooner was there a Seventies revival than there was a return in the dance market to Eighties sounds and values. This was followed more recently by blatant nods in the direction of Seventies disco, signalling a long-awaited comeback for Afro wigs, white flared trousers and all the fashion icons which for so many years endured bad press. Of course, this does beg the question: if there was to be a Nineties revival, what in heaven's name would be revived?

Probably The Best Studio In The World

Although the AIR Studios of Oxford Circus is now dead and gone, the company made history in January 1993 with the first recording session at what is widely regarded as the finest studio in the world – AIR Lyndhurst Hall in Hampstead. Throughout the Eighties, the problems associated with working in Oxford Circus had become intolerable. The West End had become progressively dirtier, parking was a nightmare, bomb scares became commonplace and towards the late Eighties, there was the threat of a massive rent rise. For the first time since 1969, AIR was on the lookout for a new London recording venue, but this time it was with the combined financial assistance of Chrysalis and Pioneer who have a fifty per cent shareholding.

It was clear that Lyndhurst Hall would deliver everything its Oxford Circus predecessor did and much more, and it was built to the highest possible specifications to serve its purpose. Dave Harries, the studio's technical director before joining Decca in 1995, says, "Chrysalis and Pioneer put a lot of faith and money behind us, so we had to make sure everything was perfect. It's an historical building and the restoration work cost a fortune. But from the very outset it was designed to be a flagship studio and there were no corners cut. If you're an existing studio, all the expensive acoustic work is already taken care of. But when you come to a new building you have to start all over again. In a building such as this, which is very close to a residential area, you have to make absolutely sure there's not going to be an acoustic problem. It will only take one of the studios to not be properly isolated and a neighbour to complain about the noise at three in the morning, and the council will close you down. You also have to meet all the new fire regulations which are horrendously stringent. We spent over £300,000 on doors alone but without them there is no studio. I'm sure that's the reason why there aren't many new studios."

AIR Lyndhurst could well be the last all-new major recording studio to be built in London. Number One studio (a direct copy of Studio One at Oxford Circus) retains the seventy-two-channel, AIR-customised Rupert Neve/Focusrite console from AIR's previous home, while Number Two studio with its seventy-two-channel SSL 8000 G+ console, incorporating Ultimation and Total Recall automated fader systems, and accurate Dynaudio monitoring, provides the ultimate environment for mixing. ("SSL certainly put together a marvellous desk there," says Harries.) Studio Three is dedicated to digital mixing, again with a Dynaudio monitoring system, and has an AMS Neve Logic II 4 x 48 input digital console for mixing. AIR has also expanded into television post-production with the building of three on-site dubbing suites. Suite A has a twenty-four-input AMS Logic II digital console with a sixteen-output Audiofile Spectraplus hard-disk editing system, while the Preparation Room has a thirty-two-channel AMS Logic III desk with thirty-two channels and Audiofile, and Studio Three boasts yet another Logic III console.

But of all its rooms, the most impressive by far has to be Lyndhurst Hall itself. Previously a congregational church which seated over 1,000 people, Lyndhurst Hall can accommodate the largest symphony orchestra and chorus, and an audience if appropriate. It boasts a Neve VRP Legend seventy-two-input channel desk with flying faders, capable of film recording, classical and rock 'n' roll. The dynamic acoustics of the Hall have predictably found favour among rock producers for live drum sounds. "It really is a lovely place to work in with lots of daylight," Harries enthuses. "Chris Thomas had the drums out in the middle of the room for Sting, Rod Stewart and Bryan Adams's 'All For Love' and it was a fantastic sound. Elton John's *Made In England* album was also recorded in there but he had the drums in the booth. We managed to put in four booths, two of which are larger than some people's whole studios, and this makes the hall very versatile. Elton had the pianos out in the main room and the guitarists and other people playing with him would had their amps and drums in the booths for good separation."

It was studio manager, Malcolm Atkin's responsibility to specify and install the equipment in all of AIR's studios, and part of his plans included an estimation of where the recording business is heading in the future. "We tried to take account of as many ideas and methods that we could see changing back in 1992," he says. "Some of our predictions were correct and others haven't been quite so spot on. All the control rooms here have five-way monitoring, so it is not purely a case of having a stereo pair in front of you at the desk. It was cheaper and easier to include this during the building phase, so even in the rock 'n' roll rooms which use stereo ninety-eight per cent of the time there is five-way monitoring which allows us to do a film soundtrack mix with full surround sound. And because we have that capability it does get used.

"We also built a central apparatus room which was an idea borrowed from the large television facilities houses where a lot of the machinery is centrally housed. In the music recording business, multitrack equipment, synthesisers and rack units are generally kept in separate machine rooms because the equipment has to be brought to the client. We have to be able to provide all formats and whatever anyone requires can be found in the apparatus room. So in designing the complex we ensured that the apparatus would be central to allow easy access from each of the studios. Because the machinery will be smaller and more centralised in ten years' time, we have cabling running to that area from every control room. I have every faith that by the end of this century, the machines we are using today will largely be living in that room and we will be operating the solid state devices in the control rooms. It is already happening in Studio Three with the SSL Logic II desk which has a large hard-disk storage system that gets downloaded onto the multitrack at the end of a working day."

AIR's Lyndhurst Hall studio officially opened for business on 2 January, 1993 when the late Henry Mancini booked to record the soundtrack of the *Son Of The Pink Panther* movie. Studio Two opened the following week for the mixing of the Dire Straits live album, *On The Night*. Most of the acoustic design of the control rooms and the isolation was managed by Richard Galbraith at Sandy Brown Associates. In the hall, the integration of a moving ceiling as a "temporary" structure helped AIR manoeuvre around English Heritage's groundrules. But one of the most fascinating aspects of the studio design was that audio perfection was achieved before any of the building work commenced. "Richard is quite a traditional acoustician, but that is not to say he doesn't also innovate, and he did some interesting things which I hadn't seen done before in control rooms," Atkin comments. "The cost involved in controlling frequencies multiplies with every descending octave and all the problems are in the last three octaves, so once you are above 300Hz it is simple. From 300Hz down to 30Hz there are big problems and it becomes progressively more expensive to cure. He did a design for each of the control rooms and we installed all the bass absorbers in the bare concrete shell to his original specification. He then demanded dummy doors and windows to be installed, after which we put in a serious hi-fi system and all went in to have a listen.

"We commented, criticised and tuned the room before it was built. We spent about a week doing that and then ripped out the dummy doors and windows, took away the hi-fi system and instructed the crews to come in and start building. So all this meant that the rooms worked first time and all four control rooms were designed using that method, two of them being identical. Richard also did the extraordinary when he specified 100dB isolation between each control room. Even though we expected it to be an impossible task, he pulled it off but it cost a fortune! This, however, was the only way we were going to put rock 'n' roll *and* classical musicians together in the same building. Even a breath of sound coming from the adjacent studio would be enough to completely scare off the classical fraternity and we would have been in serious trouble if it had not worked, because our original concept was for a studio complex which could fully cater for both extremes of music. The driving message throughout the whole of the project was to get it right and be a one-stop shop for audio production. This is without doubt the best-specified studio in the UK and it would be hard to find another in the world which has so successfully managed to marry rock 'n' roll and classical music with film score work and television post-production."

New For Older

At the time I left school in the late Seventies, I would not have believed it possible that the very same school would install a fully-equipped recording studio within only a few years. Having played in rock bands all through my school days without any form of encouragement from the teaching staff, I was mortified to hear of the news, but at the same time pleased that a new generation of musicians will benefit from the support of a more understanding world. In Britain at least, a studio is standard issue in many schools and courses in music technology are commonplace. Pop music was still the only youth-orientated industry in the Seventies but in more recent years this has been diluted into videos, computer games and fashion, as manufacturers fight for a slice of the same pie. That is why to attract young potential music makers, the equipment manufacturers have been compelled to provide better products at lower prices, and this has led to increased accessibility to today's youth. For a once-only investment of just a few thousand pounds, it is now possible to make better sounding records than could be produced in a major studio fifteen years ago. The kids of today are, as Pete Townshend would say, alright.

Improvements at the high end of technology have been startling. For the recording of his 1996 album, *Older*, George Michael purchased two twenty-four-track Otari RADAR (Random Access Digital Audio Recorder) direct-to-disk recorders and had them temporarily installed in Studio Two at SARM West, his favourite sounding room in London. Engineer Paul Gomersall says that not only did it change Michael's usual way of working, but it also meant less hands-on engineering work. "George is now doing all his own drop-ins on vocal sessions," says Gomersall. "I just leave the remote controller in the room with George and if he isn't happy with something he has just sung, he'll just cue up the machine again and do another take, so it saves quite a bit of time." In practical terms, Gomersall digitally backs up all recordings on the RADAR on to Exabyte tapes, two of which contained the whole album. "The good thing about the system is that we can cut, paste and copy sections around once everything is on the hard disk. The songs are no longer in a static format and having had quite a bit of experience working with a Pro Tools system to edit music digitally on computer, I can now reconstruct a song in any order in about five minutes. Try doing that with tape!"

The making of *Older* saw Michael more active than ever as a musician, using little outside assistance from the session players he once regularly used on his previous albums *Faith* and *Listen Without Prejudice (Volume One)*. "We are using a lot more computers and modules than before, now that the technology has improved so much," Gomersall says. "It's the same with most artists once they build up their confidence. In the past, there would be about five musicians waiting for George to call and get them down to the studio, once he had an idea for something. But now, a musician will only come in if George has a specific idea. So now in the studio, it's just George, myself and the programmer who looks after the equipment. We have specialist musicians in occasionally, like Steve Sidwell, the trumpet player, but George has worked things out on the keyboard in advance and knows exactly what he wants to hear from the trumpet. Steve will just spend a couple of hours in the studio and go away again."

Gomersall, who began engineering at SARM in 1984 ("I learned eighty per cent of the job within the first three months just through enthusiasm"), says that Michael retained complete control of the production and mixing of *Older*. "When it comes to mixing, I set up the desk and get a mix going to a reasonable stage, then George will come in and we work on it together," he says. "It can be quite alarming to some people who sit in on a mix because it can sound chaotic for the first few hours. I never just start with the drums, I just flitter round between things and whatever sticks out in a song at any given moment is what I focus on. But with George he tends to write, record and mix in one process which is very unusual. I enjoy doing that because it's very fresh."

Tony Visconti was a major force behind T-Rex and David Bowie's move to a more electric-based sound in the early Seventies

Electric Light Orchestra frontman and influential producer, Jeff Lynne

This photo ain't big enough for the both of us! Russell and Ron Mael, aka Sparks

Session bassist, Mo Foster, thumbs his way through a 1976 session at Olympic Studios for the original album of Tim Rice and Andrew Lloyd Webber's *Evita*

Craig Leon (here recording with Scarlet at Chipping Norton Studios in 1996) led the New York uprising against "dead" acoustics in the late Seventies

Dire Straits, flag wavers for the Eighties CD generation

Vocalist Lenny Zakatek and Alan Parsons working at Abbey Road on The Alan Parsons Project's *Eye In The Sky* album in 1982. Note the Fairlight CMI keyboard in the foreground

With assistance from Hugh Padgham, Phil Collins' big, gated drum sound became a template for others to emulate

Hugh Padgham, a major figure behind Sting's success, from The Police's *Ghost In The Machine* to his *Mercury*

Midge Ure in his studio in Chiswick, West London

Ultravox's Billy Currie and the "difficult" synthesisers and machinery of the early Eighties, working at AIR in

Swing Out Sister and Was Not Was producer Paul Staveley-O'Duffy

Paul Hardcastle took sampling to a new level with his hit, '19'

Trevor Horn's lavish productions characterised the excess of the Eighties

Founder member of The Human League, Heaven 17 and the British Electric Foundation, producer Martin Ware finds plenty to talk about

Boy George puts his feet up in the control room of AIR Studios, Montserrat

One third of Stock-Aitken-Waterman: Pete Waterman in his PWL "Hit Factory" Studios

Brian Eno, officially Britain's Best
Producer in 1996

Nine Inch Nails, PJ Harvey and U2
producer, Flood

Messrs Clayton, Evans, Mullen Jr and
Hewson – just one of the many bands
to benefit from Eno's oblique strategies

Like David Bowie, Manchester's James
simultaneously recorded two albums
when working with Eno at Real World

Lyndhurst Hall, Hampstead – a church built in 1880, now home to AIR Studios

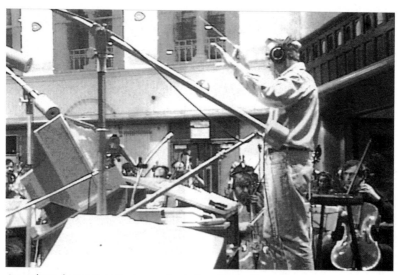

An orchestral session in the impressive hall at AIR Studios

The control room of AIR Studio One, Lyndhurst Hall

Paul Gomersall at SARM West with the Otari Radar twenty-four-track hard disk recording system used to make George Michael's *Older* in 1996

Les Negresses Vertes took over an old casino in southern France and hired Soundfield Studios' modern recording facilities to record one of their albums

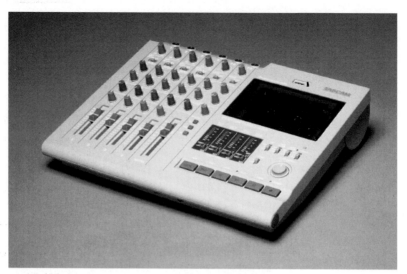

The Tascam Portastudio 424, one of the latest versions along the four-track compact cassette recorder theme

ADAT and the Tascam DA-88 provide expandable systems to bridge the gap between analogue and digital hard disk recording

Like many of their Brit Pop contemporaries, Oasis's Noel Gallagher and Ian Broudie of The Lightning Seeds wear their Sixties and Seventies influences proudly

After the success of his Unplugged album, *From The Cradle* completed Eric Clapton's back to basics approach to the blues in 1994

A portrait of the author at Nomis Studios, 1995

A view of the "Big Room" and SSL console at Peter Gabriel's Real World Studios in Box, Wiltshire

Elton John and Gus Dudgeon at the console during the 1976 sessions for the *Blue Moves* album. In the background are Kiki Dee and Bernie Taupin

Cast recorded demos for their first album, *All Change*, at John Entwistle's private studio, with assistance from long-time Who engineer Bobby Pridden (centre)

John Paul Jones, Robert Plant and John Bonham at the same session, recording a percussion track

Led Zeppelin favoured "location" recording at Headley Grange in the early Seventies, with Jimmy Page often using his trademark Les Paul

The unmistakable Jimi Hendrix – already a studio veteran before the fame days

Free's rock anthem, 'All Right Now', has invaded the singles charts on several occasions since its original

Above: John Leckie, the Brit
award-winning producer who
has been a guiding light for
bands including Radiohead and
Cast

Right: The influence of The
Small Faces – pictured here
recording 'Lazy Sunday' in 1968
– has been felt in a big way in
the Nineties

Below: Roni Size – the drum 'n'
bass ambassador. His album,
New Forms, scooped the Mercury
Music Prize in 1997

Paul Weller's albums *Wild Wood,*
Stanley Road and *Heavy Soul* defined
the mood of the mid Nineties

Radiohead's Thom Yorke

The Manics' James Dean Bradfield

Crispian Mills of Kula Shaker, whose
'Tattva' hit of 1996 propelled the band
to the forefront of the British guitar
pop renaissance

Taking The Studio To The Music

Today, we are witnessing an acute fragmentation of styles and there is no longer one way to make records. While it is common for some types of artists to record almost wholly at private home bases, there are also records which can only be made in a studio. For Scarlet's latest album, producer Craig Leon recorded the band live in a conventional manner at Chipping Norton Studios with two guitars, bass and drums. But as soon as that project was completed, Leon found himself working at the other extreme with Jean Luc de Meyer from Front 242 on his Cobalt 60 project. "A lot of our tracks have been shuttled back and forth to each other via the Internet, between his home in Belgium and mine on the Oxfordshire-Buckinghamshire border," Leon says. "So before we have even set foot in the studio together, most of the work would have been done over the telephone system and in the post, sending each other samples and exchanging disks. All that is left to do is to show up in England now that we have got the thing the way we like it, and he will put the vocals down in the studio."

It is precisely for reasons of artistic freedom that mobile recording is beginning to enjoy a new lease of life in the mid-Nineties for projects other than live albums. The first noted use of mobile equipment was on 28 June, 1888 when a recording machine was set up in the press gallery at the Crystal Palace in London to record a performance of 'Israel In Egypt' during the Handel Festival. It became fashionable during the Seventies to "get it together in the countryside" at a famous friend's mansion or farm and hire mobile facilities from the Manor, The Rolling Stones or Abbey Road. Two classic examples of such decadent recording behaviour from 1971 were The Who's 'Won't Get Fooled Again' (from *Who's Next*) and Led Zeppelin's fourth album, which included 'Rock And Roll', 'Stairway To Heaven' and 'When The Levee Breaks' – the song which features John Bonham's famously sampled drum pattern, originally recorded at Headley Grange in Hampshire with a pair of microphones suspended over a stairwell, picking up the drums being played in the middle of a wooden hall.

'Won't Get Fooled Again' was recorded at Mick Jagger's country retreat, Stargroves. "We did it in his big hall and had the Stones' mobile outside," John Entwistle says. "We were trying to get a more live sound. After *Live At Leeds*, which was done on eight-track, we were after as much of a live sound as possible and that was difficult in a lot of the dampened studios at that time. We tended to use mobiles quite a lot because it was rare to find a studio that we really liked. We recorded *Quadrophenia* with Ronnie Lane's mobile in a silver airstream caravan. Our studio in Battersea wasn't finished but we had the studio floor to work on. So we ran the wires out of the building and across the pavement to Ronnie's caravan."

Former Eurythmics' engineer, Jonathon Miles is currently carving a full-time career from his Soundfield Studios mobile service, which offers everything from the specification of equipment to finding the right venue for recording, as well as fixing catering and accommodation. Working closely with London-based audio hire company, FX Rentals, Miles is surprised to find that most acts booking his services demand not the most modern but older, even vintage recording equipment, from analogue twenty-four-track machines to Neve modules and Pultec EQ units. Many, it seems, want all the right ingredients with which to recreate a Sixties/early Seventies feel. One such artist was notorious retro equipment aficionado, Lenny Kravitz, who hired Soundfield's services for the recording of his *Circus* album in 1995.

"We were trying to find a venue which would give Lenny and Henry Hirsch [engineer] the kind of space and environment which artists like the Stones, Led Zeppelin and Jimi Hendrix enjoyed at Olympic, the large room which had amazing acoustics that made that kind of rock record spring to life," Miles says. "We eventually found an old seventeenth century chateau just outside Paris with fourteen bedrooms and two huge ballrooms, which were fantastic for what we needed, and we took a a Helios console, a 3M analogue sixteen-track machine and a selection of valve mics and pre-amps."

Hirsch himself says, "We didn't want to record the *Circus* album conventionally. We used drapes and baffles to treat the rooms and were aiming for a sense of space without it sounding too live. Living and working for several weeks in this great location was really fun and I think the performances took on a raw, experimental feel. It's a brilliant way to work."

Producer Rupert Hine also took advantage of Soundfield's location services when he took Les Negresses Vertes to an old, deserted casino in southern France. "When I'm recording people I want them to be passionate, yet remain as natural as possible," he says, "and these feelings are very hard to generate in a conventional studio because it's such an unnatural environment."

Recording at places other than standard studios certainly seems to suit Jeff Lynne, who has a tendency to gatecrash people's living rooms. "The last Traveling Wilburys album was done in a Spanish house in the hills in LA and it's a very relaxed way of doing things," he says. "You find yourself walking from room to room, checking out the atmosphere and acoustics, and thinking, 'Right, this bedroom'll be great for the guitars,' or, 'The drums will sound great in the dining room.' You get some nice little echoes and reflections that you wouldn't get in a proper studio."

Another band to record on location was Radiohead whose 1997 classic *OK Computer* (voted "The Greatest Album Ever" by readers of *Q* magazine in February 1998) was at least partly created in actress Jane Seymour's palatial mansion in England. *The Bends* had already secured the band's future with its challenging aural atmosphere and mournful lyrics, but *OK Computer* took Radiohead to another level. Delivering an awesome soundscape of melancholy and aggression, and described by guitarist Ed O'Brien as what might have been the work of a "troubled Spector", this was the kind of music which could have resulted from an unlikely collaboration between Roger Waters-era Pink Floyd and REM. And yet tracks such as 'Airbag', 'Paranoid Android', 'No Surprises' and 'Karma Police' are unmistakably Radiohead, and provide yet another watershed in both modern production and songwriting.

About Turn

Despite the wealth of modern recording technology available to someone of Martyn Ware's stature, he ignores much of it in the belief that restrictions are important in generating creativity. "It's difficult to appreciate it where you are in the middle of a recording, but the more restricted you are, the more creative you have to be and the more you are focused on the job in hand," he says. He is also sceptical about the efficacy of the assumed advances in the design of synthesisers and comments that in striving for improvement, manufacturers are overlooking key issues. As a result, Ware has increasingly turned to aging (he hates the term "vintage") technology. "Vince Clarke, who was a big fan of the early Human League, gave me an original Roland System 100 as a Christmas present when I worked on [Erasure's] *I Say, I Say, I Say*," he says. "I had traded mine in about fifteen years beforehand but he'd tracked this one down in America and I was gob-smacked! It's monophonic and you need outboard MIDI just to get it to play in sync with the track you're working on, but I'm using that all the time now. I've also bought a Jupiter 4 from a newspaper ad and that was an early synth, one of which I used to own. It sounds fantastic and the limitations that you have with those things are very stimulating. Each button doesn't have fifteen functions and you don't have an infinite number of patches to go through, but it does make you work to get a sound that is indicative of what's in your mind.

"I feel that today's synth technology has made too many decisions for people. Designers are making sounds that may be okay in a test room but are less appealing to the creative musician, while the manufacturers are putting as much processing power on to chips as possible because the unit cost per chip is virtually nothing. They try to make everything look clean and efficient, whereas what we really need are loads of knobs and switches, each with a separate function. I have made A/B comparisons between contemporary synthesisers and old ones which I have re-purchased recently and the difference in standard shocks me. The oscillators are better in the older ones, the sounds are better, there's much more performance capability, you get instant feedback and you can modify the sounds as you go along. I am a futurist in a musical sense and I'm constantly looking to see how I can make things sound new and different, but where synthesiser technology is concerned, something has been lost along the way."

Sampling, or rather the overuse of it, is another area which is criticised by Ware. "As a production tool sampling is quite useful, but creatively it bores me to death," he says. "It is now possible to create the impression of anything, given a sampler and a half decent sample library. So the temptation is not to stretch yourself and think of different ways of working, and be satisfied with creating something which approximates your aim, but really it isn't that good. The degradation of the quality of individual components like this has led us now into a lower quality aural environment, where something which is half okay will suffice. If you try to create the sound of a saxophone on an analogue synthesiser, of course it sounds nothing like a saxophone, but the end result is so interesting and bizarre that it spices it all up. Whereas now, you might have a sample of a soprano sax and if you want it to sound like a tenor, you can alter the pitch and the attitude will be, 'That sounds close enough,' but it might not actually sound *interesting* because it's too close to reality."

Computers and editing systems have presented artists and producers with a new range of possibilities – one of which is perfection. More than ever, perfect tempo, pitch and general performance can be achieved, even though it is often at the sacrifice of soul. Some manufacturers have propagated the myth that computers increase the speed of the recording process which, until the arrival of systems like the Fairlight MFX-3 hard-disk system, was not the experience of most producers. Of course, for many, the real enjoyment of recording is not derived from guaranteeing perfection, but from attempting to achieve it. There is a difference. "One of the joys of recording for me is when you don't have control, especially when working with a drummer," Manfred Mann comments. "He either plays it right or he doesn't. It may take a while to set a drum kit up in the studio, but I find it takes a lot less time than trying to recreate a hi-hat part on a computer. On one recent session I was doing a keyboard solo and we were trying to fly it in from a computer. This was just in case I did a great solo but played a wrong note in the middle and it would allow me to correct it. But the computer was cocking it all up and we were spending ages on it. I thought, 'Bugger it, I'll play it live and if I make a mistake after eight bars, I'll just stop and drop in.' It's difficult when you have that kind of control to just let it be."

Home, Sweet Home

For most musicians, the dream of having their own professional-standard recording facilities at home, where they can quite literally fall out of bed and start creating, is one which is constantly pursued. Today, it is both cheaper and easier to achieve than ever before, and it will *continue* to be easier. Sting is one of the many stars who have taken the step to largely forsake recording in London and other major musical capitals, and stay at home to work. For his album, *Ten Summoner's Tales*, Sting approached Solid State Logic to design and build a flightcased, portable studio which enabled him and engineer, Hugh Padgham, to record the entire album at his Wiltshire home. "But," Padgham says, "I tried to mix it at his house but the room was too reverberant and it was obvious we needed a professional studio, so we had to go to the Townhouse. For *Mercury Falling*, we converted his cow shed into a mixing room and I got a friend of mine in to look after the acoustic design. We continued to record in his dining room and then packed the equipment into the flight cases and wheeled everything down the drive and over to the cow shed."

This, Padgham feels, is an extremely healthy work ethic for Sting, who clearly enjoys being in the family environment, as opposed to spending long periods in London studios. "It suits him fine although it does have the reverse effect on other artists," Padgham says. "The people who really lose out are the commercial recording studios because suddenly a lot of the top artists, like Sting and Peter Gabriel, are getting wise to the economics of equipping themselves at home and it must have made the big London studios suffer. It's a once only investment and if Sting can pay for the recording of the albums himself, the amount he will save over a long period will be colossal. We spent four months at Sting's house doing the new album and the budget for doing that at a London studio would have been massive. It does make sense to buy your own gear if you can afford it."

AIR Studios' Malcolm Atkin profusely disagrees with Padgham's diagnosis of the situation and emphasises that the home recording habits of stars like the ex-Policeman will have little effect on the welfare of major studios. "It is difficult even for someone of Sting's stature to go out and spend something approaching £1 million on a very large SSL desk, two forty-eight-track machines and other peripheral equipment," he says. "You also have to employ a full-time technician to keep that kind of kit in shape. He then has to start writing that off and that kit is going to be out of date and virtually worthless within seven or eight years. That means he is going to have to make it work and if you tried to write a business plan around that kind of investment, you would quickly make the assumption that it was a dumb idea and it would be better to go somewhere that already has this equipment. That is why places like AIR exist to attract the Elton Johns and Dire Straits of this world. They may do a certain amount of pre-production in their home environment but when it comes down to doing it properly, they come here."

There are, Atkin says, a great many artists who have fulfilled their dream to record independently, à la Sting, but have ended up as commercial studio owners, realising some years later that their investment had been so heavy, they had to attract revenue from outside clients. "The real cost is not just in the equipment, it's in the buildings," Atkin observes. "A good example of that is Real World which began as Peter Gabriel's private studio and then had to go commercial, as did Fisher Lane [the Farm]. It isn't advertised but once you get through to the Genesis organisation, you realise that it can be hired during downtime."

Keyboard player and producer, Paul "Wix" Wickens installed his own enviable studio in his Muswell Hill home in 1995, but appreciates that a heavy investment will tie a musician down too tightly to one environment, and that a regular change of scenery is healthier for inspiration. "People still like to get out of the house and go to a place where you are at work and that's important," he says. "I've known a couple of people who have built all-singing, all-dancing studios at home, and they've fallen out of love with the sound of them, because it's the same four walls, same pair of monitors, same outboard gear. If you're out in different environments it helps your creative flow. I like to regard the home studio as being somewhere professional enough to do work that you can carry on and develop outside, or bring in from an outside studio to work on at home. But building a home studio with a view to never going anywhere else to record, even if you have the advantage of lots of money, is limiting, because going somewhere else can stimulate you in a different way. Even going abroad or in the countryside and working in a different environment can be stimulating and help you look at your approach to recording differently. It's about creativity and to a large extent, you are shutting the doors on creativity by locking yourself away."

Regardless of the freedom which home studio facilities provide, Gary Langan believes that this will not ultimately lead to more artists producing themselves. "Anyone with any sense knows that it's always good to have somebody come in from outside the band to see a project from a different angle," he says. "That's what a producer does and although he isn't part of the band, he's still in there giving it 100% and overseeing the big picture. Bands tend to only be able to visualise a song one way, the way it was written, and it's hard for them to be objective."

Andy Jackson, meanwhile, believes that the gradual move to the project studio scenario with artists more regularly producing themselves will ultimately affect the independent producer, whose role he feels will be more organisational than musical. But one area in which he predicts the skills of producers will become in demand is multimedia. "Music producers will probably find that they need to diversify in order to survive," he says. "It may be a situation where one person is coordinating a multimedia project, or there are several producers in charge of separate elements like sound, video and graphics. Already, there are recording studios which are now branching out into CD-ROM and I am sure that a number of producers will firstly see it as a good sideline, and then eventually become heavily involved."

ISDN

A new method of connecting artists and producers in studios at opposite ends of the globe made its mark in the early Nineties when Phil Ramone produced Frank Sinatra's *Duets* album and invited the likes of U2's Bono to send his vocal contribution from Ireland to America in real-time. The enabling system, ISDN (Integrated Services Digital Network), utilises the digital telephone system as a channel for the passing of digitised information, but so far the system has not been adopted to the extent that Ramone first imagined. His interest in ISDN and satellite links began after noticing how Steven Spielberg and George Lucas dubbed film from Santa Monica to San Francisco, while actors were "phoning in" voice-overs from various parts of the world. However, Ramone recalls that it was during his engineering of the Paul and Linda McCartney *Ram* sessions in New York in 1971 that he initially fantasised about such a remote method of recording.

"I asked the guys who had made this possible if we could try to do a record where we could interconnect people," he says. "Of course, we did the most bizarre thing – I recorded the rhythm section in LA, with an orchestra and vocal group in San Francisco and Gloria Estefan in Miami, thinking that if I could pull that off, I can do anything. It worked. When I produced Frank Sinatra's *Duets* album, the joke that prevailed was that people would phone their parts in to the studio. But now many people have that kind of fibre optic capability in their homes, and it has improved as digital compression and the technology becomes more advanced."

Ramone helped to create another world first when, in the spring of 1995, he produced a session with Japanese guitarist Hotei at Singapore's Form Studios, linked to Jesus Jones at Real World near Bath via Solid State Logic's WorldNet system. It was the very first time a single had been recorded and mixed *simultaneously* over ISDN lines, with two artists separated by over 7,000 miles and two different time zones. However, at the moment, this use of ISDN appears to be isolated.

AIR Studios has ISDN capability in each of its studios, although Malcolm Atkin claims it is rarely used at present. Like many studios, AIR believes it is a facility it *should* have, but in real terms it may not be an area of technology which will become truly relevant for some time. "I don't actually think it will be used for much more than the audio equivalent of a fax machine," he says, "purely because we are human and we really need to be in the same room as each other to achieve a rounded performance. That's the exciting part about this business. Fashions come and go, and maybe the generation will have different philosophies, but it is the intimate communication between musicians which makes for great music."

But already in the commercial advertising world it has become common for voice-over artists to "phone" their parts to large city-based advertising studios or radio broadcast production facilities without even leaving their homes. All that is required on the part of the artist is a small investment in an ISDN unit, a soundproofed vocal booth and a quality microphone. Trevor Horn, who has ISDN lines in his St John's Wood and Los Angeles home studios, received an ISDN feed in February 1996 from actor, Antonio Banderas, whose voice was used on Tina Turner's *Wildest Dreams* album. And the system proved useful to Hugh Padgham when he mixed several tracks in London for Los Angeles-based Melissa Etheridge and sent them to her for approval via ISDN.

It is exactly this type of development which excites and inspires Craig Leon, as he sees the rapid breakdown of distances between music creators. "In ten years, the technology would have improved at such a pace that we will probably have video links to enable on-line sessions between people in different cities," he says. "And with the ability to record digitally on hard disk, you will be able to involve live musicians and bring about a global workshop. That is definitely the way I see recording heading and in some ways it will help to keep costs down because the equipment will continue to get cheaper and a greater number of people will be encouraged to make music and present demos in an instantly accessible way."

Producer Fears

It is most likely that in the future, record shops as we know them may cease to exist as the method of accessing music will be via a cable or satellite-linked global jukebox, where the listener "rents" a track for playback on their multimedia entertainment system. It is a frightening thought for producers who rely on royalties from the point of sale, because renting does not contribute a sale and in terms of royalty collection, it will be an area which could be difficult to monitor. Problems are already being experienced with the upsurge in video productions.

But there is one producer-friendly organisation which formed in 1984 to keep a close eye on this and other fair-play topics, and is now spreading its influence all over the world: Re-Pro, otherwise known as

The Guild of Recording Producers, Directors and Engineers. Founder member, Alan Parsons says that the organisation was criticised in its early days for being an elitist club for the UK's top producers, but its doors have since widened significantly to welcome those at all levels of the industry and represent a variety of real issues. "The main aim when we started was purely to establish communication between ourselves because most of us had never met," Parsons says, "let alone talked to each other. One producer would leave a studio as another walked in, like passing ships. So we now know our common aims, grievances and fears, and we actively pursue certain issues which affect our work. Now that we have a voice within the industry, we are looking at the future of the producer's role within copyright and entertainment law. We have already been of financial benefit to many producers by simply making them aware of previously unseen royalty opportunities, which may be substantial."

"It's certainly a good organisation for the future because it won't be long before people download new records from the Internet into their home computer [it's already happening]," Hugh Padgham adds. "And producers' royalties have to be protected. Our methods of income will have to encompass different mediums and having a recognised body which can represent our tiny profession is good for solidarity."

For these reasons, the communications revolution is giving many producers cause to lose sleep over the possible side effects on their livelihoods, and Gary Langan is particularly keen that something is done immediately to address the Internet issue. But, he feels, being British is a sight handicap in that respect. "I'm very worried about this country because we're so slow to change – the British are dreadful in that respect," he says. "There should have been a levy on blank tapes years ago. I don't have a solution, but as someone who survives on royalties from the music he produces, of course I'm worried about how I'm going to earn from having music available on the Internet and pay per listen systems."

One solution might be for producers to receive a once-only overall fee on completion of a project, but Langan is in the majority when he dismisses the very suggestion. "I don't think you'd find many people who would want to sanction that totally," he claims. "If you really care about a project you put an awful lot into it, and whilst you can walk away from it at the end and carry it around with you like the artist, you have still invested a lot of your heart and soul. So I think it is fully justifiable to have a royalty structure in place and it would be wrong to take that away. It would be extremely difficult to set a fee per track or per album, because no one knows how an album is going to sell and there's the huge risk of at least one party being upset. If you agree to an outright buy-out fee instead of three to four per cent of ninety per cent of the gross retail sales and the album sells seven million copies, boy, are you going to be an unhappy camper! The royalty structure is there to deliver a fair reward based on an album's commercial performance and I think it's a wonderful thing."

chapter twelve

postscript: full circle

"Passion has come back into music. Real instruments played by musicians who are thinking again; records made by producers who are in tune with human beings, rather than machines. It's a renaissance."

Paul Weller

A look at the records which have dominated mainstream airwaves over the last few years may lead some to believe that all possible permutations of popular musical styles have at last been exhausted, and that artists are now forced to reinvent the past. Even if this is true it may be no bad thing.

The flagbearers of Nineties British pop/rock – Oasis, Ocean Colour Scene, Blur, Kula Shaker, Manic Street Preachers, Supergrass, Radiohead, The Lightning Seeds, Cast, Pulp and former Jam and Style Council leader turned solo artist, Paul Weller – may be criticised at times for wearing their Sixties and Seventies influences too obviously, but what of guitar legends Eric Clapton and Peter Green whose styles were based wholly on the music of pre-war bluesmen? Or The Beatles, who built their early songwriting around the hooks and chordal patterns learned from their heroes Buddy Holly, Carl Perkins and Little Richard, and Berry Gordy's new stable of Motown artists. One always seems to be able to detect a blueprint from years before, but as Cast's John Power once told me, "If it ain't broken, why fix it?

If it works, do it!"

What today's technology can do is increase the range of raw materials on the producer's palette and by drawing on old musical influences, flavours and even the actual sounds themselves, it may be possible to mould the ingredients of previous styles into what appears to the current young generation as music that is fresh and inspiring. It is already happening with artists such as Portishead, whose stark and eerie mood music is a direct descendant of John Barry's achievements more than thirty years ago, and The Manic Street Preachers, whose Mike Hedges-produced anthem 'A Design For Life' and album *Everything Must Go* could never have happened if it were not for the huge, ambient, orchestrated records made by Phil Spector. "I could hear strings in my head all the way through writing it...the song pretty much chose that treatment itself. It was never going to be a small-sounding number," says singer/guitarist James Dean Bradfield of 'A Design For Life', the track which launched the Manics' new epic sound – a departure from their earlier work before member Richey James mysteriously disappeared in February 1995.

Then, of course, there is Roni Size and his band Reprazent. Size's album *New Forms*, the winner of the prestigious Mercury Music Prize in 1997, earned unanimous acclaim from critics in the UK, America and beyond. It could be said that the drum 'n' bass style (the close relation of jungle, the dance genre noted for its frantic drum machine sequences) for which Size is a prime ambassador has its roots in production ethics which were in evidence during the Seventies (reggae, jazz-soul) and certainly the early Eighties' synth pop era. Reprazent are actually one of the few drum 'n' bass acts to incorporate a *real* bass and *real* drums when out on the road. Size himself, along with core Reprazent members Suv, Die and Krust, is a self-confessed "technology freak" who in his youth would always take note of the brand of samplers, keyboards and drum machines used by bands, but would rarely recall the musicians' names or indeed the songs they were performing. It's no surprise then that his music is technology driven – "All of us use samplers as naturally as someone else would play their guitar," Size comments.

In general terms though, mainstream rock music has taken a noticeable step backwards from being technology-driven in the

Nineties, although some might say that it has been a temporary reaction to the constant bombardment of new, improved equipment models on artists and producers. "Back to basics" has been the watch-phrase for many bands who have tended to record their most recent albums with a live approach in around three weeks, as opposed to the several months of extensive overdubbing and close analysis of previous work.

A reference point for many Nineties artists – especially Weller, Ocean Colour Scene and Blur – has been The Small Faces, a band whose recordings are now widely regarded as being ahead of their time. Drummer Kenney Jones observes, "It's almost like we peered into the window of the future, had a good look around and made our music to fit. It amazes today's musicians that us four blokes could make such a big sound with just two-, four- or eight-track recorders. The look we had was so great in its heyday and a lot of bands have taken that look and adapted it for the Nineties. What I really love about the BritPop movement, or whatever you want to call it, is that the bands are honest, they can all play very well, and there are no drum machines. It's all pure band stuff and the movement has become so much like the Sixties that it's almost like a renaissance."

Tony Visconti made a welcome return to the charts in 1997 as the producer of ex-Stone Roses guitarist John Squire's new band, The Seahorses – another new outfit to re-discover the joys of traditional songwriting values and simplistic arrangements. Visconti now feels that the once obsessive use of modern technology is finding a comfortable level.

"I've noticed on [recent] albums that everyone wants to get back to 'real' recording again, although I feel that MIDI is necessary," he says. "I now record quite often without a click track, very dangerously. But because of the sophistication of the programmes these days, you're able to lock up anything with anything. I might tap a steady tempo on a keyboard along with the drum track, which the computer will recognise and learn. Then you can use MIDI to do certain overdubs. Maybe I'll record the keyboards using MIDI and later I'll tailor the sound. At least I've got the keyboard player's performance unquantised but synched up to the track. Then I'll put together a lot of modules until I get the right sound. So I use MIDI as a useful tool but I don't live by it and I don't need it to make all my records."

Eric Clapton began to adopt a more sequenced approach to his own brand of rock music with Eighties albums *August* and *Journeyman*, but he has also reverted to grass roots methods of late, despite the availability of more sophisticated machinery. Clapton bassist, Dave Bronze, recalls the sessions at Olympic for the 1994 blues album, *From The Cradle*. "The overriding criteria was that all the numbers were to be recorded completely live, as the original bluesmen would have intended and Eric wouldn't do any overdubs at all," he says. "In the Thirties and Forties, this would have been normal, but these days it's quite extraordinary. So we had to get everything down in one hit. The track obviously had to be cooking with Eric's vocal bang on the nail all the way through, and if anyone of us screwed up, we had to do the number again. Consequently, over a period of months, we recorded dozens of takes of each song and Russ Titelman [producer] had to find the best one, and make sure that Eric agreed with it."

Many of the sessions would begin with the band members listening to original recordings by Willie Dixon, Elmore James and Freddie King, before undertaking fresh arrangements in the studio. "Some numbers would take longer to cook, but on 'Reconsider Baby' and 'Third Degree', it was pretty much instantaneous really, doing a take within an hour or so," Bronze continues. "Sometimes we would rattle off as many as seven numbers in a day, but obviously there is a limit to the number of vocals that you can deliver, so we could only work for as long as Eric's voice held out. Elmore James's tunes are pitched very high so Eric set aside days for doing those because of the strain on the voice."

It should be noted that Clapton returned to a more glamorous production style with his 1998 album *Pilgrim*, which he co-produced with Simon Climie.

American guitar virtuoso, Joe Satriani is another musician to have favoured traditional approaches, a decision he had arrived at after recording both digitally and analogue. "When technology first comes out you tend to gravitate towards it, and if it's fun you'll work with it," he says. "But most modern technology has its inevitable limits. Analogue recording really doesn't because it's literally a mirror of what you are doing and the imaging is so perfectly reproduced, whereas it's not with digital recording. It has some great things going for it but one of its disadvantages is that its imaging is lousy. Even CDs are lousy and if you want to hear how a piece of music sounded in the studio when it was first mixed, it pales in comparison to tape. Analogue allows you the freedom of continually playing with miking techniques and you get on tape what you put into it, so there is a constant payback. It's an unlimited form when it comes to recording an event."

Much of Paul Weller's solo material, such as 'Sunflower' and 'The Changingman' which were recorded at the Manor shortly before its demise, has evoked the post-psychedelic feel of the late Sixties and early Seventies. Its organic flavour is as out of line with today's technology as one can achieve, but he insists it is a sound which comes naturally to him. "Basically, we're all playing real instruments and I don't like all that digital bollocks," he says. "A lot of modern, so-called rock bands go for that really hard, toppy production which makes the songs sound transparent. I like to hear raw emotion, the sound of human beings interacting on tape. We don't, for instance, record with a click track and that's immediately breaking the rules of modern recording. If you're playing together regularly and you're a tight unit, you shouldn't need to be forced into regimented time-keeping by a click. When a musical performance is truly exciting it is bound to waver slightly in tempo, that's natural."

In spite of the backlash in some quarters of the rock field towards digital recording, Midge Ure can appreciate both sides of the story but believes that the cleanliness and clarity of digital wins at the end of the day. "I know engineers who have grand debates about whether analogue is better than digital, because analogue compresses drums and distorts and has a hiss which is all part of real music," he says. "But when I'm recording digitally it sounds great to me. I haven't really changed my opinions on technology. My sense of musical ethics remains the same regarding the use of synthesised and acoustic music. The whole outlook of Ultravox was about using whatever instrumentation we had to achieve the sound we wanted. That could just as easily have been about banging two Coke cans together, as using the world's most expensive synthesiser.

"I hated the statement that The Smiths made, that the day they used a synthesiser on a record would be the day they broke up. It was incredibly narrow-minded to ignore a whole area of musical instrumentation. It was like saying you intend never to use your right hand to make this album, that you will do it all with your left hand, which is bloody ridiculous! So I've always said that I'll use electronics and experiment with drum machines and synths. But at the end of the day, the thing that makes it all work is when I sit down and strap on a guitar and play the way I like to play, because first and foremost, I am a guitarist."

In a career that has lasted more than fifty years, Tom Dowd has worked with more artists than he could ever mention and believes that it is not necessarily the advances in technology which will have the most impact on music-making, but the attitude and interaction of the musicians themselves. "I am disappointed somewhat in the musicianship involved in a lot of the groups today," he says. Becoming a guitar player, a drummer or lead singer today is something that you strive for and you do for four or five years, and if you hit it big, then great. If not, well, at least you had a good time trying and you go on to do whatever you're gonna do, like be a doctor or a lawyer or a garbage man. Historically, many years ago, when people took up the guitar or any instrument, it was their liberation. They never planned to do it for just five years, this was getting them out of the ghetto or the steel mill or the cottonfields, into the limelight where they could bathe and eat every day. The motivation behind today's musician and his devotion is different. There is more of an emphasis on being better, faster and louder as a musician, and the relationship between players contributing equally to form a whole piece of music has been gradually torn apart. It's a sport thing. I sometimes have to figure out whether the bass player is trying to compete with the guitarists. Does he know what a bass part is? A bass part to me is something that lays a melodic foundation, but too often today, especially since we've had five- and six-string instruments, many bass players have no idea what a bass part is. They think they're just there to prove they can play as fast as the lead guitarist! But it's not a criticism, it's an observation of a style change."

Recent years have seen Trevor Horn move slightly away from the machinery which helped him achieve his initial success as a producer in the early Eighties, and employ the skills of session musicians whom, despite Dowd's claims, he finds to be generally more user-friendly than ever. "Maybe I'm mellowing but I like musicians much more than I ever did before," he admits. "I used to be one! Studio musicians have improved enormously and they are generally more able to help producers in terms of achieving key sounds. There's better training available to musicians now and they have to be better because they have to compete with computers and programmers.

"Whatever happens with technology, people will still like nice songs that they can listen to in the car. When there was less technology and you were fighting, then it was a case of doing whatever you could do within your constraints. There are no longer any constraints and it's like a menu. How do you want your rhythm track? Cooked? Lightly done? Medium rare? That can be a little bit daunting at times. I have every confidence that there will always be a demand for a good album, regardless of fashion and technological advance. There doesn't have to be any interactive bullshit to make them enjoy it more. That's why people like pop stars because they get simple pleasure from listening to a piece of music."

Brit Power

From the release of their debut album *Definitely Maybe*, Oasis have dominated both the record charts and the media. While Liam Gallagher has successfully forged a reputation as the bad boy of British pop, his big brother, lead guitarist Noel, has earned equal notoriety as one of the most important songwriters to have emerged over the last decade, even if he has occasionally displayed signs of being a "magpie" – 'Shakermaker' bore an uncanny resemblance in places to The New Seekers' 'I'd Like To Teach The World To Sing', and the closing harmonies of 'She's Electric' could have even been directly lifted from end of The Beatles' 'With A Little Help From My Friends'.

The Oasis "wonderwall" of sound has become increasingly reliant on the thick layering of Noel Gallagher's guitars. By their second album, *(What's The Story) Morning Glory?*, Gallagher's guitar dubs were occupying up to ten channels on the multitrack at Rockfield

Studios in Wales, even without the additional rhythm guitar playing by Bonehead (aka Paul Arthurs). *Be Here Now*, their much-hyped 1997 follow-up, co-produced by the omnipresent Owen Morris, was recorded at a variety of studios including Abbey Road, AIR and Ridge Farm, and the in-your-face bombardment of the guitar playing reached a new saturation point, particularly on 'D'you Know What I Mean'. Gallagher's concrete sound on this track was enhanced by a string section (recorded at AIR) which Morris fed to a Marshall guitar stack and distorted. Shades of The Beatles? Surely not.

If proof was needed that guitar-led pop music had reached a new level of popularity in the mid-1990s, one only had to look at John Leckie rising to the lectern to take the title of "Best Producer" in the 1997 Brit Awards, almost twenty-seven years to the day when he first walked through the doors of Abbey Road Studios as a new EMI recruit. For those who cared deeply about the welfare of honest-to-goodness, "organic" pop/rock, it was as if music had come home. "I think it's a really good sign that I got it rather than Trevor Horn!" joked Leckie at the time. This was no personal jibe at Horn, but rather an appreciation of the strength of character displayed by today's bands.

Since producing tracks such as 1989's seminal 'Fools Gold' by The Stone Roses, Leckie has gone on to help define the sound of today's British guitar pop music with Radiohead, Cast, Kula Shaker, Ride and others, although he is the first to concede that finding an identity for each of these bands has been the result of a two-way partnership. "I feel that my input as a producer can only work if the band's music is already of a high standard before I step in," he says. "The bands I choose to work with are those who are halfway towards the sound that will happen on record because of their live work, and I think I contribute the other half in terms of communicating ideas for them to act upon or guiding them in that direction."

This "other half" may include flavouring music with Leslie speakers, Mellotrons and other exotic hardware which first found favour among bands and their listeners during the psychedelic era. "Both Cast and Kula Shaker are known for their use of Leslies and Mellotrons," he admits, "and that comes from me. I just turned on the Leslie one day and they loved it. I might choose to set the

Symphonic effect on an SPX-90 and speed it up, but when when you make the effort to use a real Leslie and you can find one that doesn't rattle or hum, it is a very special sound because it's the Doppler effect and it has a life of its own. Knowing when to use it is part of the secret. [Cast frontman] John Power instantly fell in love with the sound and, of course, there were all kinds of observations like, 'It sounds just like [The Beatles'] "Blue Jay Way".' The way I record drums and get a certain sound also appeals to them. What I hope I can do above everything else is capture the spirit of a band on stage so that when you see them play live after liking their record, it's not a big disappointment."

On several occasions since the mid-Seventies, Leckie had received offers of work from the USA, but declined, visualising Britain as the place where the majority of inventive, thought-provoking music was being made. "American music tends to be a little too conventional for me," he says. "The contrast between the UK and US dance scenes is a good example. In the UK it is a thriving market with some incredible, creative music that is more than just music to dance to; it is constantly breaking down the boundaries and everything I aspired to when I was at college in the late 1960s. It's all about fantastic sounds and there is immense control, but it seems that the best things happen when it goes out of control. That's when I get a buzz from dance music. I'm not inspired when I hear it thumping away in a predictable manner. It's the same with humans playing guitars and drums in bands, and American musicians probably find it more difficult to get out of control than their British counterparts. What's happening in dance music today is not too dissimilar from what Pink Floyd were thinking about in 1968 but they didn't have the simple technology that people now have at their disposal to create the sound. If they or Hendrix had used it then, the results would have been phenomenal."

Cast's 1995 first album *All Change* was briefly the biggest-selling debut in the history of Polydor Records, and legend has it that immediately upon hearing their demos, an impressed Leckie headed straight for Liverpool, urging the band to hire him as their producer. What was it that attracted him? "The first thing I noticed was the quality of the songs and John's voice which I knew anyway having produced The La's," he says. "I could tell where John's head was at.

When I heard 'Walkaway' it was a very scratchy acoustic guitar demo but I could tell it had the potential to be a classic record."

Nearly two years on, Cast returned with their second album *Mother Nature Calls*, an incredibly mature and diverse collection of songs and styles with Leckie once again at the production helm. The major difference between the albums (apart from the fact that Mark "Spike" Stent mixed the latter) was in the approach to the sessions. Whereas *All Change* consisted of material routined on the road before recording, *Mother Nature Calls* relied almost totally on new, previously unperformed songs which were arranged with Leckie's input during a two-week stretch of rehearsals. There was also a glimmer of complacency to overcome. "We made the first album for ourselves and there was a lot more excitement," Leckie admits. "This time there was the comfort factor which came from knowing that whatever we did was ultimately going to sell a substantial number of records. But I still wanted to make a great album and they needed a bit of a kick from me to get going!"

Backing tracks for *Mother Nature Calls* were recorded over four weeks at RAK Studio One in the room which Leckie eagerly describes as "the best in the country – we used their old API console made by Boeing around 1975 and I don't think it has been turned off since!" After a Christmas break, Cast relocated to the Sawmills in Cornwall where they re-worked the backing for 'Free Me', 'I'm So Lonely', 'She Sun Shines' and 'Mirror Me', and recorded guitar overdubs. It was at this point when it seemed that the clock was ticking too fast for comfort.

"Our original plan was to do all the backing tracks at RAK, the vocal and guitar overdubs at Sawmills and then mix in Studio Three at Abbey Road where they've got my favourite desk – an SSL G Series 8000," Leckie says. "But somewhere down the line we ran out of time and ended up doing more recording when we got to Abbey Road. That included B-sides, for Christ's sake! Right at the end of the project when 'Free Me' was about to be mastered for the single, the label were saying, 'Give us as many B-sides as you've got, a minimum of four and a maximum of six. We need them now, finished and mixed, for the dual format CD singles.' So I suggested to Cast that every night after dinner we should go back into the studio at nine pm and bang out a B-side by midnight, and by the end of the week we'd have five of them. I had the same problem with Radiohead where a single was brought out before the album was finished, so you have to abandon the album for a while until you've delivered these bonus tracks. This is a major distraction to your focus on the main event. So my advice to any band is to get the B-sides recorded and out of the way before you concentrate on the album, otherwise your judgment can be damaged."

Much acclaim has been reserved for the guitar sounds Leckie captures in the studio. His miking technique usually involves the mixture of either an SM58 or 57 dynamic mic with an 87 or 67 condenser. "There's obviously an amazing difference in the sound and coloration you get from adjusting the balance of each of those mics," he says, "and you can get radically different textures depending on your mix of the two. I always have the mics positioned right up close to the guitar cabinet, literally touching the speaker cloth, and never two feet back, no matter how loud the cabinet's being driven. Whether you have the mics in the centre of the speaker or to the side, off-axis, is a matter of experimentation. I tend to prefer a 58 because I'm not overly keen about the top lift of a 57. A lot of it is down to perfect tuning and the tone you get on the amp in the first place, because if you have a shitty sounding amp, it'll still sound bad no matter what you do in the control room. If the guitar sounds great in the room, then that is most of your battle won. Very rarely do I use any ambient miking away from the cabinet. I might do on the odd solo or for a special effect, but it certainly is not the rule."

Leckie informs that many of the guitar tracks on *Mother Nature Calls* (including the main riff of 'Free Me') were recorded with a £30 battery-powered miniature Fender Twin replica. "It wasn't out of laziness but because it sounded so great!" he insists. "I placed a 58 on the speaker and just added a touch of low-end EQ on the desk because you don't get too much bass out of those toys! One of the things about recording guitars is that although there are no rules, you have to be careful with EQ. You generally know if you're going wrong in the room itself, if you're over-compensating for something by adding lots of top end."

Maybe as a throwback to the era in which Leckie began his

career, he is an enormous fan of the psychedelic-hued backwards guitar. This is mirrored in the Cast track 'She Sun Shines'. "I normally turn the multitrack tape over and get the guitarist to play completely spontaneously, do a few passes, then use the most interesting sections," he says. "The most difficult aspect of recording in this way is to know where you are in the song and the result essentially depends on where the guitarist's head is at on the day. That's the beauty of the whole backwards guitar thing – you never know what you're going to get until you turn the tape back over and play it. It's full of surprises and often if you are lost for an idea, the backwards thing might just produce a magical phrase that sends a track in a new direction.

"You can, of course, sample some guitar licks and reverse them via a sampler, and if it sounds good, then great. But if the whole point is to have a random feel then the old manual method of turning the tape is the best. One of the features of 'She Sun Shines' is Skin's backwards guitar riff which we spent a lot of time on and is actually a sample loop that was used by Brendan Lynch on the original demo of the song. However, if Skin had played to the reversed multitrack I'm sure a lot more strange ideas would have evolved."

Obviously, working with guitars has its limitations and there are few ideas and sounds left for Leckie to discover. It is not surprising, therefore, that he is constantly on the lookout for unique touches to add to his clients' tracks. His subtle contribution to Cast's 'Live The Dream', a wispy, swampy sound which appears in gaps between the vocal lines, is a typical example. "It was a sound I discovered on a Roland Sound Canvas and I just pushed it up to the highest possible octave so that it no longer sounded musical, but instead produced an effect," he explains. "I just love taking things to the edge and I've often stayed up all night listening to some of the craziest noises to see if they'll fit. Suddenly you'll hear something that totally captivates you and you then try to see how you can incorporate it without it sounding false. It's great to work with people who'll allow you to do that. One of the things about working with guitar bands is that rarely will you have a band member who is a real keyboard player. You'll get someone saying they can play Hammond organ but is he a genuine Hammond organ player. There is a big difference, as you'd note if you heard Georgie Fame." Or possibly Kula Shaker's Jay Darlington.

'Tattva'

Kula Shaker – now, there's a band who have thoroughly embraced the Sixties, particularly the influences of 'Magical Mystery Tour'-era Beatles, Pink Floyd, Grateful Dead, The Doors and Hendrix, and produced a sound fit for the Nineties. Their single 'The Sound Of Drums', the perfect marriage of all of these influences, was one of the most exciting records to emerge in 1998, but it was their single of 1996, 'Tattva', which first brought the band to wide public attention.

Singer/guitarist Crispian Mills, the son of actress Hayley and grandson of veteran actor Sir John Mills, wrote the Eastern-flavoured song (and named his band) following an experience in India. "I'd heard the phrase 'Achintya Bhedabheda Tattva' in India, but I got a friend of mine who I met there and was my guide to explain it to me," he recalls. "I was trying to work some things out in my head about life at the time. Then someone else who was called Kula Shaker rang me and said, 'Just remember Achintya Bhedabheda Tattva.' I thought that was fucking weird how he said exactly the same sentence, with the same pace to it as well. I then had the idea of getting something together with the band with this mantra coming in and out of it. We started working out the music and it sounded so good that we had to make a whole track out of it. It was very organic.

"We recorded 'Tattva' at first in a Kilburn eight-track studio with the riff going round and round. That's when we were learning about recording and we did some full-on psychedelic rock epics on eight-track, I'll tell you! The 'St George's Day' version of 'Tattva' [available on the CD single] was recorded at a place called Eastcote and it was the first time we'd used a Mellotron. It wasn't Nineties enough for where we're at now, but the charm and magic of it was wonderful. It was the first time that song really started to happen as a possible single."

"There were two demos," John Leckie recalls. "The very first one had no verses and it was more of a jam with tabla and a drum loop, and it was pretty wild-sounding. Then they did a demo which had verses and still had all of the ingredients but it had a much lengthier structure, lasting about ten minutes. I knew it was a brilliant single but it sounded a bit tame to me at this stage, so we went back into rehearsals with it and formed a new arrangement before going into Townhouse Two to record the single. Crispian had the idea for the slide solo even though no one definite solo existed; he plays it differently every time they play live and it was a question of picking the right one for the mix. What makes Kula Shaker great is that they work really hard at their music and there is always room for spontaneity and improvisation. Crispian has a classic musician's soul ethic and nothing scares him. He'll happily make mistakes in pursuit of something outstanding and he'll instinctively know when it's right.

"Unlike a lot of today's keyboard players, Jay Darlington is not ruled by synths and MIDI. He keeps to his Hammond and provides keyboard colours for the rest of the band to fall back upon. And he's bloody good! Despite how it might appear, we didn't use any esoteric valve gear to record *K* [the band's debut album], but instead did it more or less totally on SSLs at different modern studios like Eden, Livingstone and Townhouse Two."

The Changing Face Of The Producer's Role

Brian Eno believes that as musicians increase their familiarisation with studio practices and the technology behind the recording process, the traditional producer is gradually becoming a thing of the past. This switch, he says, was triggered by the introduction of MIDI and is now in an advanced stage.

"One of the things that has happened over the last fifteen years is that production as we understand it has actually become part of the province of what musicians do," he says. "When people sit at home with their home studios, banks of synthesisers and sequencers, and so on, they are in a way looking after the territory that used to be the province of producers a lot more, which is this quasi-artistic, quasi-technical ground that a lot of rock music is made in. So in one sense, the idea of the producer as someone who mediates and converses between the completely non-technical musician and the completely non-artistic engineer, which was the old picture, is now dead because most musicians now occupy all three of those roles to some extent. Most of today's musicians who play an electric instrument are partly engineers – they have some feeling about how things should connect together and how things should sound. That kind of producer is now on the way out. But I think there is another kind coming into existence who is not an interface between the artistic and technical, but an interface between different areas of the existing culture."

Muff Winwood foresees a time in the very near future when even the most successful producers will take a more back seat, consultative role, rather than assume responsibility for a project from start to finish. "In some ways, we could see a return to the A&R man of the Fifties who didn't really have any creative input, but kept an eye on things like a father figure," he suggests. "Artists are now quite capable of getting their backing tracks down on their own and they might seek the opinion of the A&R man who would offer advice on how to improve the recording and arrangement – maybe suggest a middle eight here, a better bass part there.

"A reasonably musical A&R man could probably by-pass the job of the independent record producer that has grown up since the Sixties, and the only outside person needed would be someone to mix the tracks. I tend to be working that way all the time now, as an *executive* producer. I'm involved in the signing of the act, the choosing of material, in discussions on whether the material works or doesn't work and in getting the material down on tape. I check to see if the choruses come in right, if the intros work and if the vocals are good enough. But that's what a record company would pay an independent record producer to do. The only time where I think you will need an outside producer is in the case of out and out commercial pop records, where the Pete Waterman types are independent producers, doing what both an artist *and* an A&R man do."

In spite of Winwood's predictions, the likelihood of Brian Eno giving up his hands-on studio for an in-house consultant's post is slim. He will remain far too busy with his conceptualising. "Nothing is obvious anymore," he states. "If you were making a beat record in 1963, there wouldn't be much question about what to do. You'd know you were making a pop record and it had to fit into a particular culture, so there were certain guidelines. But with the moving on of time, the field has become so wide and there are so many edges to it, and so many ways you can have a successful career doing this, that it isn't obvious which course you're on and where your music fits in. So that's an area in which producers can work. But an artist is always going to need to rely on a pair of experienced ears to say if something doesn't work or if it is time to stop overdubbing because the song is getting lost. Regardless of developments, some traditions have to be maintained for the sake of common sense."

The Retirement Of An Icon

At the time of my original interview with George Martin for this book's first edition in 1996, he had just turned seventy years of age and was just a few months away from receiving his long-deserved knighthood – an acknowledgement both of his unrivalled contribution to twentieth century music, and the matured appreciation of the art of record production. Indeed, Her Majesty The Queen saw fit to bestow the same honour on Paul McCartney and Elton John the following year – further proof that rock 'n' roll was at last a respectable pillar of society!

Sir George had "threatened" to retire several times over the previous couple of years, and assured me that he would in that summer of 1996. However, a number of projects would prevent this, in particular a single which would become not only his thirtieth UK Number One production but also the biggest-selling single of all-time.

Elton John's 'Candle In The Wind', a highlight of the Gus Dudgeon-produced *Goodbye Yellow Brick Road* album, had been a major hit in the spring of 1974. But under the most tragic of circumstances, he and lyricist Bernie Taupin re-worked the song as 'Goodbye England's Rose' aka 'Candle In The Wind 1997', a tribute to the late, lamented Diana, Princess of Wales, performed live by the singer one time only – at the Princess's emotional funeral at Westminster Abbey in September 1997. Sir George recalls the making of the single: "My wife [Judy] and I were holidaying in Turkey when we heard the news of Diana's death on the radio, and we flew back that day. A couple of days later, Elton rang me up and said, 'I'm going to do a special song in the Abbey; Bernie has re-written the lyrics of 'Candle In The Wind' and I want to record it and give all the royalties to Diana's fund. Would you produce it for me?'

"Well, I always regarded Elton as a great singer and this was a super song, but I did wonder if this was the right thing to do. It was a tough decision, but I could hardly say no because Elton is a very genuine person; I'd worked with him before and trusted his judgement entirely."

On the afternoon of Diana's funeral, John left the Abbey and headed straight for the Townhouse's Studio One which had already been set up for the singer's on-going sessions for his album *The Big Picture*. Waiting for his arrival was Sir George and his assisting son Giles (an up and coming producer in his own right), engineer Pete Lewis and assistant engineer Andy Green. After a brisk run-through for John's voice and piano levels, the basic track was recorded digitally in one take, using the studio's SSL G+ seventy-two-channel desk and Sony 3348 and 3324 digital machines.

"We put down his voice and [Bosendorfer] piano quite quickly, and then he added the string quartet and a couple of woodwind that I specially wrote scores for in haste at the session," Sir George recalls. "Within just a few hours we had mixed the track and made the master which was couriered to the factory, and at the end of the week we'd already sold a quarter of a million records."

Away from his still busy studio life, Sir George even found time to organise and appear at a major live show that September – "Music For Montserrat" – at the Royal Albert Hall. The concert, which featured Sir Elton, Sir Paul, Eric Clapton, Phil Collins, Sting, Midge Ure, Arrow, Jimmy Buffet, and Carl Perkins (who sadly died in 1998), was probably the most expensive gathering of talent since Live Aid and achieved its aim of raising more than £1 million for the victims of Montserrat's Soufriere volcano disaster of July 1997.

Despite this activity, Sir George did finally retire from record production in the spring of 1998 at the age of seventy-two. His last project, released on 23 March, 1998, was the album *In My Life*, a collection of his favourite Beatles songs, performed by a bewildering array of celebrities (including Sean Connery, Robin Williams, Jeff Beck, Jim Carrey, Goldie Hawn, Celine Dion, John Williams, Phil Collins, Vanessa Mae and Billy Connolly) and boasting exquisite orchestral arrangements that could only have come from the Martin pen.

Recorded mainly at his AIR Lyndhurst Studios in Hampstead, *In My Life* was, he says, his way of expressing his deep gratitude to all the artists he had worked with in his staggering forty-eight-year production career – not least The Beatles. Just as the Fabs knew *Abbey Road* was going to be their last album, Sir George's *In My Life* was always going to be his studio swansong and its recording had been gradually taking place over a two-year period. (Unknown to me at the time, Jeff Beck's session for his version of 'A Day In The Life' was in progress at AIR on the afternoon that I originally interviewed Sir George in 1996.)

"I wanted to make a definite full stop to my career rather than a comma," he says, "and singles-wise it was very pleasing to have achieved my thirtieth Number One, rather than staying on twenty-nine forever – it's a rather odd number, don't you think? Inevitably there had to be a final album, and I had the freedom to decide exactly what that should be. I wanted it to be one I would remember with affection, one that would be enjoyable to make as well as hear. So I asked some of my friends and heroes, people I had always liked and admired, to join me in music that has been a big part of my life. It would be a salute to them, too.

"It was natural that I should choose Beatle music, because whether I wanted it or not I'm associated with The Beatles eternally, and it's not bad music either! The Beatles, of course, are my friends and heroes, but they could hardly be part of it [as a group] and for a number of reasons I didn't actually seek their involvement. Instead I could select their songs and fit them to some unlikely voices. It was partly inspired by the record I made with Peter Sellers performing 'A Hard Day's Night', when I persuaded him to use his Laurence Olivier voice in a great Richard III send-up. I thought, 'Well let's do something like that...let's have a giggle!' After producing lots of other people all my life, I thought it was time to finish with something that was just for me, and I think it has rounded off my career in the nicest possible way."

Retiring from the studio has not meant the absolute end of Sir George's working life – he maintains his role as the head of AIR Studios, and there are his other business interests such as his involvement with London radio station Heart 106.2FM and the

Montserrat relief fund, as well as his continued concert appearances and work in television. No pipe and slippers for this man!

His reasons for quitting the session life are clear, however. "I'm now quite old," he says, in spite of a spirit which belies his age, "and I don't want to spend the rest of my life in the recording studio. It takes too long to do things now and there are so many other things I'd rather be doing. I've been in the business now since 1950 and that's a long time; I can't remember how many records I've made. If you turn me upside down, musical notes will fall out of my ears, so I'm rather full up with it now – I simply don't want to make records anymore.

"Record production is such a different game now, although to be successful some fundamental attributes still apply – you've got to get on with and relate to artists; you've got to make them feel secure in their talent. I've been awfully lucky because I think timing is everything in life and I started in the business when there were only about ten people in the country who you could describe as record producers. Walk down the street now and you'll find that one in three is a record producer, and it's different technology, it's different music. I think records are made more for vision now than they are for sound. You can't sell a record without being seen and image is everything. So, the record producer of today has to be a different kind of animal to the one I was."

Ending this edition of *Good Vibrations* with the retirement of Sir George Martin is my own personal way of thanking him for the great inspiration he has given to me and millions of other creative spirits across the globe. "A cross between your favourite school teacher and your father," is how Midge Ure describes Sir George, through his experience of recording with him on Montserrat in 1982. Whether one has had the pleasure of either working with or simply meeting Sir George, an instant impression is formed of the perfect English gentleman. When I eagerly questioned him about the making of 'Strawberry Fields Forever', for instance, I was painfully aware that this was far from being the first time he had told the story. Yet he remained perfectly affable, genuinely modest and happy to assist with a detailed account. One almost has to be reminded that this was the man who recorded the twentieth century's most enduring pop records. Quite simply, he *is* the history of record production.

The doors to the recording myth have been kicked wide open. Teenage music makers in the Nineties laugh wildly at the notion that professional musicians in the Sixties had no idea of the process of getting music on to tape. The bubble has burst and no longer does a musician have to rely on the tradition that in order to make a quality recording, one *must* book a commercial studio, a producer and an engineer. With a little technical insight and a great deal of imagination, it is possible to record music on one's own terms and doorstep. Technology has been a major focus in this book, but it should be put in perspective. IT IS NOT AS IMPORTANT AS THE MUSIC. Unless we grasp this very important point, there is every possibility that future generations of musicians and producers will be no more than computer programmers with the musical sensitivity of robots. The technology is secondary and it should always be seen as a *channel* for the making of music, not the *reason*. So far, so good. In fact, we've done brilliantly.

100 classic albums of the rock era

In August 1995, to celebrate the fortieth anniversary of the launch of the long-playing album, the popular UK music magazine, *Mojo*, listed its "100 Greatest Albums Ever Made" survey results, based on the collective votes of more than seventy of its editorial contributors, researchers and associates. The ground rules given to all those voting were simple: the albums were not to include compilations of singles and greatest hits, or bootlegs (no matter how good), and that all should be from the wide rock genre.

The results were fascinating and while many of those albums included would appear in many a rock fan's personal Top 100, there are several entries which provoked lively debate (and an equal number of worthy contenders which are conspicuously absent). As a reference guide, the full list from Number One to 100 is reproduced here (with the kind permission of *Mojo*) with label and original year of release information, and producer and studio credits (where available). For this updated version of *Good Vibrations*, I have also listed a further ten more recent albums which in years to come may be considered as worthy of a place in this hotly contested chart.

Title – Artist (Label/Year Of Release/Producer)
Recording Studios

1   **Pet Sounds – The Beach Boys** (Capitol/1966/Brian Wilson)

Western Sound Recorders, Sunset Sound, Gold Star Studios, California

2 **Astral Weeks – Van Morrison** (Warner Bros/1968/Lewis Merenstein)
Century Sound Studios, New York City

3 **Revolver – The Beatles** (Parlophone/1966/George Martin)
EMI Abbey Road Studios, London

4 **Exile On Main Street – The Rolling Stones** (Rolling Stones/1972/Jimmy Miller)
Rolling Stones Mobile, Nellcote, France

5 **Highway 61 Revisited – Bob Dylan** (CBS/1965/Bob Johnston & Tom Wilson)
Columbia Studios, New York City

6 **What's Going On – Marvin Gaye** (Tamla Motown/1971/Marvin Gaye)
Hitsville (Motown Studios) and Golden Studios, Detroit

7 **Let It Bleed – The Rolling Stones** (Decca/1969/Jimmy Miller)
Olympic Sound Studios, London

8 **Blonde On Blonde – Bob Dylan** (CBS/1966/Bob Johnston)
Columbia Studios, New York City and Columbia Music Row Studios, Nashville

9 **The Velvet Underground & Nico – The Velvet Underground** (Verve-MGM/1967/Andy Warhol)
Anonymous Manhattan studio and TTG Studios, Los Angeles

10 **Horses – Patti Smith** (Arista/1975/John Cale)
Electric Lady Studios, New York City

11 **Forever Changes – Love** (Elektra/1967/Arthur Lee & Bruce Botnick)
Sunset Sound and Leon Russell's Skyhill Studio, Los Angeles

12 **Are You Experienced? – The Jimi Hendrix Experience** (Track/1967/Chas Chandler)
CBS Studios, Olympic Sound Studios, De Lane Lea and Kingsway Studio, London

13 **Countdown To Ecstacy – Steely Dan** (ABC/1973/Gary Katz)
Village Recorders, Santa Monica and Caribou Ranch, Nederland, Colorado

14 **Electric Ladyland – The Jimi Hendrix Experience** (Track/1968/Jimi Hendrix)
Olympic Sound Studios, London and The Record Plant, New York City

15 **The Band – The Band** (Capitol/1969/John Simon)

Poolhouse Studio, Los Angeles and The Hit Factory, New York City

16 **Fun House – The Stooges** (Elektra/1970/Don Gallucci & Brian Ross-Myring)
Elektra Sound Recorders, Los Angeles

17 **Marquee Moon – Television** (Elektra/1977/Andy Johns & Tom Verlaine)
A&R Studios, New York City

18 **Blue – Joni Mitchell** (Reprise/1971/Joni Mitchell)
A&M Studios, Los Angeles

19 **The Beatles – The Beatles** (Apple/1968/George Martin, plus – unaccredited – Chris Thomas)
EMI Abbey Road Studios and Trident Studios, London

20 **Innervisions – Stevie Wonder** (Motown/1973/Stevie Wonder, Bob Margouleff & Malcolm Cecil)
The Record Plant, Los Angeles and Media Sound Inc, New York City

21 **Station To Station – David Bowie** (RCA/1976/David Bowie & Harry Maslin)
Cherokee Studios, Los Angeles

22 **Never Mind The Bollocks – The Sex Pistols** (Virgin/1977/Chris Thomas & Bill Price)
Wessex Studios, London

23 **London Calling – The Clash** (CBS/1979/Guy Stevens)
Wessex Studios, London

24 **Abbey Road – The Beatles** (Apple/1969/George Martin)
EMI Abbey Road Studios, London

25 **Hunky Dory – David Bowie** (RCA/1971/Ken Scott)
Trident Studios, London

26 **Beggars Banquet – The Rolling Stones** (Decca/1968/Jimmy Miller)
Olympic Sound Studios, London

27 **Rubber Soul – The Beatles** (Parlophone/1965/George Martin)
EMI Abbey Road Studios, London

28 **Trout Mask Replica – Captain Beefheart & His Magic Band** (Straight/1969/Frank Zappa)
Whitney Studios, Glendale, California and The Magic Band's house, San Fernando Valley

29 **The Rise & Fall Of Ziggy Stardust & The Spiders From Mars – David Bowie** (RCA/1972/David Bowie & Ken Scott)

Trident Studios, London
30 **The Doors – The Doors** (Elektra/1967/Paul A Rothchild)
Sunset Sound, Los Angeles
31 **Otis Blue/Otis Redding Sings Soul – Otis Redding**
(Atlantic/1965/Tom Dowd & Jim Stewart)
Stax Studio, Memphis
32 **Live At The Apollo Vol 1 – James Brown & The Famous Flames**
(King/1963/James Brown)
Apollo Theatre, New York City
33 **Nevermind – Nirvana** (Geffen/1991/Butch Vig & Nirvana)
Sound City Studios, Van Nuys, California
34 **The Velvet Underground – The Velvet Underground**
(MGM/1969/The Velvet Underground)
TTG Studios, Los Angeles
35 **Sign 'O' The Times – Prince** (Paisley Park/1987/Prince)
Paisley Park, Minneapolis, Sunset Sound, Los Angeles and partly live in Paris
36 **The Notorious Byrd Brothers – The Byrds** (CBS/1968/Gary Usher)
Columbia Studios, Los Angeles
37 **Automatic For The People – REM** (Warner Bros/1992/Scott Litt & REM)
Bearsville Studio, New York, Criteria Studios, Miami, John Keane Studio, Athens, Georgia, Kingsway Studio, New Orleans and Bosstown Recordings, Atlanta
38 **The Who Sell Out – The Who** (Track/1968/Kit Lambert)
IBC Studios, Kingsway Studios, De Lane Lea and CBS Studios, London, Talent Masters Studios, New York and Columbia and Gold Star Studios, Los Angeles
39 **Blood On The Tracks – Bob Dylan** (CBS/1975/Bob Dylan)
Columbia and A&R Studios, New York City and Sound 80 Studio, Minneapolis
40 **Third – Big Star** (Aura-PVC/1978/Jim Dickinson)
Ardent Studios, Memphis
41 **Born To Run – Bruce Springsteen** (CBS/1975/Bruce Springsteen, Mike Appel and Jon Landau)
914 Sound Studios, Blauvelt, New York and The Record Plant, New York City

42 **Grievous Angel – Gram Parsons with Emmylou Harris**
(Reprise/1974/Gram Parsons)
Wally Heider Studios and Capitol Studios, Los Angeles

43 **Ramones – The Ramones** (Sire/1976/Craig Leon)
Plaza Sound, Radio City Music Hall, New York City

44 **Lust For Life – Iggy Pop** (RCA/1977/Bewlay Bros-David Bowie)
Hansa Ton Studios, Berlin

45 **Transformer – Lou Reed** (RCA/1972/David Bowie & Mick Ronson)
Trident Studios, London

46 **In A Silent Way – Miles Davis** (CBS/1969/Teo Macero)
Columbia Studios, New York City

47 **Younger Than Yesterday – The Byrds** (CBS/1967/Gary Usher)
Columbia Studios, Los Angeles

48 **Trans-Europe Express – Kraftwerk** (Capitol/1977/Ralf Hutter &
Florian Schneider)
*Klingklang Studio, Dusseldorf, Russel Studio, Hamburg and The Record
Plant, Los Angeles*

49 **New York Dolls – The New York Dolls** (Mercury/1973/Todd
Rundgren)
The Record Plant, New York City

50 **Moby Grape – Moby Grape** (CBS/1967/David Rubinson)
CBS Studios, Hollywood

51 **Sgt Pepper's Lonely Hearts Club Band – The Beatles**
(Parlophone/1967/George Martin)
EMI Abbey Road Studios and Regent Sound Studios, London

52 **Sticky Fingers – The Rolling Stones** (Rolling Stones/1971/Jimmy
Miller)
Olympic Sound Studios, London and Muscle Shoals, Alabama

53 **Closer – Joy Division** (Factory/1980/Martin Hannett)
Britannia Row Studios, London

54 **Darkness On The Edge Of Town – Bruce Springsteen**
(CBS/1978/Jon Landau & Bruce Springsteen)
Atlantic Studios and The Record Plant, New York City

55 **We're Only In It For The Money – The Mothers Of Invention**
(MGM/1968/Frank Zappa)
Mayfair Studios and Apostolic Studios, New York City

56 **The Nightfly – Donald Fagen** (Warner Bros/1982/Gary Katz)

Soundworks Digital Audio/Video Recording Studios and Automated Sound, New York City, and Village Recorders, Los Angeles

57 **Bringing It All Back Home – Bob Dylan** (Columbia/1965/Tom Wilson)
Columbia Studios, New York City

58 **The Clash – The Clash** (CBS/1977/Micky Foote)
CBS Studios, London

59 **For Your Pleasure – Roxy Music** (Island/1973/Chris Thomas)
AIR Studios, London

60 **Hounds Of Love – Kate Bush** (EMI/1985/Kate Bush)
Windmill Lane Studios, Dublin and EMI Abbey Road Studios, London

61 **Something/Anything? – Todd Rundgren** (Bearsville/1972/Todd Rundgren)
ID Sound, Los Angeles, Bearsville Sound, Bearsville, New York and The Record Plant, New York City

62 **Future Days – Can** (United Artists/1973/Can)
Inner Space Studio, Cologne

63 **With The Beatles – The Beatles** (Parlophone/1963/George Martin)
EMI Abbey Road Studios, London

64 **Clear Spot – Captain Beefheart & His Magic Band** (Reprise/1972/Ted Templeman)
Amigo Studos, Los Angeles

65 **Stand! – Sly & The Family Stone** (Epic/1969/Sly Stone)
Sunset Sound, Los Angeles

66 **Here Come The Warm Jets – Eno** (Island/1974/Eno)
Majestic Studios, London

67 **Catch A Fire – The Wailers** (Island/1972/Bob Marley & Chris Blackwell)
Dynamic Sound, Harry J Studios and Randy's Studios, Kingston , Jamaica and Island Studios, London

68 **Blue Lines – Massive Attack** (Wild Bunch/1991/Massive Attack with Jonny Dollar)
Coach House and Cherry Bear Studios, Bristol, Eastcote and EMI Abbey Road Studios, London

69 **This Year's Model – Elvis Costello** (Radar/1978/Nick Lowe)
Eden Studios, Chiswick, London

70 **I Want To See The Bright Lights Tonight – Richard & Linda Thompson** (Island/1974/Richard Thompson & John Wood)
Sound Techniques Studio, Chelsea, London

71 **Talking Book – Stevie Wonder** (Motown/1972/Stevie Wonder, Bob Margouleff & Malcolm Cecil)
AIR Studios, London, Electric Lady Studios, New York City, Crystal Studios and The Record Plant, Los Angeles

72 **The Modern Dance – Pere Ubu** (Blank/1978/Pere Ubu & Ken Hamann)
Cleveland Sound Studios and Suma Studios, Cleveland

73 **Can't Buy A Thrill – Steely Dan** (ABC/1972/Gary Katz)
Village Recorders, Los Angeles

74 **There's A Riot Goin' On – Sly & The Famliy Stone** (CBS/1971/Sylvester Stewart & Sly Stone)
John Phillips's house, Bel Air, California

75 **It's Too Late To Stop Now – Van Morrison** (Warner Bros/1974/Van Morrison & Ted Templeman)
Live at the Troubadour, Los Angeles, Santa Monica Civic, Santa Monica and the Rainbow Theatre, London

76 **It Takes A Nation Of Millions To Hold Us Back – Public Enemy** (Def Jam/1988/Hank Shocklee & Carl Ryder)
Greene Street Recording, Chung King House of Metal, Sabella recording and Spectrum City Studios, New York City

77 **The Piper At The Gates Of Dawn – The Pink Floyd** (Columbia/1967/Norman Smith)
EMI Abbey Road Studios, London

78 **The Hissing Of Summer Lawns – Joni Mitchell** (Asylum/1975/Joni Mitchell)
Burbank, Los Angeles

79 **The Stooges – The Stooges** (Elektra/1969/John Cale)
Elektra Studios, New York City

80 **Songs In The Key Of Life – Stevie Wonder** (Motown/1976/Stevie Wonder)
Crystal Industries Inc and The Record Plant, Los Angeles, The Hit Factory, New York City and The Record Plant, Sausalito, California

81 **A Hard Day's Night – The Beatles** (Parlophone/1964/George Martin)

EMI Abbey Road Studios, London

82 **Bitches Brew – Miles Davis** (CBS/1970/Teo Macero)
Columbia Studios, New York City

83 **Tonight's The Night – Neil Young** (Reprise/1975/David Briggs, Neil Young, Tim Mulligan & Elliot Mazer)
Studio Instrument Rentals Rehearsal Hall D, Los Angeles and Broken Arrow Ranch, California

84 **Good Old Boys – Randy Newman** (Warner Bros/1974/Lenny Waronker & Russ Titelman)
Warner Bros Studios, Hollywood

85 **Steve McQueen – Prefab Sprout** (Kitchenware/1985/Thomas Dolby & Phil Thomally)
No specified studio details, though recorded in Newcastle-upon-Tyne and London

86 **Here, My Dear – Marvin Gaye** (Motown/1978/Marvin Gaye, Delta Ashby & Ed Townsend)
Marvin Gaye Studio, Hollywood

87 **Spirit Of Eden – Talk Talk** (Parlophone/1988/Tim Friese-Greene)
Wessex Studios, London

88 **Miss America – Mary Margaret O'Hara** (Virgin/1988/Mary Margaret O'Hara & Michael Brook)
Rockfield Studios, Wales, Windmill Lane Studios, Dublin, Phase One and Comfort Sound Studios, Toronto

89 **Hot Rats – Frank Zappa** (Reprise/1969/Frank Zappa)
Whitney Studios, TTG and Sunset Sound, Los Angeles

90 **Gaucho – Steely Dan** (MCA/1980/Gary Katz)
Soundworks, A&R Studios, Sigma Sound and Automated Sound Studios, New York, Village Recorders, Los Angeles and Producers' Workshop, Hollywood

91 **The Village Green Preservation Society – The Kinks** (Pye/1968/Raymond Douglas Davies)
Pye & IBC Studios, London

92 **Dusty In Memphis – Dusty Springfield** (Philips/1969/Jerry Wexler, Tom Dowd & Arif Mardin)
American Studios, Memphis and Atlantic Studios, New York City

93 **A Wizard, A True Star – Todd Rundgren** (Bearsville/1973/Todd Rundgren)

Secret Sound, New York
94 **The Smiths – The Smiths** (Rough Trade/1984/John Porter)
Pluto and Strawberry Studios, Manchester and Eden and Matrix Studios, London
95 **Hard Again – Muddy Waters** (Blue Sky/1977/Johnny Winter)
The Schoolhouse, Boston
96 **Physical Graffiti – Led Zeppelin** (Swansong/1975/Jimmy Page)
Headley Grange, Hampshire, Mick Jagger's house (Stargroves), Berkshire, Olympic Sound Studios and Island Studios, London, Electric Ladyland, New York
97 **Odessey & Oracle – The Zombies** (Epic/1968/Rod Argent & Chris White)
EMI Abbey Road Studos, London
98 **Raw Power – Iggy & The Stooges** (CBS/1973/Iggy Pop with David Bowie)
CBS Studios, London and Western Sound Recorders, Los Angeles
99 **Led Zeppelin IV – Led Zeppelin** (Atlantic/1971/Jimmy Page)
Headley Grange, Hampshire, Island and Olympic Sound Studios, London and (mixed at) Sunset Sound, Los Angeles
100 **Rock Bottom – Robert Wyatt** (Virgin/1974/Nick Mason)
The Manor, Shipton-on-Cherwell, Oxfordshire and The Manor Mobile at Delphina's Farm, Little Bedwyn, Wiltshire

The Author's Suggestions For Future Top 100 Contenders:

1 **OK Computer**
– Radiohead
2 **Odelay**
– Beck
3 **Urban Hymns**
– The Verve
4 **Time Out Of Mind**
– Bob Dylan
5 **BloodSugarSexMagik**
– Red Hot Chili Peppers

off the record: producer and engineer credits

In this section, selected credits from the careers of a wide range of producers and engineers interviewed and/or featured for this book are listed.

ROY THOMAS BAKER

Queen	*A Night At The Opera*
The Cars	*Candy-O*
Foreigner	*Head Games*
T'Pau	*Bridge Of Spies*
Cheap Trick	*One On One*
Devo	*Potato Head*

GERRY BRON

Manfred Mann	'Ha Ha Said The Clown'
Uriah Heep	*Demons & Wizards*
Gene Pitney	'Something's Gotten Hold Of My Heart'
The Bonzo Dog Doo-Dah Band	'The Intro And The Outro'
Colosseum	*Those About To Die*
Osibisa	'Sunshine Day'

JOHN BURGESS

Manfred Mann	'Pretty Flamingo'
John Barry Seven	'James Bond Theme'
Adam Faith	'What Do You Want?'
Cliff Bennett &	'One Way Love'
The Rebel Rousers	
The Pipkins	'Gimme Dat Ding'
The Congregation	'Softly Whispering I Love You'

RICHARD JAMES BURGESS

Landscape	*From The Tea Rooms Of Mars...*
Spandau Ballet	*Journeys To Glory*
Adam Ant	*Strip*
Five Star	*Silk And Steel*
Living In A Box	'Living In A Box'
King	'Love And Pride'

TONY CLARKE

Pinkerton's Assorted	'Mirror Mirror'
Colours	
The Moody Blues	*Days Of Future Passed*
Equals	'Baby Come Back'
Four Tops	'Simple Game'
Justin Hayward &	*Blue Jays*
John Lodge	
Clannad	*Legend*

STUART COLMAN

Shakin' Stevens	'This Old House'
Cliff Richard & Phil Everly	'She Means Nothin' To Me'
Jeff Beck	'Crazy Legs'
The Young Ones & Cliff	'Living Doll'
Nanci Griffith &	'Do You Wanna Be Loved'
The Crickets	

Little Richard   'Great Gosh A'Mighty'

TOM DOWD

Otis Redding	*Otis Blue/Otis Redding Sings Soul*
Aretha Franklin	'Respect'
Derek & The Dominoes	*Layla & Other Assorted Love Sougs*
Rod Stewart	*Atlantic Crossing*
Lynyrd Skynyrd	*Gimme Back My Bullets*
Primal Scream	*Give Out But Don't Give Up*

GUS DUDGEON

The Strawbs	*Strawbs*
David Bowie	'Space Oddity'
Elton John	*Goodbye Yellow Brick Road*
John Kongos	'He's Gonna Step On You Again'
Chris Rea	*Whatever Happened To Benny Santini?*
Elkie Brooks	*Pearls I & II*

BRIAN ENO

Eno	*Here Come The Warm Jets* (as producer and artist)
Various Artists	*Help*
U2	*The Joshua Tree*
Talking Heads	*Remain In Light*
James	*Laid*
David Bowie	*Outside:1*

STUART EPPS (engineering)

Chris Rea	*Espresso Logic*
Elton John	'Song For Guy'
Led Zeppelin	*Coda*
Lindisfarne	'Run For Home'
Bill Wyman/Rhythm Kings	*Struttin' Our Stuff*

Voyager   'Halfway Hotel'

COLIN FAIRLEY

Elvis Costello   *Blood & Chocolate*
The Bluebells   'Young At Heart'
The Fabulous   *T-Bird Rhythm*
Thunderbirds
Madness   'It Must Be Love' (engineered)
Judie Tzuke   'Stay With Me Till Dawn' (engineered)
The Teardrop Explodes   'Reward' (engineered)
Japan   *Gentlemen Take Polaroids* (engineered)

FLOOD

P J Harvey   *To Bring You My Love*
Depeche Mode   *Violator*
Nine Inch Nails   *The Downward Spiral*
U2   *Zooropa*
The Charlatans   *Weirdo*
Jesus And Mary Chain   'Some Candy Talking' (engineered)

PAUL GOMERSALL

Phil Collins   *Serious Hits Live* (engineered)
Eric Clapton   *August* (engineered)
Kate Bush   *The Sensual World* (engineered)
George Michael   *Older* (engineered)
Aztec Camera   *Dreamland* (engineered)
Blur   'To The End' (mixed)

DAVID HENTSCHEL

Carly Simon   *No Secrets* (engineered)
Genesis   *And Then There Were Three*
Renaissance   'Northern Lights'
Mike Oldfield   *QE2*

Yellowjackets	*Politics*
Andy Summers	*The Golden Wire*

TREVOR HORN

The Buggles	*The Age Of Plastic*
ABC	*The Lexicon Of Love*
Yes	*90125*
Frankie Goes To Hollywood	*Welcome To The Pleasuredome*
Seal	*Seal (I & II)*
Rod Stewart	*A Spanner In The Works*

JOHN HUDSON (Mixing/engineering)

Gary Glitter	'I'm The Leader Of The Gang (I Am)'
Slik	'Forever And Ever'
Tina Turner	*Private Dancer*
A-ha	'The Sun Always Shines On TV'
Bryan Adams	'Everything I Do (I Do It For You)'
Pulp	'Disco 2000'

ANDY JACKSON

Fields Of The Nephilim	*Elizium*
Heroes del Silencio	*Avalancha*
The Dream Academy	'Life In A Northern Town' (engineered)
The Boomtown Rats	'I Don't Like Mondays' (engineered)
Roger Waters	*The Pros And Cons Of Hitch-hiking* (engineered)
Pink Floyd	*The Division Bell* (engineered)

JEFF JARRATT

Simon Dupree & The Big Sound	'Kites' (engineered)
The Beatles	'Something' (engineered)

Billy Preston	'That's The Way God Planned It' (engineered)
London Symphony Orchestra	*Classic Rock*
Royal Philharmonic Orchestra	'Hooked On Classics'
Barbra Streisand & Michael Crawford	'The Music Of The Night' (associate producer)

GLYN JOHNS (Engineering)

Small Faces	*Ogdens' Nut Gone Flake*
The Beatles	*Let It Be*
Led Zeppelin	*Led Zeppelin*
The Who	'Won't Get Fooled Again'
Rolling Stones	'Honky Tonk Women'
Joan Armatrading	*Show Some Emotion*

GARY LANGAN

Spandau Ballet	*Through The Barricades*
Public Image Limited	*Happy?*
Art Of Noise	'Close (To The Edit)'
Queen	'Bohemian Rhapsody' (engineered)
Rock Aid Armenia	'Smoke On The Water'
Scritti Politti	'Hypnotise' (mixed)

JOHN LECKIE

George Harrison	*All Things Must Pass* (tape op)
Pink Floyd	*Meddle* (engineered)
Be Bop Deluxe	*Sunburst Finish*
XTC	*White Music*
Radiohead	*The Bends*
Cast	*All Change*

CRAIG LEON

Blondie	*Blondie*
The Ramones	*Ramones*
Jesus Jones	*Liquidizer*
The Bangles	*Bangles*
Doctor And The Medics	'Spirit In The Sky'
Suicide	*Suicide*

GEORGE MARTIN

The Beatles	*Sergeant Pepper's Lonely Hearts Club Band*
Cilla Black	'Anyone Who Had A Heart'
Jeff Beck	*Blow By Blow*
Paul McCartney	*Pipes Of Peace*
Larry Adler & Various Artists	*The Glory Of Gershwin*
Elton John	'Candle In The Wind 1997'

JOE MEEK

Emile Ford & The Checkmates	'What Do You Want To Make Those Eyes At Me For?'
The Blue Men	*I Hear A New World*
John Leyton	'Johnny Remember Me'
The Tornados	'Telstar'
The Honeycombs	'Have I The Right'
Heinz	'Just Like Eddie'

PAUL STAVELEY O'DUFFY

Swing Out Sister	*It's Better To Travel*
Was (Not Was)	*What Up Dog*
Danny Wilson	'Mary's Prayer'
Curiosity Killed The Cat	'Ordinary Day'
Tom Verlaine	*A Town Called Walker*
Hipsway	'The Honeythief'

HUGH PADGHAM

Yes	*Drama* (engineered)
Peter Gabriel	*Peter Gabriel 3* (engineered)
Genesis	*Invisible Touch*
Sting	*Mercury Falling*
XTC	*English Settlement*
Police	*Ghost In The Machine*

ALAN PARSONS

The Beatles	*Abbey Road* (engineered)
Pink Floyd	*The Dark Side Of The Moon* (engineered)
Steve Harley & Cockney Rebel	'(Come Up And See Me) Make Me Smile'
Pilot	'January'
John Miles	'Music'
The Alan Parsons Project	*Eye In The Sky* (as producer and artist)

SAM PHILLIPS

Elvis Presley	'That's All Right'
Johnny London	'Drivin' Slow'
Carl Perkins	'Blue Suede Shoes'
Jerry Lee Lewis	'Whole Lot Of Shakin' Going On'
Roy Orbison	'Chicken Hearted'
Johnny Cash	'Cry! Cry! Cry!'

PHIL RAMONE

Billy Joel	*An Innocent Man*
Paul Simon	*Still Crazy After All These Years*
Nilsson	'Everybody's Talkin''
Barbra Streisand	'Evergreen (Theme From A Star Is Born)'
John Barry (with Larry Adler)	'Theme From Midnight Cowboy'
Frank Sinatra	*Duets*

PHIL SPECTOR

The Crystals	'He's A Rebel'
Various Artists	*A Christmas Gift For You*
Righteous Brothers	'You've Lost That Lovin' Feelin''
Ike And Tina Turner	'River Deep, Mountain High'
George Harrison	*All Things Must Pass*
John Lennon	*Imagine*

STOCK-AITKEN-WATERMAN

Mel And Kim	'Respectable'
Rick Astley	'Never Gonna Give You Up'
Kylie Minogue	'I Should Be So Lucky'
Hazell Dean	'Whatever I Do'
Bananarama	'I Heard A Rumour'
Princess	'Say I'm Your Number One'

CHRIS THOMAS

The Beatles	*The Beatles/White Album* (uncredited producer and musician)
Pink Floyd	*The Dark Side Of The Moon* (mixing supervisor)
Roxy Music	*Siren*
Sex Pistols	*Never Mind The Bollocks*
Pretenders	*Pretenders*
Pulp	*Different Class*

MIKE VERNON

John Mayall's Blues Breakers with Eric Clapton	*Blues Breakers*
Fleetwood Mac	'Black Magic Woman'
Focus	'Sylvia'
Dr Feelgood	*Doctor's Orders*
Level 42	*In Pursuit Of Accidents*
Sherman Robertson	*I'm The Man*

TONY VISCONTI

Joe Cocker	'With A Little Help From My Friends' (mixed)
T-Rex	'Get It On (Bang-A-Gong)'
Sparks	*Indiscreet*
David Bowie	*Heroes*
Hazel O'Connor	*Breaking Glass*
Seahorses	*Do It Yourself*

MARTYN WARE

The Human League	*Reproduction* (as producer and artist)
Heaven 17	*Penthouse & Pavement* (as producer and artist)
BEF	*Music Of Quality And Distinction Vols 1 & 2*
Terence Trent D'Arby	*The Hardline According To...*
Erasure	*I Say I Say I Say*
Tina Turner	'Let's Stay Together'

NB Credits are for production/co-production unless otherwise specified.

studio lingo: a glossary of terminology

A cappella
Unaccompanied singing.

Acetate
A disc made direct from a master tape, used either for demonstration or review purposes, but not for processing.

A/D Convertor
A device which converts analogue waveforms into digital code. A D/A converter does the reverse.

ADT
Artificial Double Tracking. Invented at EMI Abbey Road Studios in 1966. Involves electronic methods to simulate the manual form of double-tracking. Flanging, a phrase originated by George Martin and John Lennon, is a variation on the ADT technique whereby the two identical signals are moved slightly wider apart.

Ambience
The acoustic characteristics of sound reverberating in a room or space.

Amp

Abbreviation of amplifier.

Analogue

The waveform format of sound.

AOR

Adult-Orientated Rock.

A&R

Artistes & Repertoire (as in A&R man).

Arpeggio

The notes of a musical chord, played in sequence.

Assistant Engineer

The person responsible for supporting the engineer, especially at the mixdown stage but also with the placement of microphones and connection of equipment.

ATOC

Automatic Transient Overload Control. An EMI-designed version of limiting.

Attack

The beginning of a sound which varies from instrument to instrument: eg a snare drum or picked guitar string both have a fast attack, while bowed string instruments have a slow attack, their sound developing over a comparatively longer period.

Attenuator

A control device used to trim the gain of an input signal.

Backing Track

The instrumental background music prepared in advance of a vocal recording.

Backline

This normally refers to the amplification used for individual guitars, basses and keyboards. Can also include drums.

Baffles

Isolation screens which provide soundproofing (separation) between instruments playing together in a studio.

Balance Engineer

See Engineer

Banding

The assembly of a chain of recordings in an arranged order, in advance of mastering an album.

Bar

a) A division of a musical score, determined by the time signature of a composition;
b) favoured meeting place of musicians.

Board

See Mixing Console.

Bottom End

The bass end of the frequency spectrum.

Bouncing

A method whereby an increased amount of audio information can be stored on the recording medium. This is achieved by balancing the sounds from two or more individual tracks and transferring them to one track, freeing the original tracks for the recording of further sound.

Break

In musical arrangement terms, this refers to a passage in a song where an instrumentalist takes a solo.

Breakdown

The end of an incomplete take.

Bridge

Transitional passage between a verse and a chorus. See also Middle Eight.

Bumping

Bouncing between two tracks.

Buss

An audio routing circuit which allows either one or a group of signal inputs to be delivered to one or more outputs.

CCIR

A European equalisation standard for tape machines.

Chorus

a) The repeated hook line or refrain of a song;
b) A thickening effect caused by two or more identical signals being transmitted at slightly different times. A similar effect to flanging. See also ADT.

Click Track

A tempo guide, normally provided by a rhythm box or drum machine, by which musicians can keep perfect time. Also referred to as the pulse which drives a sequencer.

Compression

The control of the output dynamics of an input signal. Used on the human voice, for example, compression will smooth the volume peaks of a performance to deliver a more even signal to the recording medium.

Console

See Mixing Console.

Crossfade

The controlled passing of signals from two tape machines to one tape machine.

Cue

a) An indication to begin a performance;
b) A system, normally integrated into a mixing console, which allows the communication between individuals in the control room and the studio.

Cutting Lathe

An electro-mechanical item of equipment which cuts a lacquer. See Lacquer.

Decay

The retardation in amplitude of either a whole piece of music, a single note or a reverberated sound.

Delay

The slowing down of the introduction of a signal, which can be used for echo effects.

Decibel (dB)

A unit of measurement relating to the power of sound levels.

Demo

A raw example of an intended piece of music. Today, with affordable but sophisticated home equipment, it is common for most demos to sound like a finished product.

Desk

See Mixing Console.

Digital

The encoded form of sound.

Direct Injection (DI)

The direct connection of instruments to a mixing console, sometimes via an intermediary box, by-passing the need for microphones.

Dolby Noise Reduction

A system invented by Raymond Dolby which eliminates hiss on analogue recordings, while maintaining high frequencies.

Double Tracking

Two identical performances recorded separately and merged to deliver a more substantial sound.

Drop In/Drop Out

A method of "patching up" mistakes in a recording. An engineer will temporarily put a tape machine into record (drop in) while a musician replaces a faulty part of a performance, and then switch off the record mode (drop out), leaving a composite, perfect performance on tape.

Dry

A signal which has been recorded without the addition of effects processing.

Dub

a) See Overdub;
b) A reggae production style which employs high levels of echo delay and reverb;
c) A common phrase in the TV and film world, referring to the amendments of a soundtrack.

Echo Chamber

A room with reflective surfaces into which sound is fed by one or more speakers, picked up by one or more microphones and sent back to the control room. Digital effects processors have largely outweighed the need for such rooms.

Echo Plate

A large, thin steel plate suspended in a framework which vibrates when sound is fed to it; these vibrations are received by two microphones and delivered to the mixing console. The length of the vibrations is determined by the degree of pressure applied by a mechanical dampening device.

Edit

a) The point at which two spliced recordings meet;
b) an abridged or shortened piece of music, normally produced to facilitate radio airplay.

Editing

See Splicing.

Eight-track

Generally refers to the multitrack recording machine which allows the recording of eight individual signals which can subsequently be balanced.

EMT Plate

See Echo Plate.

Engineer

The person responsible for the technical aspects of a recording session, by operating the mixing console and ensuring that all sounds are transferred to the recording medium in the correct way.

Envelope Generator

A feature of synthesisers allowing the shaping of sounds via the attack, decay, sustain and release parameters.

EQ or Equalisation

The adjustment of frequency response to tailor a desired quality of sound.

Fade Out

Either refers to the gradual decrease in the volume level of a particular instrument within a recording, or the decrease in the overall volume level of a recording at the end of a performance, achieved by closing down all of the faders on the mixing console.

Fade In

The opposite of Fade Out. The Beatles' 'Strawberry Fields Forever' and Traffic's 'Paper Sun' are two popular examples of a fade in at the end of a recording.

Fader

The finger-drive device on a mixing console which allows the increase or decrease in volume level of an individual signal.

Fairchild

A brand of limiter named after its inventor, Sherman Fairchild.

False Start

See Breakdown.

Feedback

A howling sound normally the result of a microphone picking up its own signal from a nearby speaker.

Filter

This boosts or cuts selected frequencies.

Flanging

See ADT.

Flat

A reference to 0dB frequency response.

Foldback

In studio terms, this refers to the feed of sound to a performer's headphones.

Foldback Speakers

Same as Foldback, but refers to a time before headphones were standard issue.

Four-track

See Eight-track

Frequency Response

The range of frequencies handled and delivered by audio equipment, eg most microphones have a frequency response of 40Hz to 20kHz.

Front End

The beginning of a signal chain.

Fuzz Box

A foot-operated distortion effect pedal mainly used by guitarists.

Gain

The amplification of an input signal.

Gig

Musicians' slang for a performance booking, either live or in the studio. Apparently an abbreviation of "giggle", but then maybe not.

Glass Master

The vital ingredient from which a compact disc is produced.

Graphic EQ

An equalisation unit where manufacturer-defined frequencies are each represented by a cut/boost fader and displayed graphically.

Hard Disk

A medium for the recording of digital audio.

Harmonizer

A device which allows the pitch of a signal to be altered without affecting the speed of its reproduction.

Hertz (Hz)

a) A unit of frequency measurement;
b) Handy at airports.

Impedance

Refers to the amount of current flowing in a circuit when a certain voltage is applied.

Input

The point at which a signal enters an item of audio equipment.

Internet

The international communications network which links its users via computer terminals and the telephone system, allowing the distribution of information by digital means.

IPS

Inches per second – a measurement of tape speed.

ISDN

Integrated Services Digital Network. This allows the delivery of an audio signal from one studio to be sent to another in real time, regardless of its international location.

Jam

An impromptu performance by a group of musicians, normally based around a fixed chord sequence to allow free expression. Not referred to in America as "a jelly".

Jangle

A honky-tonk type of piano.

Lacquer

A high quality aluminium disc used in the cutting process of vinyl records.

Layering

See Overdub.

Leader Tape

Not a Gary Glitter master, but a normally-coloured piece of non-magnetic tape which is used at the beginning and end of a spool of an analogue recorded tape, to allow its loading on to a machine without the need to handle the actual recorded part of the tape.

Leakage

The transference of sound from one instrument's microphone to another by the result of close proximity and poor separation.

LED

Light Emitting Diode – used for indicating purposes on audio equipment.

Leslie Speaker

A rotating speaker favoured by organists, but also used creatively for effects on other instruments.

Level

The volume of a signal.

Limiter

Reduces the volume or gain increase of a signal to a pre-determined level to prevent overload.

Loop

A tape or other recording format which has been edited back upon itself in a seamless circle and replayed *ad infinitum*.

Master

The mixed and completed version of a recording.

Mellotron

Keyboard-based instrument which reproduces the sounds of real instruments using a tape replay system. The forerunner to the sampler.

Micro Groove Record

The original name given to the vinyl album.

Middle

The central area of the frequency spectrum, between bass and treble.

Middle Eight

A diversion in a song which normally comes between a verse and a chorus. It can sometimes usher a key change.

MIDI

Musical Instrument Digital Interface. A system which enables a communication link between electronic instruments and equipment.

Mixdown

The point during a recording project when all sounds assembled on a multitrack tape are balanced to form the desired blend.

Mixed Out

An element of a recording which is removed during the mixdown stage.

Mixing Console

The heart of the recording studio into which all audio material is delivered for adjustment of tone, volume and balance before it is sent to the multitrack machine.

Modulation

The shifting of a waveform.

Monitor

A loudspeaker designed specifically for control room playback and analysis purposes.

Monophonic/Mono

Single channel reproduction.

Mono Remix

An alternative blend of sounds from a multitrack tape, mixed on to a single channel.

Moog

A brand of synthesiser invented by Dr Robert Moog.

MOR

Middle Of The Road – the generic term for easy listening pop music.

Moving Coil Microphone

One in which sound striking a diaphragm causes a coil to vibrate within a magnetic field to create an electrical impulse.

Multitrack Tape/Production Master

The multitrack tape carries the individual unmixed sound elements which make up a whole performance; the production master is the definitive, first generation version of the final mixed performance which is then used for the mass production of CDs, cassettes and vinyl records.

Multitracking

The recording of several different signals at different times, each on a separate track.

Muting

The switching off of an input signal to a mixing console.

NAB Equalisation

American equalisation standard for tape machines.

Noise Gate

A device which only allows audio signals to be heard once they rise above a pre-determined volume threshold.

Octave

An interval between notes sharing the same name but at twice the frequency.

Oscillation

Waveform movement.

Outboard

The generic term for the audio equipment, such as signal processing and effects units, which support the mixing console and recorder.

Output

The reverse of Input.

Outtake

A performance which has been omitted from release in the public domain.

Overdub

A performance added to a previous recording.

PA

Public Address (ie PA system – a means of amplified sound reinforcement).

Pad

A normally chordal background on a recording used to fill a

sound space, normally provided by voices or a keyboard.

Panning

The positioning of sounds across the left and right channels.

Pan Pot

The common abbreviation of panoramic potentiometer, a control device on a mixing console which achieves panning.

Parametric EQ

As Graphic EQ, except that frequency bands are continuously selectable for adjustment instead of being graphically displayed.

Patch Bay

Sometimes referred to as the jackfield, where a number of patch leads connect various items of equipment together from a central matrix.

Potentiometer

A variable level controller.

Producer

The artistic director of a recording session who has the final word on the progress of the music being recorded. Not usually inclined to make the tea.

Punch In

See Drop In/Drop Out.

Quadrophonic Sound

A format of audio replay where four channels each containing different blends of sound feed to four speakers.

Release

a) the issue of musical product to the public;
b) the dying of a musical signal, normally applicable to

synthesisers.

Reduction Mix

See Bouncing.

Remix

An alternative blend of sounds from a multitrack tape. Sometimes subject to a new range of overdubs and enhancements, especially in the case of dance music.

Reverb

An abbreviation of reverberation. Refers to the natural ambient or digitally-created characteristics of a room or open space.

RF

Radio Frequency.

Rhythm Track

The rhythmical background music of a recording which normally consists of drums, bass, rhythm guitar and a keyboard.

Riff

A group of notes or musical phrase essential to a song.

Rill

The empty groove spaces in between tracks on a vinyl album or extended play (EP) record.

Roll Off

The de-emphasis of a given frequency or frequency grouping.

Rough Mix

An approximation of the final production master mix, normally prepared at the end of a session for review purposes.

Routing

The movement of input signals through the audio processing

chain and to outputs.

Royalty

An agreed percentage of record sales or publishing revenue.

RPM

Revolutions Per Minute.

Sampler

A digital device which enables the storage, manipulation and replay of sounds via a keyboard or triggering device.

Separation

Distancing instruments from each other, either in the overall sound picture or physically during recording.

Sequencer

A computer software programme or hardware unit which can replay a series of musical notes and/or drive other MIDI-linked musical equipment.

Session Fixer

A person who organises bookings for session musicians.

Session Tapes

All tapes used during a session.

Session Musician

A freelance musician, normally specialising in one instrument, available for hire to studios and producers.

Splicing

The art of joining two pieces of tape to form a seamless piece of audio material.

STEED

a) Single Tape Echo Echo Delay – an acronym for an echo

technique devised at EMI Abbey Road Studios;
b) The bowler-hatter chappie in *The Avengers*.

Stereo Remix
As Mono Remix, except it uses two channels.

Stereophonic/Stereo
Dual channel reproduction.

Superimposition
See Overdub.

Sync Head
The record head of a tape machine used in play mode.

Sync Pulse Track
One track on a multitrack tape which is reserved for a timing pulse, enabling the synchronisation of two machines.

Talkback
See Cue.

Tape Delay
The use of magnetic tape to effect a time delay.

Tape Operator
The person responsible for operating the multitrack recorder at the engineer's command. One who strives to become either an engineer or a producer.

Tape-to-Tape
The transference of audio material from one tape machine to another.

Three-track
See Eight-track.

Transport

A reference to the movement of motorised and non-motorised elements which drive the tape across the heads of a tape machine.

Tremolo

The effect of oscillation between notes. See also Vibrato.

Triplet

A group of three notes spread over the space of two.

Two-track

See Eight-track.

Varispeed

The term for varying the capstan speed of a multitrack machine to accelerate or slow down the tempo of a recording.

Vibrato

Rapid undulation of pitch by controlled vibration, giving a stylised tone.

VU Meter

Abbreviation of Volume Unit meter – a needle and scale indicator of volume level.

Wah-Wah

A foot-operated filter effect unit which alters the frequency of a signal. Mostly used by guitarists although Pink Floyd's Rick Wright used one to great effect on his electric piano part on 'Money'. Listen out, too, for the wah-wah textured congas on the Mickie Most production of Hot Chocolate's 'You Sexy Thing'.

White Label

Alternative name for a test pressing of a record.

White Noise

A rushing sound made by a signal which contains every
frequency rising in level by 6dB every octave.

appendix IV

reference section

In writing *Good Vibrations – A History Of Record Production*, information gleaned through various interviews was cross-checked using a selected library of rock music reference books and magazines, all of which are highly recommended for providing more specialised knowledge of some areas covered in this book.

Books:

What Was The First Rock 'N' Roll Record?
by Jim Dawson & Steve Propes (Faber & Faber – 1992)
Good Rockin' Tonight
by Colin Escott with Martin Hawkins (St Martin's Press – 1991)
The Legendary Joe Meek
by John Repsch (Woodford House – 1989)
Where Did Our Love Go?
by Nelson George (St Martin's Press – 1985)
Wouldn't It Be Nice – My Own Story
by Brian Wilson with Todd Gold (Bloomsbury – 1992)
Seventeen Watts? The First Twenty Years Of British Rock Guitar, The Musicians And Their Stories
by Mo Foster (Sanctuary Publishing – 1997)
Abbey Road
by Brian Southall (PSL – 1982)

The Complete Beatles Recording Sessions
by Mark Lewisohn (Hamlyn/EMI – 1988)
Revolution In The Head
by Ian MacDonald (Fourth Estate – 1994)
Summer Of Love
by George Martin with William Pearson (Macmillan – 1995)
All You Need Is Ears
by George Martin with Jeremy Hornsby (St Martin's Press – 1979)
Loving John: The Untold Story
by May Pang (Warner Books – 1983)
All You Need Is Love – The Story Of Popular Music
by Tony Palmer (Futura – 1976)
Peter Green – The Biography
by Martin Celmins (Sanctuary Publishing – 1996)
Frank Zappa In His Own Words
by Miles (Omnibus Press – 1993)
Saucerful Of Secrets: The Pink Floyd Odyssey
by Nicholas Schaffner (Sidgwick and Jackson – 1991)
The Making Of Mike Oldfield's Tubular Bells
by Richard Newman (Music Maker Books – 1993)
U2 The Rolling Stone Files
by the Editors of *Rolling Stone* (Sidgwick and Jackson – 1994)
The Guinness Book Of Recorded Sound
by Robert & Celia Dearling (Guinness Superlatives – 1984)
The Record Producers
by John Tobler (BBC – 1982)
The Top Twenty Book
Compiled by Tony Jasper (Blandford – 1991)

Consumer & Industry Magazines:

Audio Media
(UK – AM Publishing)
EQ
(USA – Miller Freeman Entertainment)
Future Music
(UK – Future Publishing)

Making Music
(UK – Nexus Media)
Mojo
(UK – EMAP Metro)
Music Week
(UK – Miller Freeman Entertainment)
Pro Sound News
(UK/USA – Miller Freeman Entertainment)
Q
(UK – EMAP Metro)
Record Collector
(UK – Diamond Publishing)
Sound On Sound
(UK – SOS Publications)
Studio Sound
(UK – Miller Freeman Entertainment)
The Mix
(UK – Music Maker Publications)
Total Production
(UK – Pulse Publications)

Music Industry Organisations:

The following organisations also provide a good source of information
and advice on studios, recording technology and production, and audio
engineering:

AES (Audio Engineering Society), PO Box 645, Slough, Berks SL1
8BJ
APRS (Association of Professional Recording Studios), 2 Windsor
Square, Silver Street, Reading, Berks RG1 2TH
*BASCA (The British Association of Songwriters, Composers &
Authors)*, 34 Hanway Street, London W1P 9DE
British Library National Sound Archive, 29 Exhibition Road,
London SW7 2AS
British Music Information Centre, 10 Stratford Place, London W1N
9AE

Joe Meek Appreciation Society, c/o Woodford House Publishing, 110 Chertsey Court, Clifford Avenue, London SW14 7BX

Musicians' Union, 60-62 Clapham Road, London SW9 0JJ

PRS (The Performing Rights Society), 29-33 Berners Street, London W1P 4AA

Re-Pro (The Guild of Recording Producers, Directors & Engineers), 68 Cleveland Gardens, London SW13 0AH

index